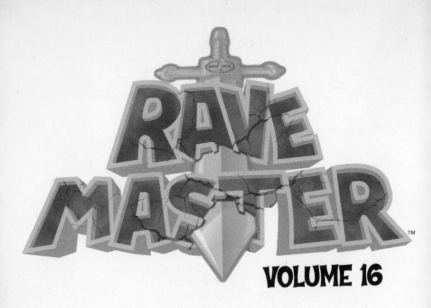

VOLUME 16

Story and Art by

HIRO MASHIMA

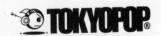

HAMBURG // LONDON // LOS ANGELES // TOKYO

THE STORY SO FAR...

Haru Glory and his companions still haven't found the fourth **Rave Stone**, but they **have** found plenty of trouble. Recently, our heroes have been busy trading blows with the most powerful baddies that the **Ghost Attack Squad** has to offer. From the undead **Cookie Crusher**, to the twisted **Wolf Doctor Mummy**, to the manipulative **Lilith Nina**, to the evil **Pumpkin Doryu** himself. While Cookie, Mummy and Lilith were all soundly defeated, Doryu has proven to be quite formidable. Hungry for the destructive might of her **Etherion**, he's taken **Elie** captive. The fiery Rave Master quickly mounted a rescue attempt, but he has paid a devastating price for his rashness. Thoroughly dominated in battle by Doryu before being violently run through by his sword, Haru's life now hangs precariously by a thread.

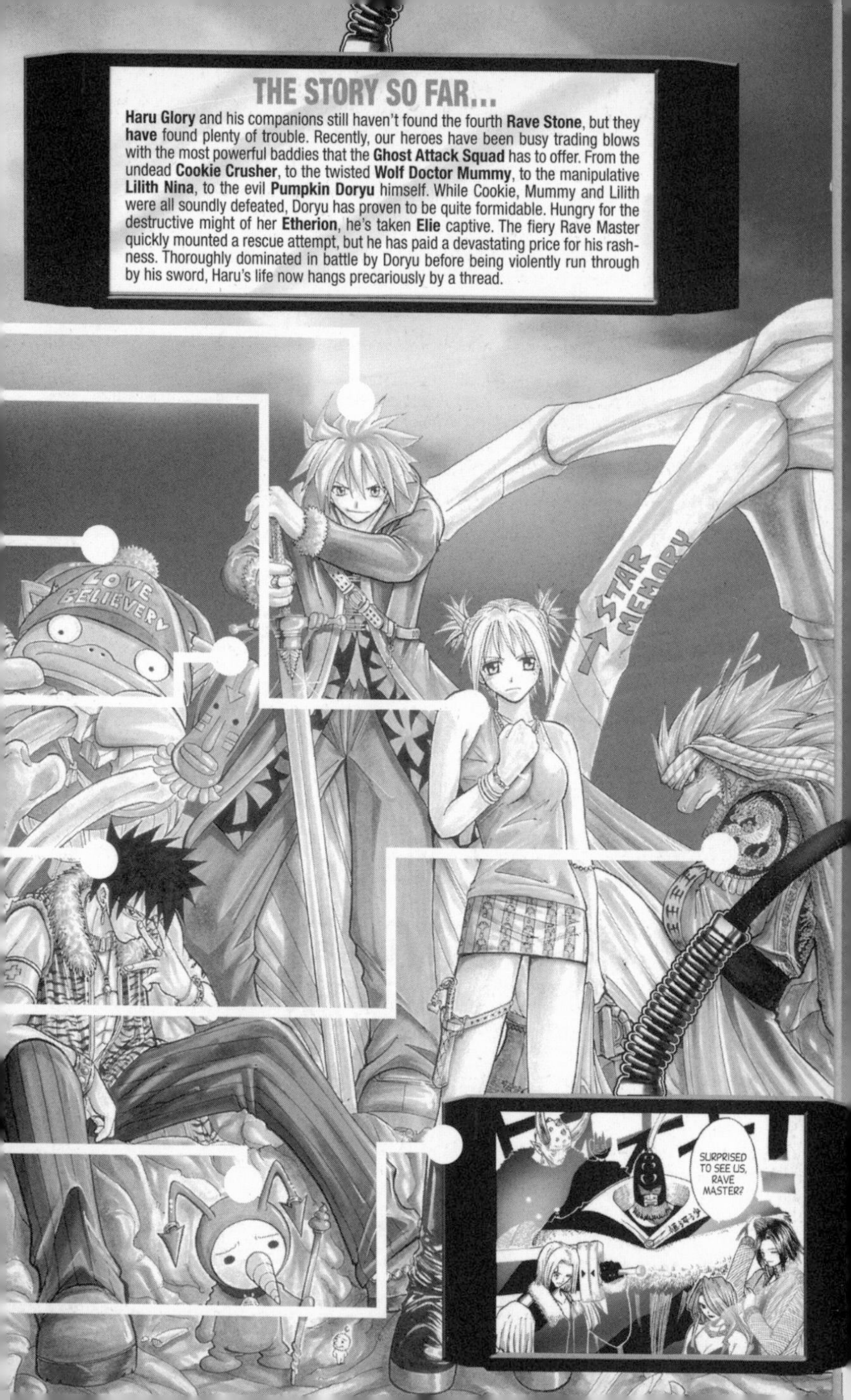
LOVE BELIEVER♥
STAR MEMORY
SURPRISED TO SEE US, RAVE MASTER?

THE RAVE MASTER CREW

HARU GLORY

A small-town boy turned savior of the world. As the **Rave Master** (the only one capable of using the holy weapon RAVE), Haru set forth to find the missing Rave Stones and defeat **Demon Card.** He fights with the **Ten Powers Sword,** a weapon that takes on different forms at his command. With Demon Card seemingly out of the way, Haru now seeks the remaining two Rave Stones in order to open the way to Star Memory.

ELIE

The girl without memories. Elie joined Haru on his quest when he promised to help her find out about her past. She's cute, spunky and loves gambling and shopping in equal measure. Locked inside of her is the power of **Etherion.**

RUBY

A "penguin-type" sentenoid, Ruby loves rare and unusual items. After Haru saved him from Pumpkin Doryu's gang, Ruby agreed to sponsor Haru's team in their search for the ultimate rare treasures: the Rave Stones!

GRIFFON KATO (GRIFF)

Griff is a loyal friend, even if he is a bit of a coward. His rubbery body can stretch and change shape as needed. Griff's two greatest pleasures in life are mapmaking and peeping on Elie.

MUSICA

A **"Silverclaimer"** (an alchemist who can shape silver at will) and a former street punk who made good. He joined Haru for the adventure, but now that Demon Card is defeated, does he have any reason to stick around?

LET

A member of the **Dragon Race,** he was formerly a member of the Demon Card's Five Palace Guardians. He was so impressed by Haru's fighting skills and pureness of heart that he made a truce with the Rave Master. After passing his Dragon Trial, he gained a human body, but his blood is still Dragon Race.

PLUE

The **Rave Bearer,** Plue is the faithful companion to the Rave Master. In addition to being Haru's guide, Plue also has powers of his own. When he's not getting Haru into or out of trouble, Plue can be found enjoying a sucker, his favorite treat.

THE ORACION SIX

Demon Card's six generals. Haru defeated **Shuda** after finding the Rave of Wisdom. The other five generals were presumed dead after King destroyed Demon Card Headquarters.

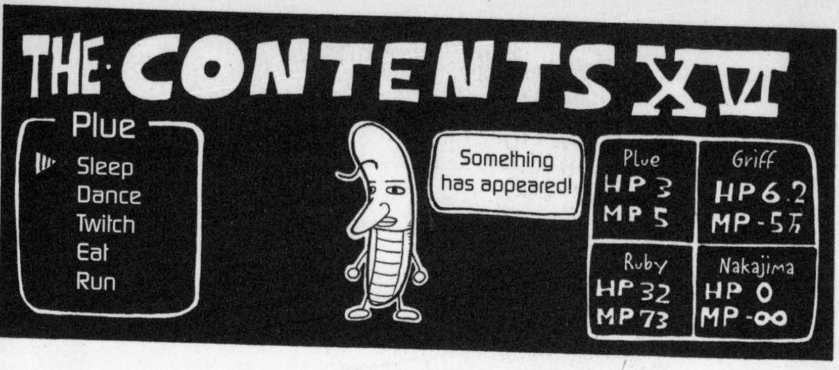

THE CONTENTS XVI

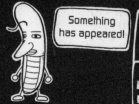

Plue
- Sleep
- Dance
- Twitch
- Eat
- Run

Something has appeared!

Plue	Griff
HP 3	HP 6.2
MP 5	MP -5兆

Ruby	Nakajima
HP 32	HP 0
MP 73	MP -∞

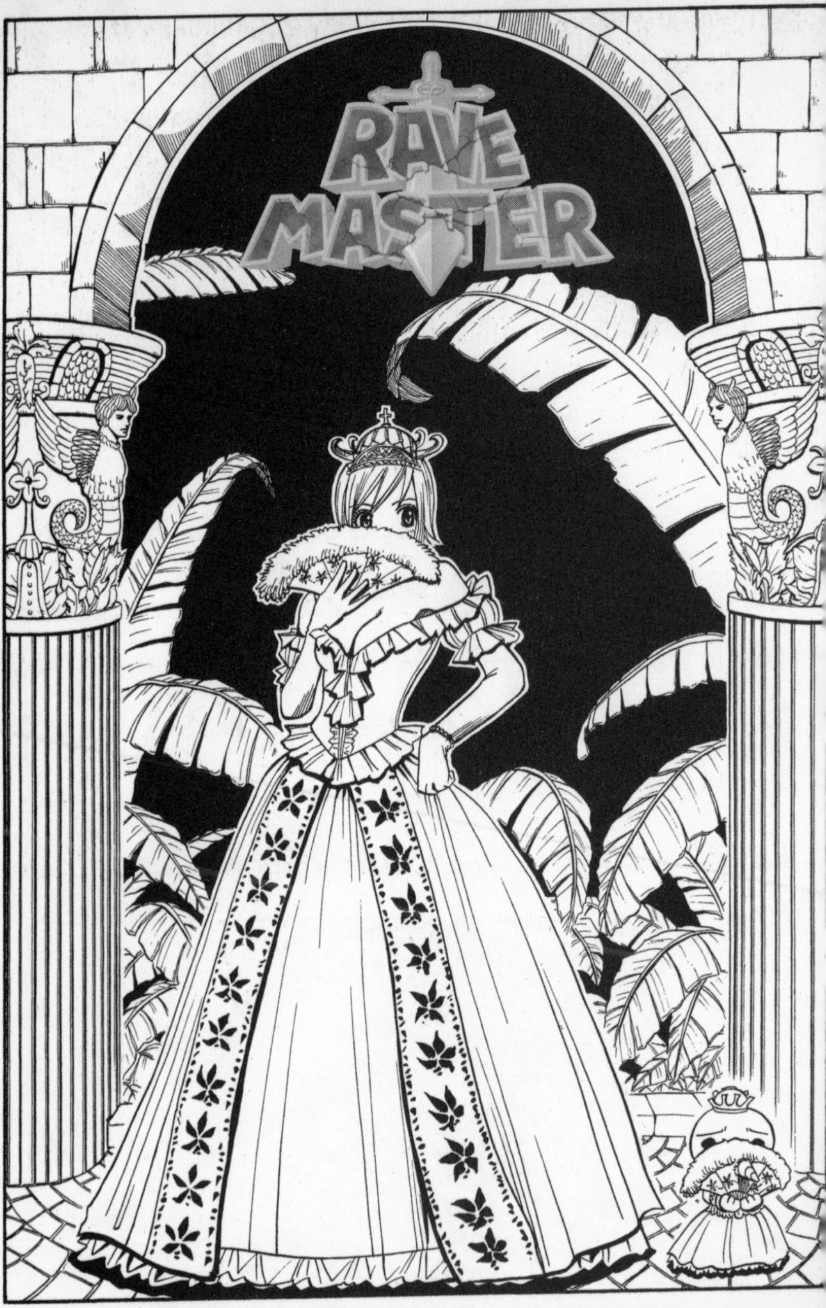
RAVE MASTER

RAVE:123 DORYU'S DARK DESIGNS

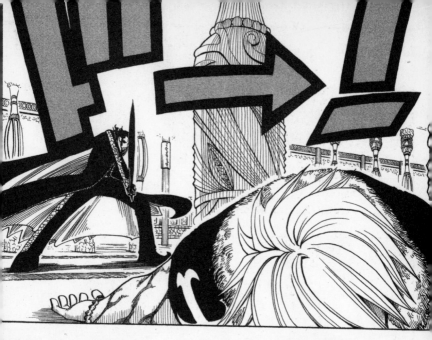

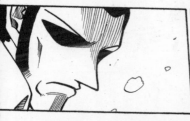

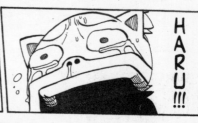

HARU!!!

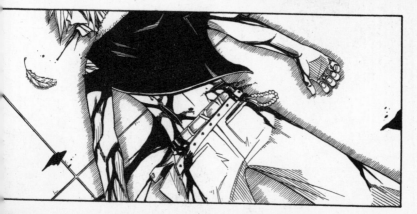

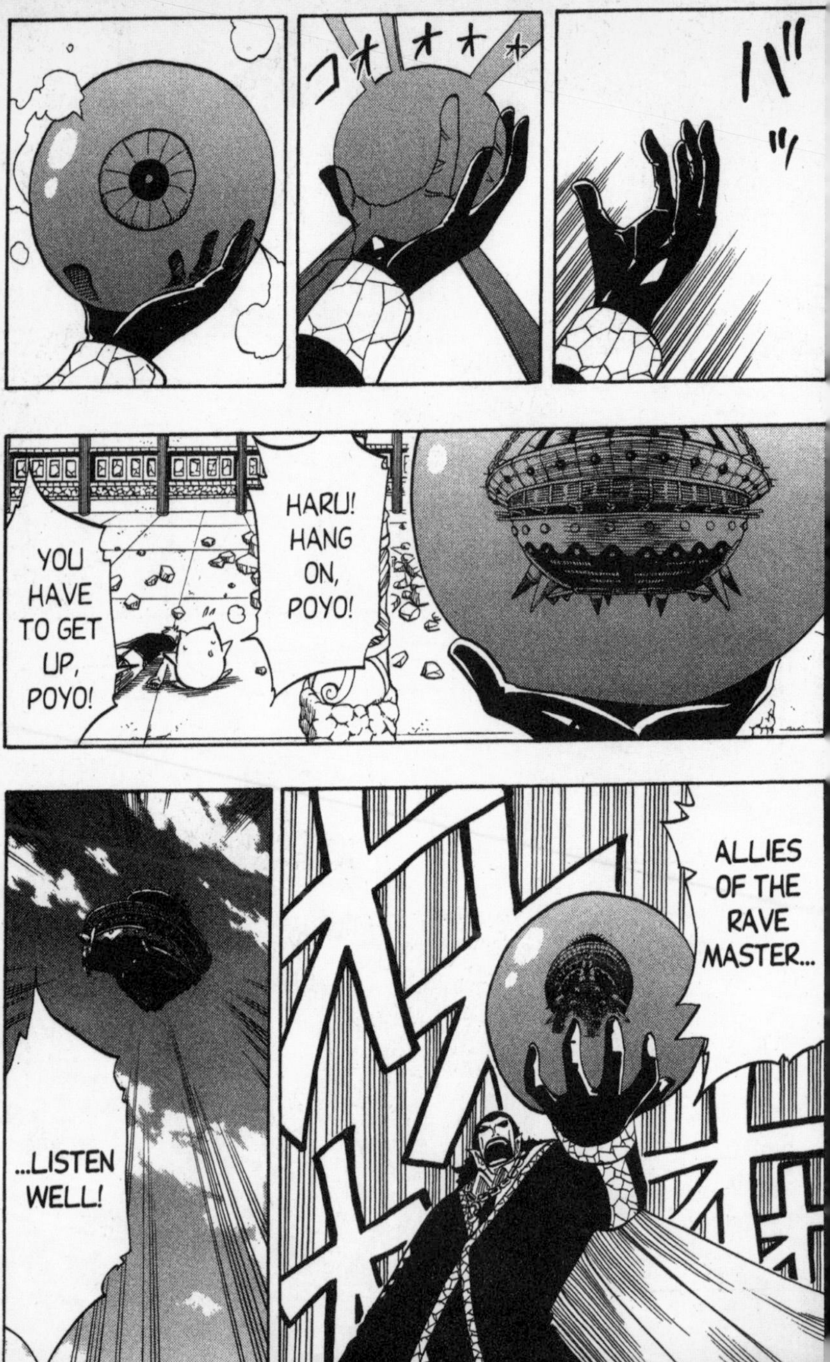
バッ
コオオオ
HARU! HANG ON, POYO!
YOU HAVE TO GET UP, POYO!
ALLIES OF THE RAVE MASTER...
...LISTEN WELL!

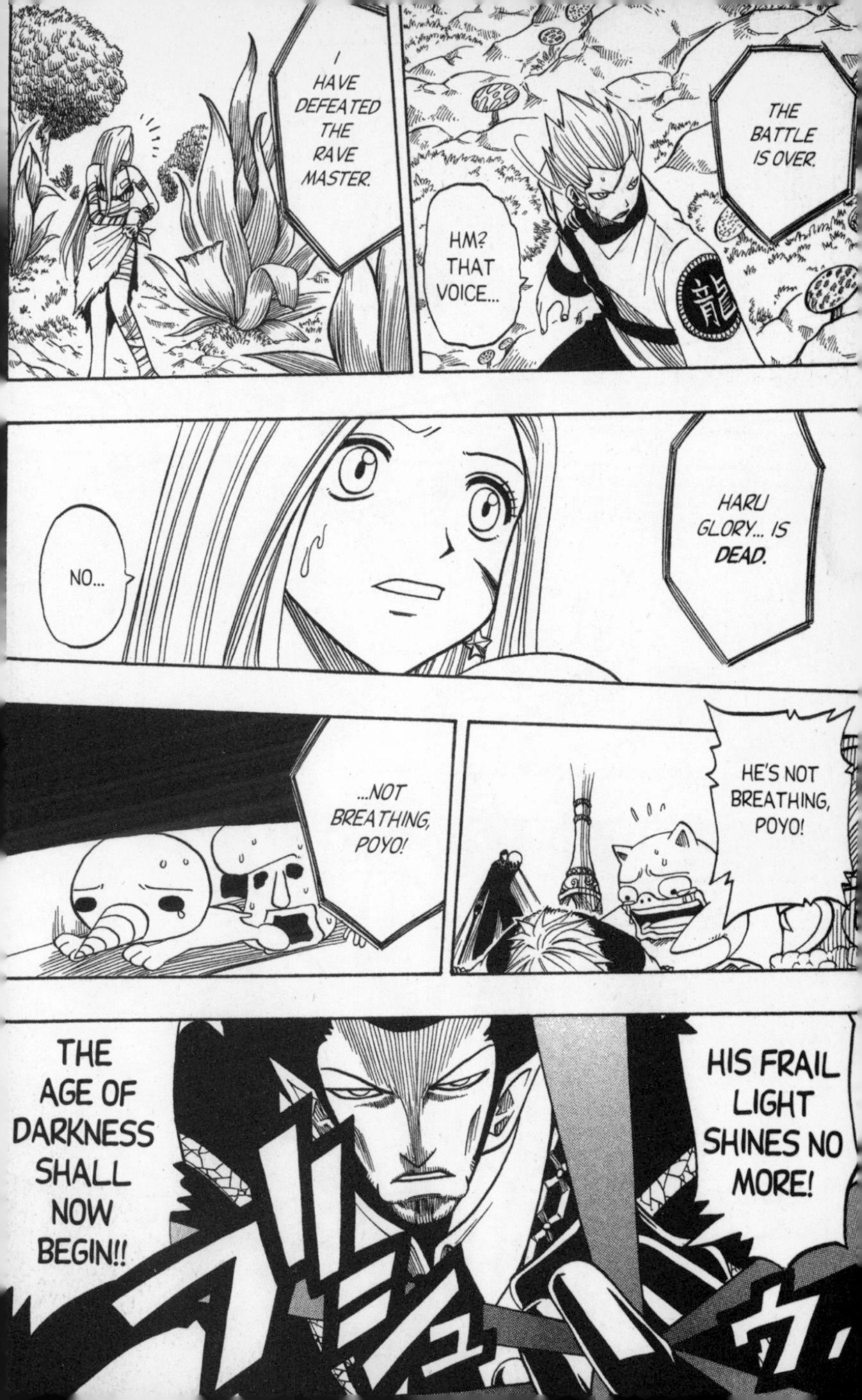
THE BATTLE IS OVER.
HM? THAT VOICE...
I HAVE DEFEATED THE RAVE MASTER.
HARU GLORY... IS DEAD.
NO...
HE'S NOT BREATHING, POYO!
...NOT BREATHING, POYO!
HIS FRAIL LIGHT SHINES NO MORE!
THE AGE OF DARKNESS SHALL NOW BEGIN!!

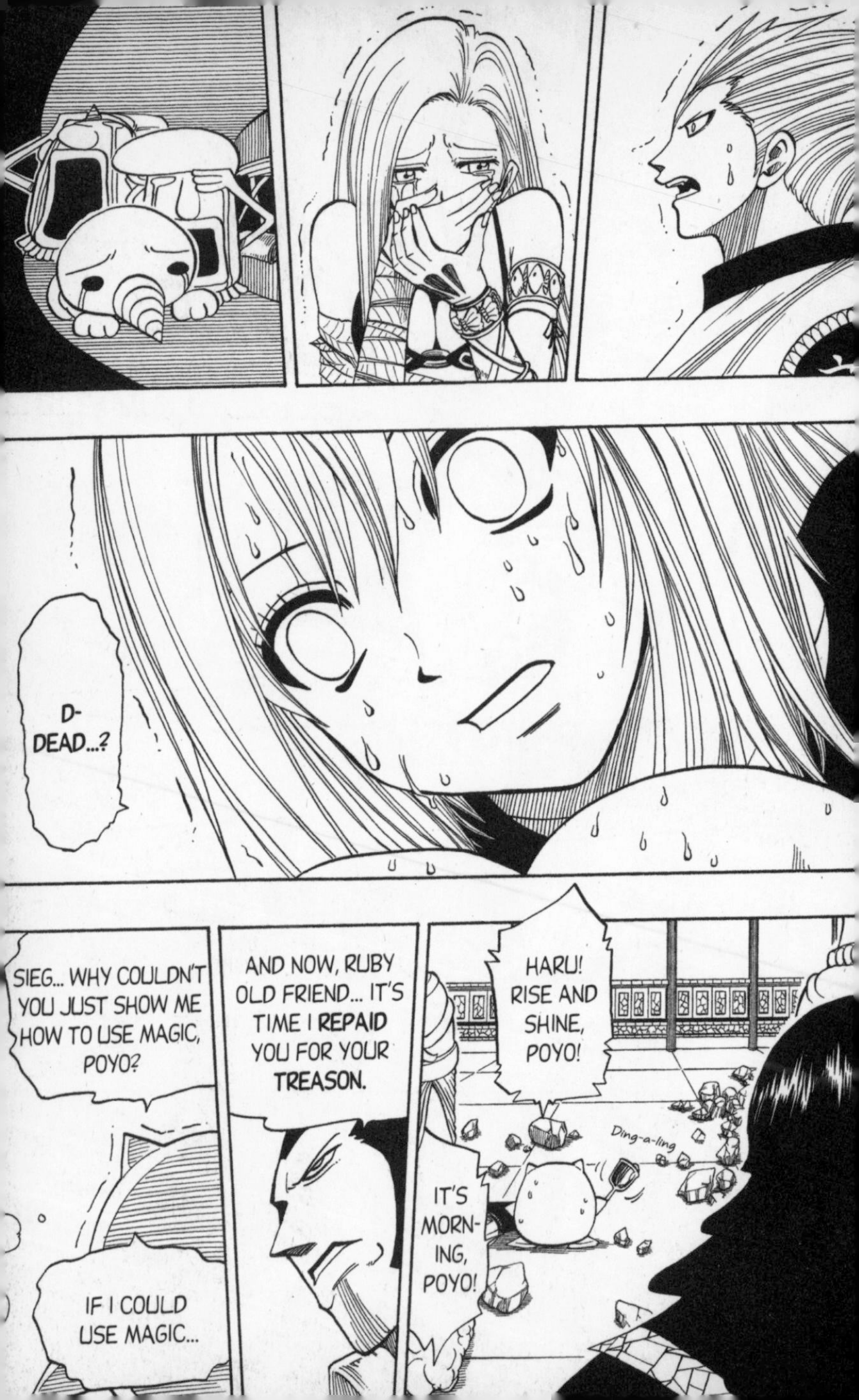
D-DEAD...?
HARU! RISE AND SHINE, POYO!
Ding-a-ling
IT'S MORNING, POYO!
AND NOW, RUBY OLD FRIEND... IT'S TIME I **REPAID** YOU FOR YOUR **TREASON.**
SIEG... WHY COULDN'T YOU JUST SHOW ME HOW TO USE MAGIC, POYO?
IF I COULD USE MAGIC...

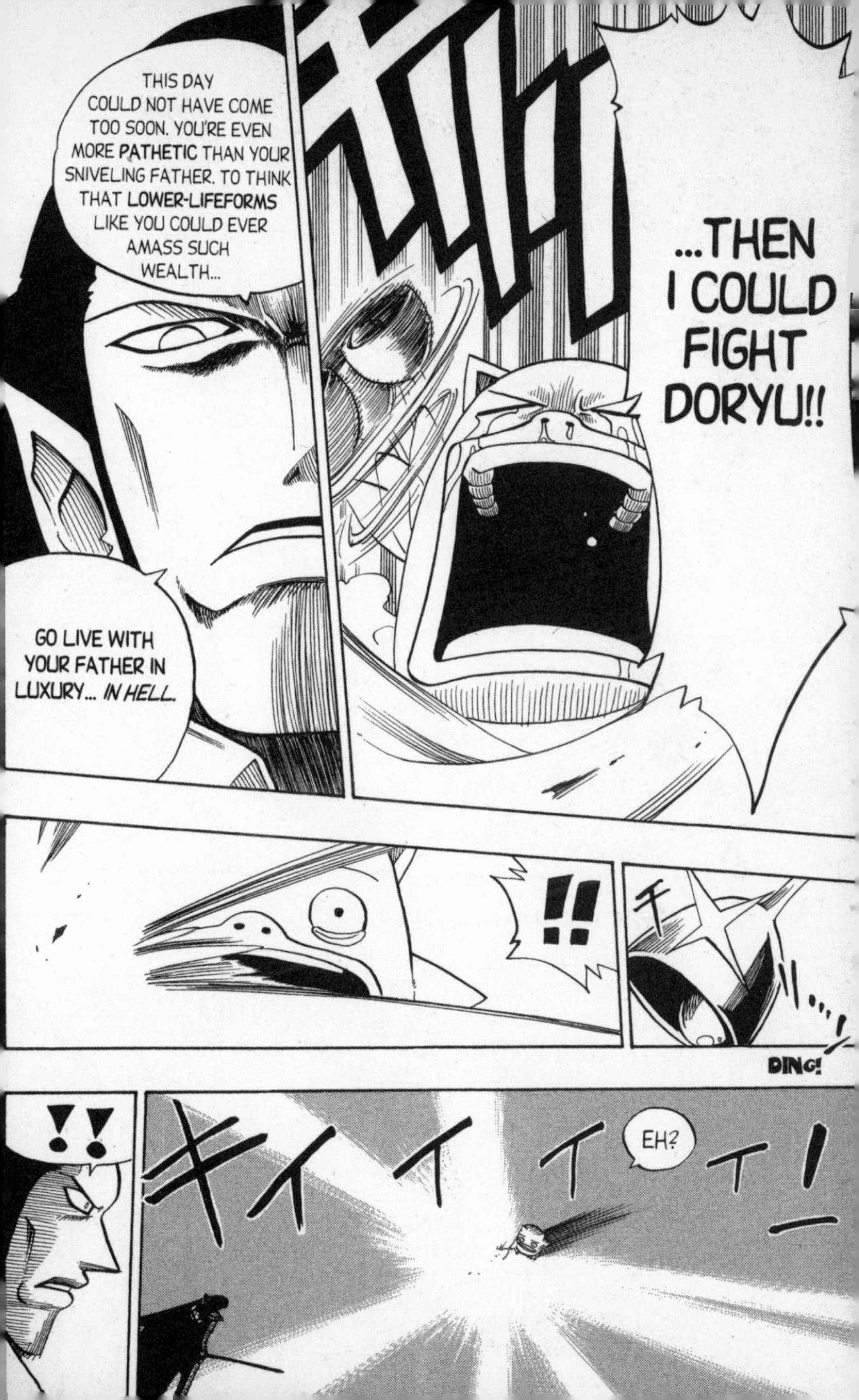
...THEN I COULD FIGHT DORYU!!
THIS DAY COULD NOT HAVE COME TOO SOON. YOU'RE EVEN MORE PATHETIC THAN YOUR SNIVELING FATHER. TO THINK THAT LOWER-LIFEFORMS LIKE YOU COULD EVER AMASS SUCH WEALTH...
GO LIVE WITH YOUR FATHER IN LUXURY... IN HELL.
DING!
!!
EH?
!!

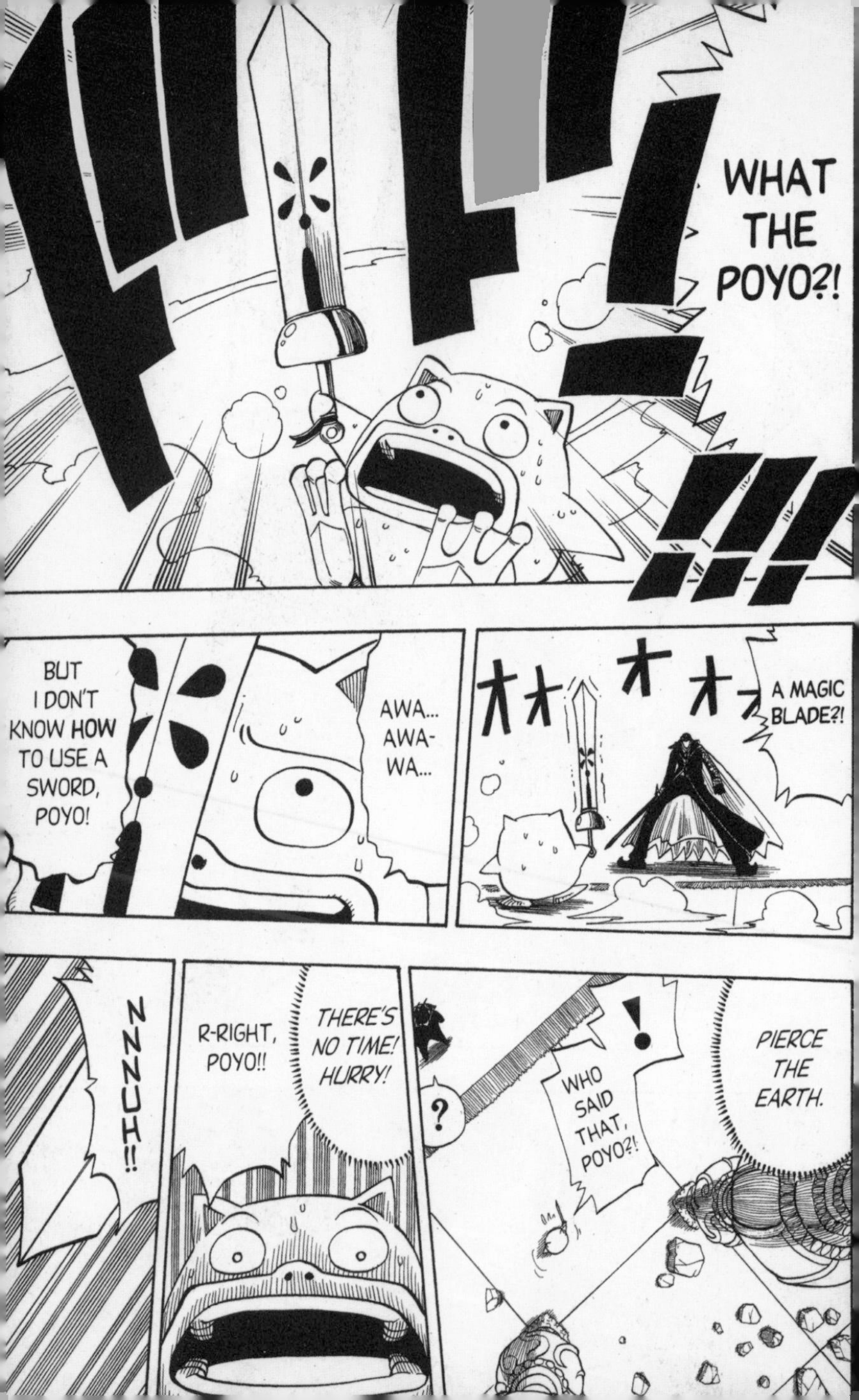
WHAT THE POYO?!
A MAGIC BLADE?!
AWA... AWA-WA...
BUT I DON'T KNOW HOW TO USE A SWORD, POYO!
PIERCE THE EARTH.
WHO SAID THAT, POYO?!
THERE'S NO TIME! HURRY!
R-RIGHT, POYO!!
NNNUH!!

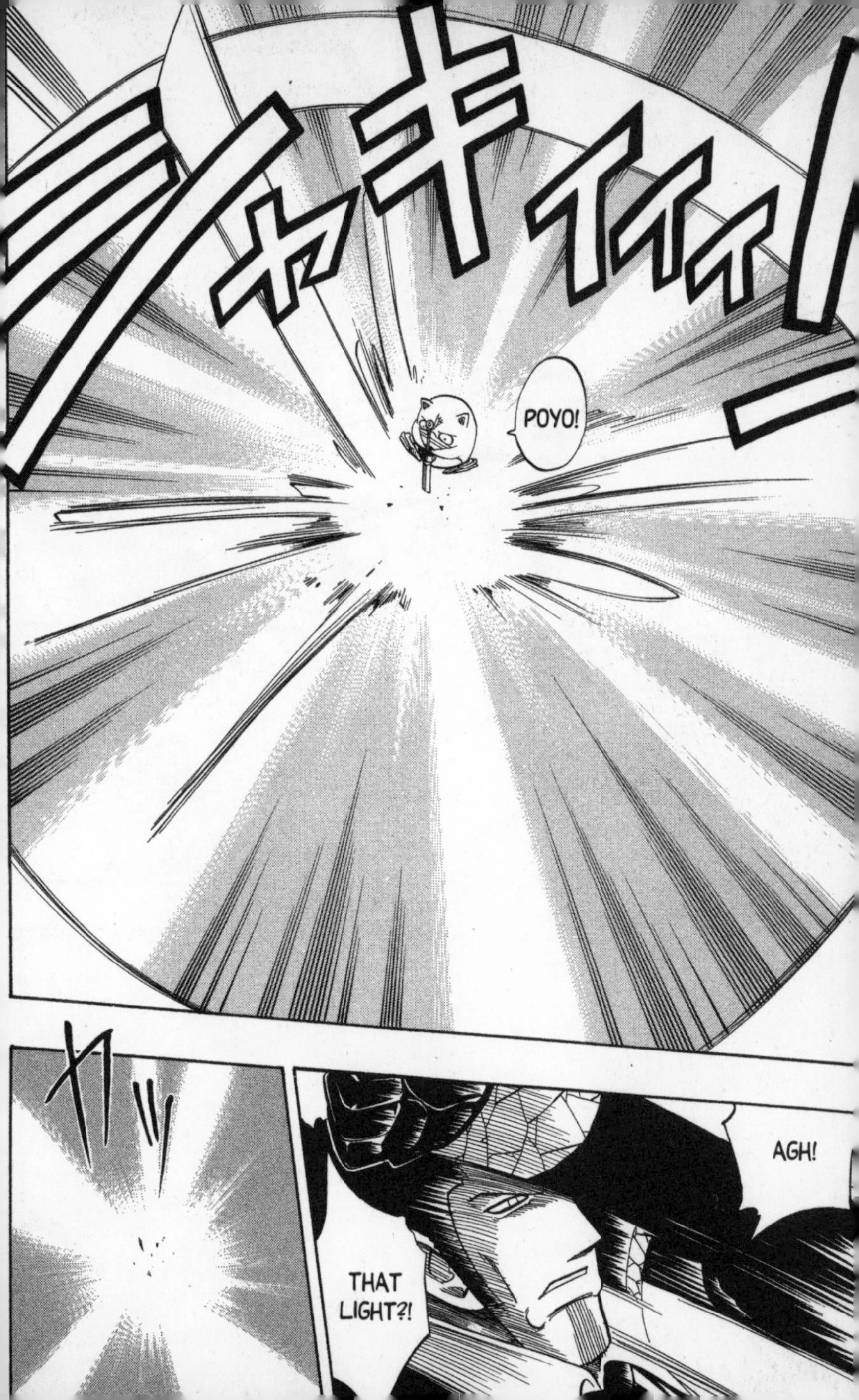
POYO!
AGH!
THAT LIGHT?!

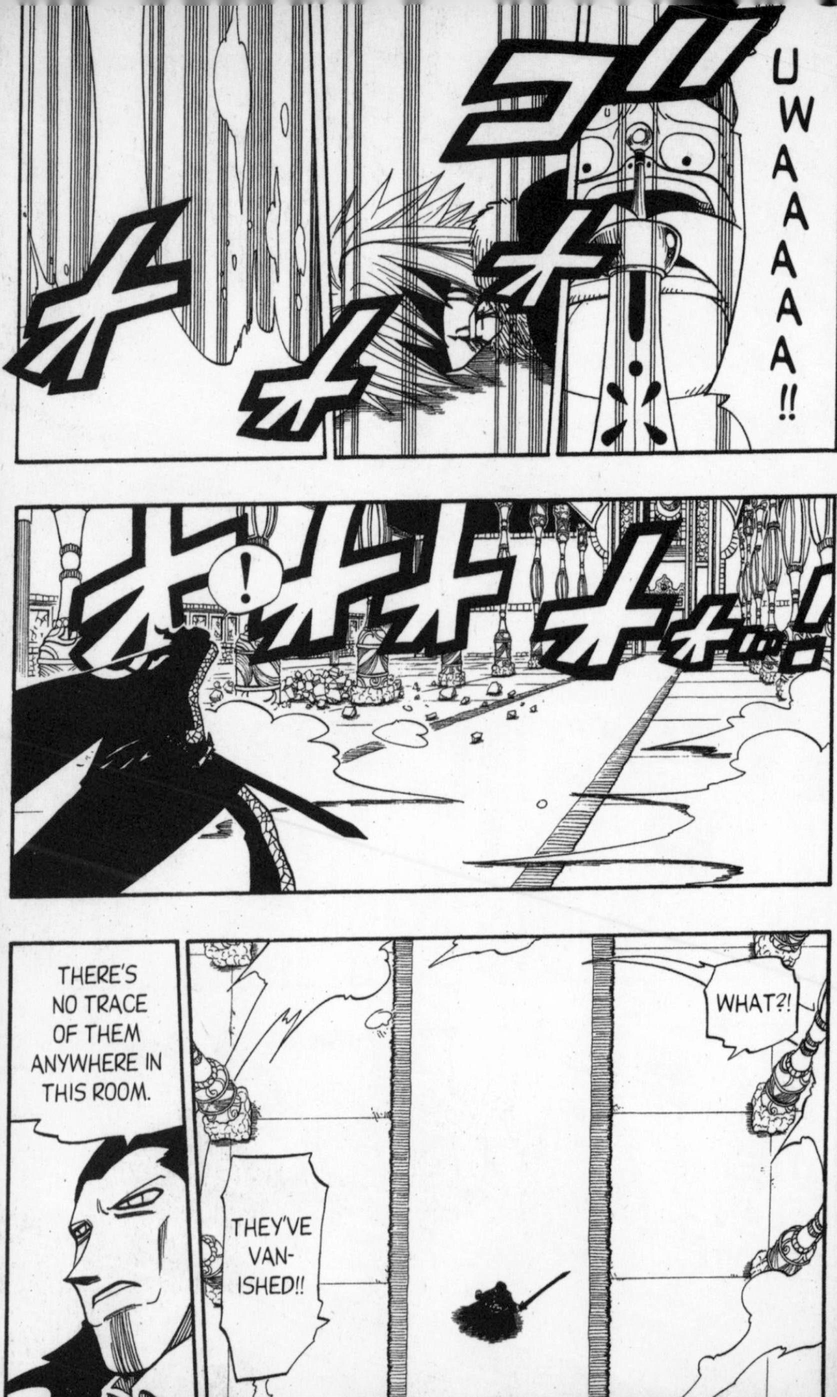
UWAAAAA!!
!
WHAT?!
THEY'VE VAN-ISHED!!
THERE'S NO TRACE OF THEM ANYWHERE IN THIS ROOM.

ゴゴ ゴ ゴゴ
POOF
!
AAAAAGH!!
THE OCEAN, POYO!!

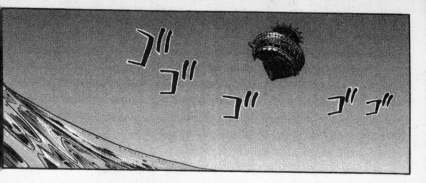

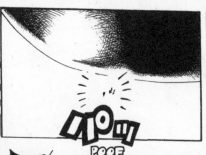

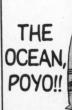

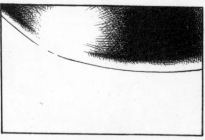

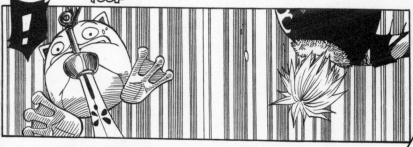

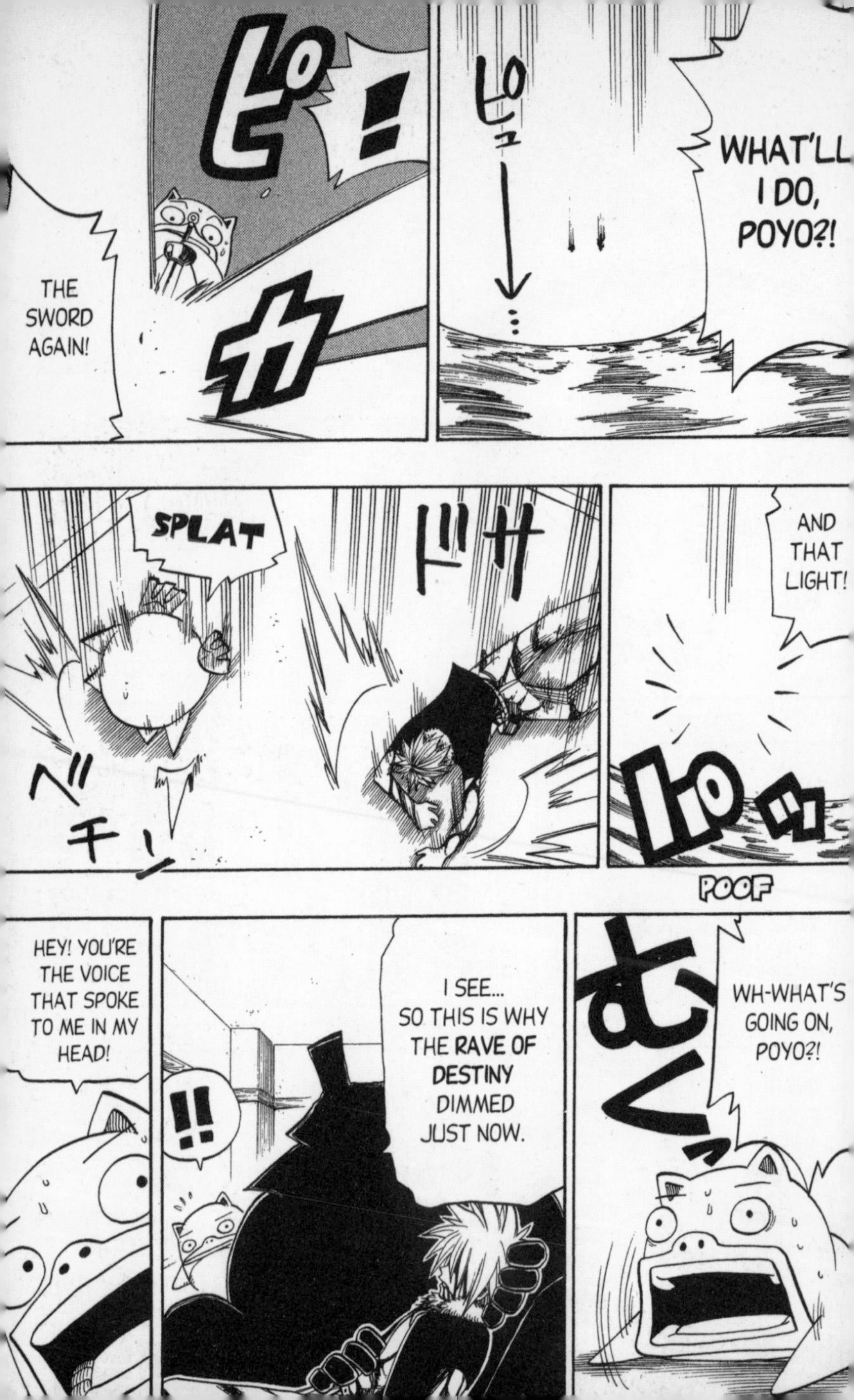
WHAT'LL I DO, POYO?!
THE SWORD AGAIN!
AND THAT LIGHT!
POOF
SPLAT
WH-WHAT'S GOING ON, POYO?!
I SEE... SO THIS IS WHY THE **RAVE OF DESTINY** DIMMED JUST NOW.
!!
HEY! YOU'RE THE VOICE THAT SPOKE TO ME IN MY HEAD!

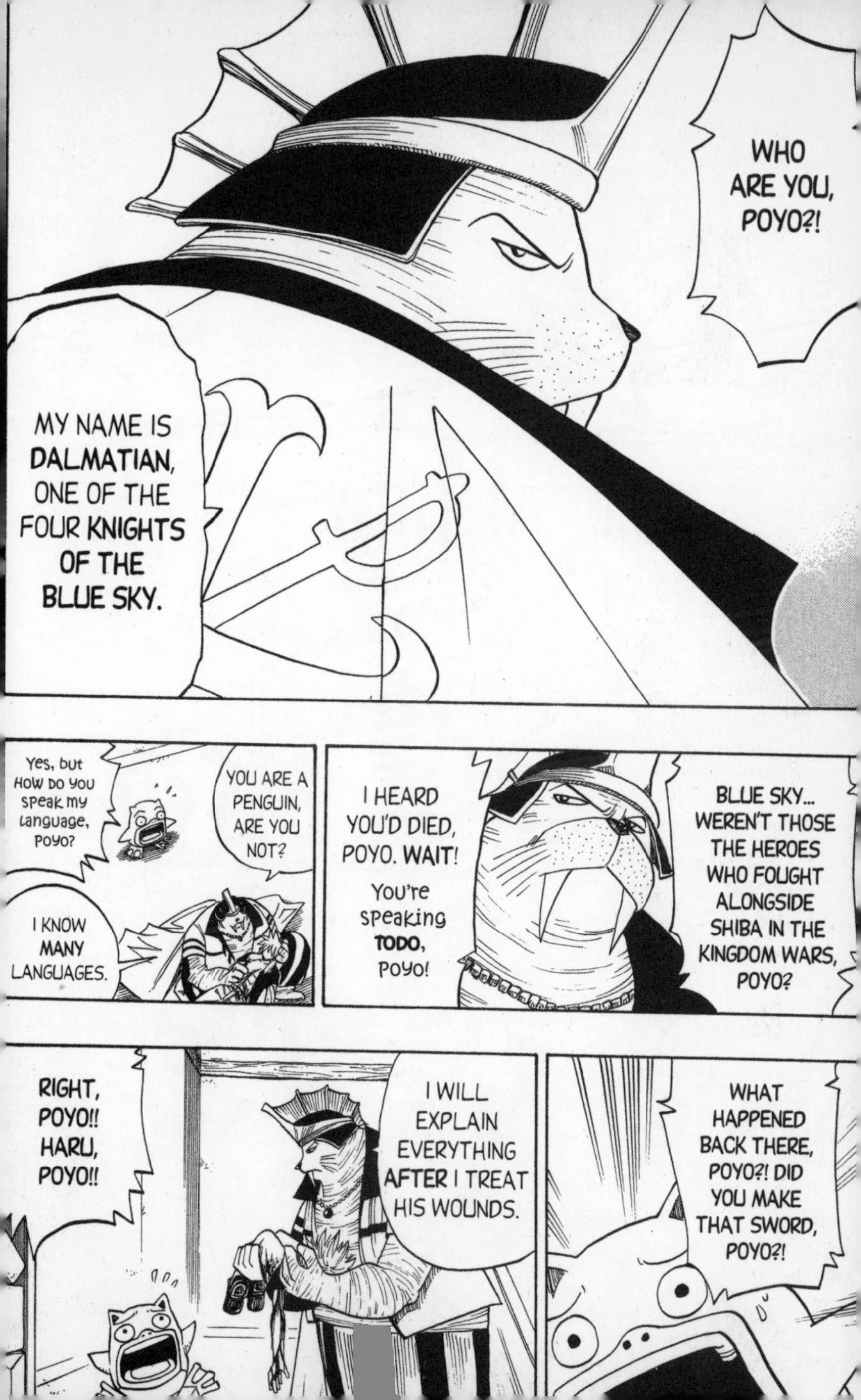
WHO ARE YOU, POYO?!
MY NAME IS DALMATIAN, ONE OF THE FOUR KNIGHTS OF THE BLUE SKY.
BLUE SKY... WEREN'T THOSE THE HEROES WHO FOUGHT ALONGSIDE SHIBA IN THE KINGDOM WARS, POYO?
I HEARD YOU'D DIED, POYO. WAIT!
You're speaking TODO, Poyo!
YOU ARE A PENGUIN, ARE YOU NOT?
Yes, but how do you speak my language, Poyo?
I KNOW MANY LANGUAGES.
WHAT HAPPENED BACK THERE, POYO?! DID YOU MAKE THAT SWORD, POYO?!
I WILL EXPLAIN EVERYTHING AFTER I TREAT HIS WOUNDS.
RIGHT, POYO!! HARU, POYO!!

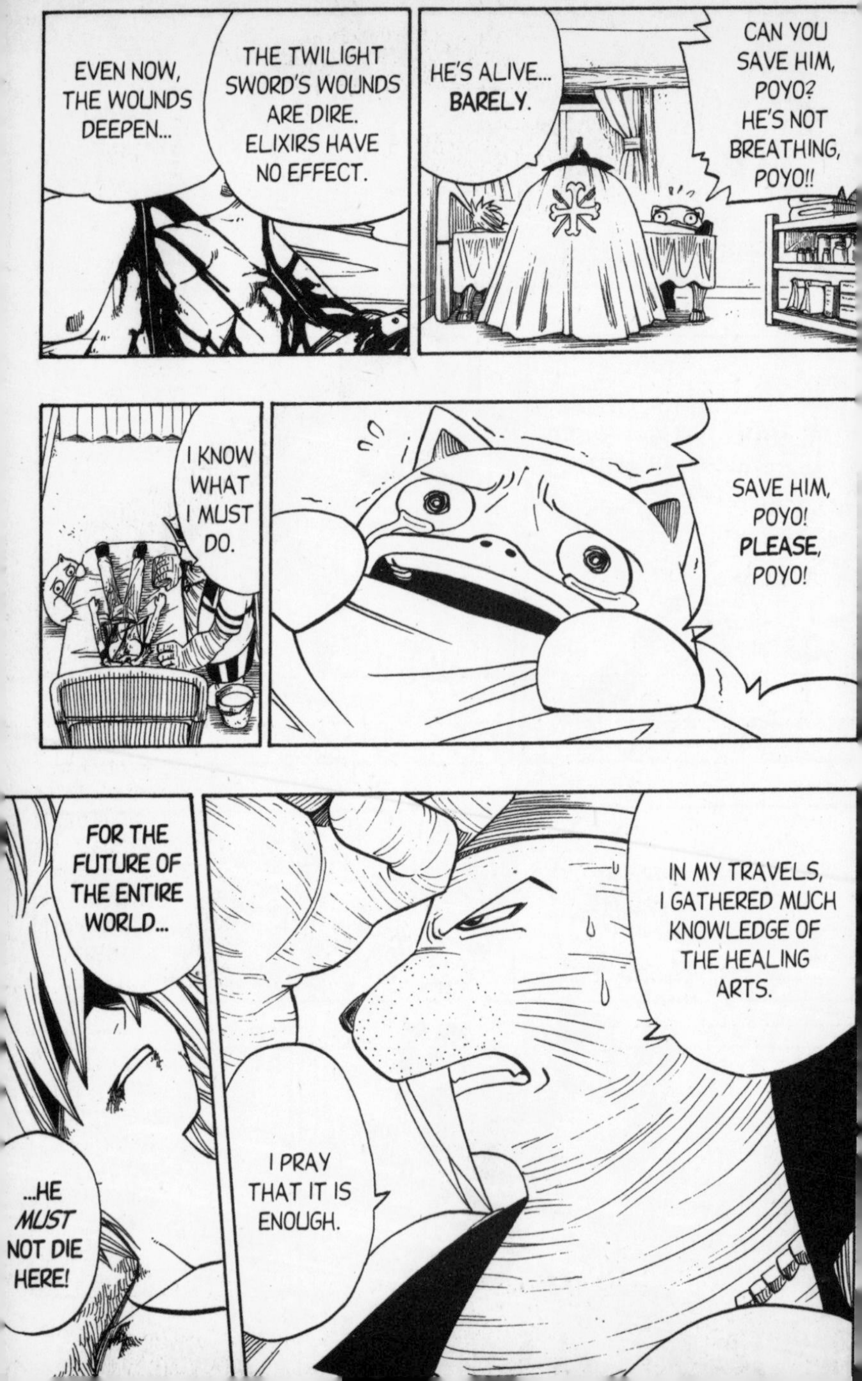
CAN YOU SAVE HIM, POYO? HE'S NOT BREATHING, POYO!!
HE'S ALIVE... **BARELY.**
THE TWILIGHT SWORD'S WOUNDS ARE DIRE. ELIXIRS HAVE NO EFFECT.
EVEN NOW, THE WOUNDS DEEPEN...
SAVE HIM, POYO! **PLEASE,** POYO!
I KNOW WHAT I MUST DO.
IN MY TRAVELS, I GATHERED MUCH KNOWLEDGE OF THE HEALING ARTS.
I PRAY THAT IT IS ENOUGH.
FOR THE FUTURE OF THE ENTIRE WORLD...
...HE *MUST* NOT DIE HERE!

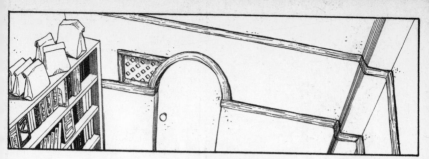

ガチャ
THE SURGERY IS FINISHED... NOW, THE REAL PROBLEM.
WOUNDS INFLICTED BY THE TWILIGHT SWORD WORSEN AS NIGHT DEEPENS.
THE TIME IS 6:21 P.M.
HARU'S LIFE HANGS IN THE BALANCE UNTIL THE PASSAGE OF MIDNIGHT.
HARU...
AND IF HE DOES LIVE, HE WON'T BE ABLE TO MOVE HIS BODY FOR A YEAR.
WE CAN ONLY KEEP FAITH.

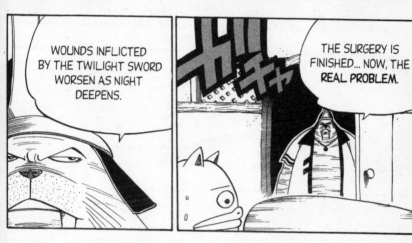

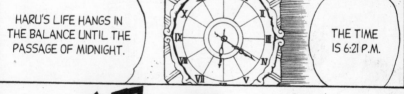

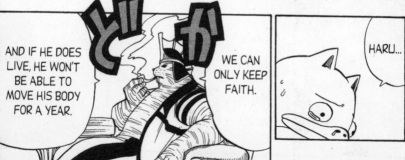

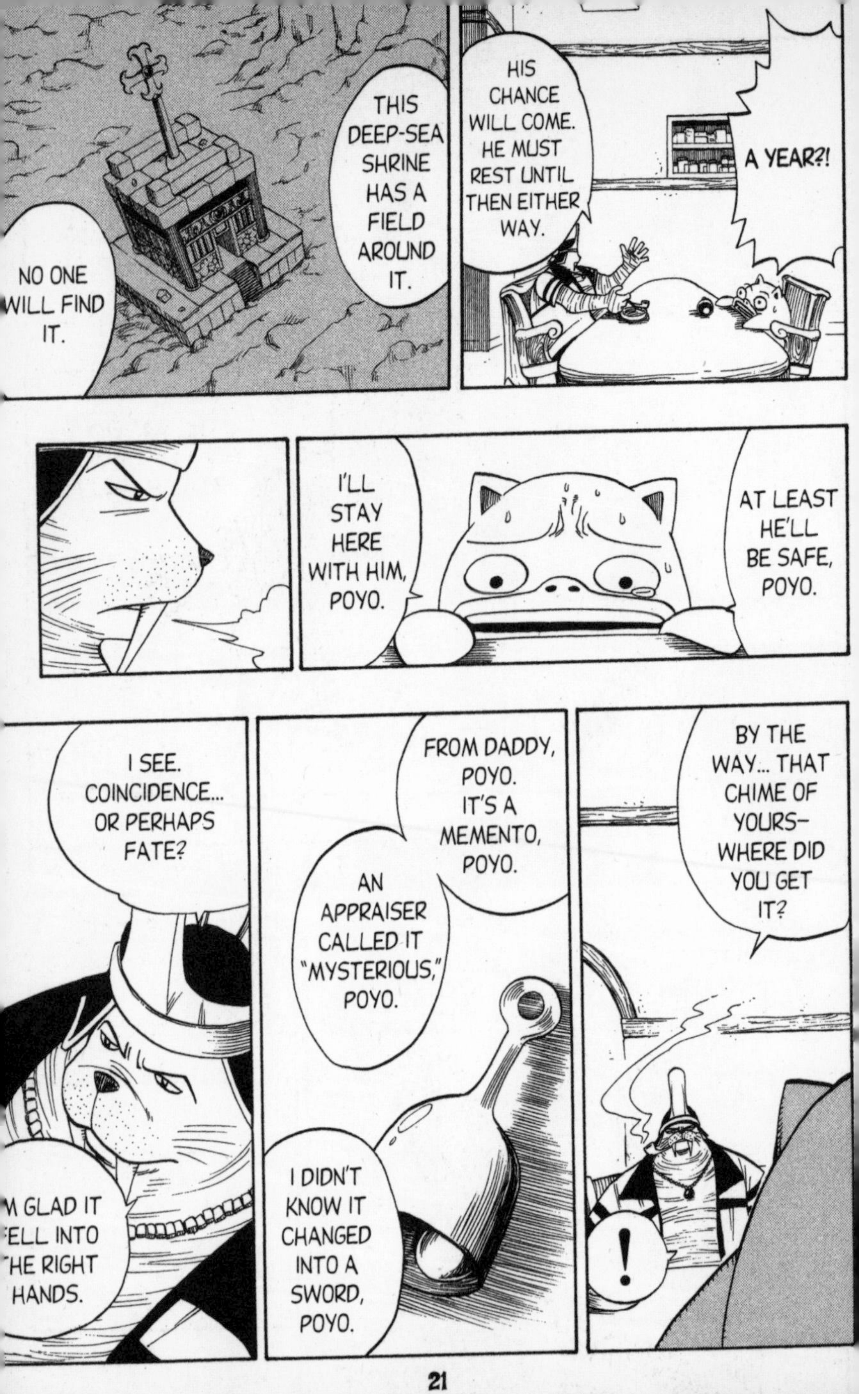
A YEAR?!
HIS CHANCE WILL COME. HE MUST REST UNTIL THEN EITHER WAY.
THIS DEEP-SEA SHRINE HAS A FIELD AROUND IT.
NO ONE WILL FIND IT.
AT LEAST HE'LL BE SAFE, POYO.
I'LL STAY HERE WITH HIM, POYO.
BY THE WAY... THAT CHIME OF YOURS— WHERE DID YOU GET IT?
!
FROM DADDY, POYO. IT'S A MEMENTO, POYO.
AN APPRAISER CALLED IT "MYSTERIOUS," POYO.
I DIDN'T KNOW IT CHANGED INTO A SWORD, POYO.
I SEE. COINCIDENCE... OR PERHAPS FATE?
M GLAD IT ELL INTO HE RIGHT HANDS.

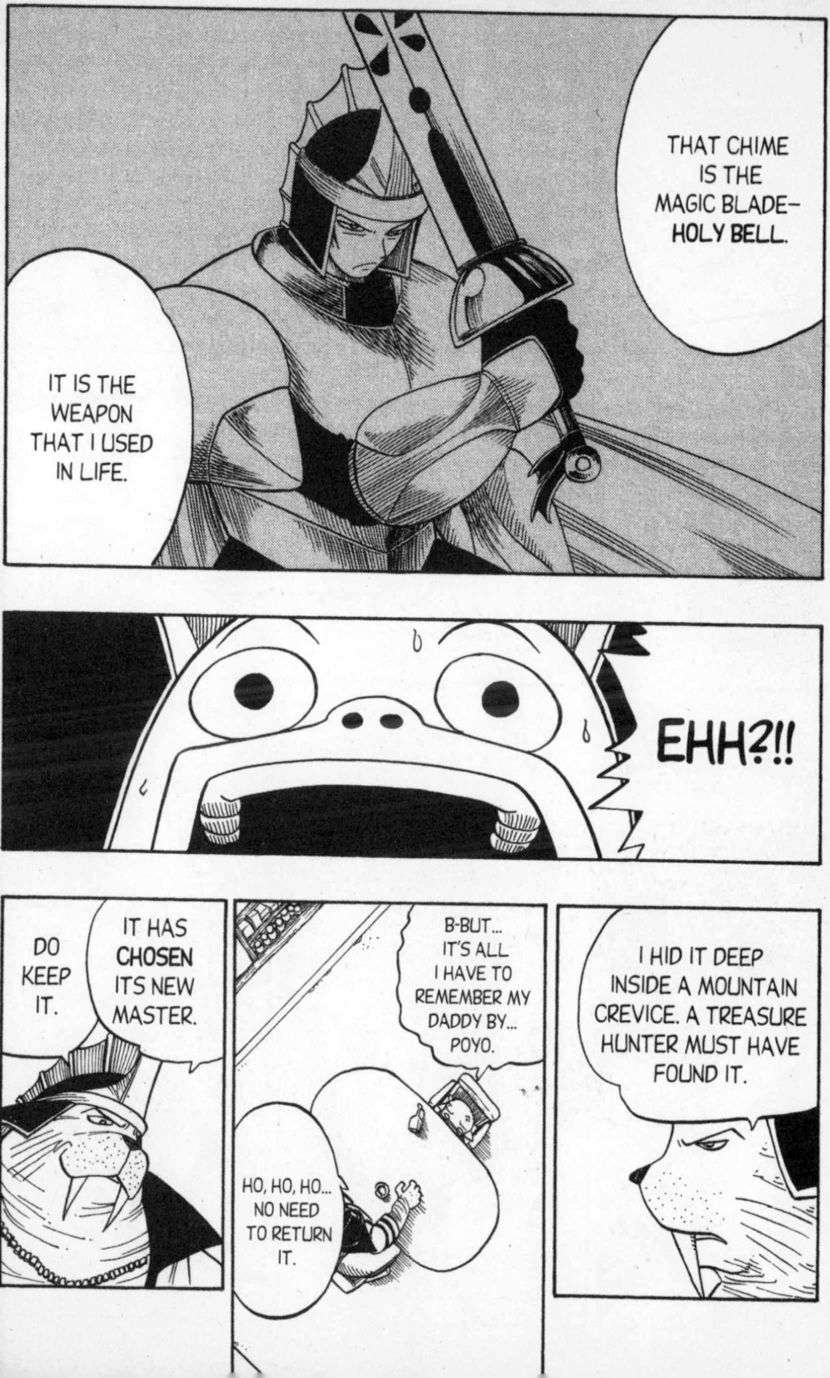
THAT CHIME IS THE MAGIC BLADE— HOLY BELL.
IT IS THE WEAPON THAT I USED IN LIFE.
EHH?!!
I HID IT DEEP INSIDE A MOUNTAIN CREVICE. A TREASURE HUNTER MUST HAVE FOUND IT.
B-BUT... IT'S ALL I HAVE TO REMEMBER MY DADDY BY... POYO.
HO, HO, HO... NO NEED TO RETURN IT.
IT HAS CHOSEN ITS NEW MASTER.
DO KEEP IT.

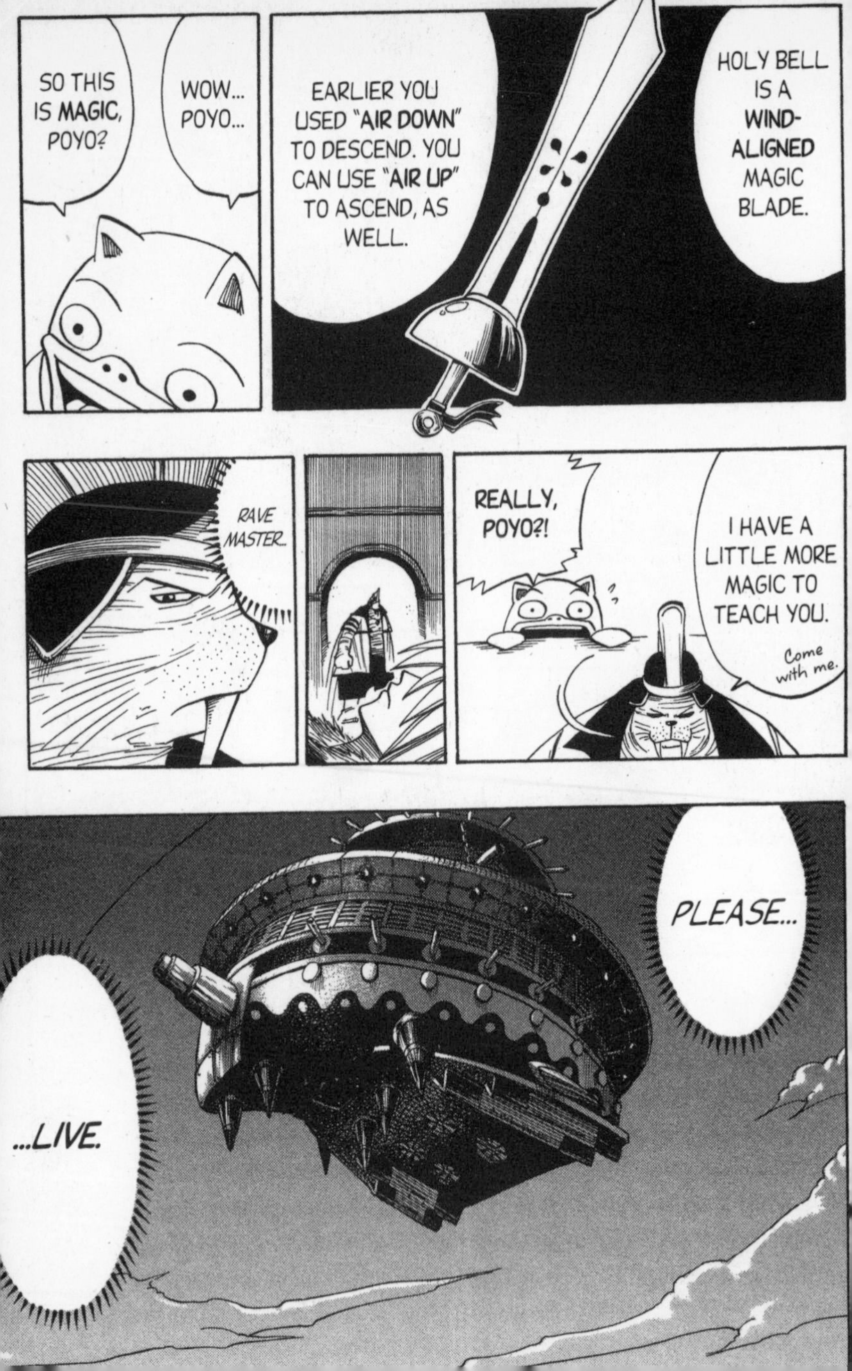
HOLY BELL IS A WIND-ALIGNED MAGIC BLADE.
EARLIER YOU USED "AIR DOWN" TO DESCEND. YOU CAN USE "AIR UP" TO ASCEND, AS WELL.
WOW... POYO...
SO THIS IS MAGIC, POYO?
I HAVE A LITTLE MORE MAGIC TO TEACH YOU.
Come with me.
REALLY, POYO?!
RAVE MASTER...
PLEASE...
...LIVE.

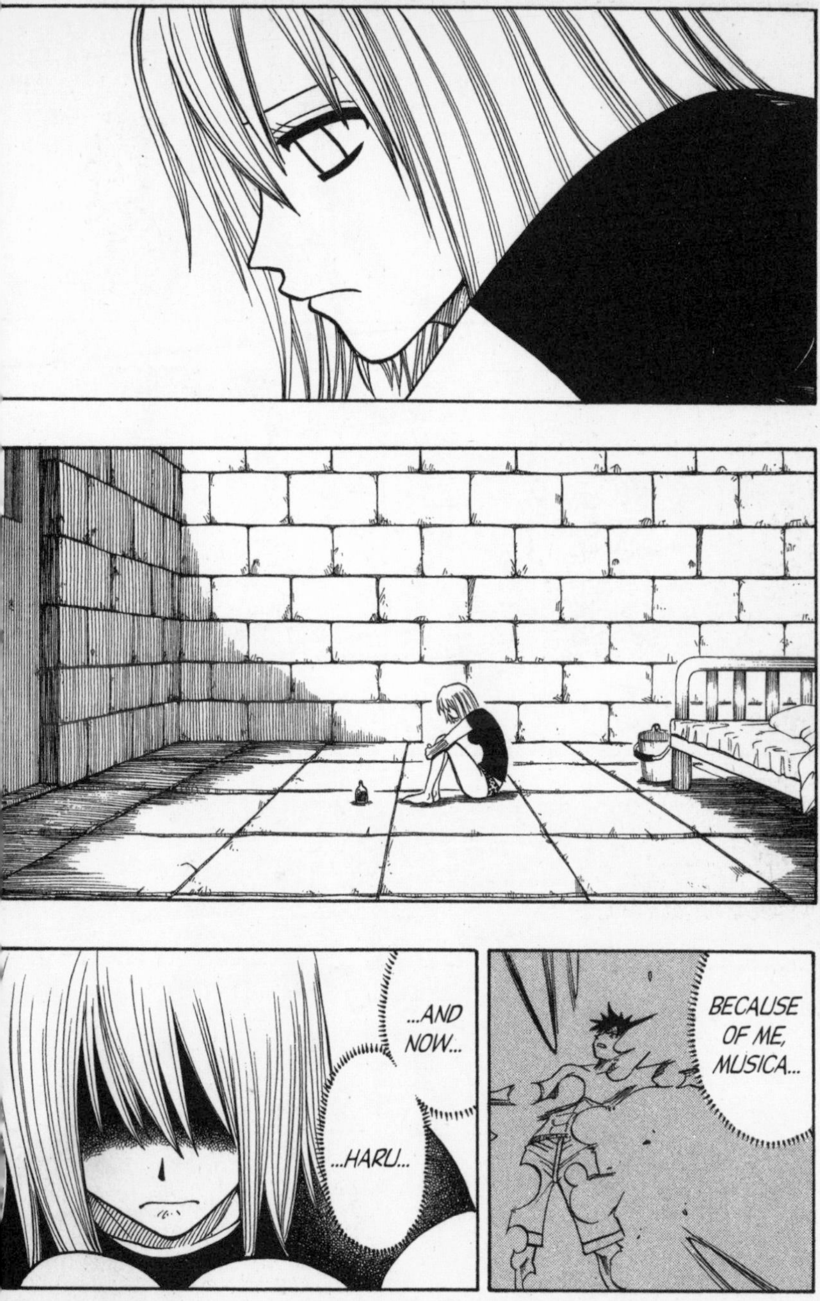
BECAUSE OF ME, MUSICA...
...AND NOW...
...HARU...

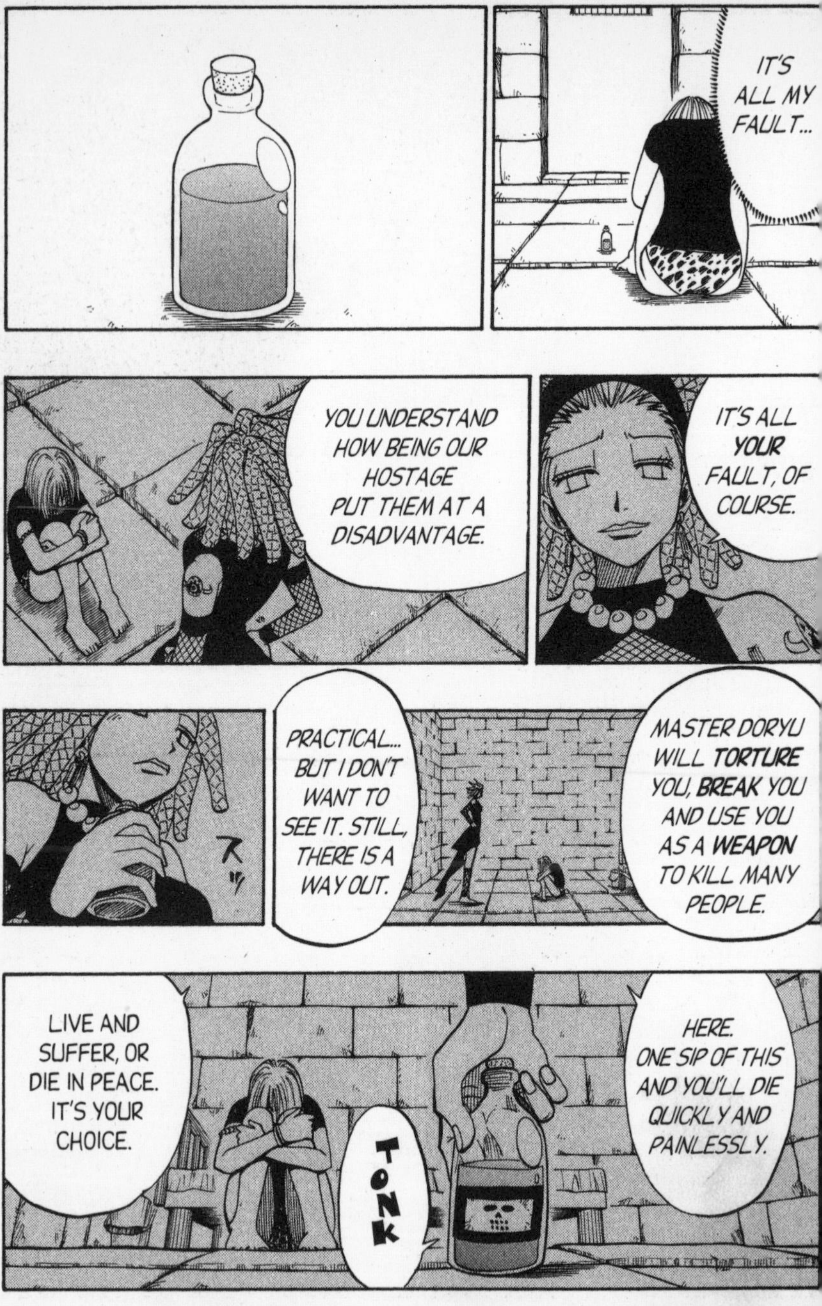
IT'S ALL MY FAULT...
IT'S ALL YOUR FAULT, OF COURSE.
YOU UNDERSTAND HOW BEING OUR HOSTAGE PUT THEM AT A DISADVANTAGE.
MASTER DORYU WILL TORTURE YOU, BREAK YOU AND USE YOU AS A WEAPON TO KILL MANY PEOPLE.
PRACTICAL... BUT I DON'T WANT TO SEE IT. STILL, THERE IS A WAY OUT.
スッ
HERE. ONE SIP OF THIS AND YOU'LL DIE QUICKLY AND PAINLESSLY.
TONK
LIVE AND SUFFER, OR DIE IN PEACE. IT'S YOUR CHOICE.

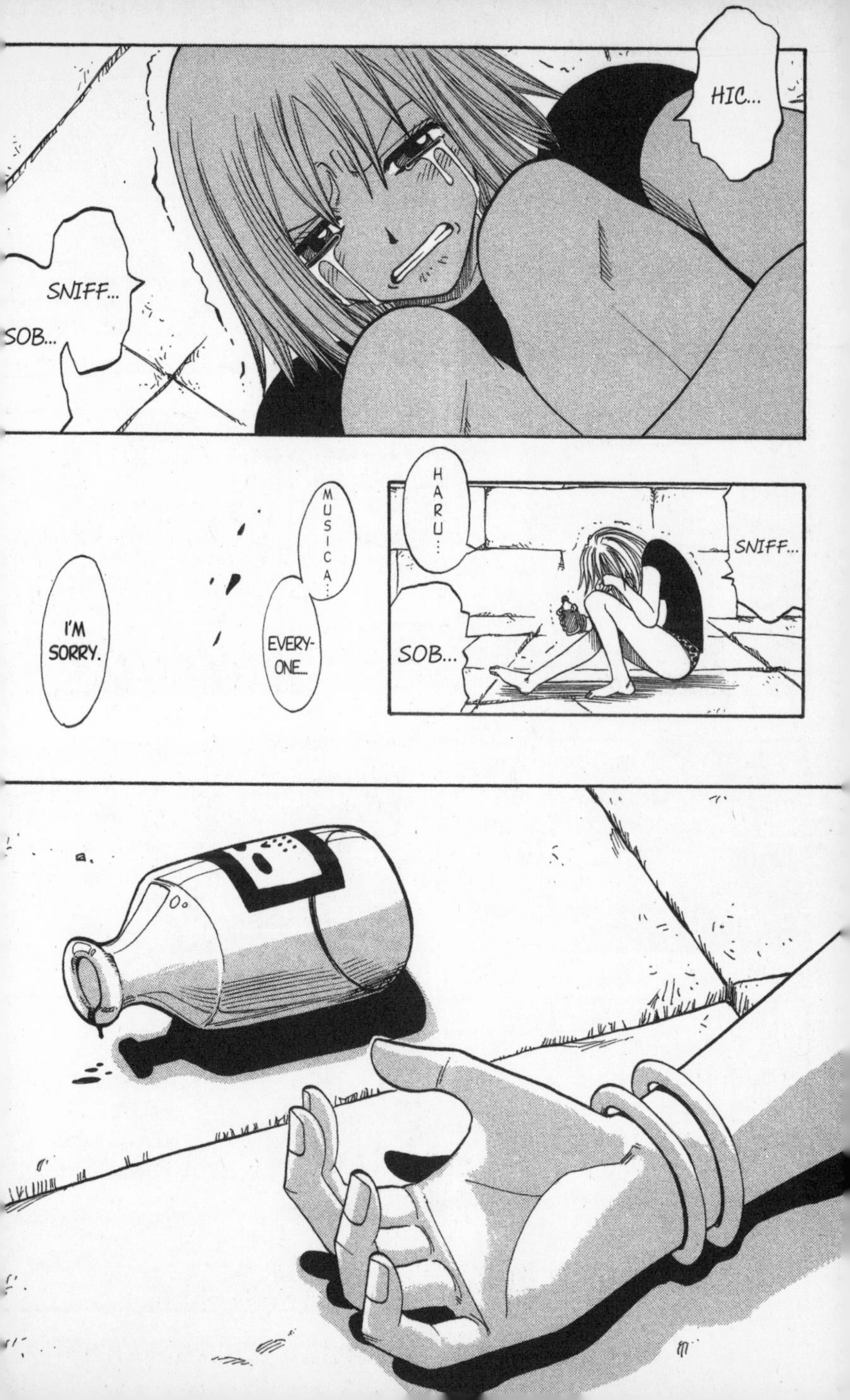
HIC...
SNIFF...
SOB...
HARU...
SNIFF...
SOB...
MUSICA...
EVERY-ONE...
I'M SORRY.

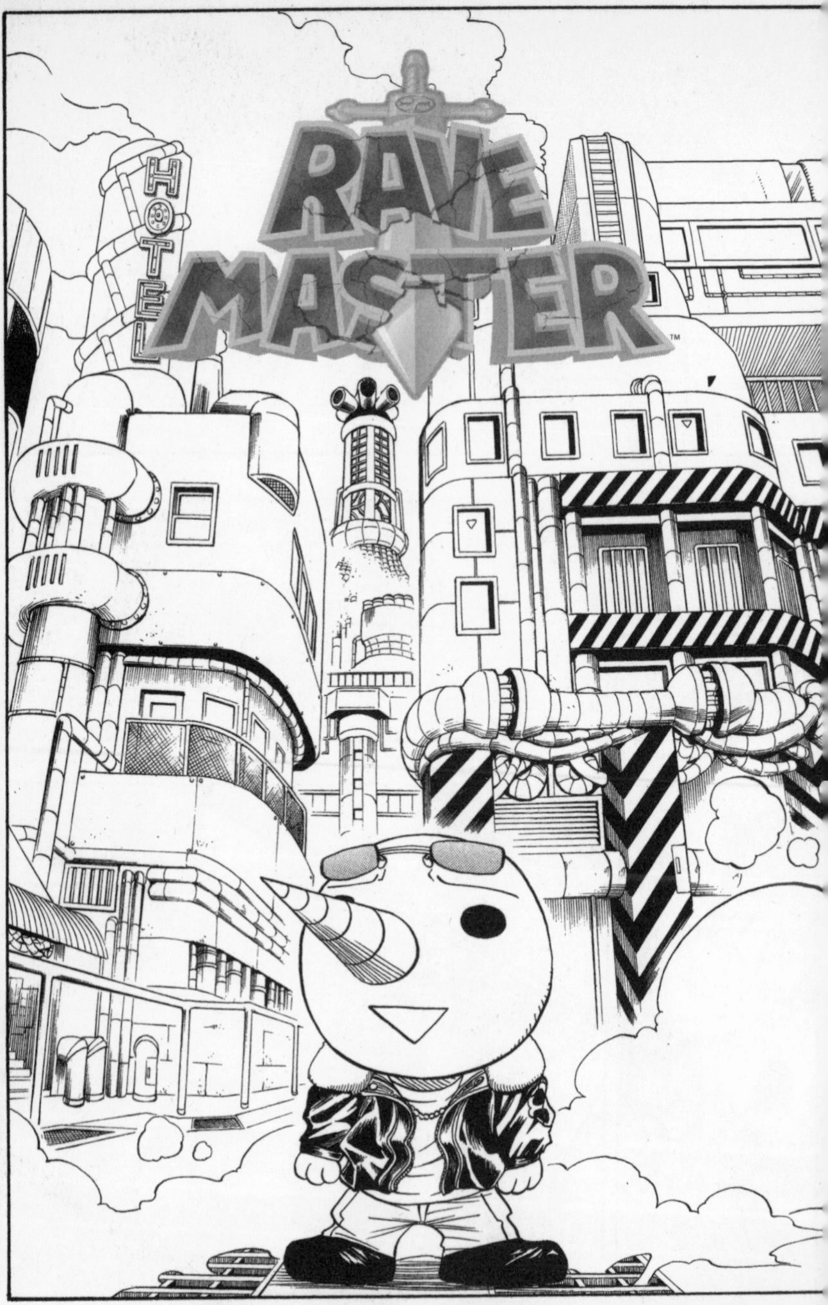
RAVE MASTER™
HOTEL

RAVE:124 CRUEL REVELATION

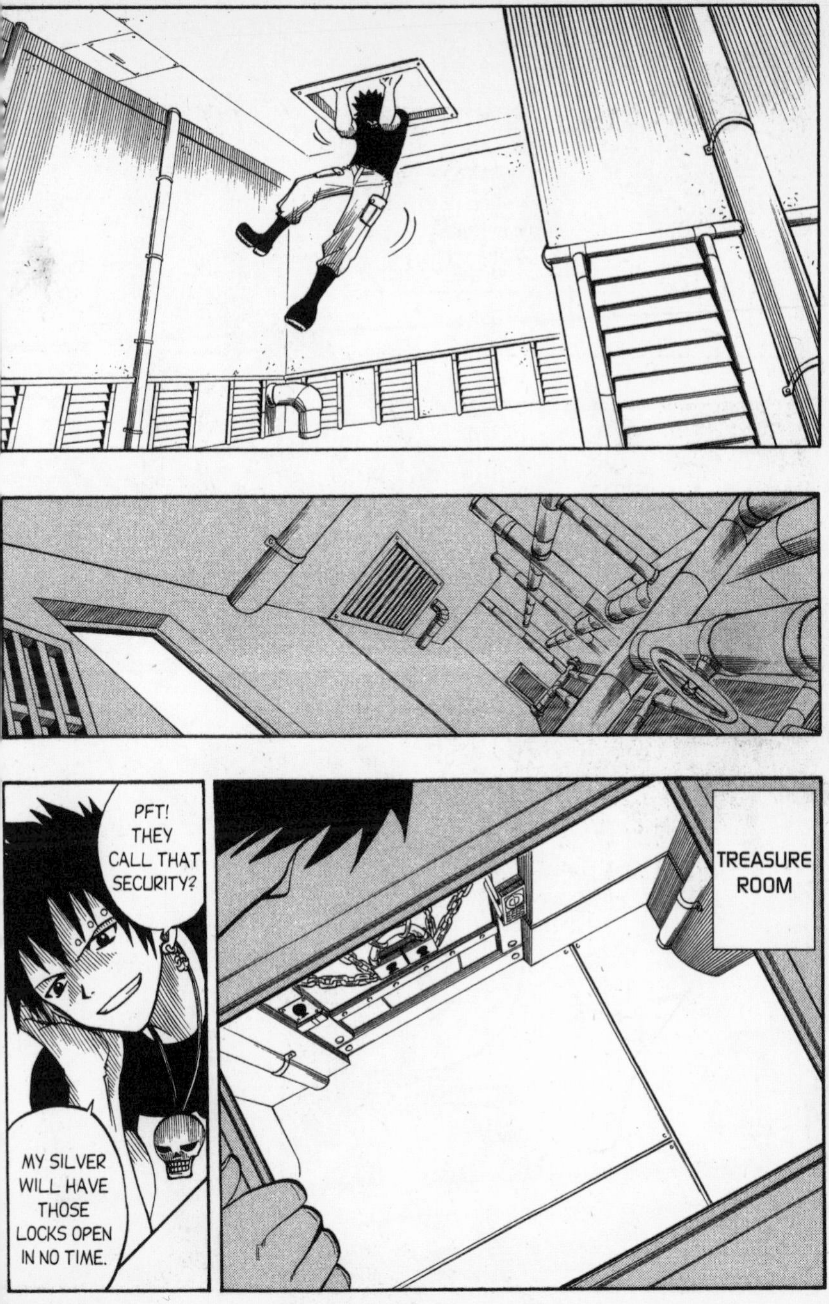
TREASURE ROOM
PFT! THEY CALL THAT SECURITY?
MY SILVER WILL HAVE THOSE LOCKS OPEN IN NO TIME.

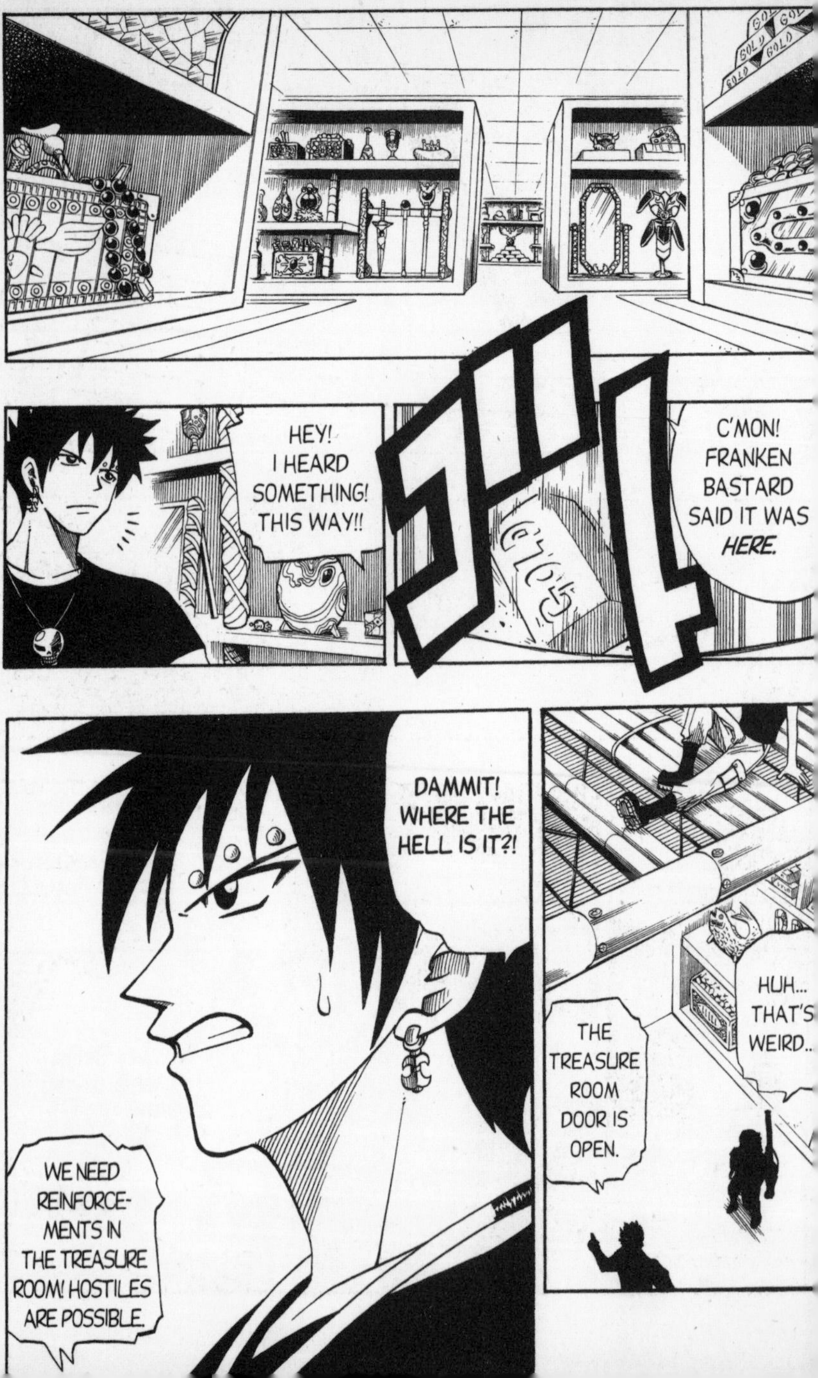
C'MON! FRANKEN BASTARD SAID IT WAS *HERE*.
HEY! I HEARD SOMETHING! THIS WAY!!
HUH... THAT'S WEIRD..
THE TREASURE ROOM DOOR IS OPEN.
DAMMIT! WHERE THE HELL IS IT?!
WE NEED REINFORCE-MENTS IN THE TREASURE ROOM! HOSTILES ARE POSSIBLE.

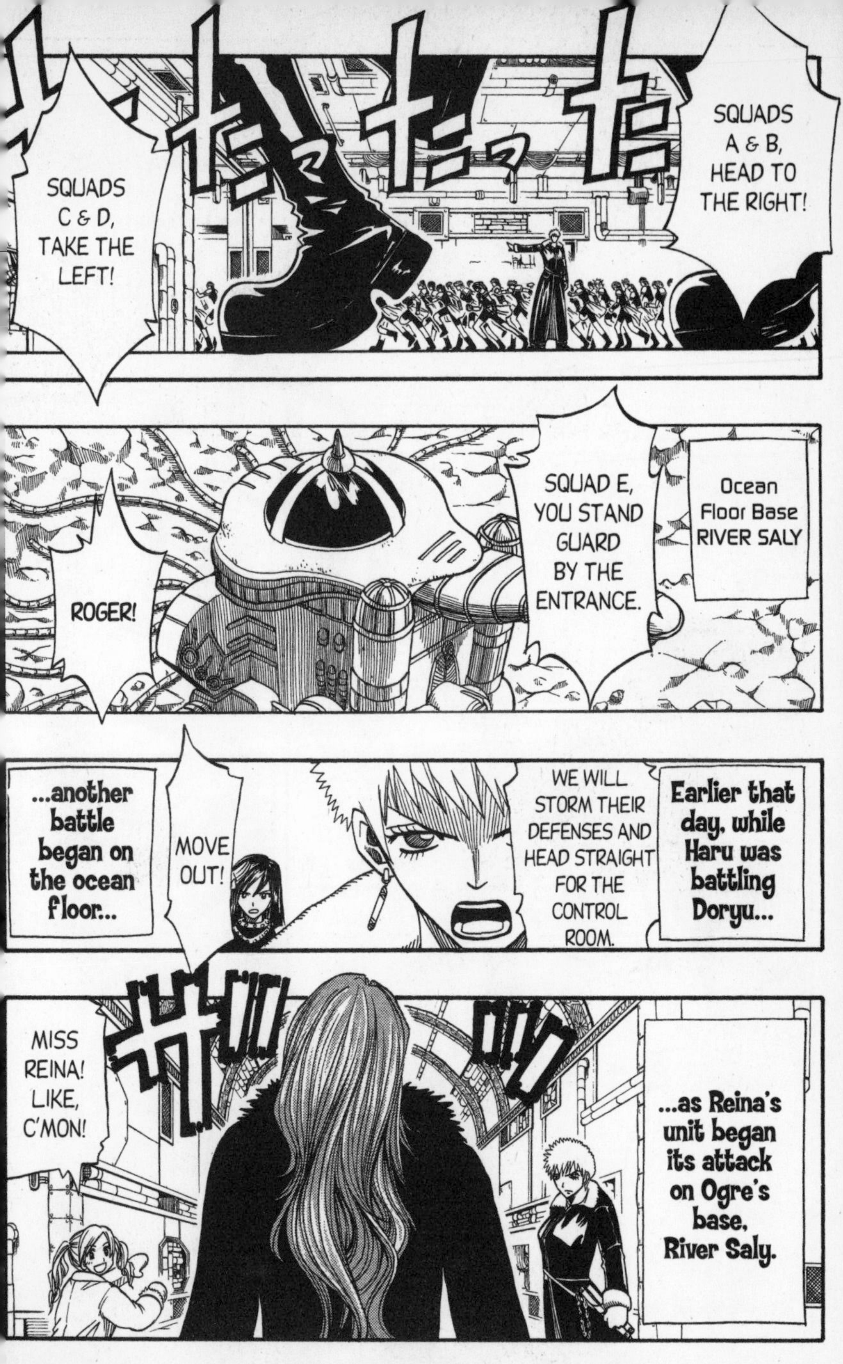
SQUADS A & B, HEAD TO THE RIGHT!
SQUADS C & D, TAKE THE LEFT!
Ocean Floor Base RIVER SALY
SQUAD E, YOU STAND GUARD BY THE ENTRANCE.
ROGER!
Earlier that day, while Haru was battling Doryu...
WE WILL STORM THEIR DEFENSES AND HEAD STRAIGHT FOR THE CONTROL ROOM.
MOVE OUT!
...another battle began on the ocean floor...
...as Reina's unit began its attack on Ogre's base, River Saly.
MISS REINA! LIKE, C'MON!

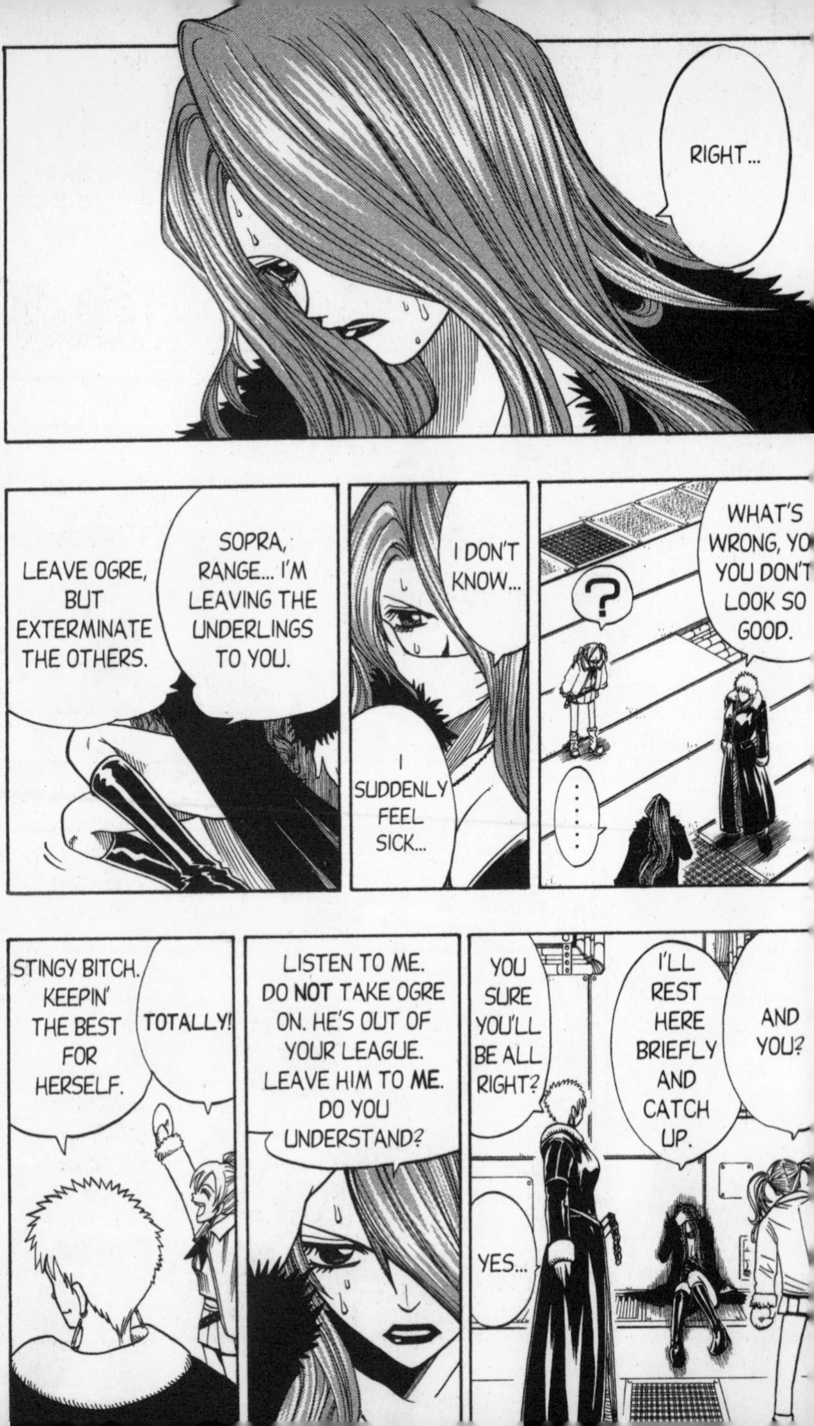
RIGHT...
WHAT'S WRONG, YO YOU DON'T LOOK SO GOOD.
?
......
I DON'T KNOW...
I SUDDENLY FEEL SICK...
SOPRA, RANGE... I'M LEAVING THE UNDERLINGS TO YOU.
LEAVE OGRE, BUT EXTERMINATE THE OTHERS.
AND YOU?
I'LL REST HERE BRIEFLY AND CATCH UP.
YOU SURE YOU'LL BE ALL RIGHT?
YES...
LISTEN TO ME. DO **NOT** TAKE OGRE ON. HE'S OUT OF YOUR LEAGUE. LEAVE HIM TO **ME**. DO YOU UNDERSTAND?
STINGY BITCH. KEEPIN' THE BEST FOR HERSELF.
TOTALLY!

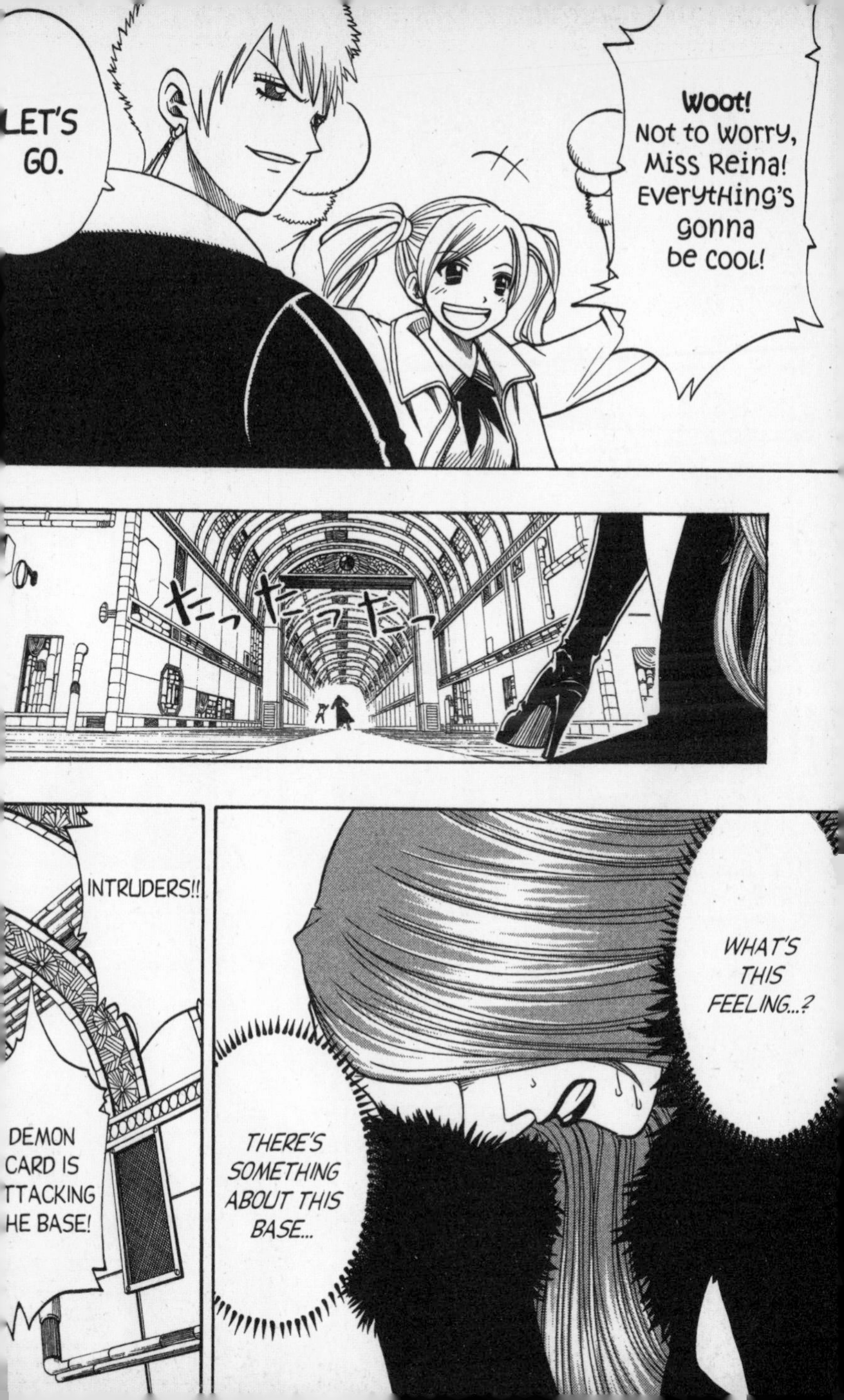
Woot! Not to worry, Miss Reina! Everything's gonna be cool!
LET'S GO.
WHAT'S THIS FEELING...?
THERE'S SOMETHING ABOUT THIS BASE...
INTRUDERS!!
DEMON CARD IS TTACKING HE BASE!

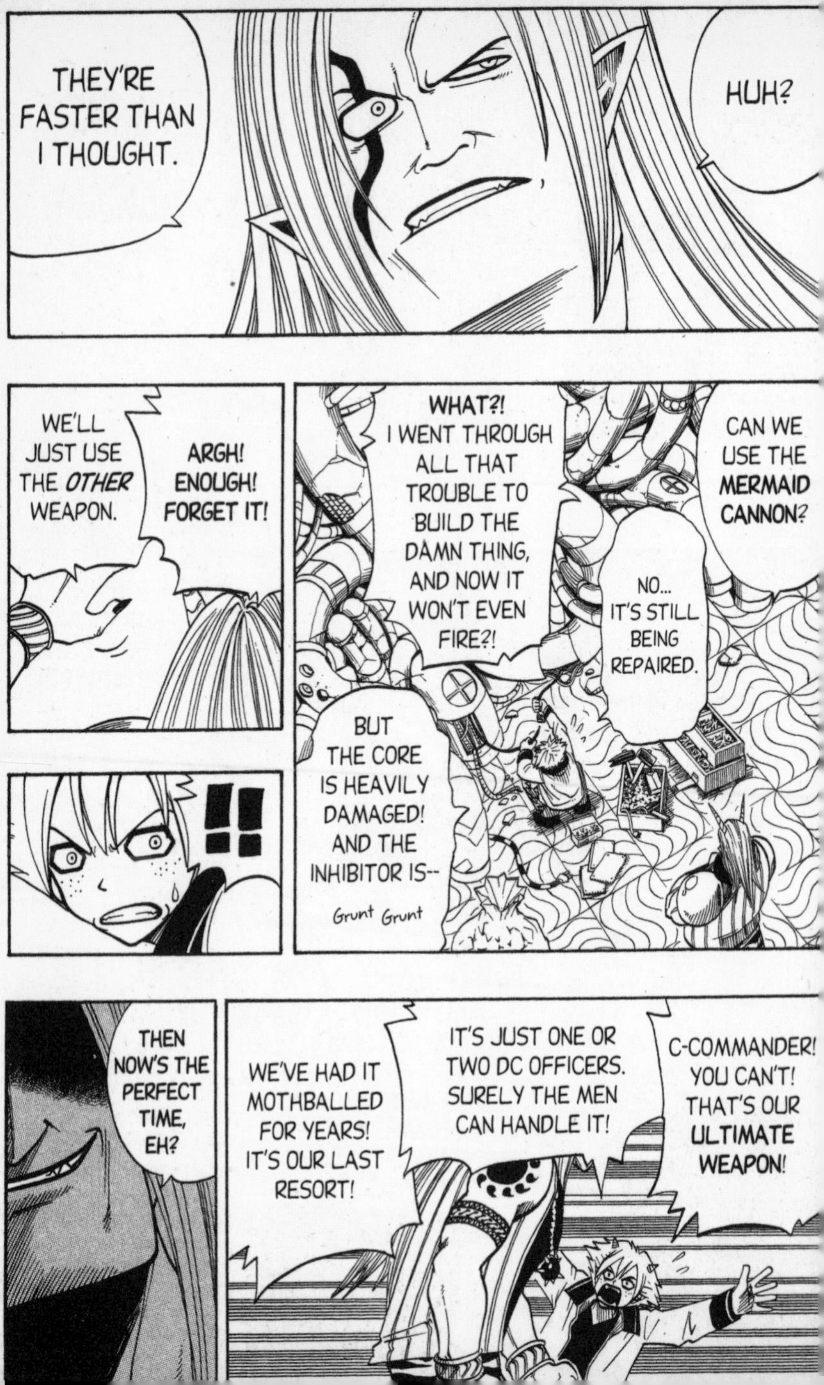
HUH?
THEY'RE FASTER THAN I THOUGHT.
CAN WE USE THE **MERMAID CANNON**?
NO... IT'S STILL BEING REPAIRED.
WHAT?! I WENT THROUGH ALL THAT TROUBLE TO BUILD THE DAMN THING, AND NOW IT WON'T EVEN FIRE?!
BUT THE CORE IS HEAVILY DAMAGED! AND THE INHIBITOR IS--
Grunt Grunt
ARGH! ENOUGH! FORGET IT!
WE'LL JUST USE THE *OTHER* WEAPON.
!!
C-COMMANDER! YOU CAN'T! THAT'S OUR **ULTIMATE WEAPON**!
IT'S JUST ONE OR TWO DC OFFICERS. SURELY THE MEN CAN HANDLE IT!
WE'VE HAD IT MOTHBALLED FOR YEARS! IT'S OUR LAST RESORT!
THEN NOW'S THE PERFECT TIME, EH?

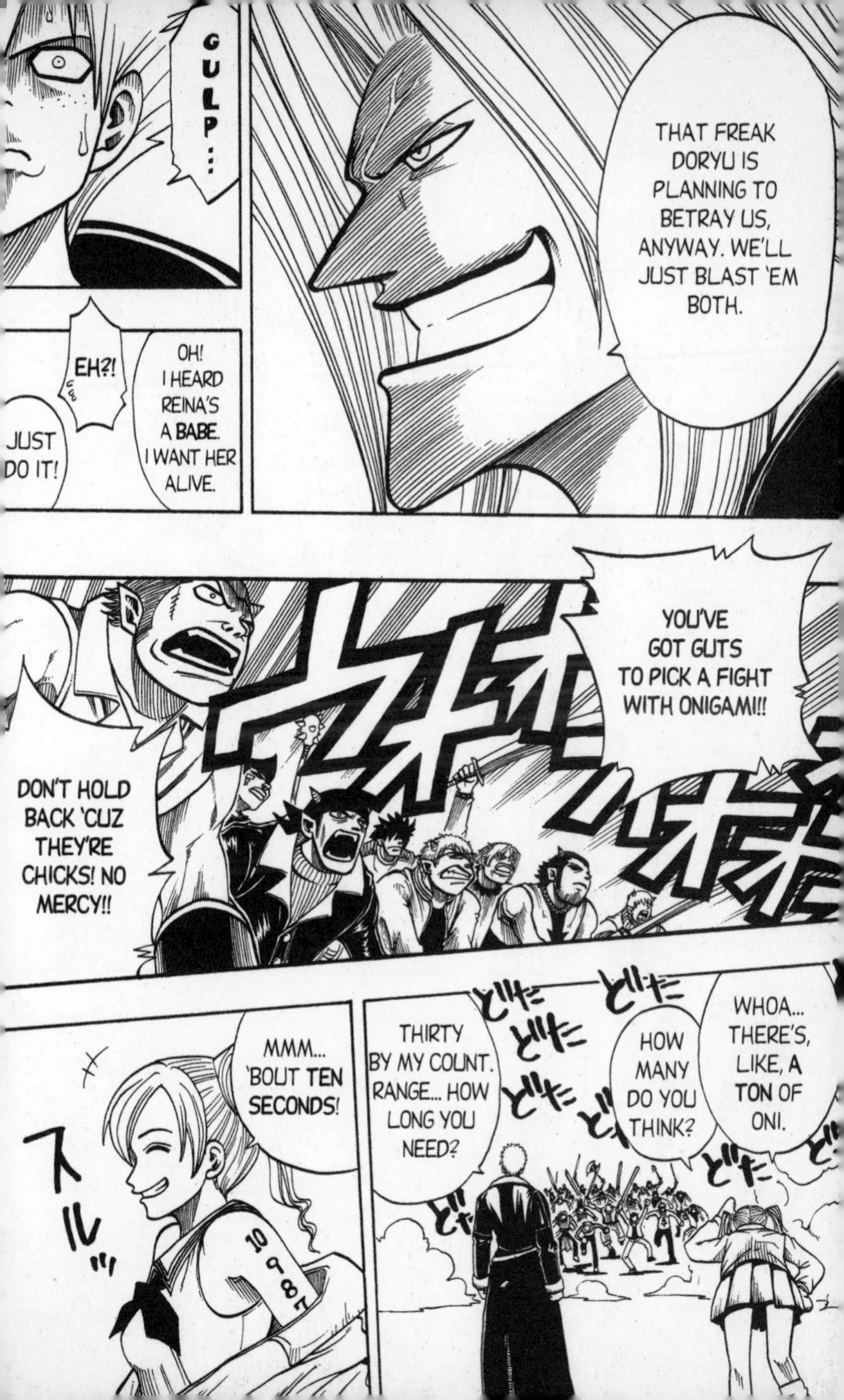
THAT FREAK DORYU IS PLANNING TO BETRAY US, ANYWAY. WE'LL JUST BLAST 'EM BOTH.
GULP...
OH! I HEARD REINA'S A BABE. I WANT HER ALIVE.
EH?!
JUST DO IT!
YOU'VE GOT GUTS TO PICK A FIGHT WITH ONIGAMI!!
DON'T HOLD BACK 'CUZ THEY'RE CHICKS! NO MERCY!!
WHOA... THERE'S, LIKE, A TON OF ONI.
HOW MANY DO YOU THINK?
THIRTY BY MY COUNT. RANGE... HOW LONG YOU NEED?
MMM... 'BOUT TEN SECONDS!

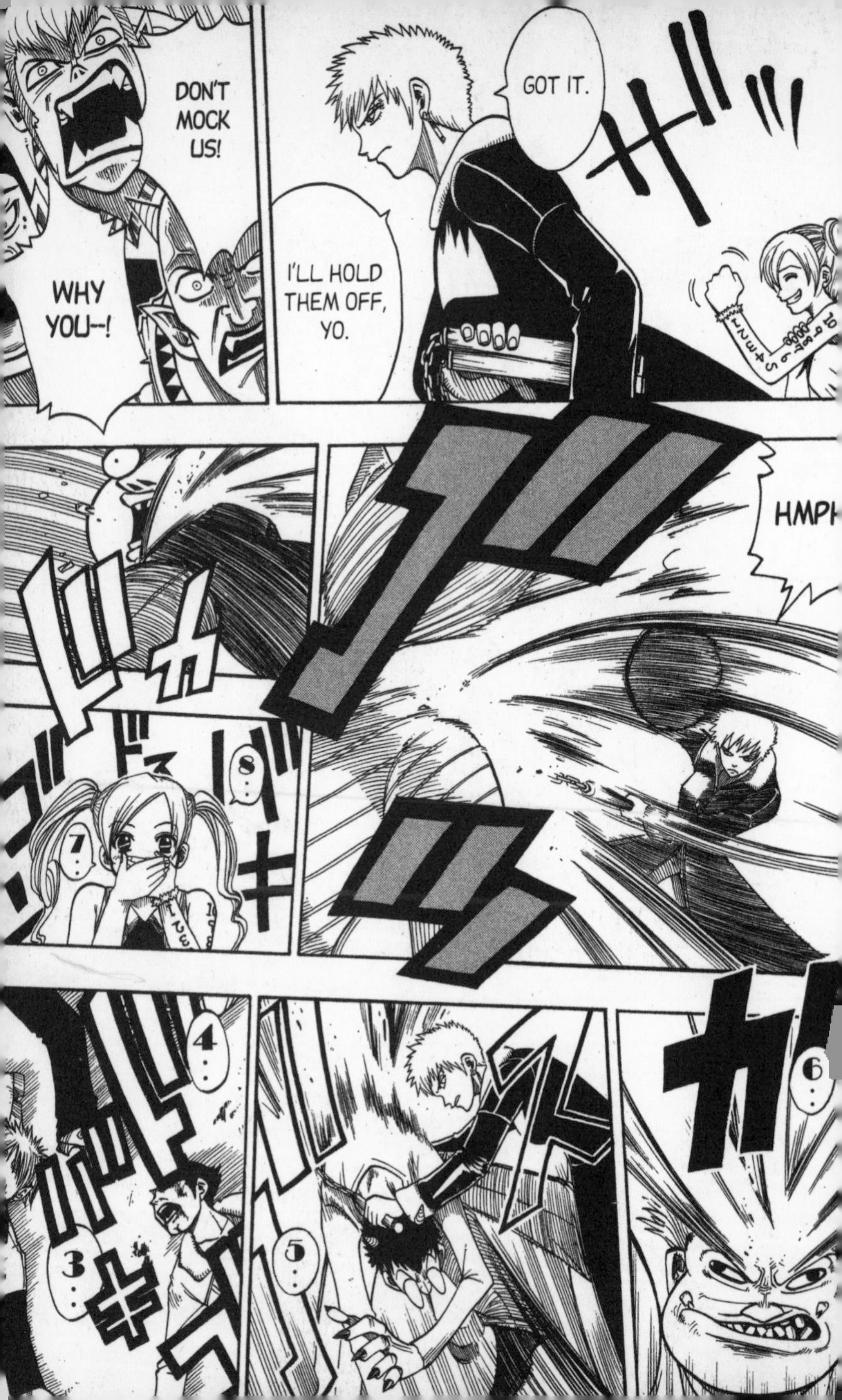
GOT IT.
I'LL HOLD THEM OFF, YO.
DON'T MOCK US!
WHY YOU--!
HMPH
8...
7...
6...
5...
4...
3...

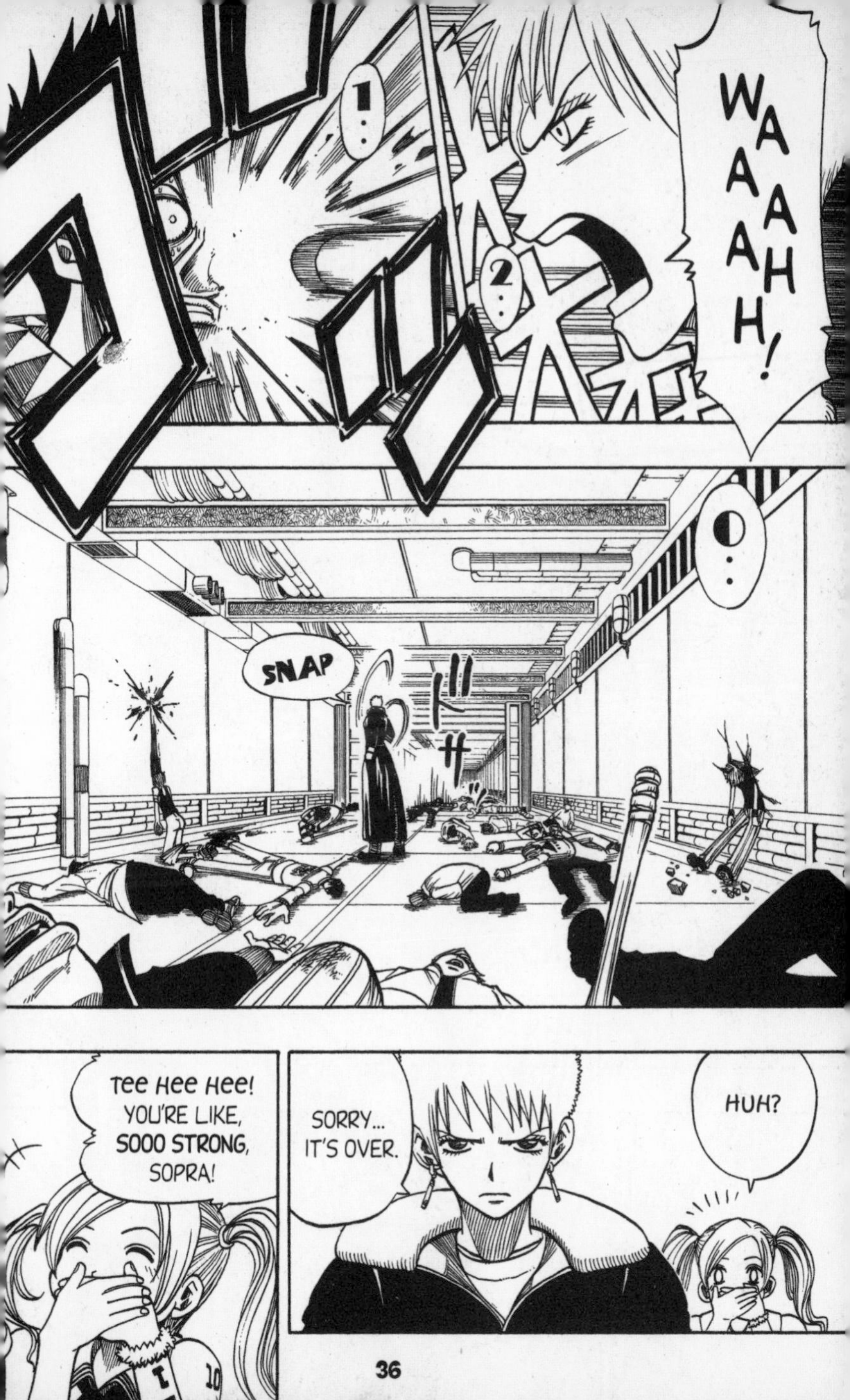
WAAAAH!
1...
2...
SNAP
HUH?
SORRY... IT'S OVER.
TEE HEE HEE! YOU'RE LIKE, SOOO STRONG, SOPRA!

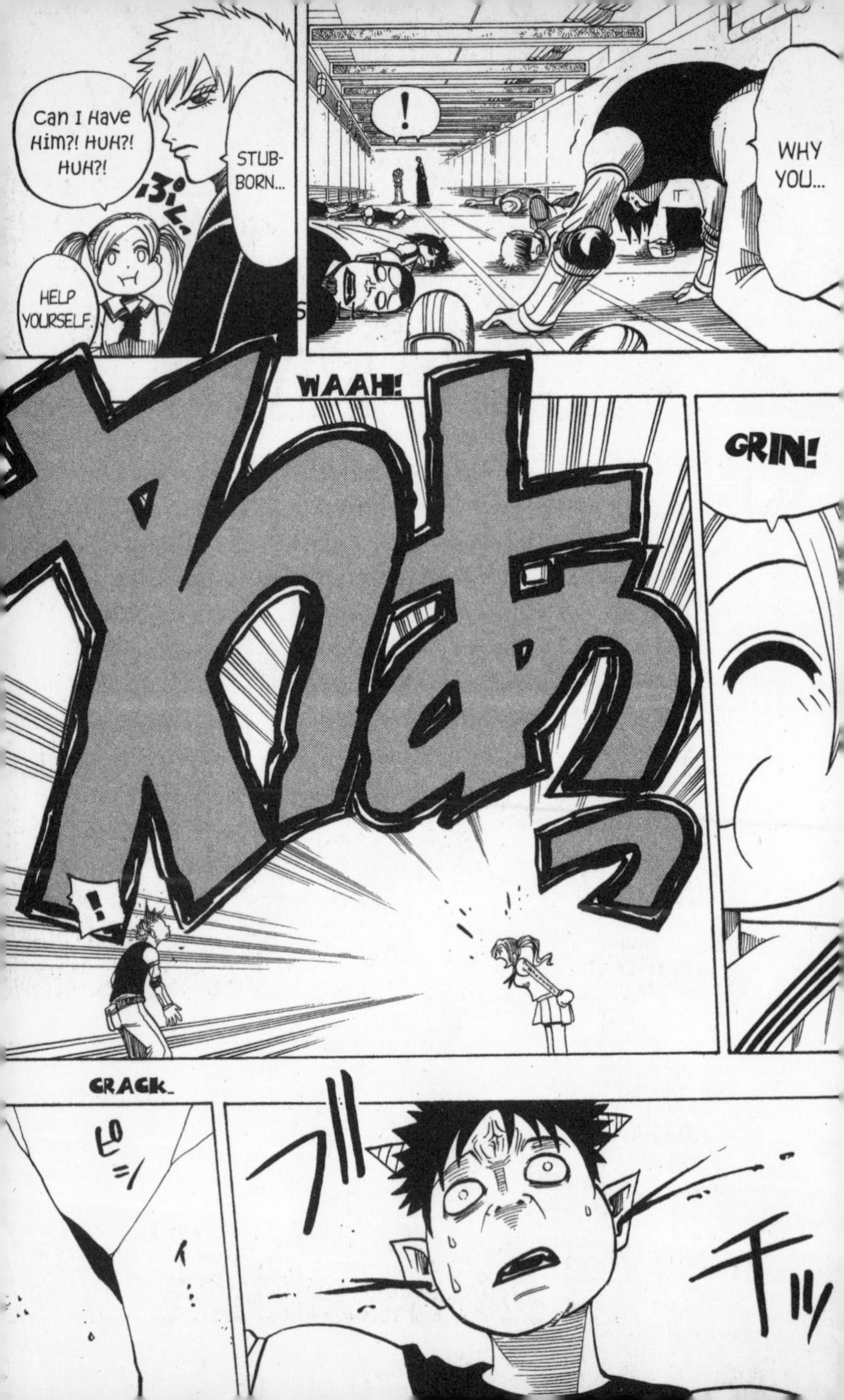
!
WHY YOU...
STUB-BORN...
Can I Have Him?! HUH?! HUH?!
HELP YOURSELF.
GRIN!
WAAH!
!
CRACK...

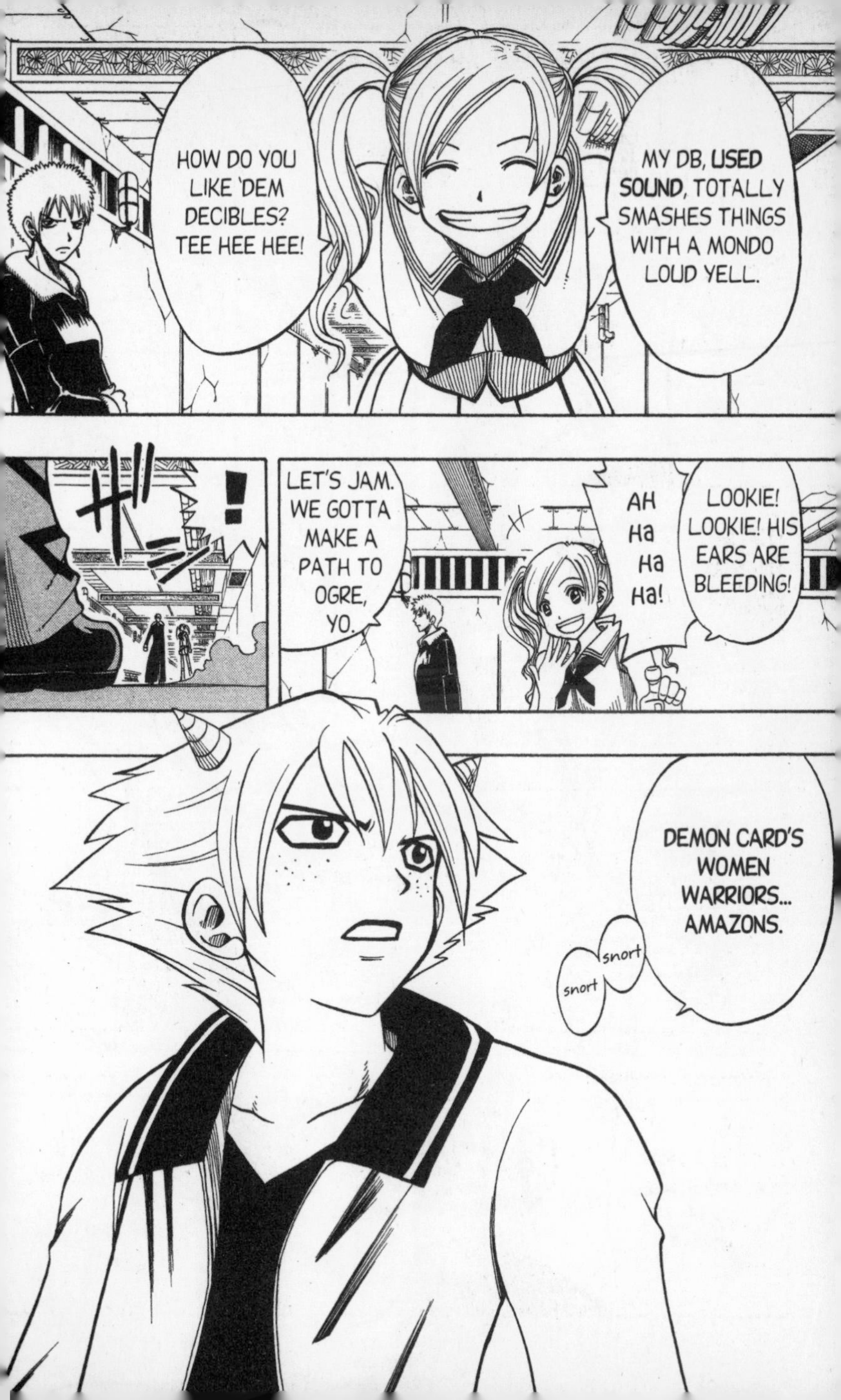
MY DB, USED SOUND, TOTALLY SMASHES THINGS WITH A MONDO LOUD YELL.
HOW DO YOU LIKE 'DEM DECIBLES? TEE HEE HEE!
LOOKIE! LOOKIE! HIS EARS ARE BLEEDING!
AH Ha Ha Ha!
LET'S JAM. WE GOTTA MAKE A PATH TO OGRE, YO.
!
DEMON CARD'S WOMEN WARRIORS... AMAZONS.
snort
snort

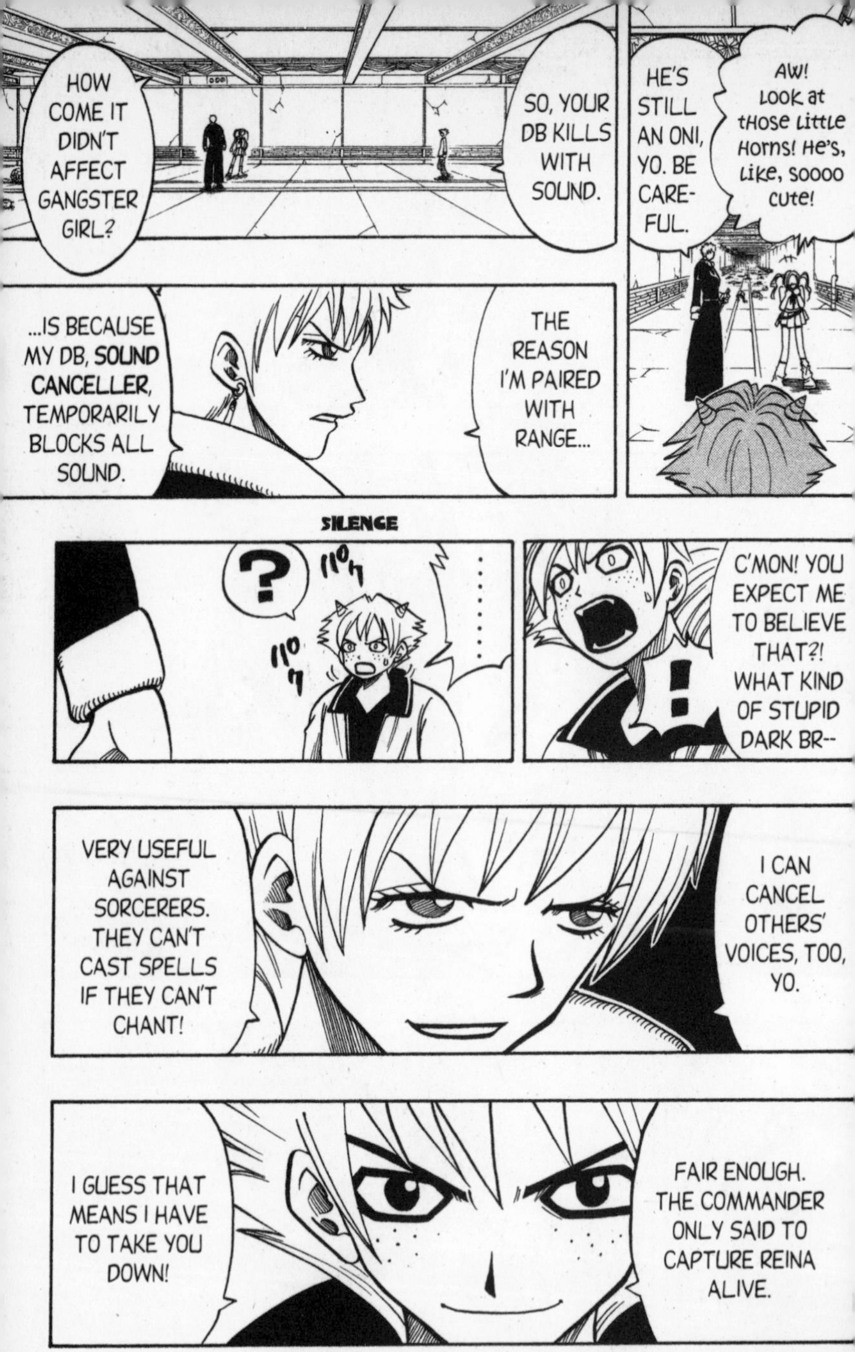
AW! Look at those Little Horns! He's, Like, soooo cute!
HE'S STILL AN ONI, YO. BE CAREFUL.
SO, YOUR DB KILLS WITH SOUND.
HOW COME IT DIDN'T AFFECT GANGSTER GIRL?
THE REASON I'M PAIRED WITH RANGE...
...IS BECAUSE MY DB, **SOUND CANCELLER**, TEMPORARILY BLOCKS ALL SOUND.
SILENCE
C'MON! YOU EXPECT ME TO BELIEVE THAT?! WHAT KIND OF STUPID DARK BR--
!
....
?
I CAN CANCEL OTHERS' VOICES, TOO, YO.
VERY USEFUL AGAINST SORCERERS. THEY CAN'T CAST SPELLS IF THEY CAN'T CHANT!
FAIR ENOUGH. THE COMMANDER ONLY SAID TO CAPTURE REINA ALIVE.
I GUESS THAT MEANS I HAVE TO TAKE YOU DOWN!

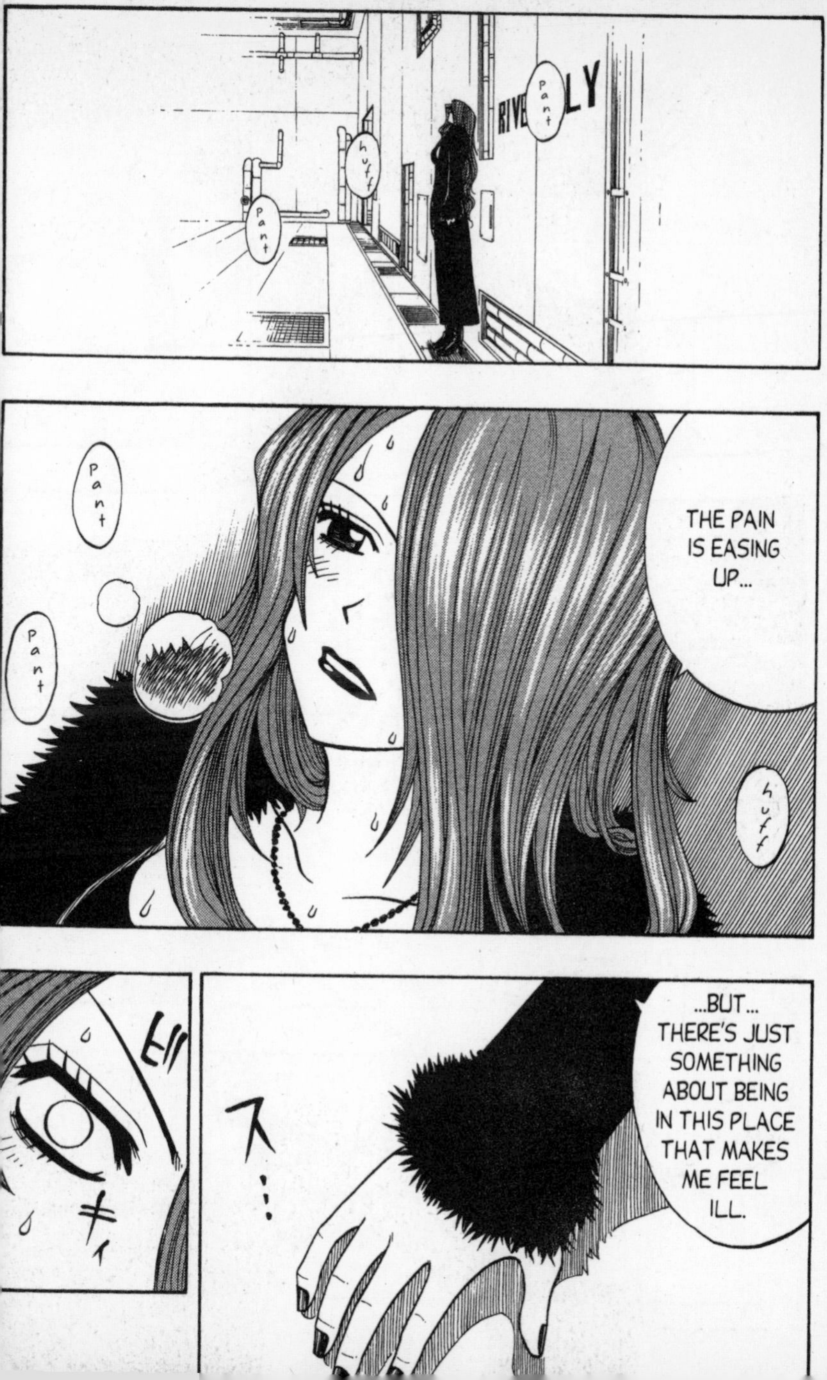
Pant
RIVE LY
huff
Pant
THE PAIN IS EASING UP...
huff
Pant
Pant
...BUT... THERE'S JUST SOMETHING ABOUT BEING IN THIS PLACE THAT MAKES ME FEEL ILL.
ス...

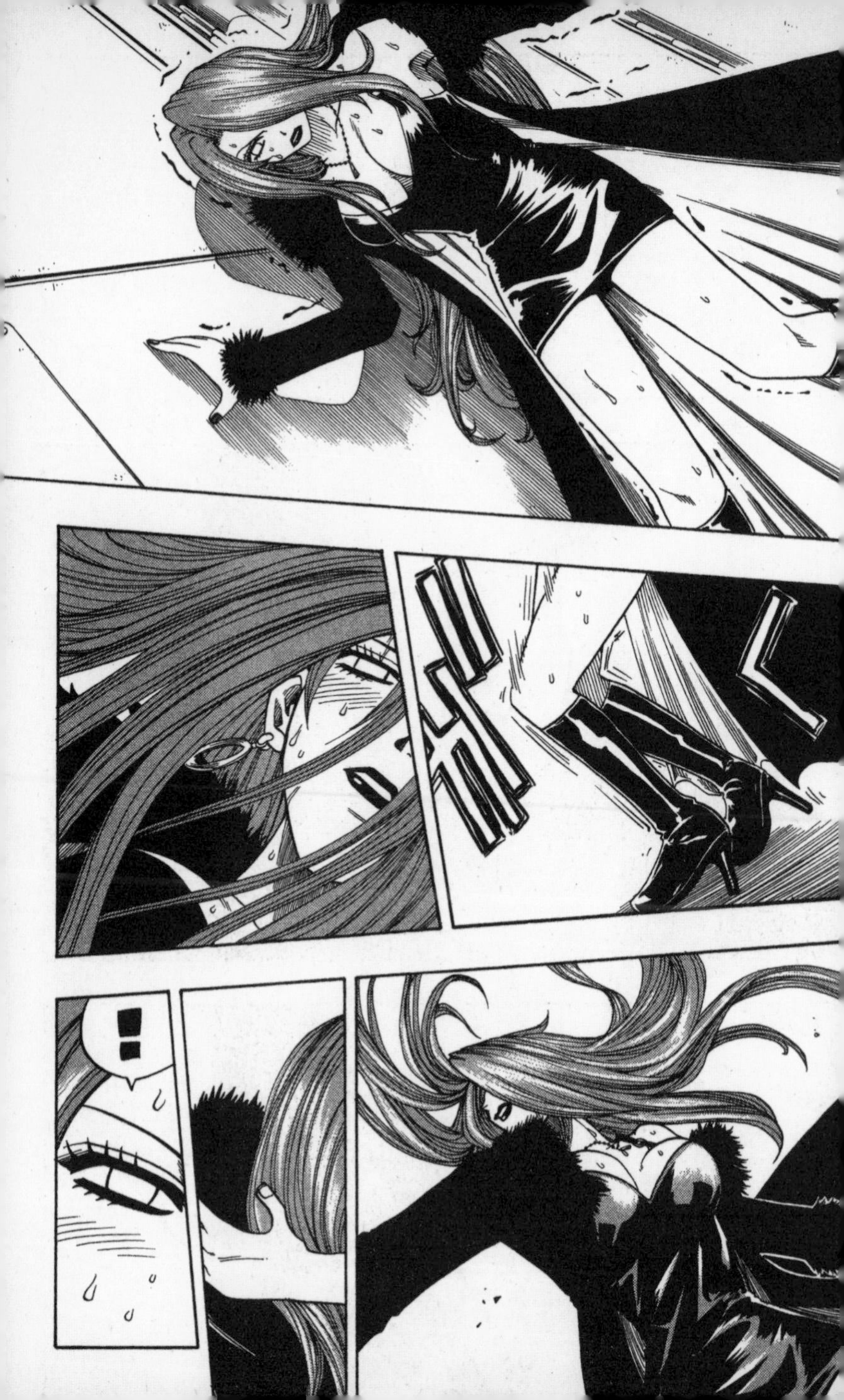
!!

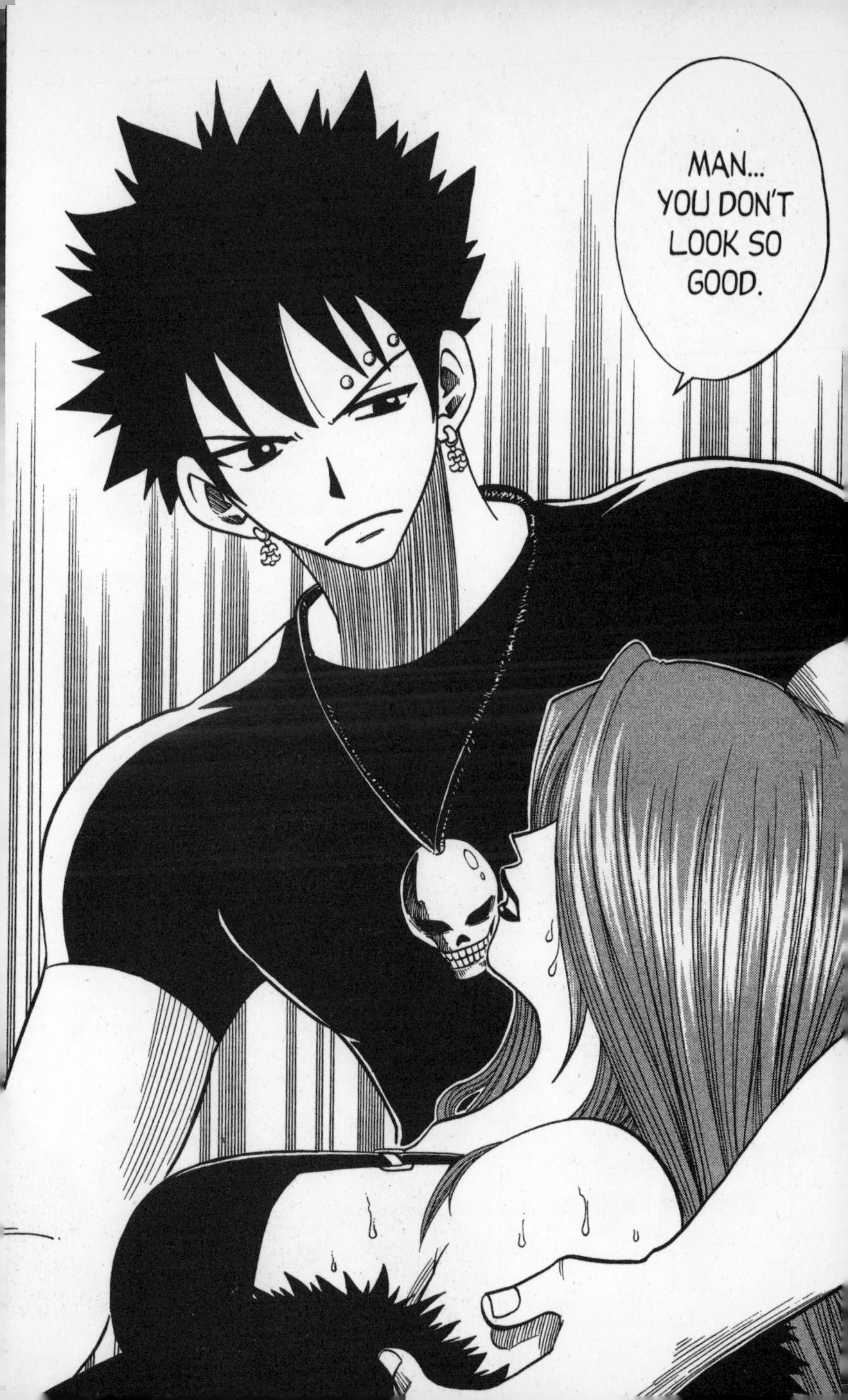
MAN... YOU DON'T LOOK SO GOOD.

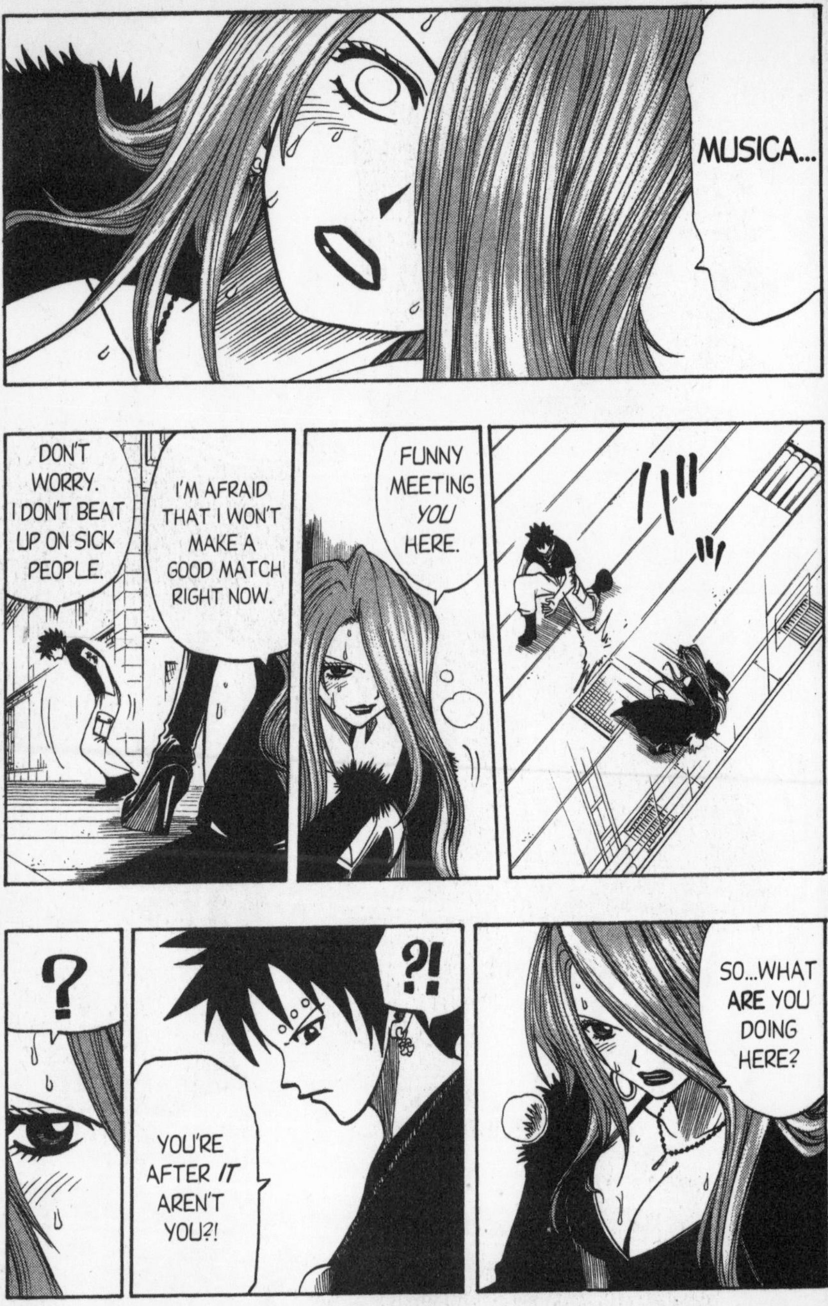
MUSICA...
FUNNY MEETING YOU HERE.
I'M AFRAID THAT I WON'T MAKE A GOOD MATCH RIGHT NOW.
DON'T WORRY. I DON'T BEAT UP ON SICK PEOPLE.
SO...WHAT ARE YOU DOING HERE?
?!
YOU'RE AFTER IT AREN'T YOU?!
?

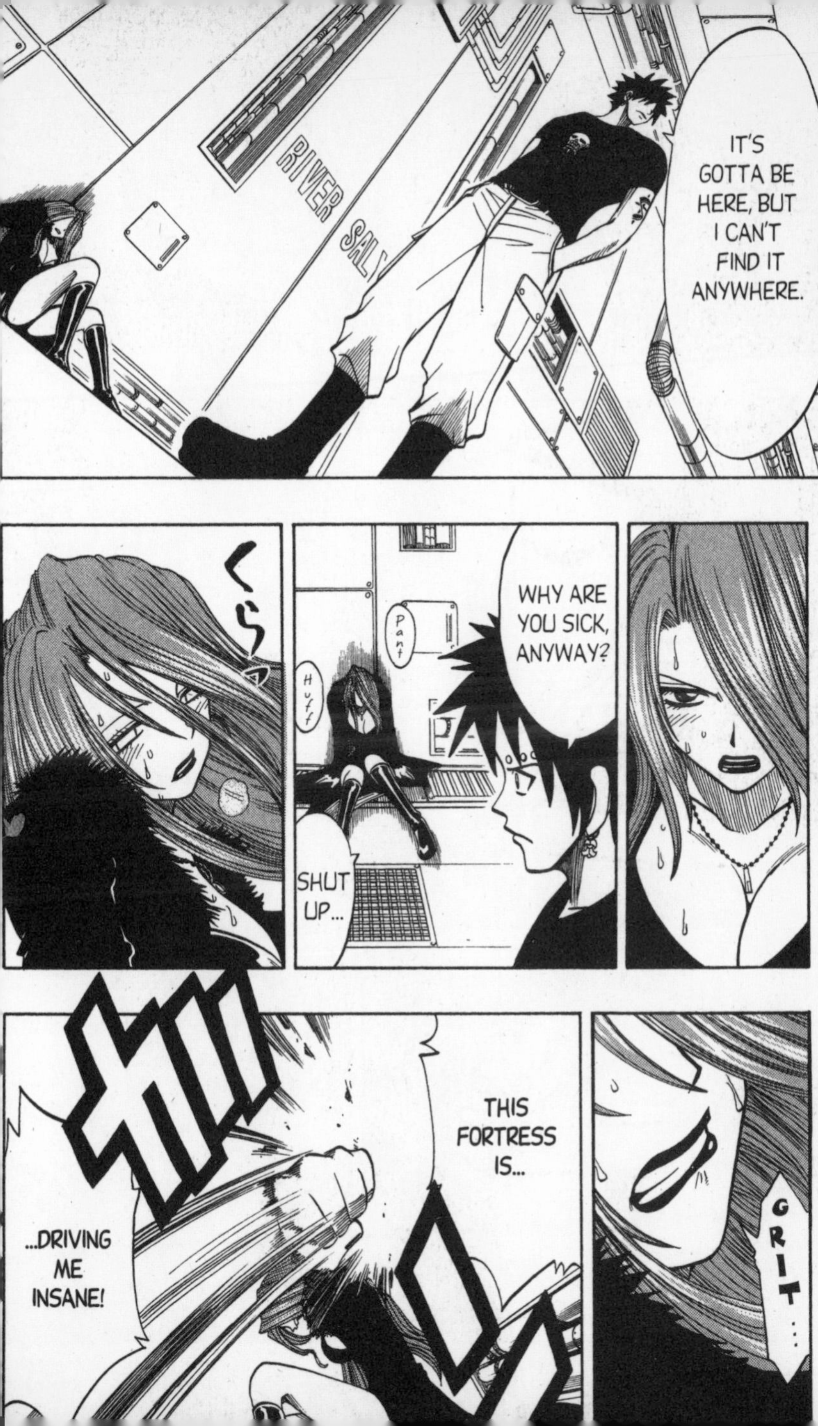
IT'S GOTTA BE HERE, BUT I CAN'T FIND IT ANYWHERE.
RIVER SALV
WHY ARE YOU SICK, ANYWAY?
Pant
Huff
SHUT UP...
くら
GRIT...
THIS FORTRESS IS...
...DRIVING ME INSANE!

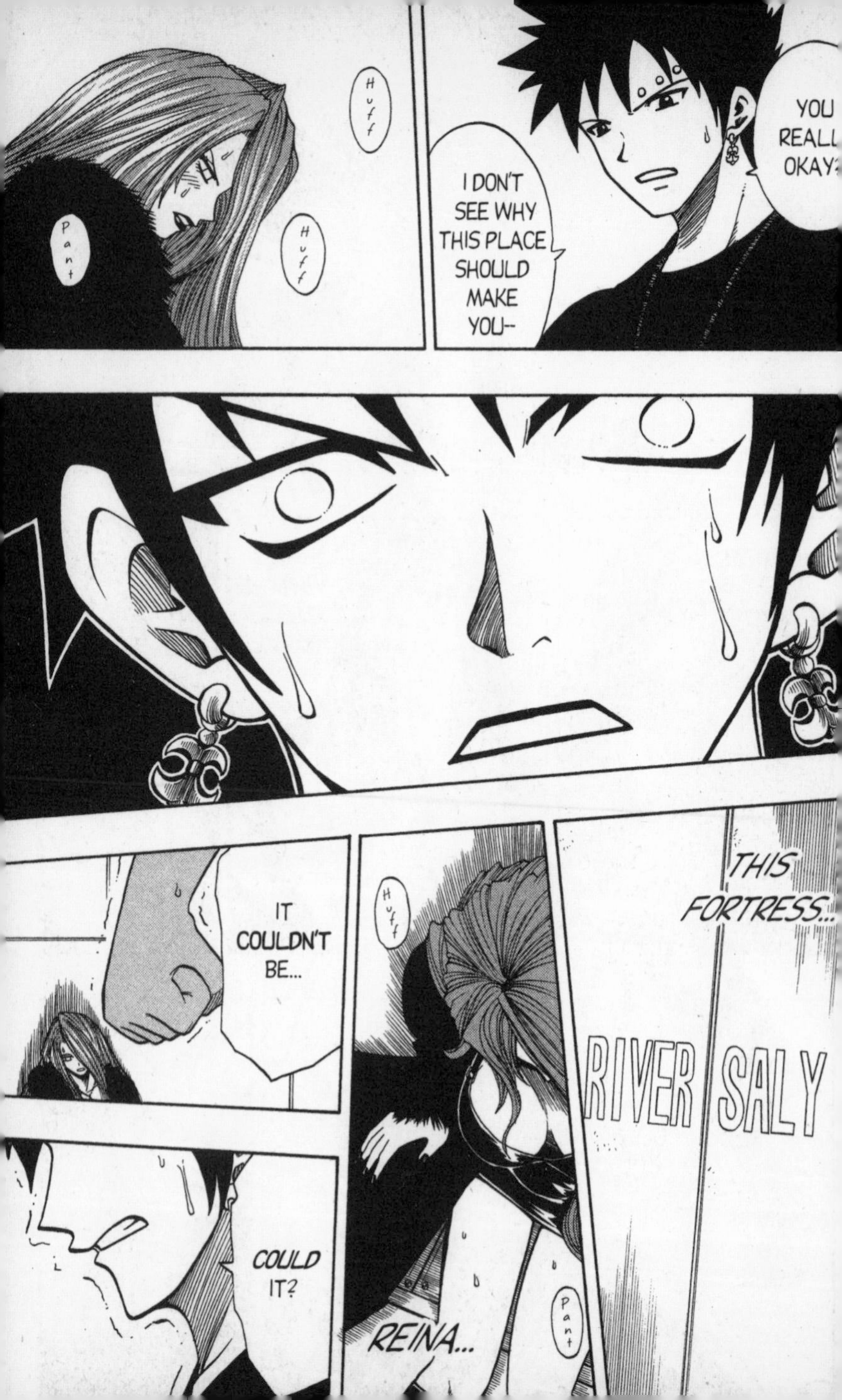
YOU REALL OKAY?
I DON'T SEE WHY THIS PLACE SHOULD MAKE YOU--
Huff
Huff
Pant
THIS FORTRESS...
RIVER SALY
Huff
Pant
REINA...
IT COULDN'T BE...
COULD IT?

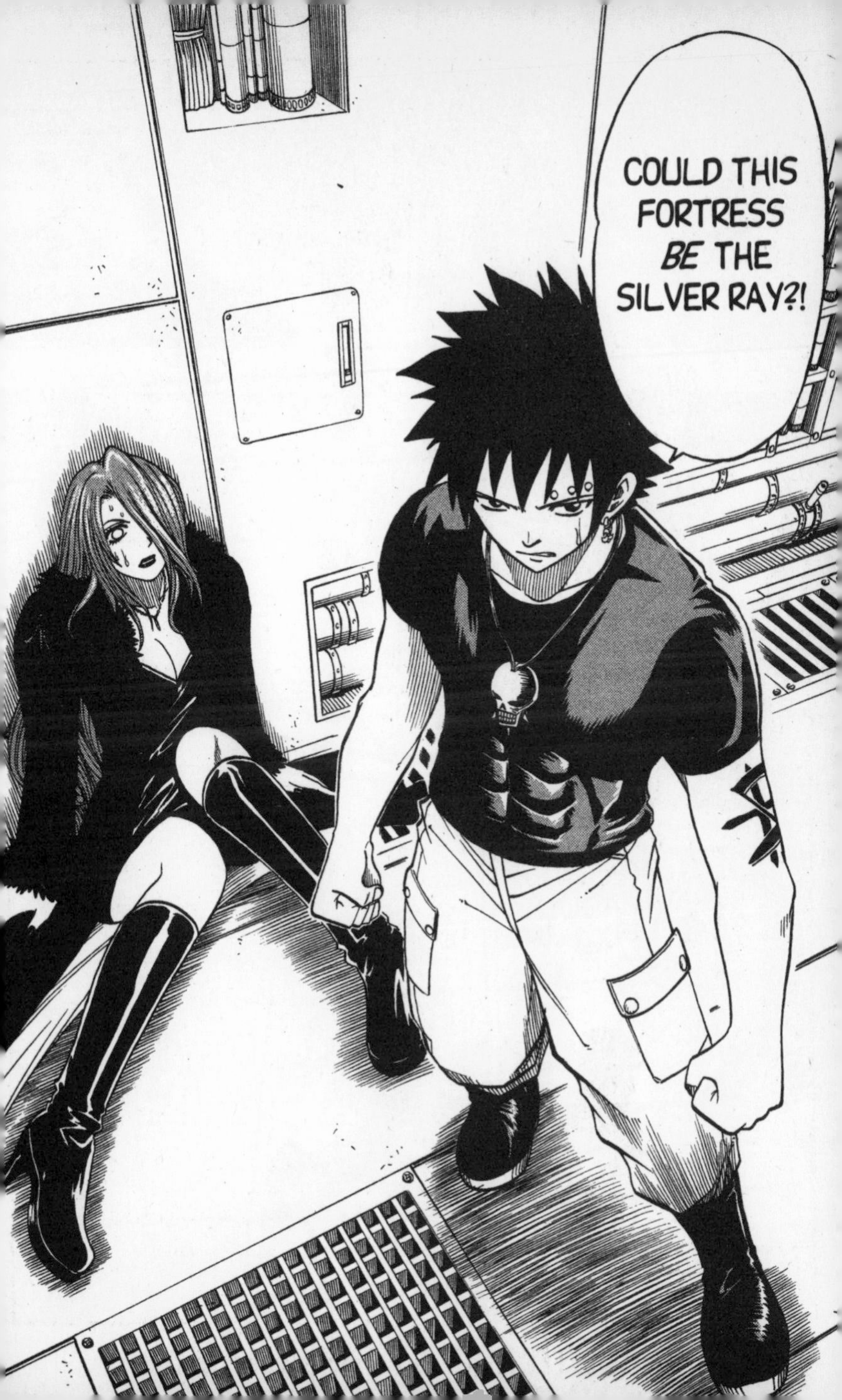
COULD THIS FORTRESS *BE* THE SILVER RAY?!

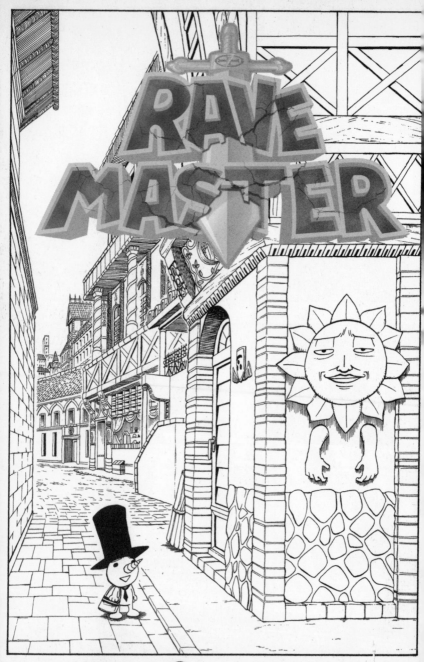

RAVE:125 ✛ **Silverclaimer Duet**

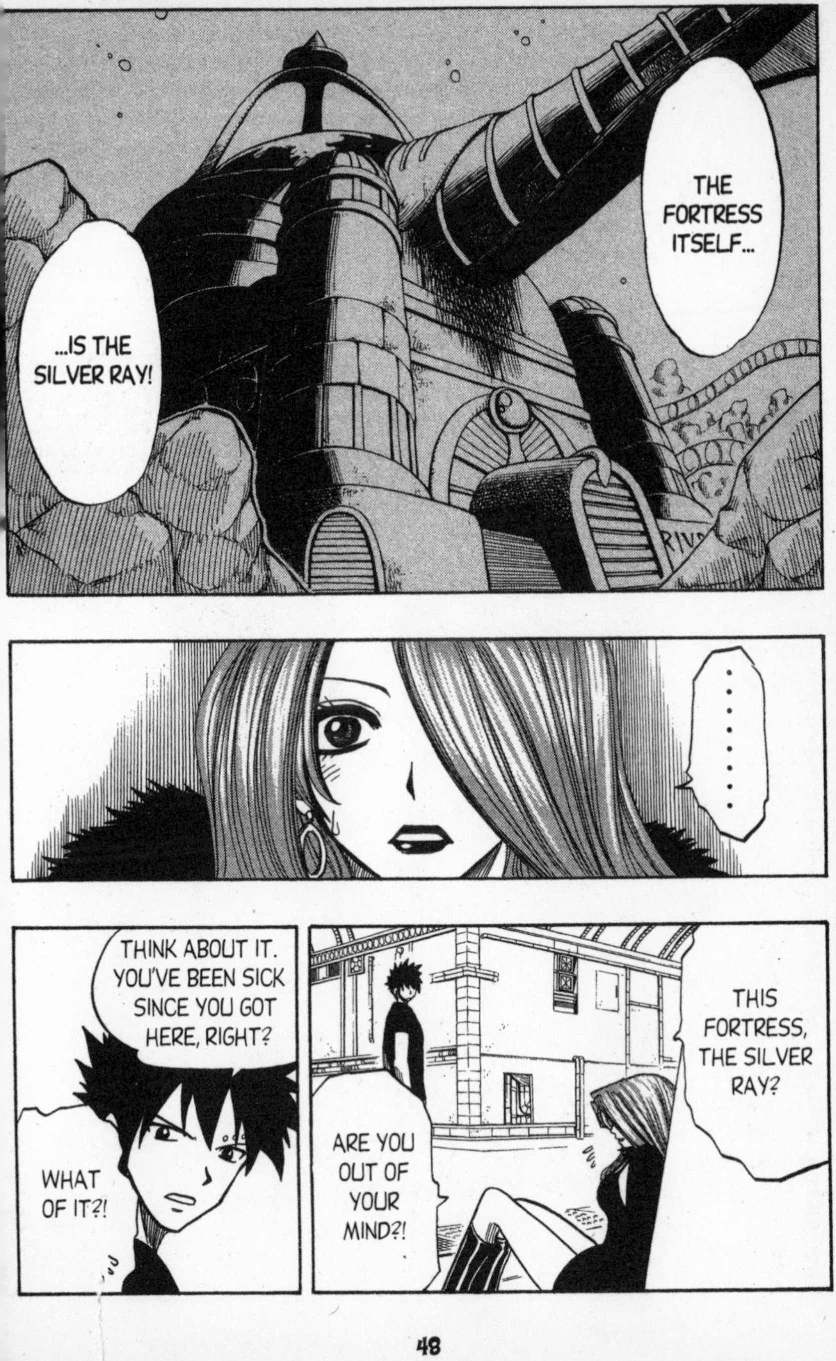
THE FORTRESS ITSELF...
...IS THE SILVER RAY!
....
THIS FORTRESS, THE SILVER RAY?
ARE YOU OUT OF YOUR MIND?!
THINK ABOUT IT. YOU'VE BEEN SICK SINCE YOU GOT HERE, RIGHT?
WHAT OF IT?!

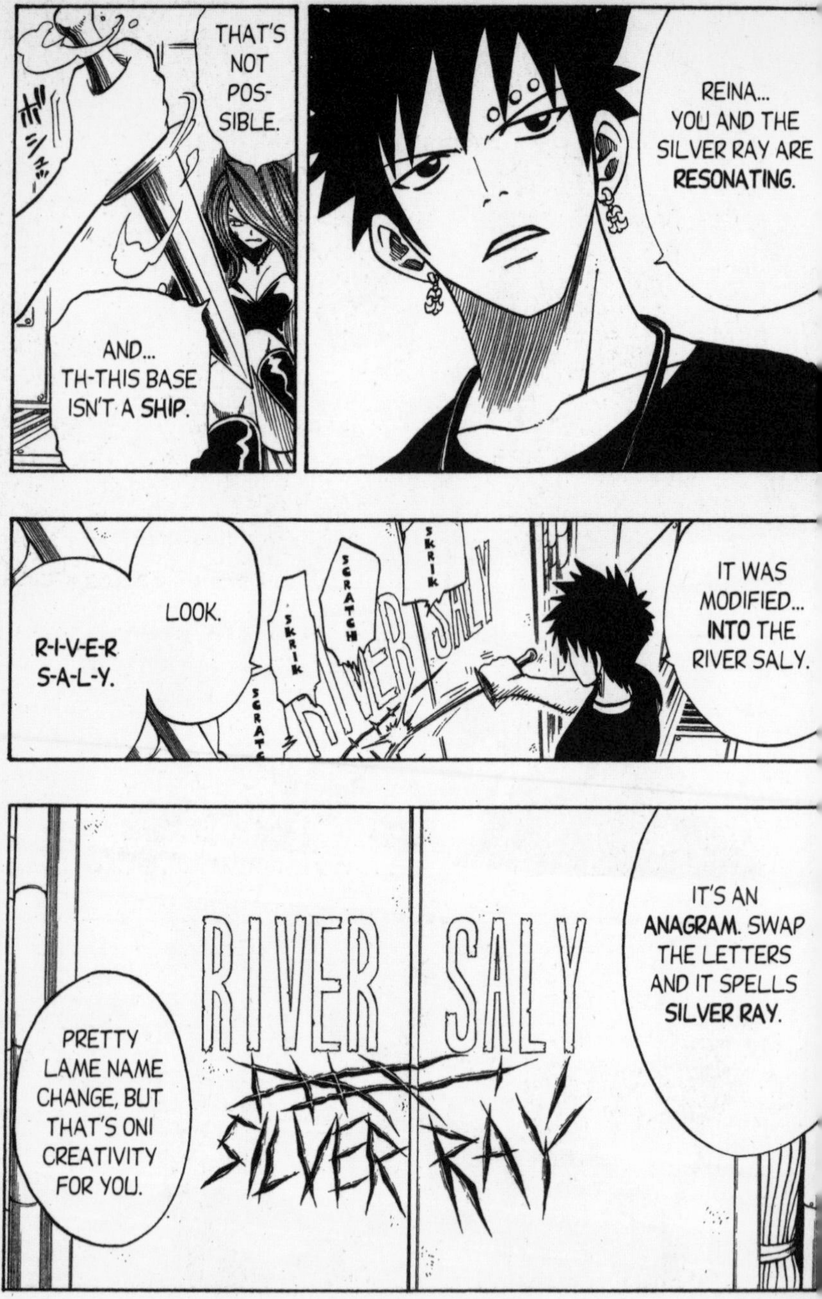

REINA... YOU AND THE SILVER RAY ARE **RESONATING.**
THAT'S NOT POSSIBLE.
AND... TH-THIS BASE ISN'T A **SHIP.**
IT WAS MODIFIED... **INTO** THE RIVER SALY.
SKRIK
SCRATCH
SKRIK
RIVER SALY
LOOK.
R-I-V-E-R S-A-L-Y.
IT'S AN **ANAGRAM.** SWAP THE LETTERS AND IT SPELLS **SILVER RAY.**
RIVER SALY
SILVER RAY
PRETTY LAME NAME CHANGE, BUT THAT'S ONI CREATIVITY FOR YOU.

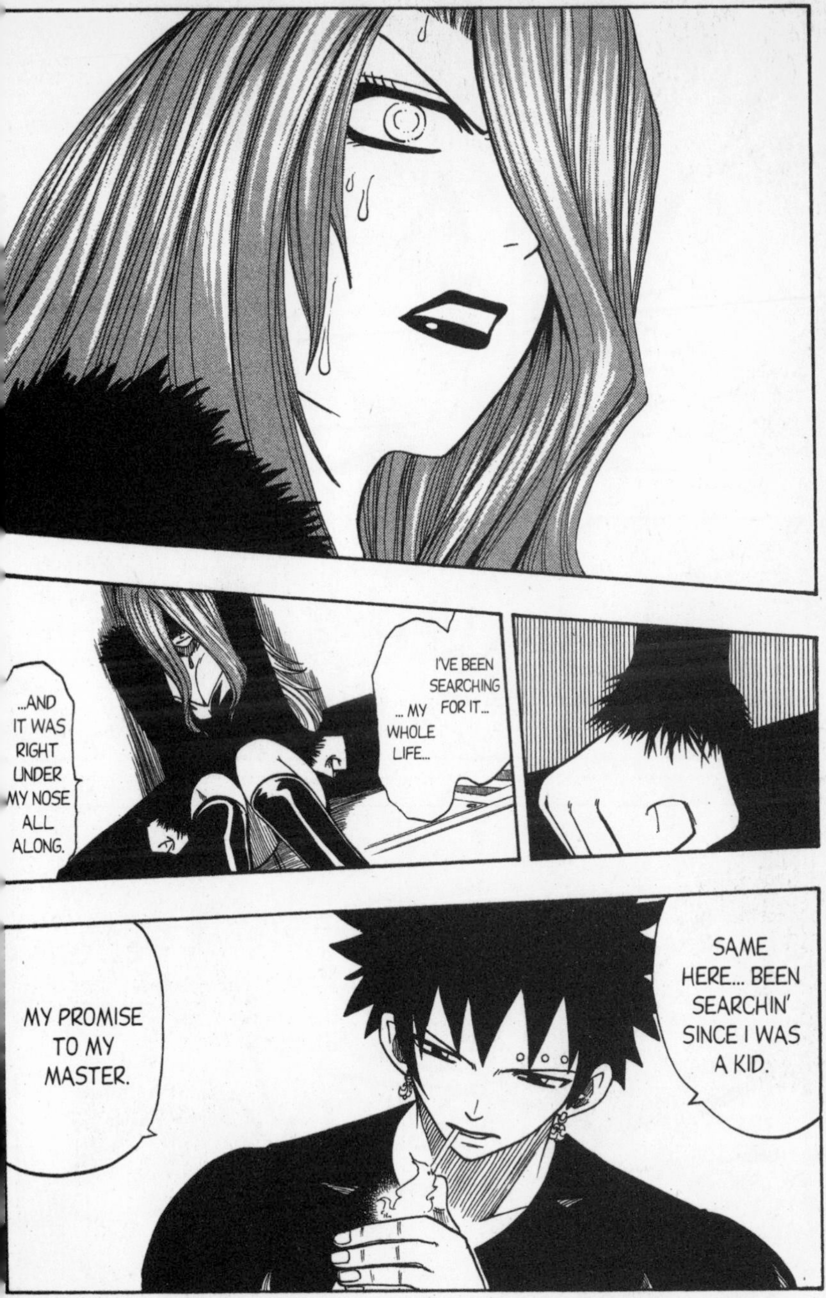
I'VE BEEN SEARCHING FOR IT... ... MY WHOLE LIFE...
...AND IT WAS RIGHT UNDER MY NOSE ALL ALONG.
SAME HERE... BEEN SEARCHIN' SINCE I WAS A KID.
MY PROMISE TO MY MASTER.

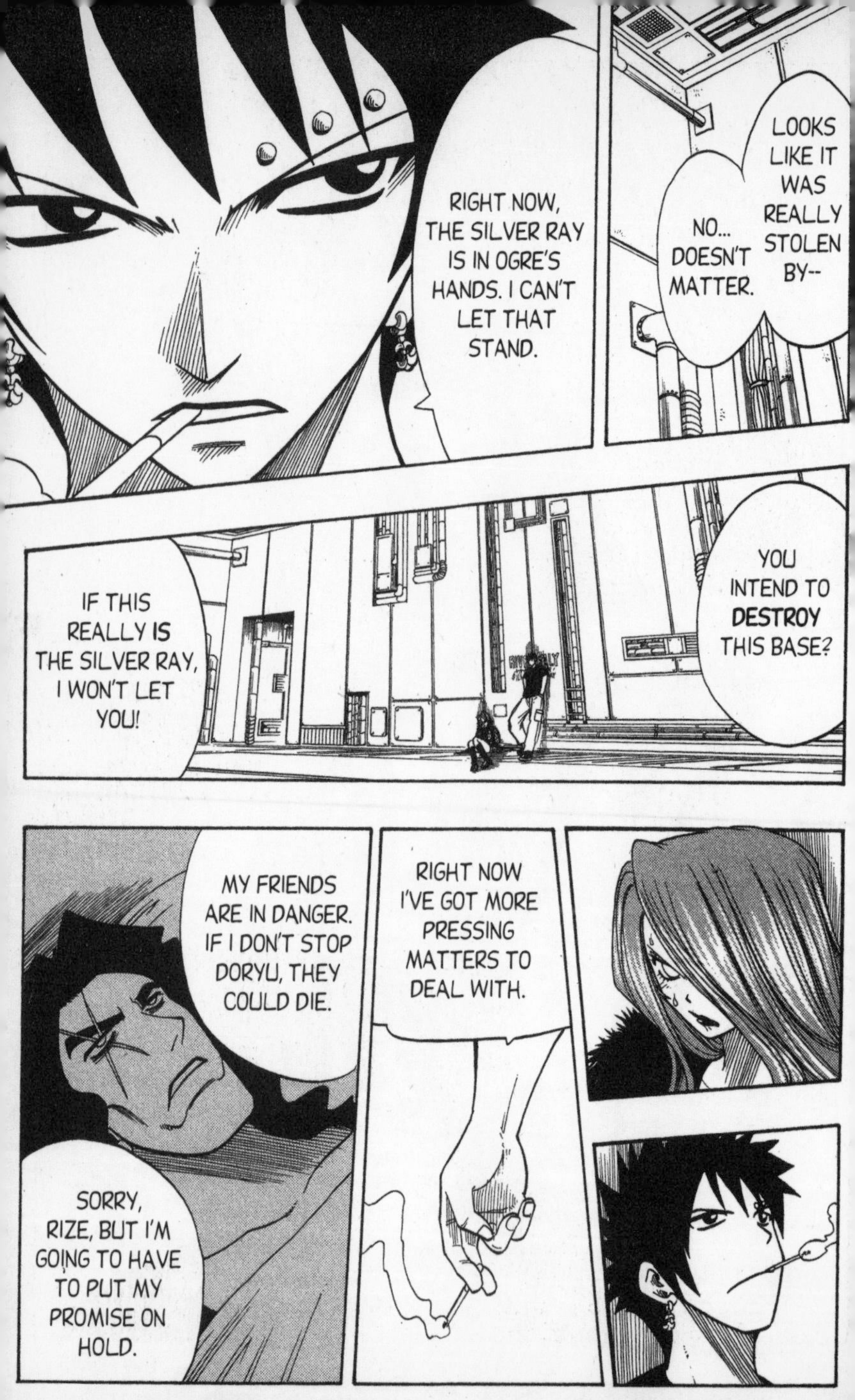
LOOKS LIKE IT WAS REALLY STOLEN BY--
NO... DOESN'T MATTER.
RIGHT NOW, THE SILVER RAY IS IN OGRE'S HANDS. I CAN'T LET THAT STAND.
YOU INTEND TO **DESTROY** THIS BASE?
IF THIS REALLY **IS** THE SILVER RAY, I WON'T LET YOU!
RIGHT NOW I'VE GOT MORE PRESSING MATTERS TO DEAL WITH.
MY FRIENDS ARE IN DANGER. IF I DON'T STOP DORYU, THEY COULD DIE.
SORRY, RIZE, BUT I'M GOING TO HAVE TO PUT MY PROMISE ON HOLD.

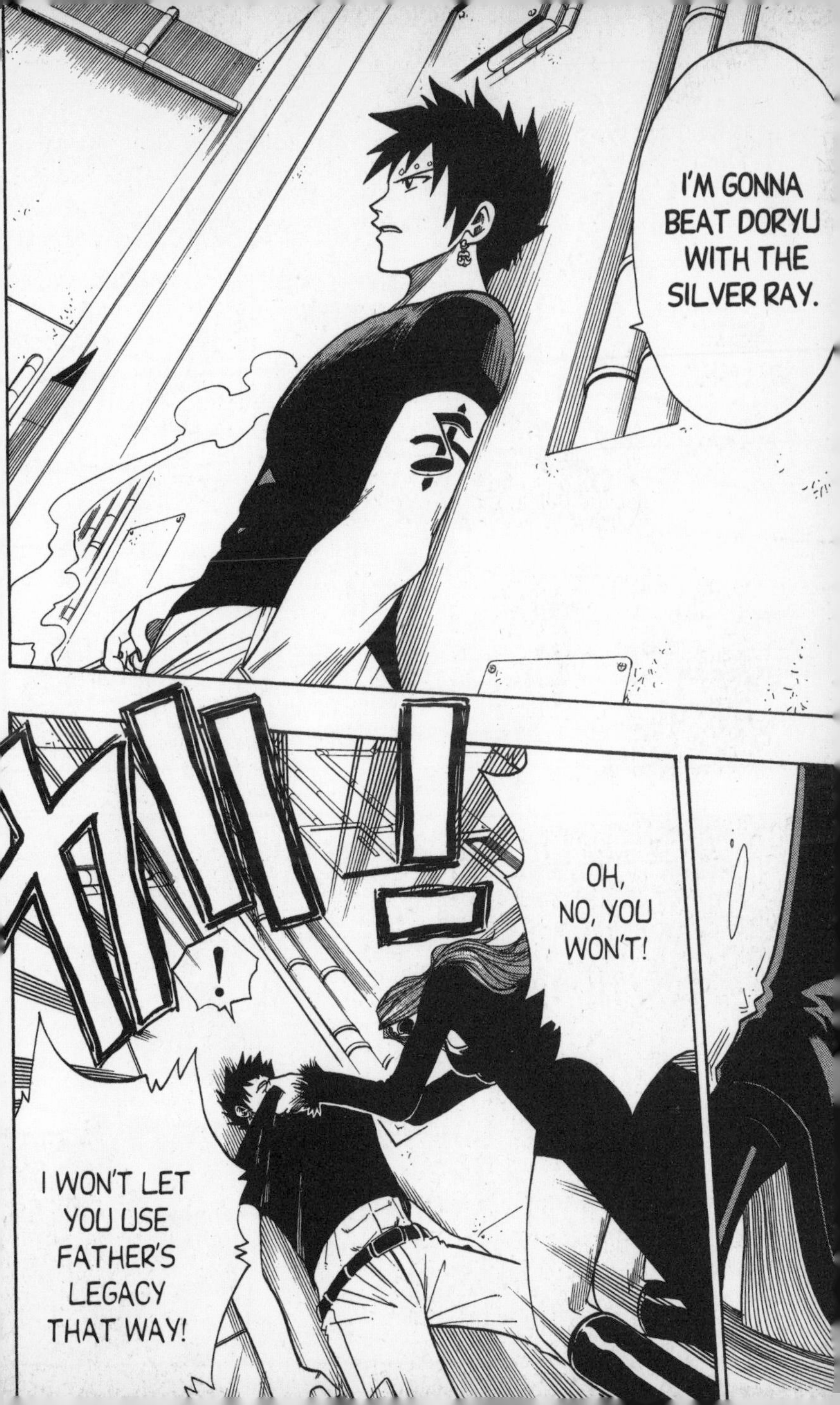
I'M GONNA BEAT DORYU WITH THE SILVER RAY.
OH, NO, YOU WON'T!
!
I WON'T LET YOU USE FATHER'S LEGACY THAT WAY!

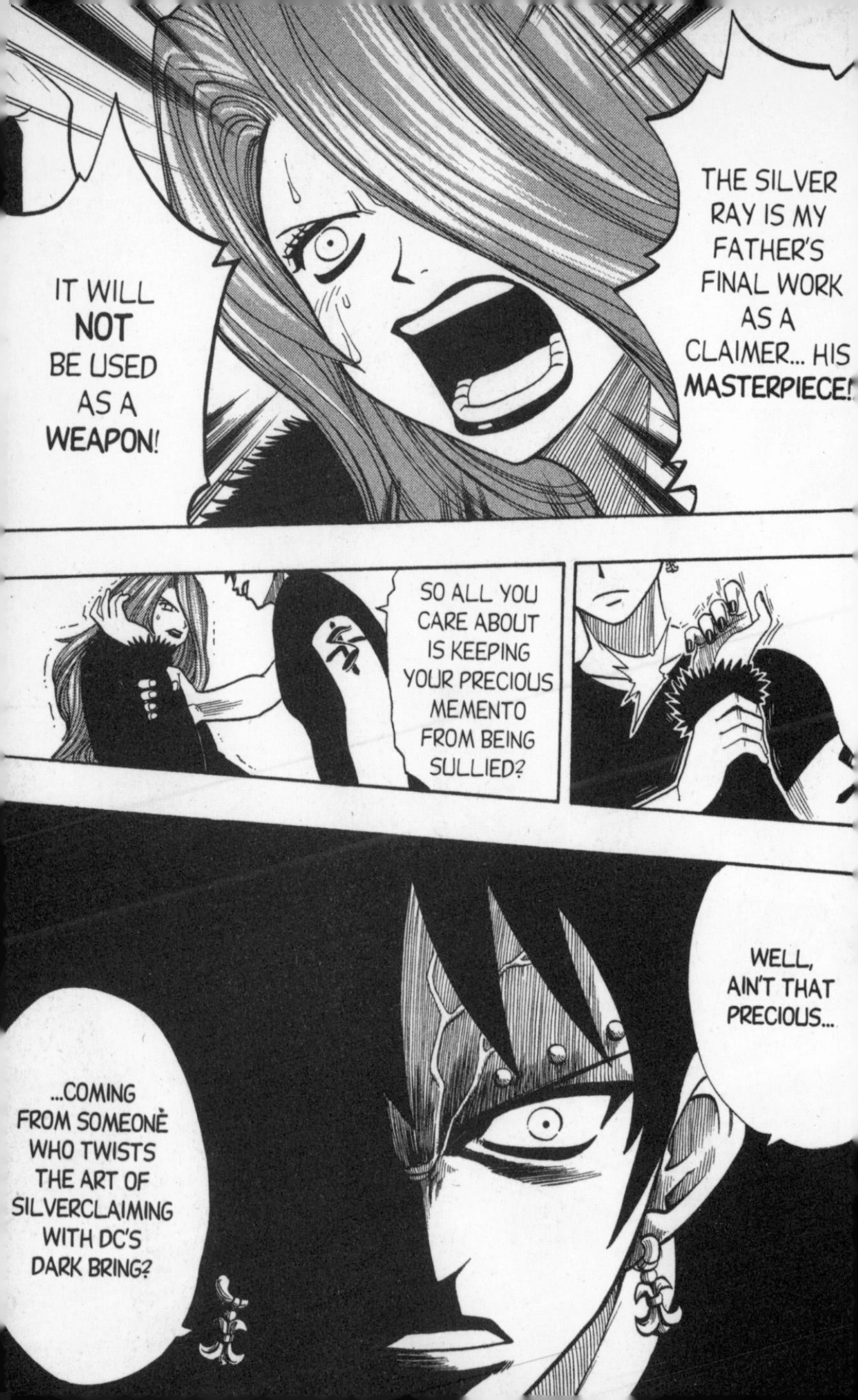
THE SILVER RAY IS MY FATHER'S FINAL WORK AS A CLAIMER... HIS MASTERPIECE!
IT WILL NOT BE USED AS A WEAPON!
SO ALL YOU CARE ABOUT IS KEEPING YOUR PRECIOUS MEMENTO FROM BEING SULLIED?
WELL, AIN'T THAT PRECIOUS...
...COMING FROM SOMEONE WHO TWISTS THE ART OF SILVERCLAIMING WITH DC'S DARK BRING?

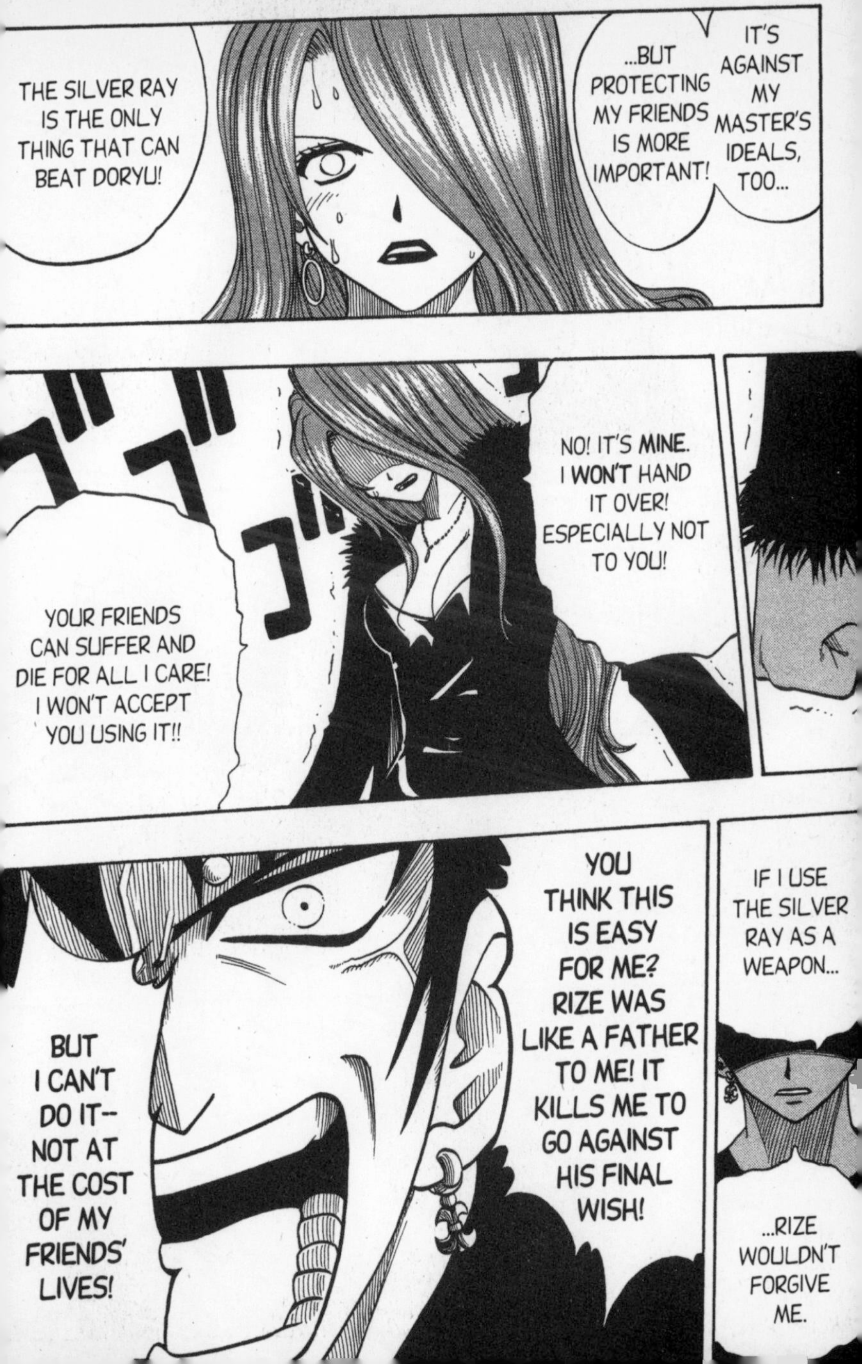
IT'S AGAINST MY MASTER'S IDEALS, TOO...
...BUT PROTECTING MY FRIENDS IS MORE IMPORTANT!
THE SILVER RAY IS THE ONLY THING THAT CAN BEAT DORYU!
NO! IT'S MINE. I WON'T HAND IT OVER! ESPECIALLY NOT TO YOU!
ゴゴゴ
YOUR FRIENDS CAN SUFFER AND DIE FOR ALL I CARE! I WON'T ACCEPT YOU USING IT!!
IF I USE THE SILVER RAY AS A WEAPON...
...RIZE WOULDN'T FORGIVE ME.
YOU THINK THIS IS EASY FOR ME? RIZE WAS LIKE A FATHER TO ME! IT KILLS ME TO GO AGAINST HIS FINAL WISH!
BUT I CAN'T DO IT-- NOT AT THE COST OF MY FRIENDS' LIVES!

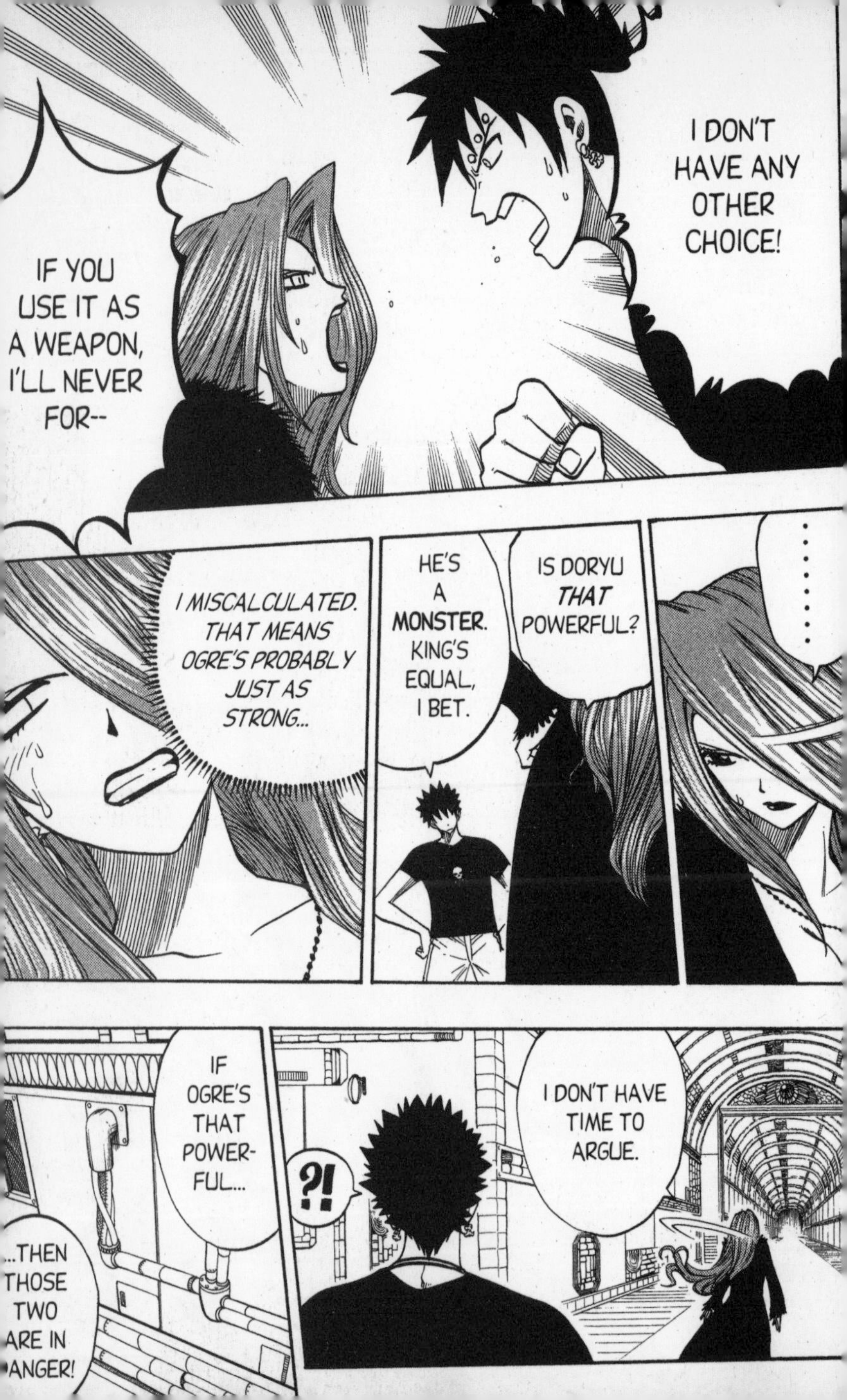
I DON'T HAVE ANY OTHER CHOICE!
IF YOU USE IT AS A WEAPON, I'LL NEVER FOR--
......
IS DORYU *THAT* POWERFUL?
HE'S A **MONSTER**. KING'S EQUAL, I BET.
I MISCALCULATED. THAT MEANS OGRE'S PROBABLY JUST AS STRONG...
I DON'T HAVE TIME TO ARGUE.
?!
IF OGRE'S THAT POWER-FUL...
...THEN THOSE TWO ARE IN ANGER!

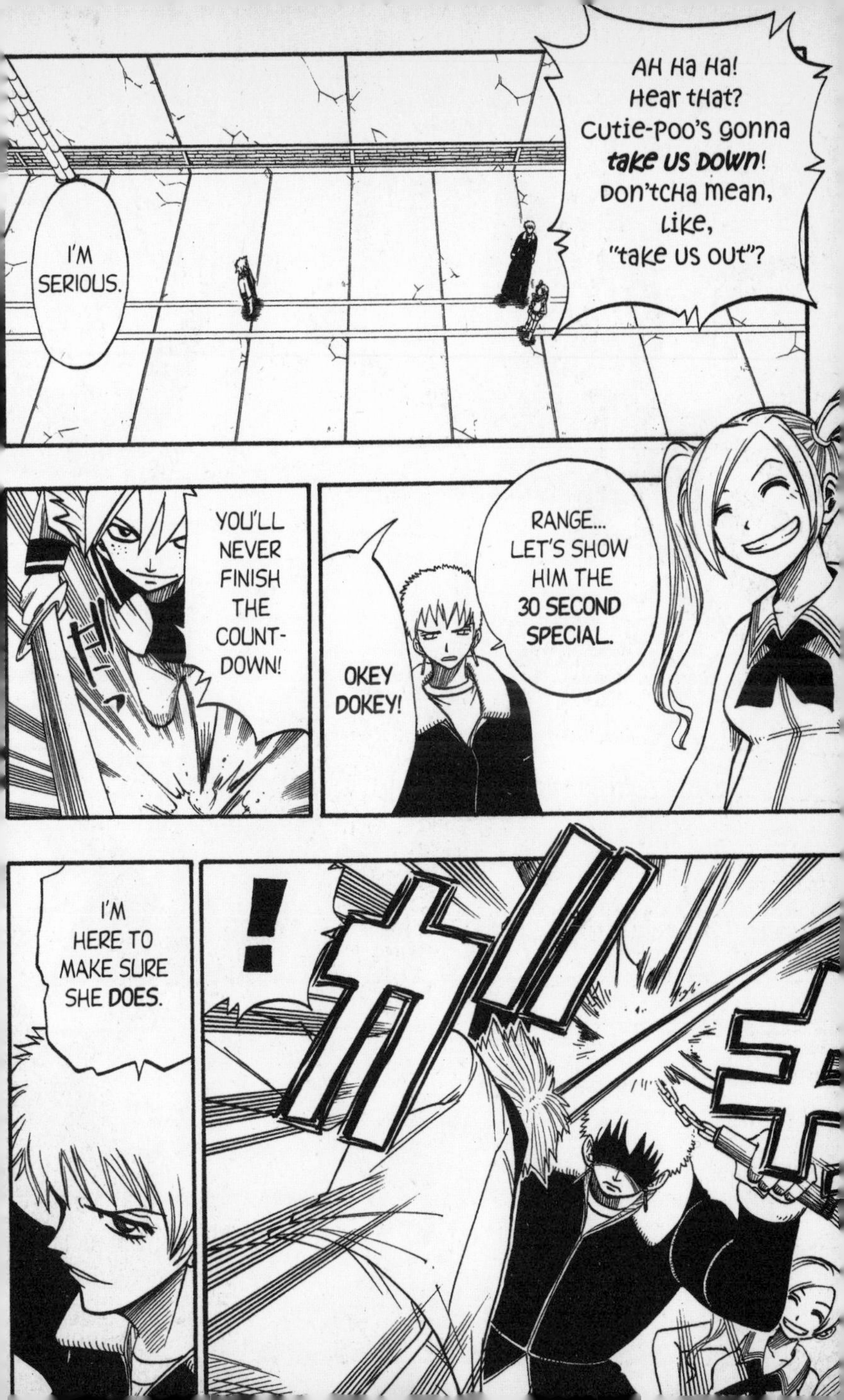
AH Ha Ha! Hear tHat? Cutie-poo's gonna **take us down**! Don'tcHa mean, like, "take us out"?
I'M SERIOUS.
RANGE... LET'S SHOW HIM THE **30 SECOND SPECIAL.**
OKEY DOKEY!
YOU'LL NEVER FINISH THE COUNT-DOWN!
!
I'M HERE TO MAKE SURE SHE **DOES.**

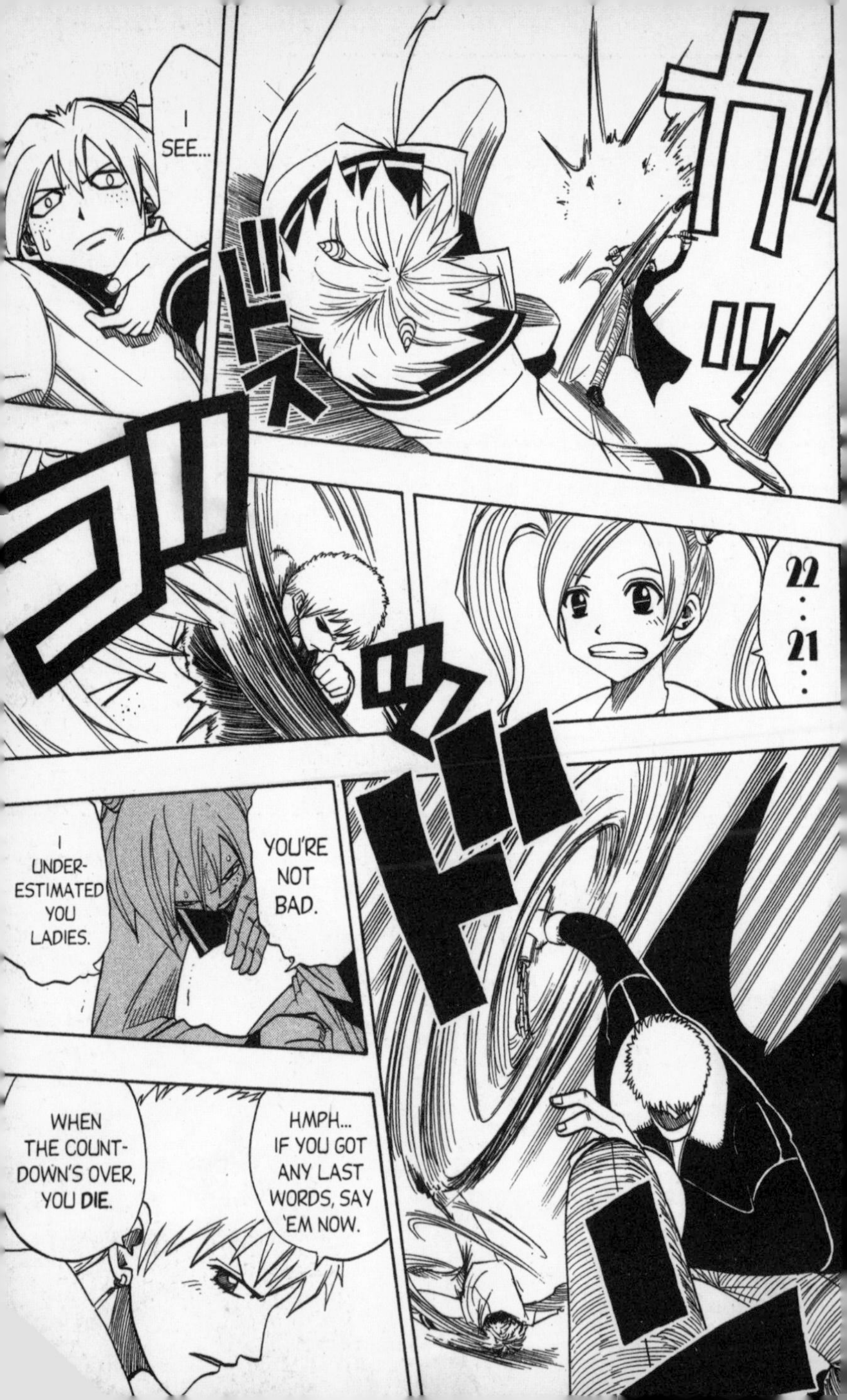
I SEE...
22 . . 21 . .
YOU'RE NOT BAD.
I UNDER-ESTIMATED YOU LADIES.
HMPH... IF YOU GOT ANY LAST WORDS, SAY 'EM NOW.
WHEN THE COUNT-DOWN'S OVER, YOU **DIE**.

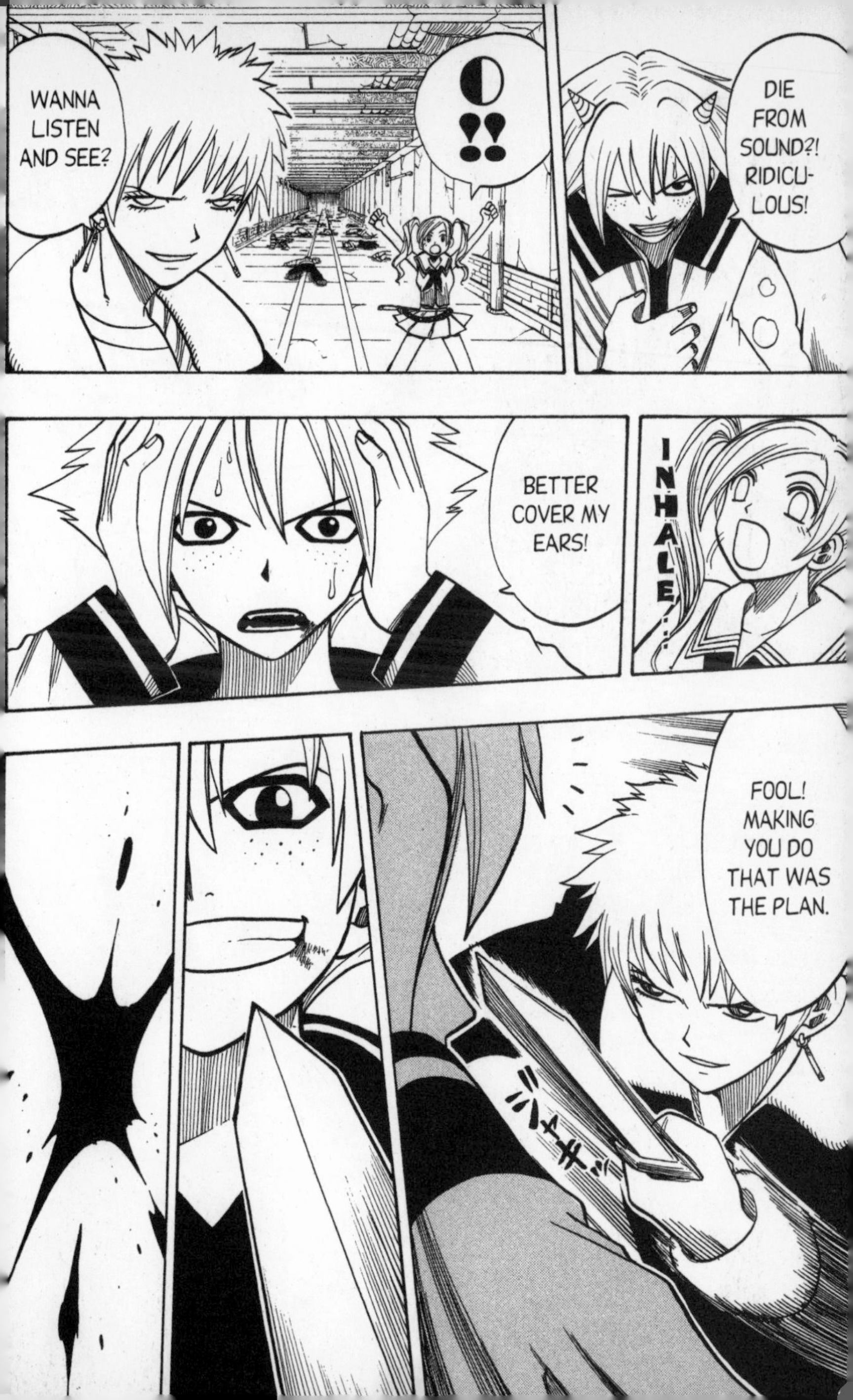
DIE FROM SOUND?! RIDICULOUS!
!!
WANNA LISTEN AND SEE?
INHALE...
BETTER COVER MY EARS!
FOOL! MAKING YOU DO THAT WAS THE PLAN.

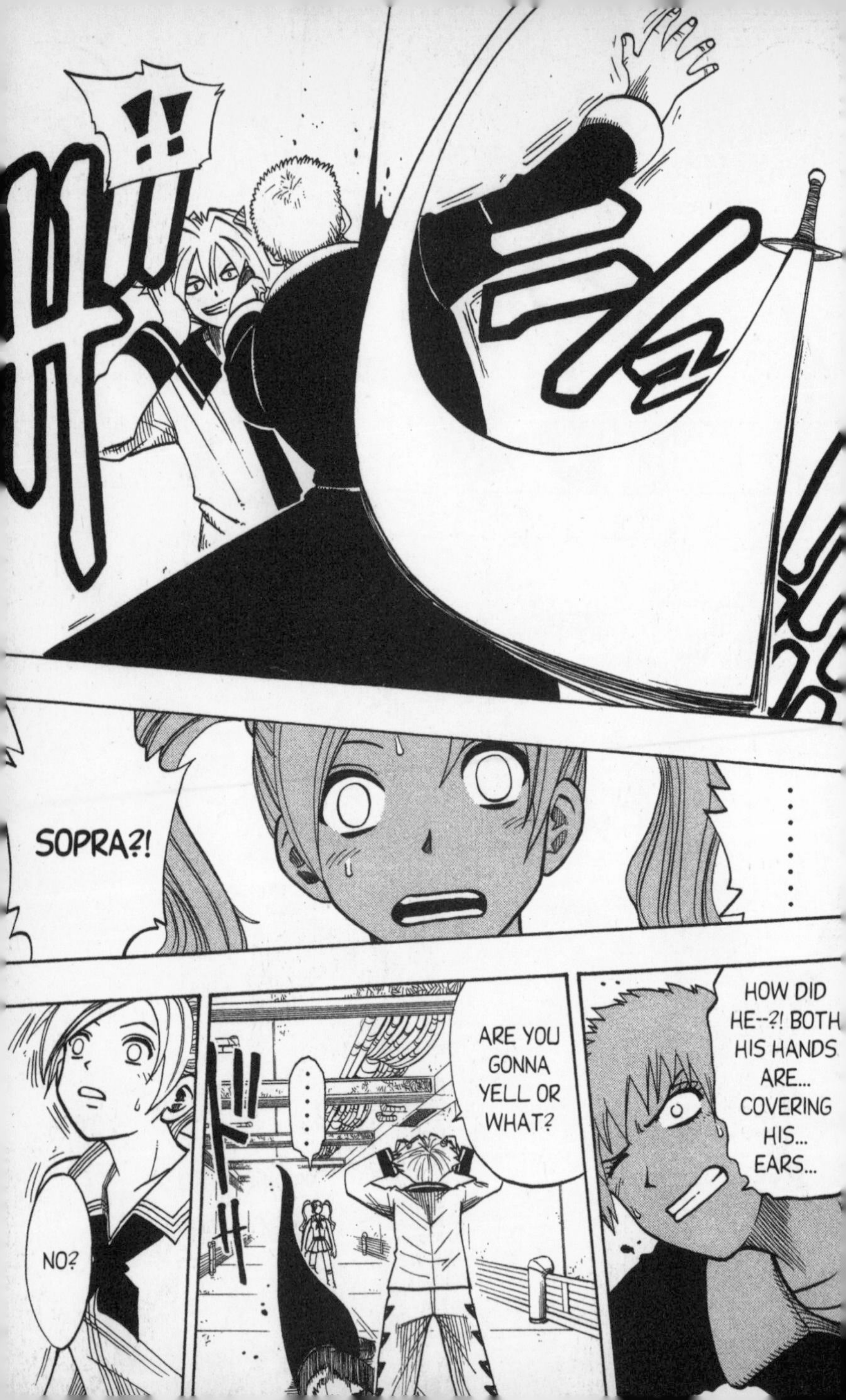
!!
......
SOPRA?!
HOW DID HE--?! BOTH HIS HANDS ARE... COVERING HIS... EARS...
ARE YOU GONNA YELL OR WHAT?
......
NO?

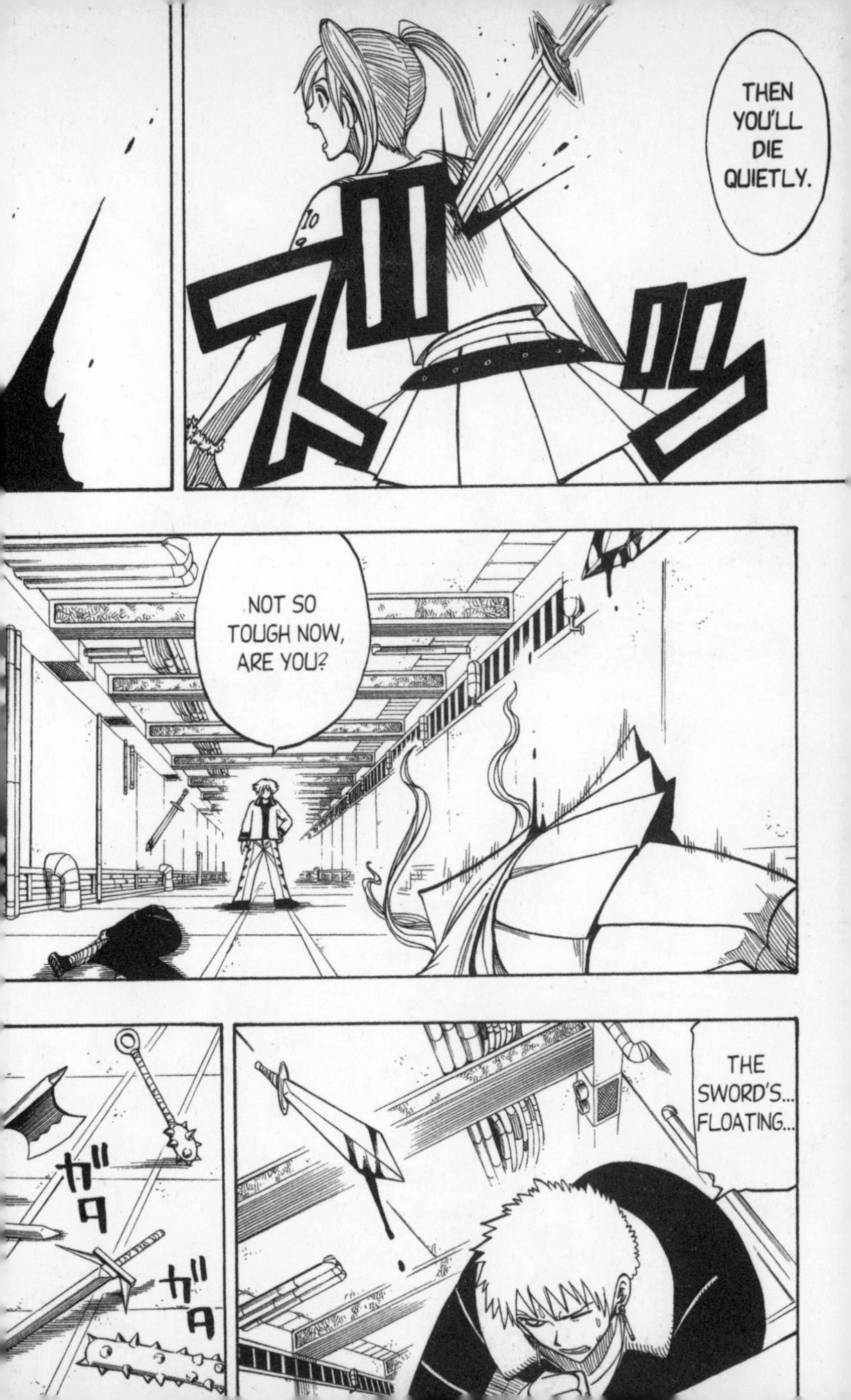
THEN YOU'LL DIE QUIETLY.
NOT SO TOUGH NOW, ARE YOU?
THE SWORD'S... FLOATING...
ガタ
ガタ

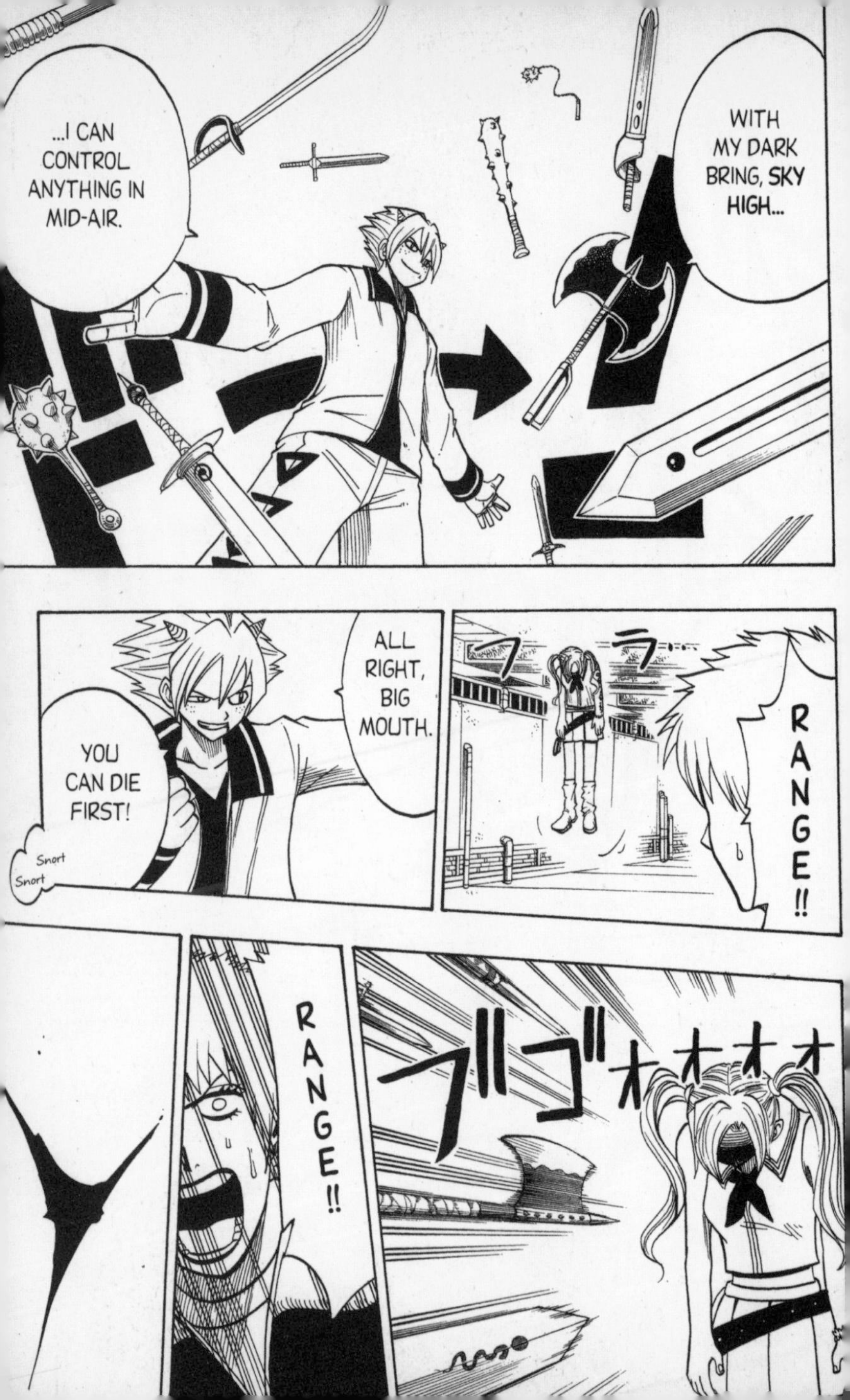
WITH MY DARK BRING, SKY HIGH...
...I CAN CONTROL ANYTHING IN MID-AIR.
フラ
RANGE!!
ALL RIGHT, BIG MOUTH.
YOU CAN DIE FIRST!
Snort Snort
ゴオオオオ
RANGE!!

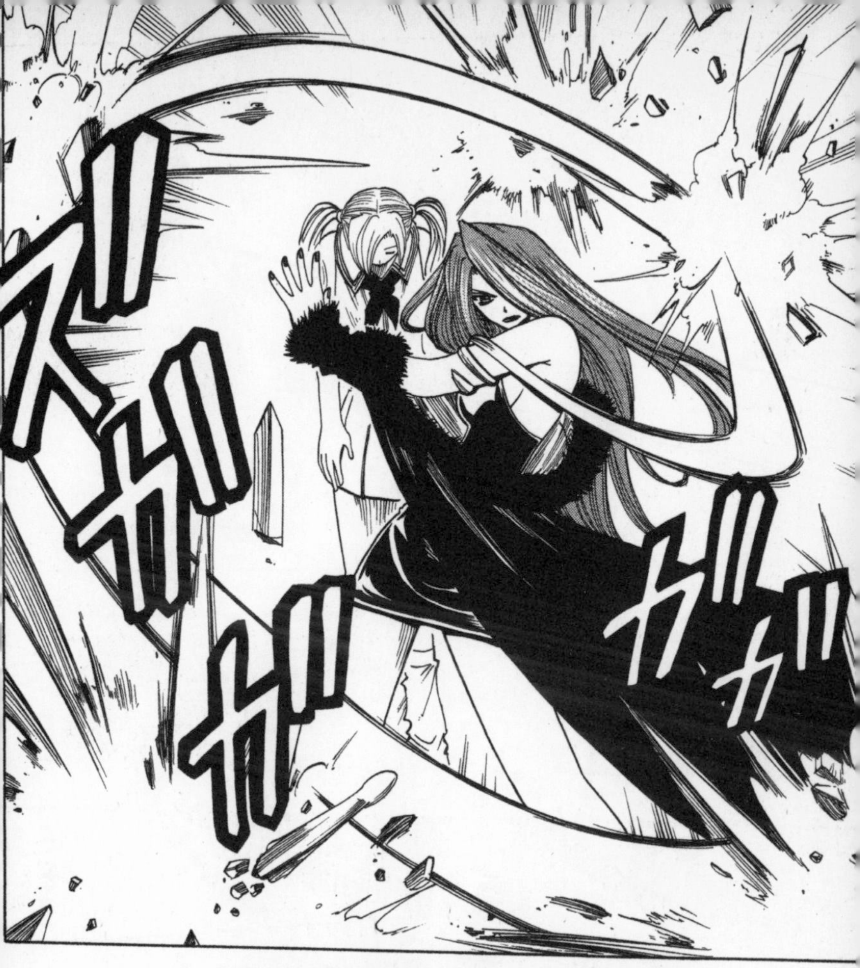
ガガ
ズガガ
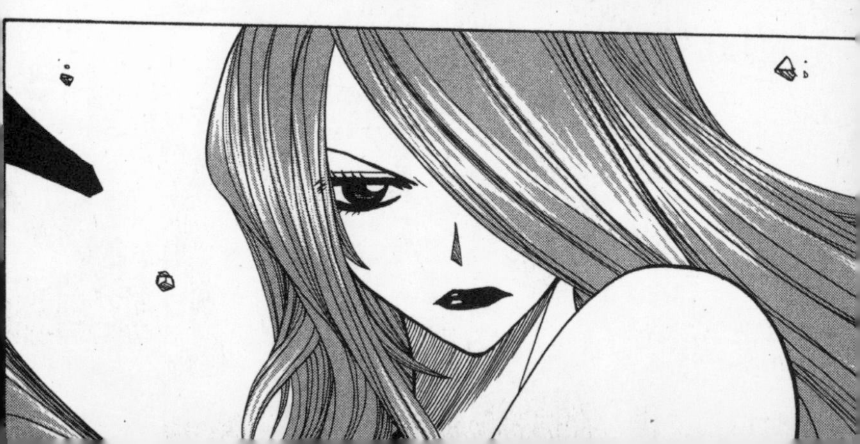

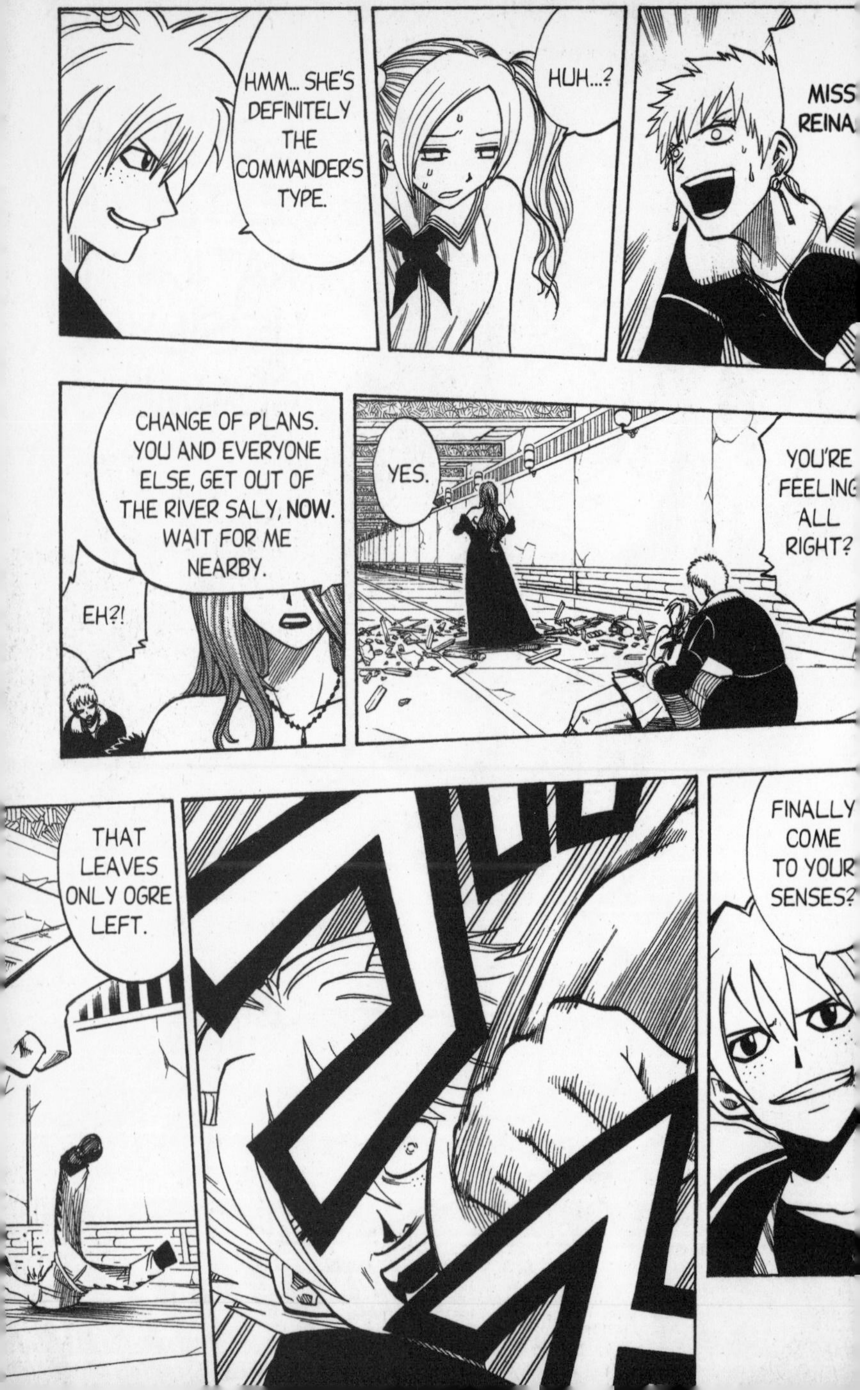
MISS REINA
HUH...?
HMM... SHE'S DEFINITELY THE COMMANDER'S TYPE.
YOU'RE FEELING ALL RIGHT?
YES.
CHANGE OF PLANS. YOU AND EVERYONE ELSE, GET OUT OF THE RIVER SALY, NOW. WAIT FOR ME NEARBY.
EH?!
FINALLY COME TO YOUR SENSES?
THAT LEAVES ONLY OGRE LEFT.

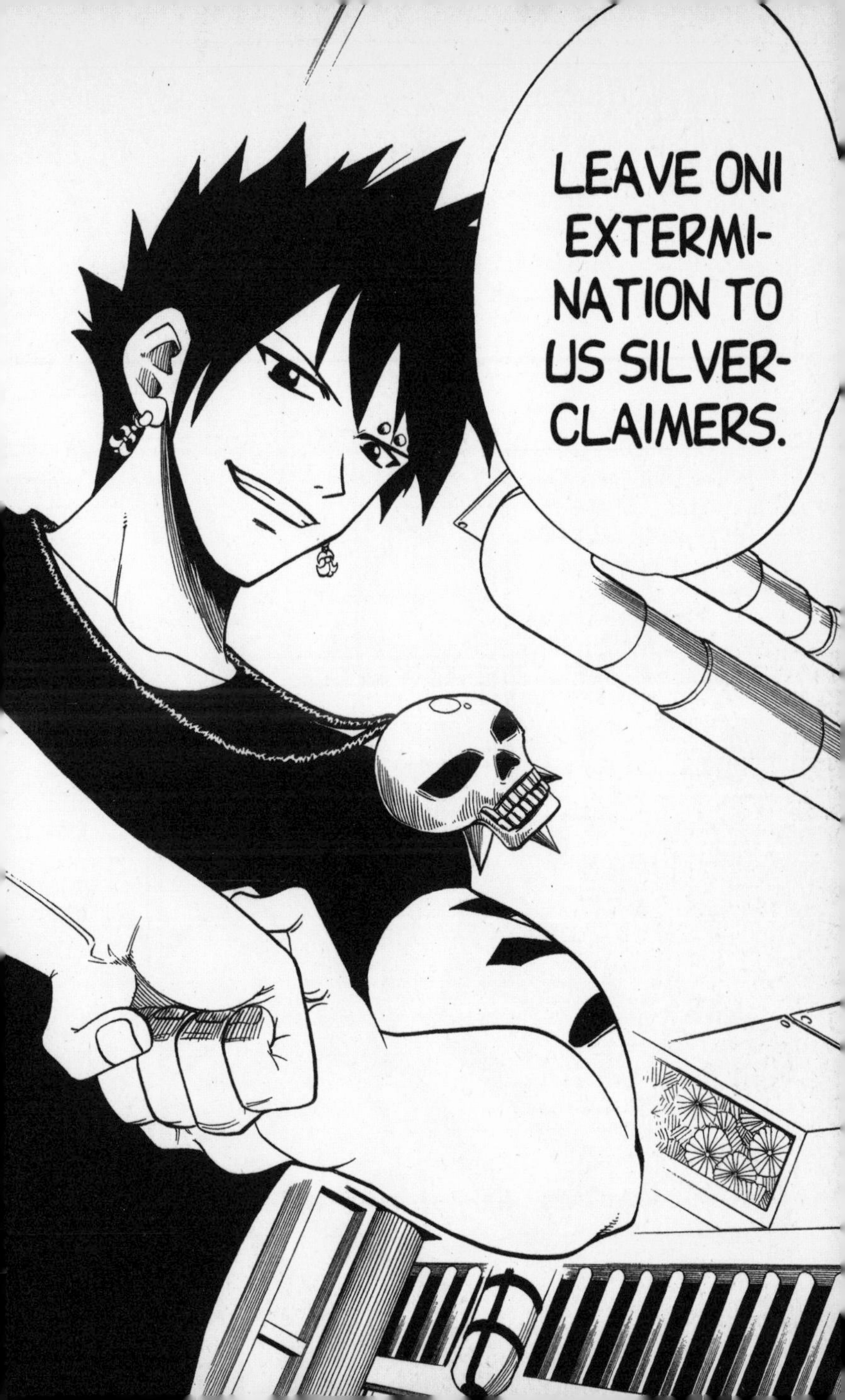
LEAVE ONI EXTERMINATION TO US SILVER-CLAIMERS.

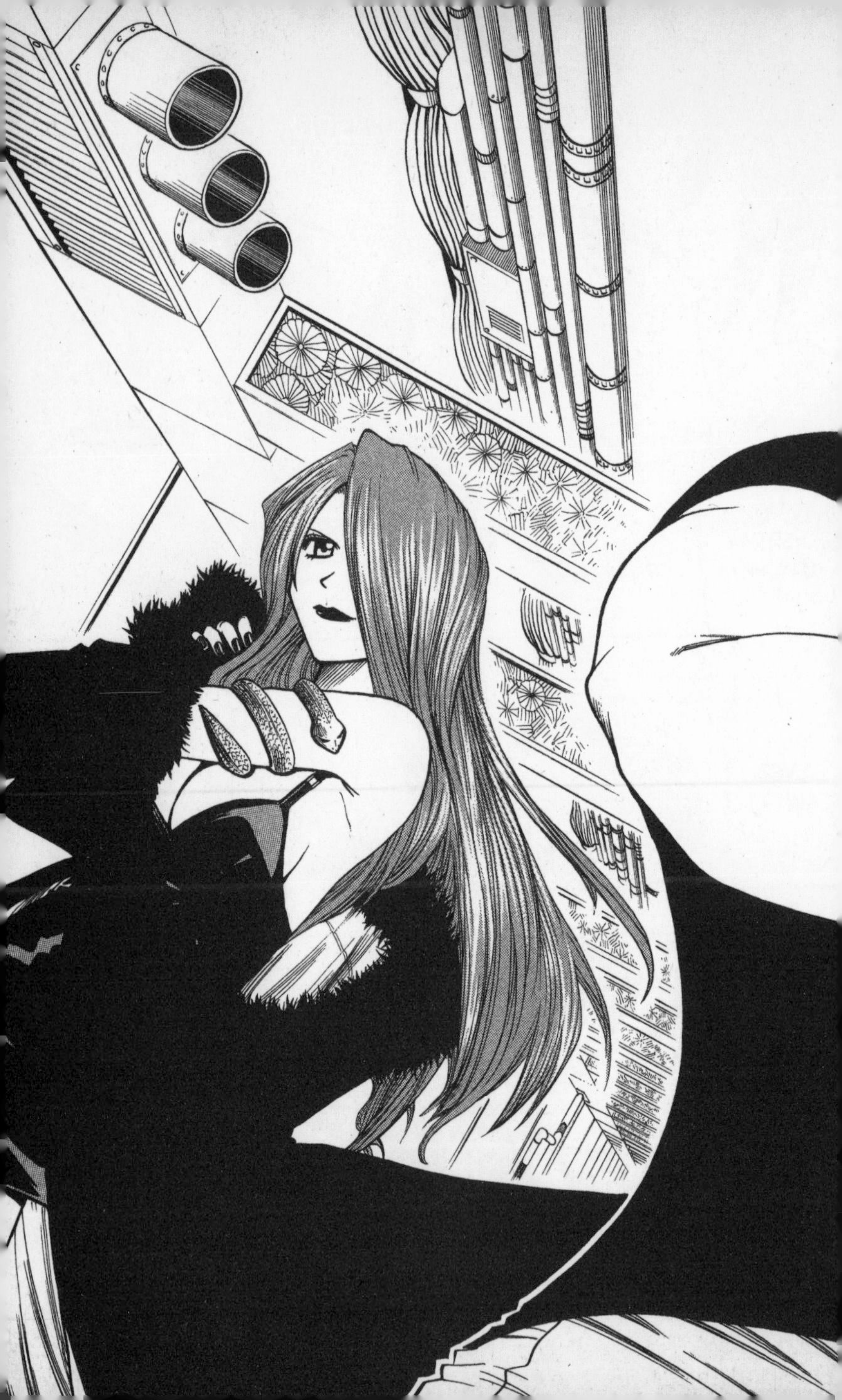

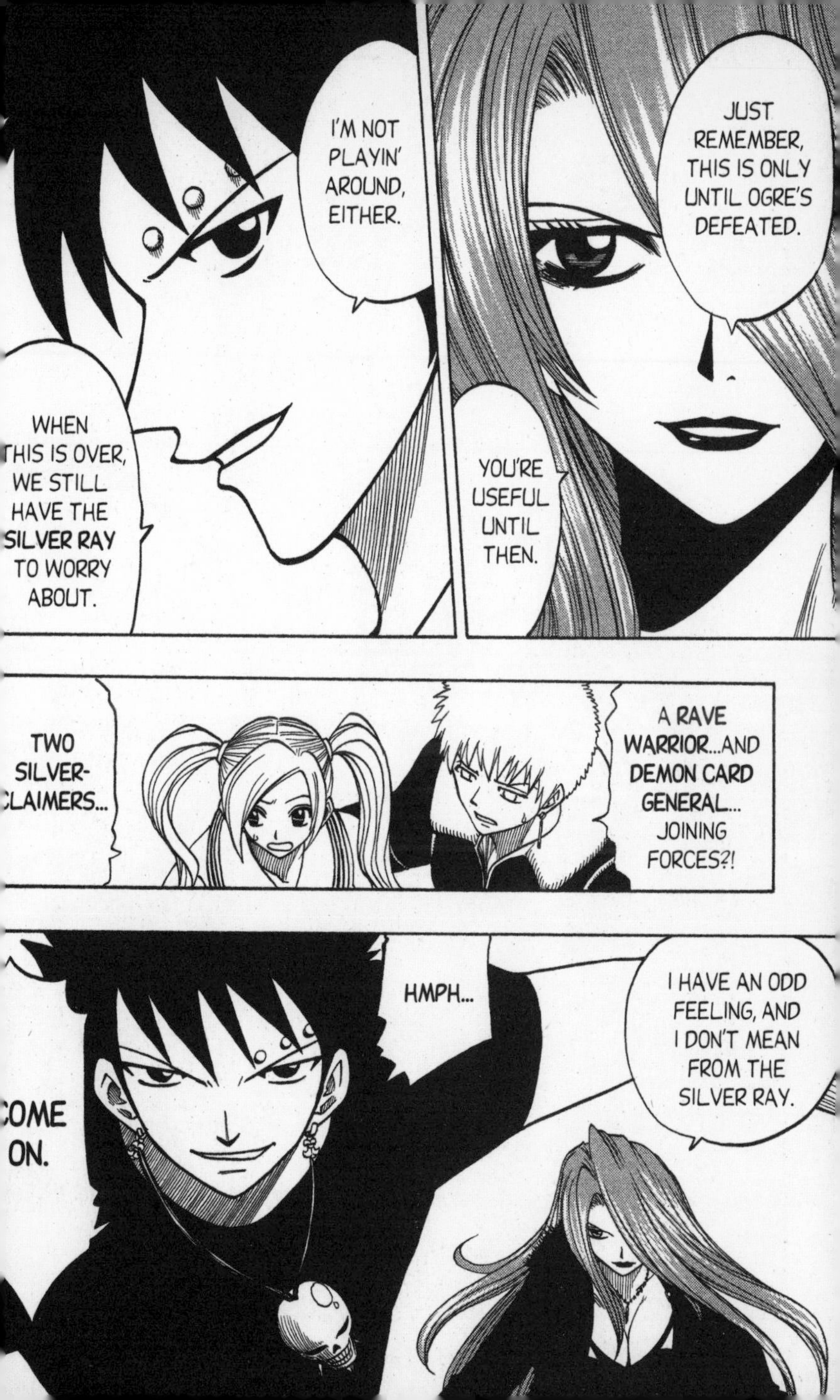
JUST REMEMBER, THIS IS ONLY UNTIL OGRE'S DEFEATED.
YOU'RE USEFUL UNTIL THEN.
I'M NOT PLAYIN' AROUND, EITHER.
WHEN THIS IS OVER, WE STILL HAVE THE SILVER RAY TO WORRY ABOUT.
A RAVE WARRIOR...AND DEMON CARD GENERAL... JOINING FORCES?!
TWO SILVER-CLAIMERS...
I HAVE AN ODD FEELING, AND I DON'T MEAN FROM THE SILVER RAY.
HMPH...
COME ON.

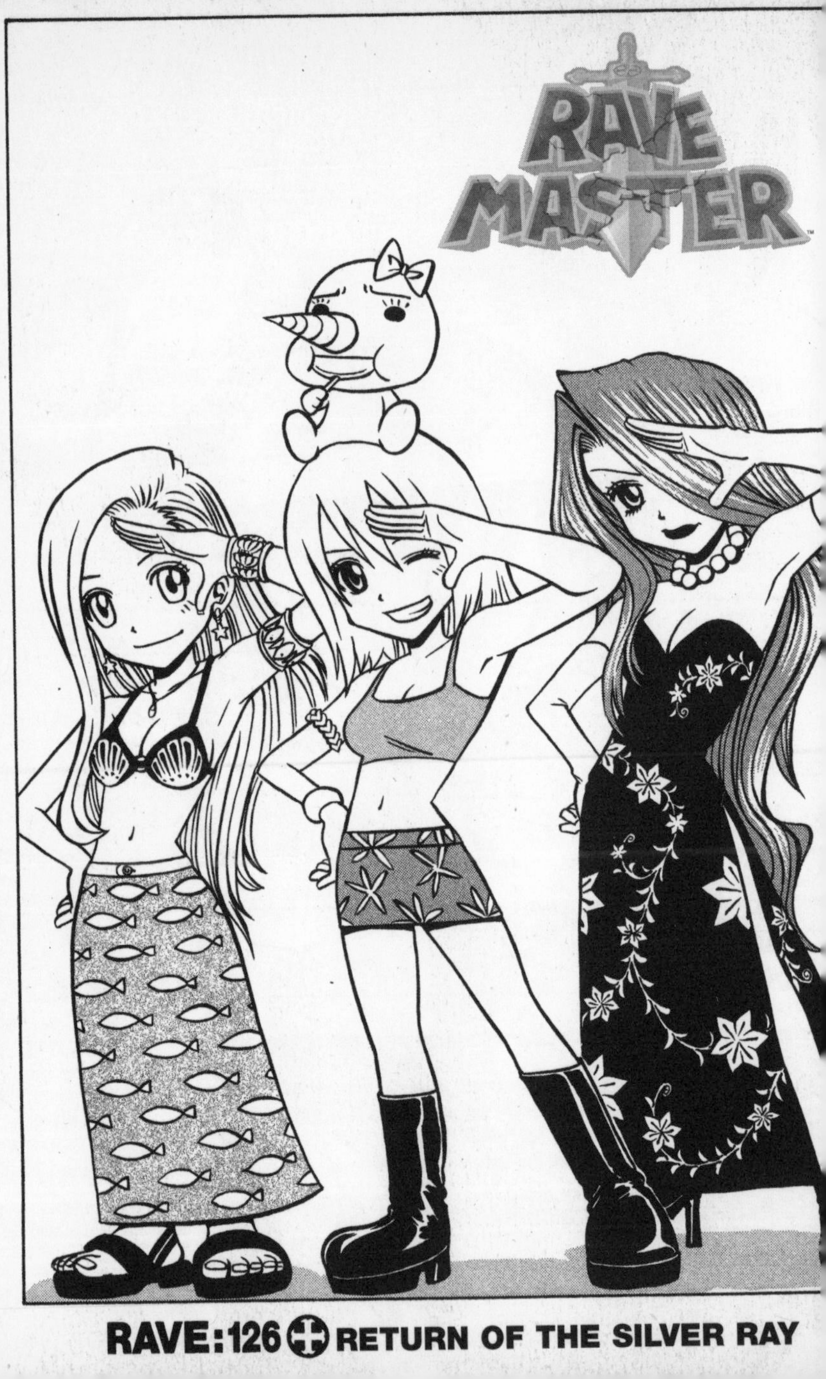
RAVE MASTER

RAVE:126 RETURN OF THE SILVER RAY

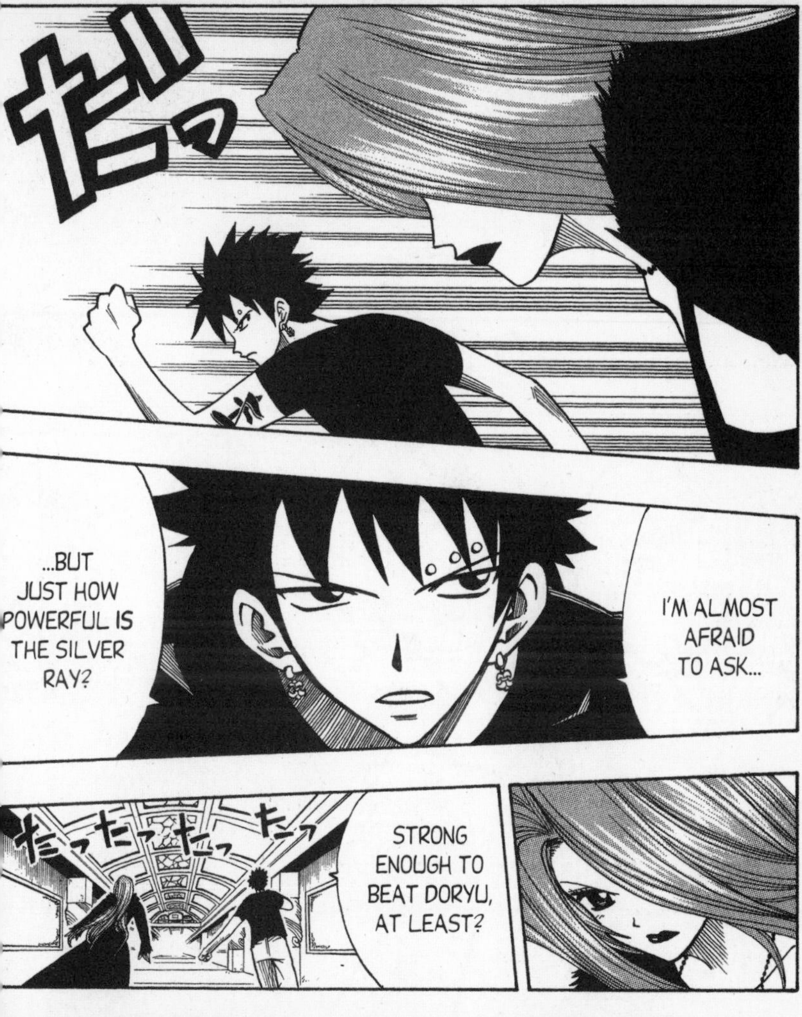

たーッ
I'M ALMOST AFRAID TO ASK...
...BUT JUST HOW POWERFUL IS THE SILVER RAY?
STRONG ENOUGH TO BEAT DORYU, AT LEAST?
たっ たっ たっ キーッ
IF YOU'RE NOT AFRAID OF LOSING ANYTHING.

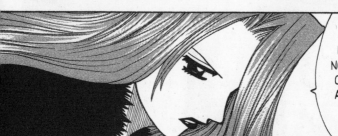

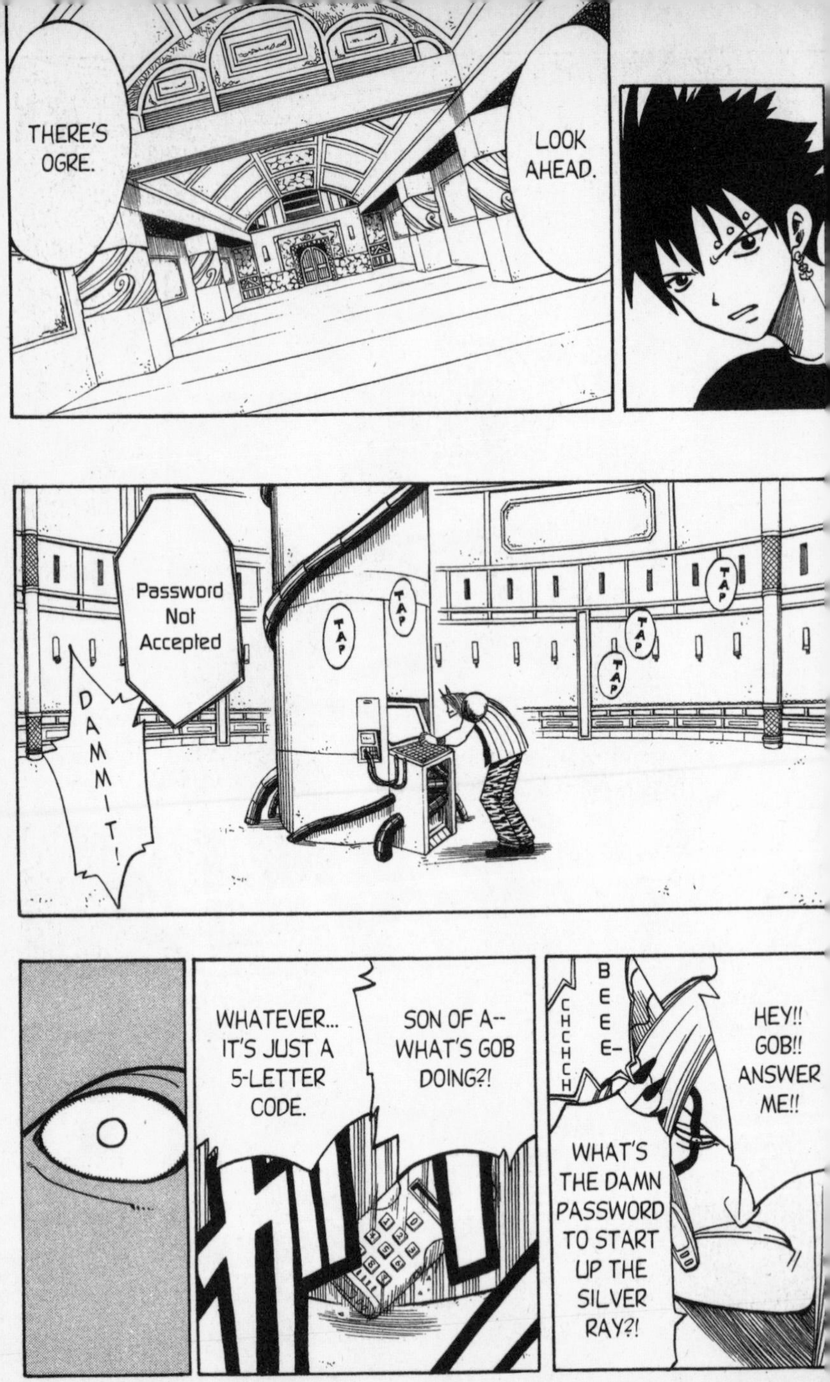
LOOK AHEAD.
THERE'S OGRE.
TAP
TAP
TAP
TAP
TAP
Password Not Accepted
DAMMIT!
HEY!! GOB!! ANSWER ME!!
BEEE-
CHCHCH
WHAT'S THE DAMN PASSWORD TO START UP THE SILVER RAY?!
SON OF A-- WHAT'S GOB DOING?!
WHATEVER... IT'S JUST A 5-LETTER CODE.

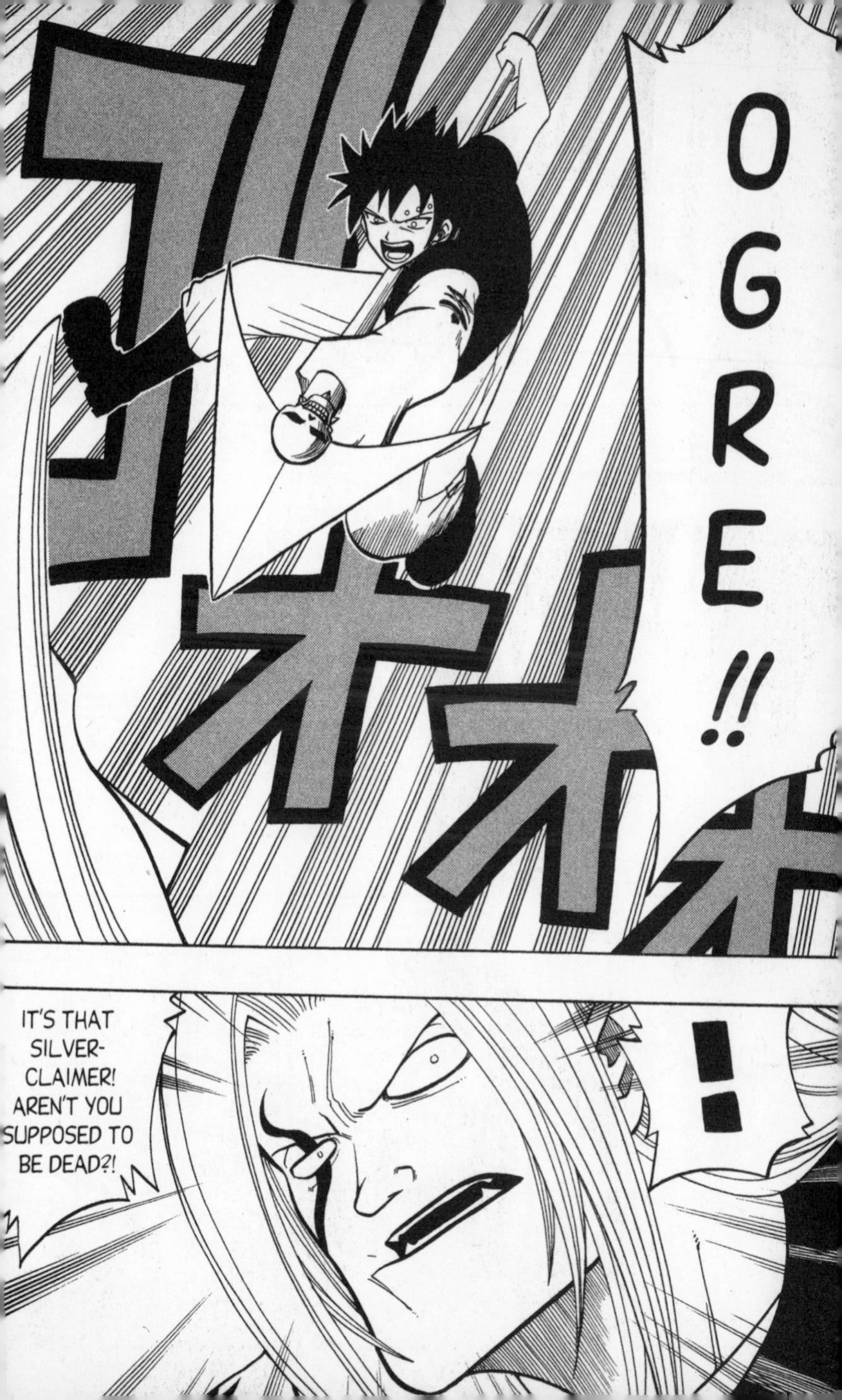
OGRE!!
IT'S THAT SILVER-CLAIMER! AREN'T YOU SUPPOSED TO BE DEAD?!
!

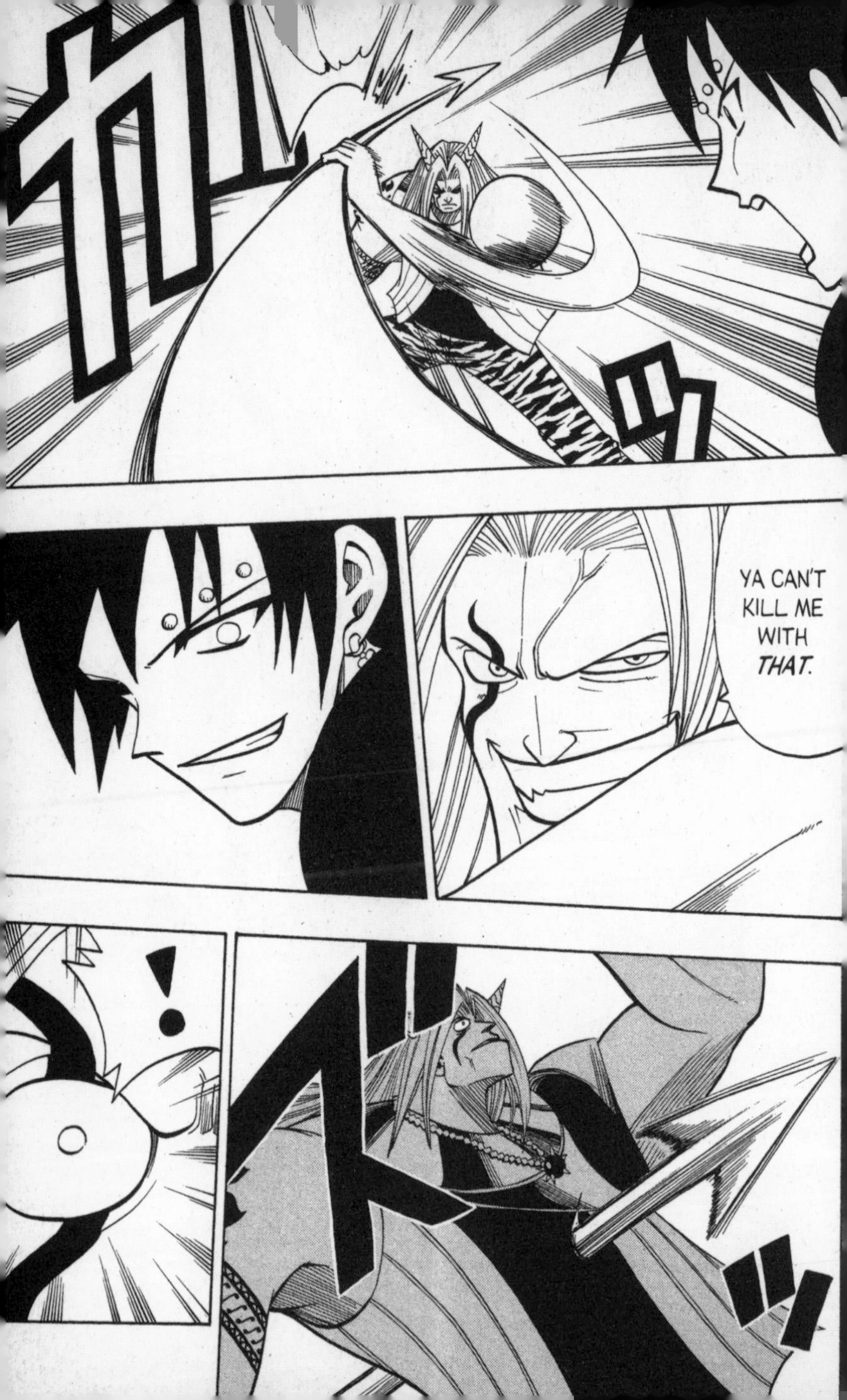
YA CAN'T KILL ME WITH *THAT*.

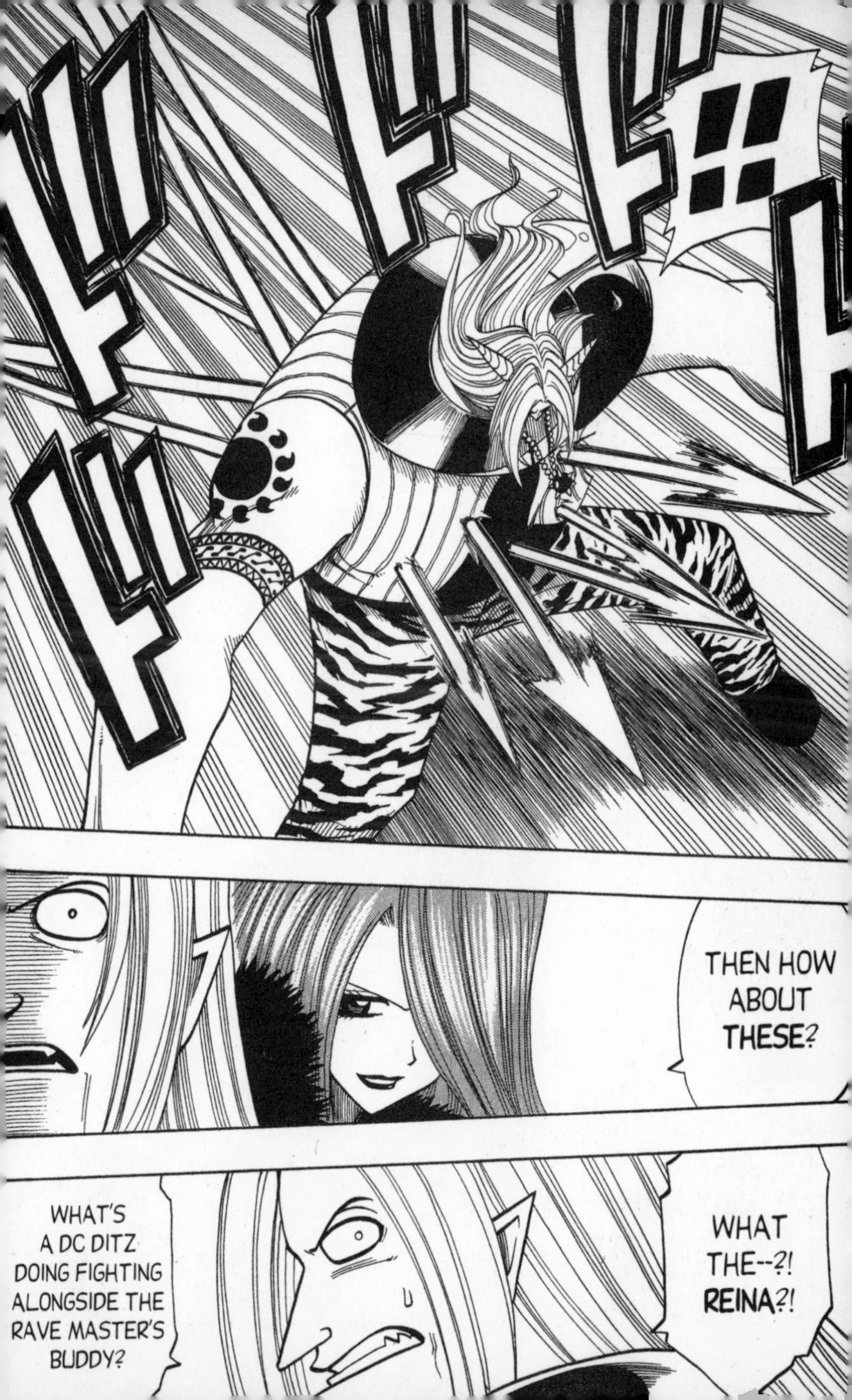
THEN HOW ABOUT THESE?
WHAT THE--?! REINA?!
WHAT'S A DC DITZ DOING FIGHTING ALONGSIDE THE RAVE MASTER'S BUDDY?

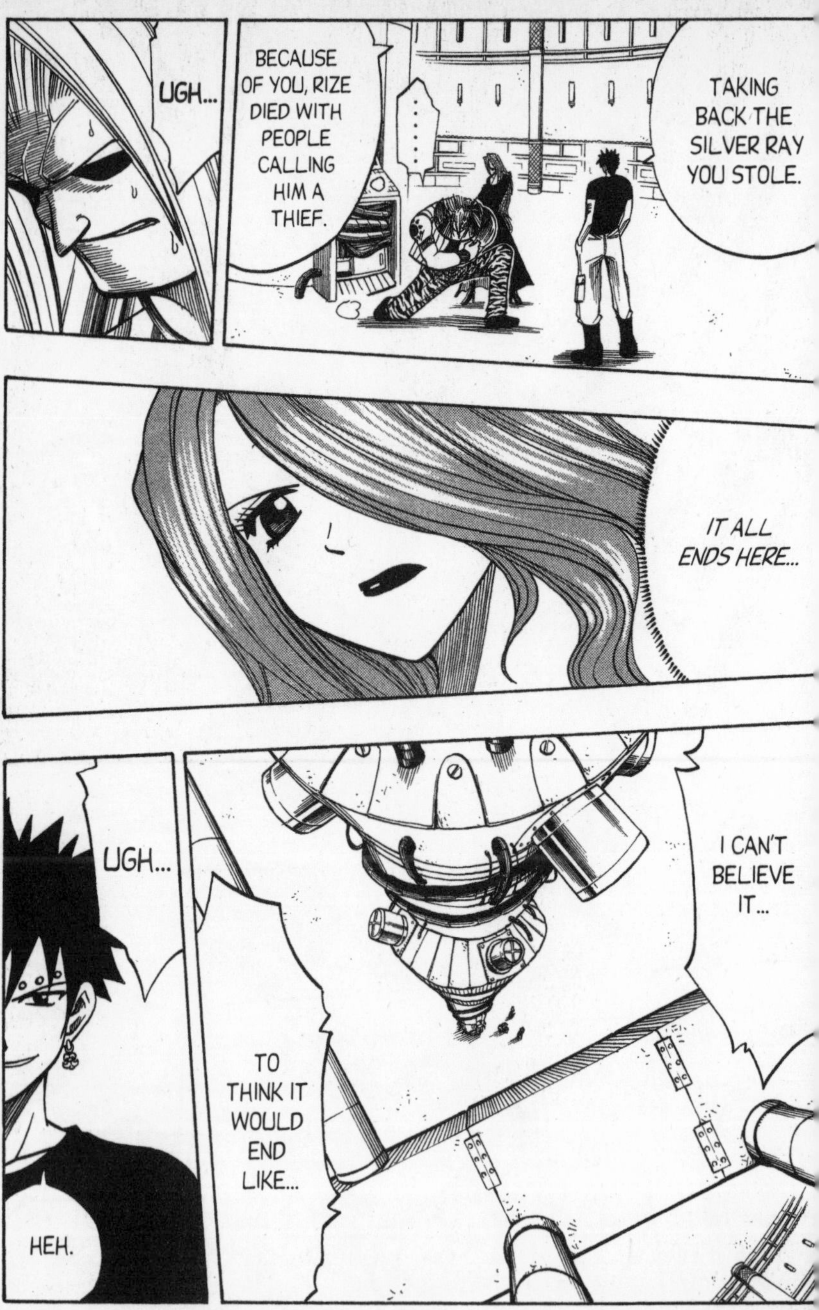

TAKING BACK THE SILVER RAY YOU STOLE.
BECAUSE OF YOU, RIZE DIED WITH PEOPLE CALLING HIM A THIEF.
......
UGH...
IT ALL ENDS HERE...
I CAN'T BELIEVE IT...
TO THINK IT WOULD END LIKE...
UGH...
HEH.

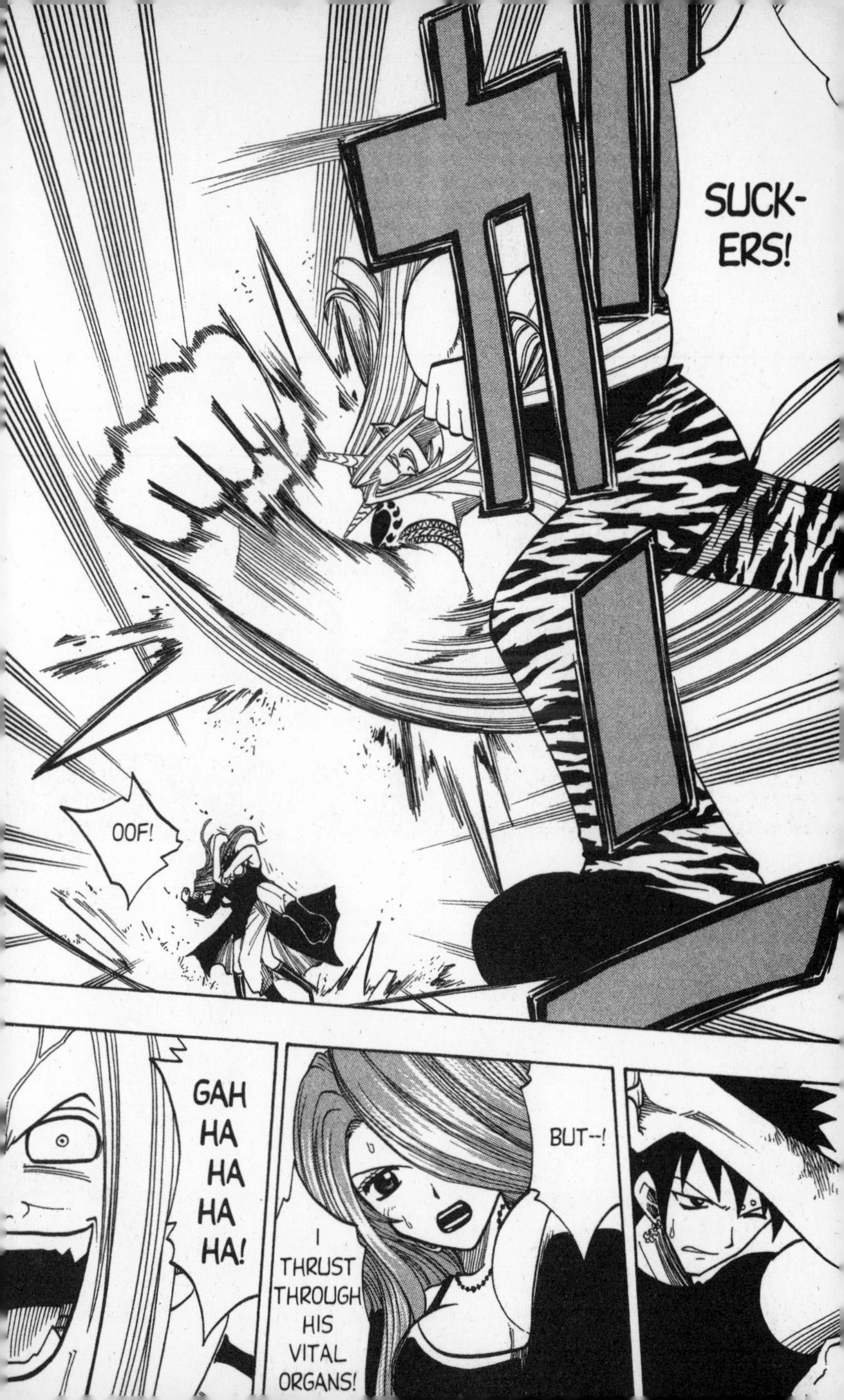
SUCK-
ERS!
OOF!
BUT--!
I THRUST THROUGH HIS VITAL ORGANS!
GAH HA HA HA HA!

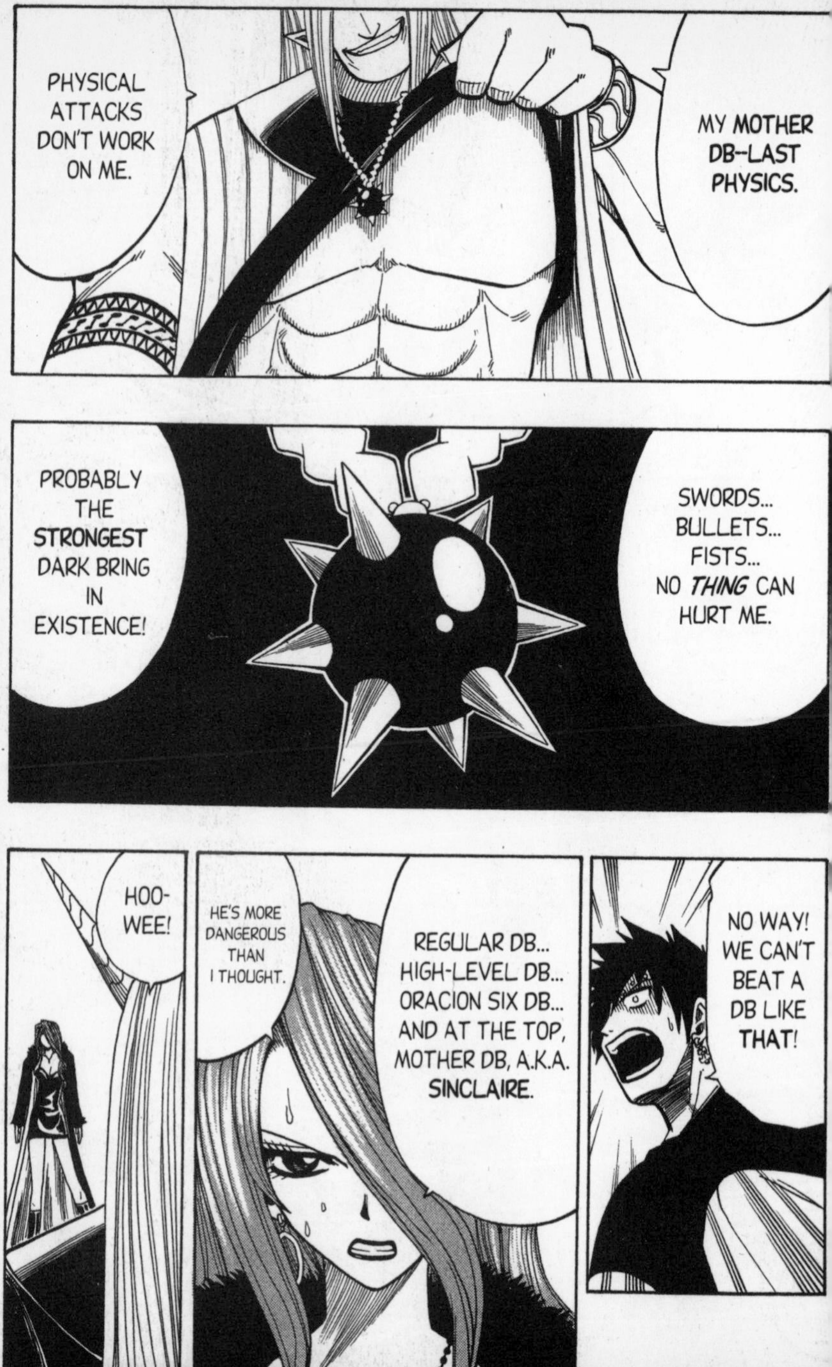
MY MOTHER DB--LAST PHYSICS.
PHYSICAL ATTACKS DON'T WORK ON ME.
SWORDS... BULLETS... FISTS... NO *THING* CAN HURT ME.
PROBABLY THE STRONGEST DARK BRING IN EXISTENCE!
NO WAY! WE CAN'T BEAT A DB LIKE THAT!
REGULAR DB... HIGH-LEVEL DB... ORACION SIX DB... AND AT THE TOP, MOTHER DB, A.K.A. SINCLAIRE.
HE'S MORE DANGEROUS THAN I THOUGHT.
HOO-WEE!

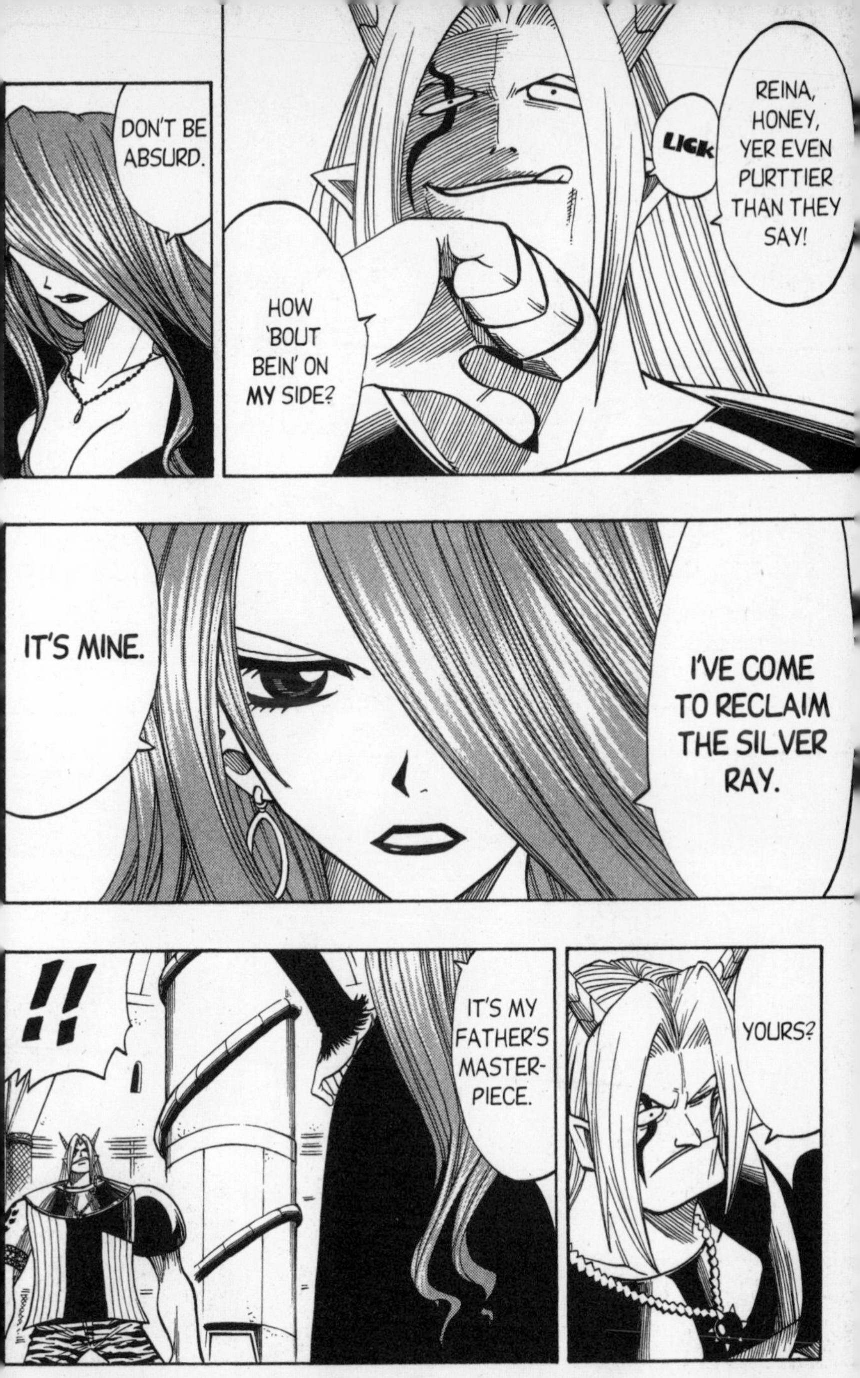
REINA, HONEY, YER EVEN PURTTIER THAN THEY SAY!
LICK
HOW 'BOUT BEIN' ON MY SIDE?
DON'T BE ABSURD.
I'VE COME TO RECLAIM THE SILVER RAY.
IT'S MINE.
YOURS?
IT'S MY FATHER'S MASTER-PIECE.
!!

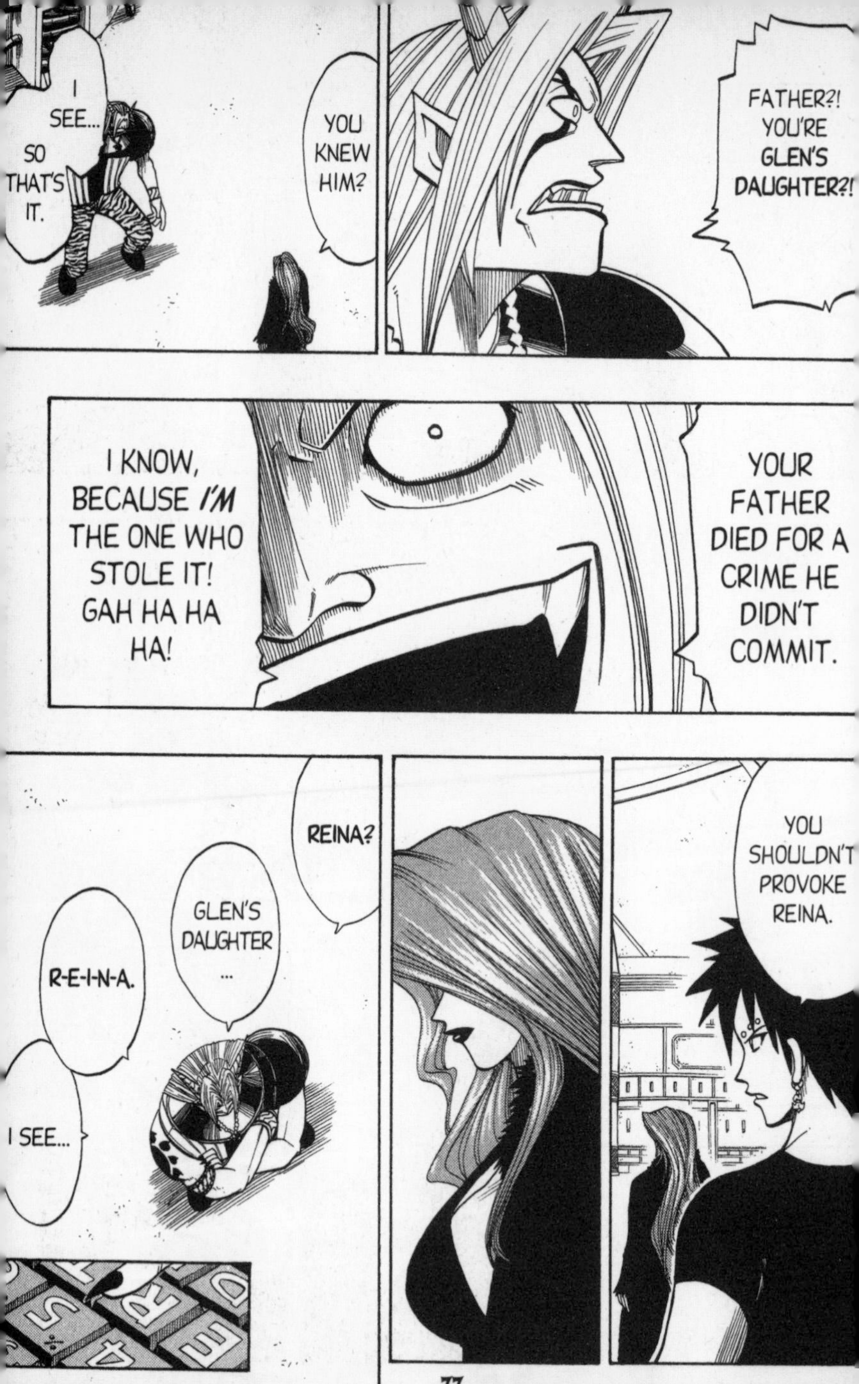
FATHER?! YOU'RE GLEN'S DAUGHTER?!
I SEE... SO THAT'S IT.
YOU KNEW HIM?
YOUR FATHER DIED FOR A CRIME HE DIDN'T COMMIT.
I KNOW, BECAUSE *I'M* THE ONE WHO STOLE IT! GAH HA HA HA!
YOU SHOULDN'T PROVOKE REINA.
REINA?
GLEN'S DAUGHTER ...
R-E-I-N-A.
I SEE...

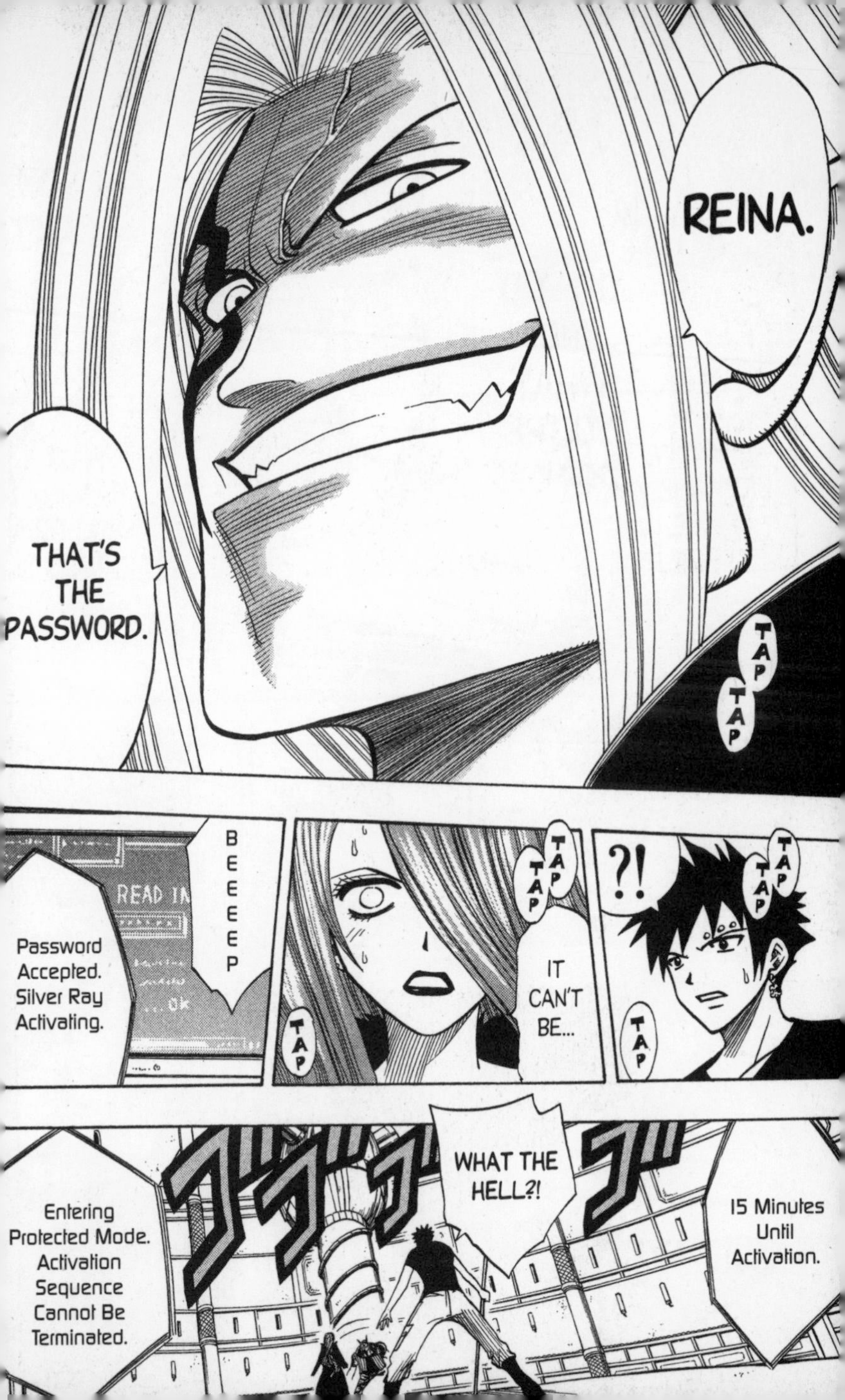
REINA.
THAT'S THE PASSWORD.
TAP TAP
?!
TAP TAP
TAP
TAP TAP
IT CAN'T BE...
TAP
BEEEEEP
Password Accepted. Silver Ray Activating.
15 Minutes Until Activation.
WHAT THE HELL?!
Entering Protected Mode. Activation Sequence Cannot Be Terminated.

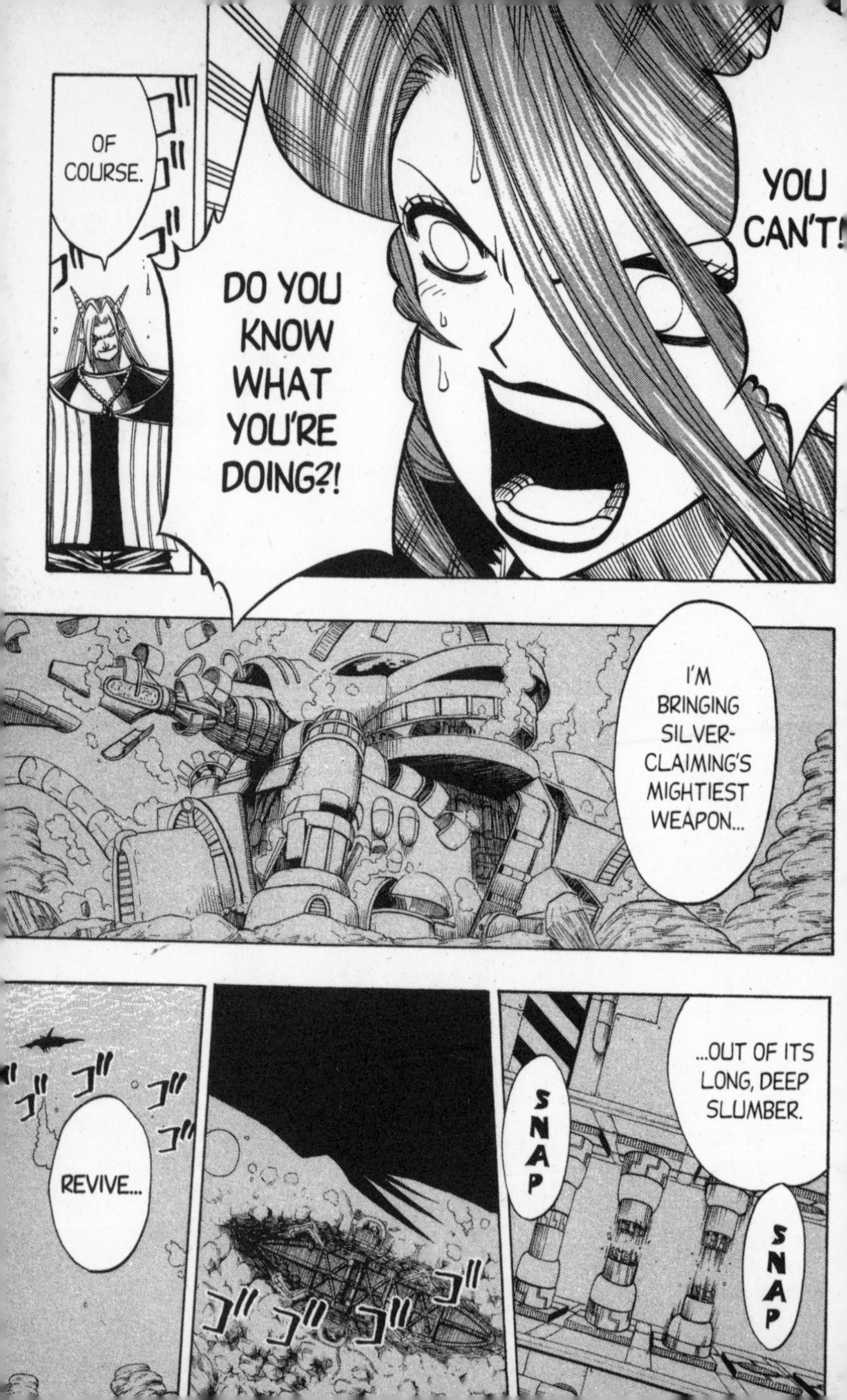
YOU CAN'T!
DO YOU KNOW WHAT YOU'RE DOING?!
OF COURSE.
I'M BRINGING SILVER-CLAIMING'S MIGHTIEST WEAPON...
...OUT OF ITS LONG, DEEP SLUMBER.
SNAP
SNAP
REVIVE...

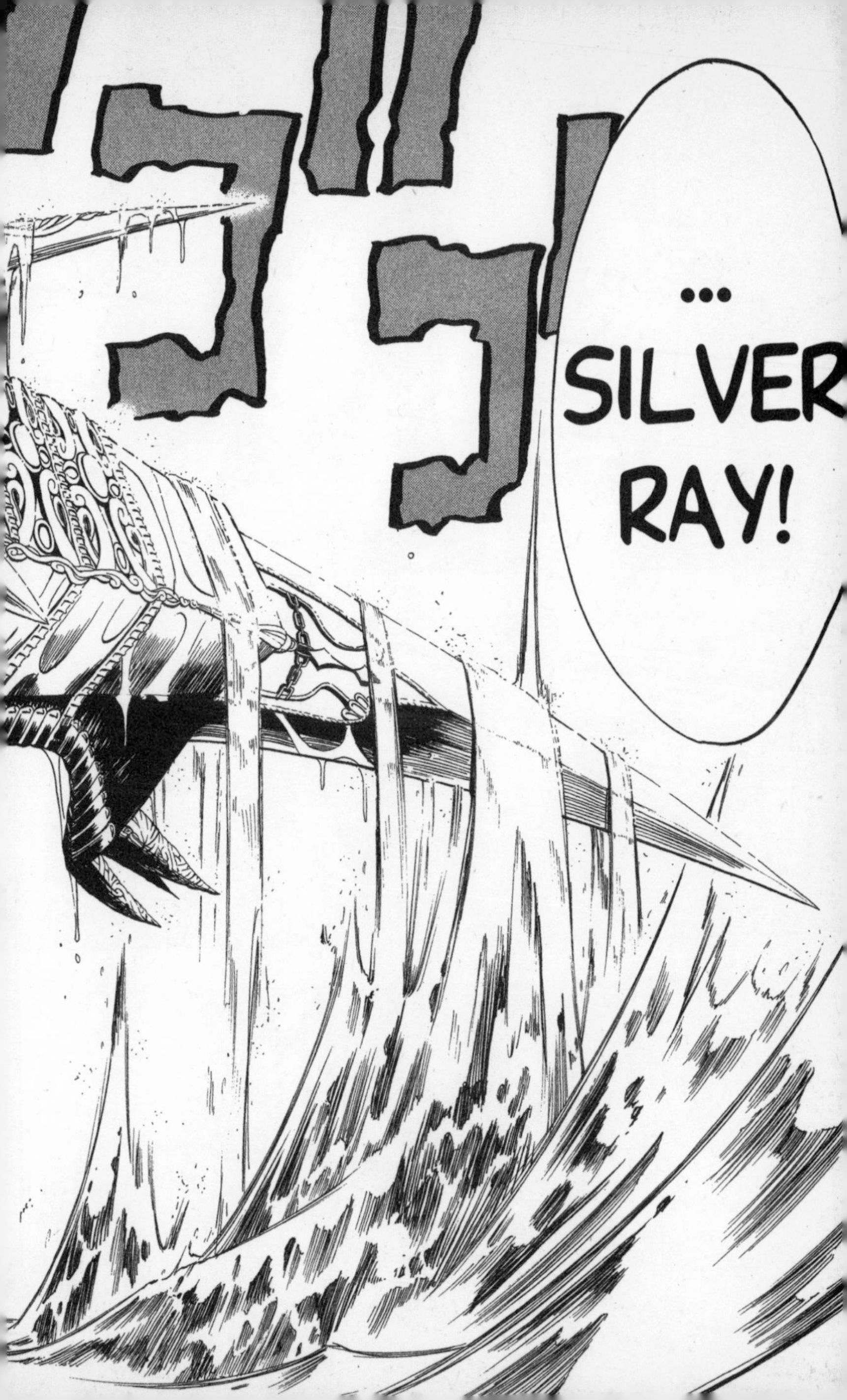
...SILVER RAY!

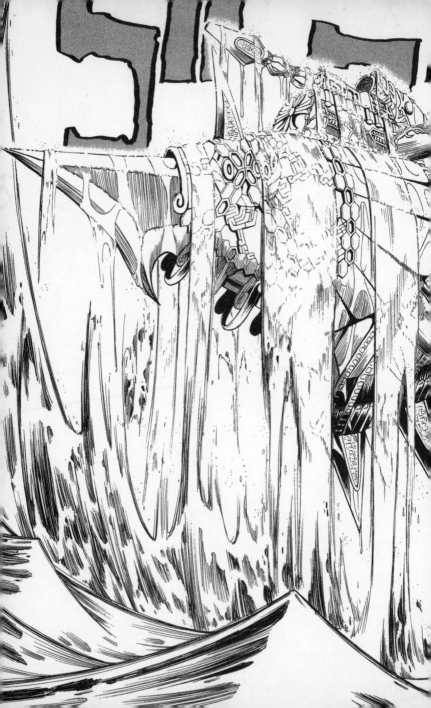

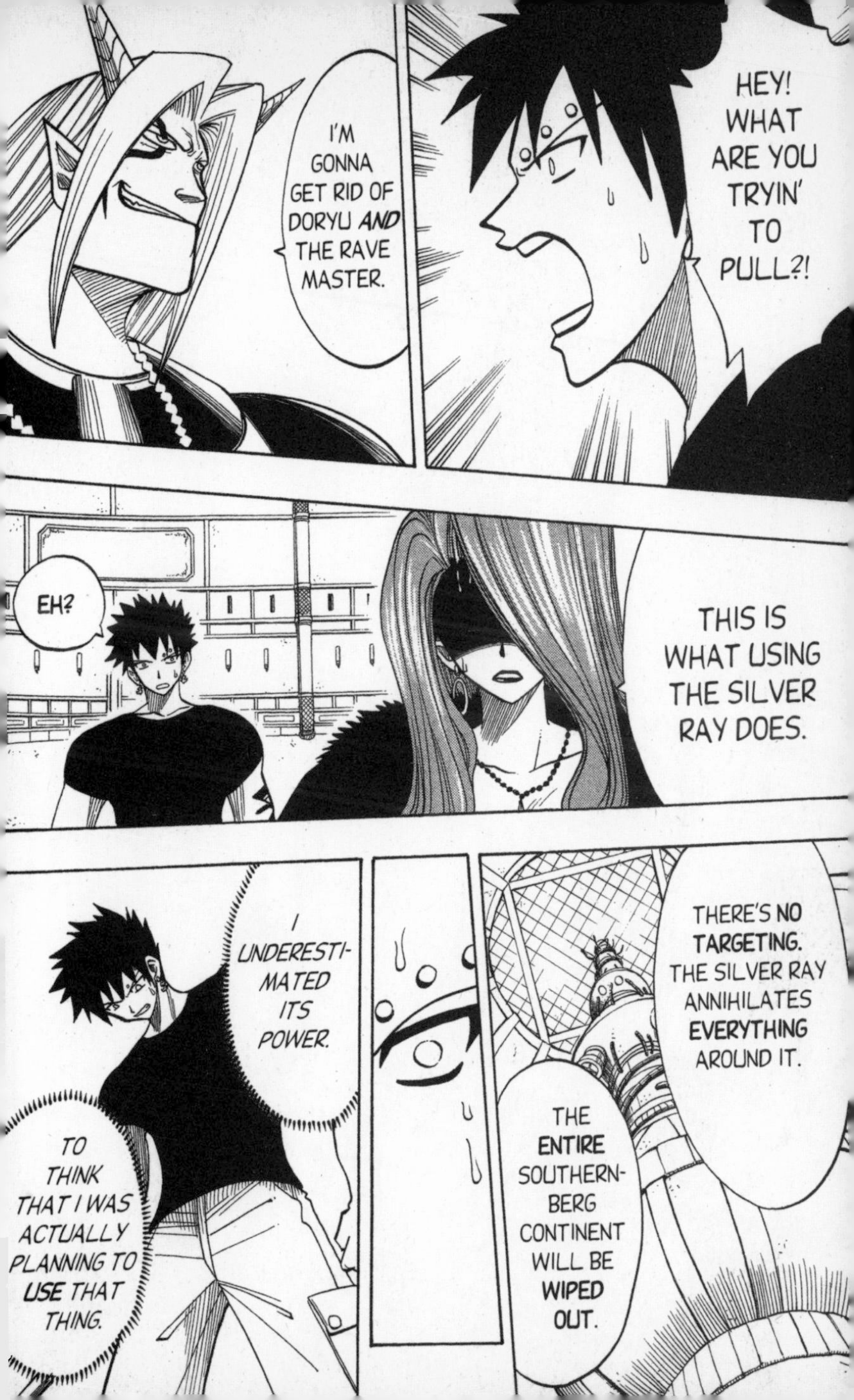
HEY! WHAT ARE YOU TRYIN' TO PULL?!
I'M GONNA GET RID OF DORYU *AND* THE RAVE MASTER.
THIS IS WHAT USING THE SILVER RAY DOES.
EH?
THERE'S **NO TARGETING.** THE SILVER RAY ANNIHILATES **EVERYTHING** AROUND IT.
THE **ENTIRE** SOUTHERNBERG CONTINENT WILL BE **WIPED OUT.**
I UNDERESTIMATED ITS POWER.
TO THINK THAT I WAS ACTUALLY PLANNING TO **USE** THAT THING.

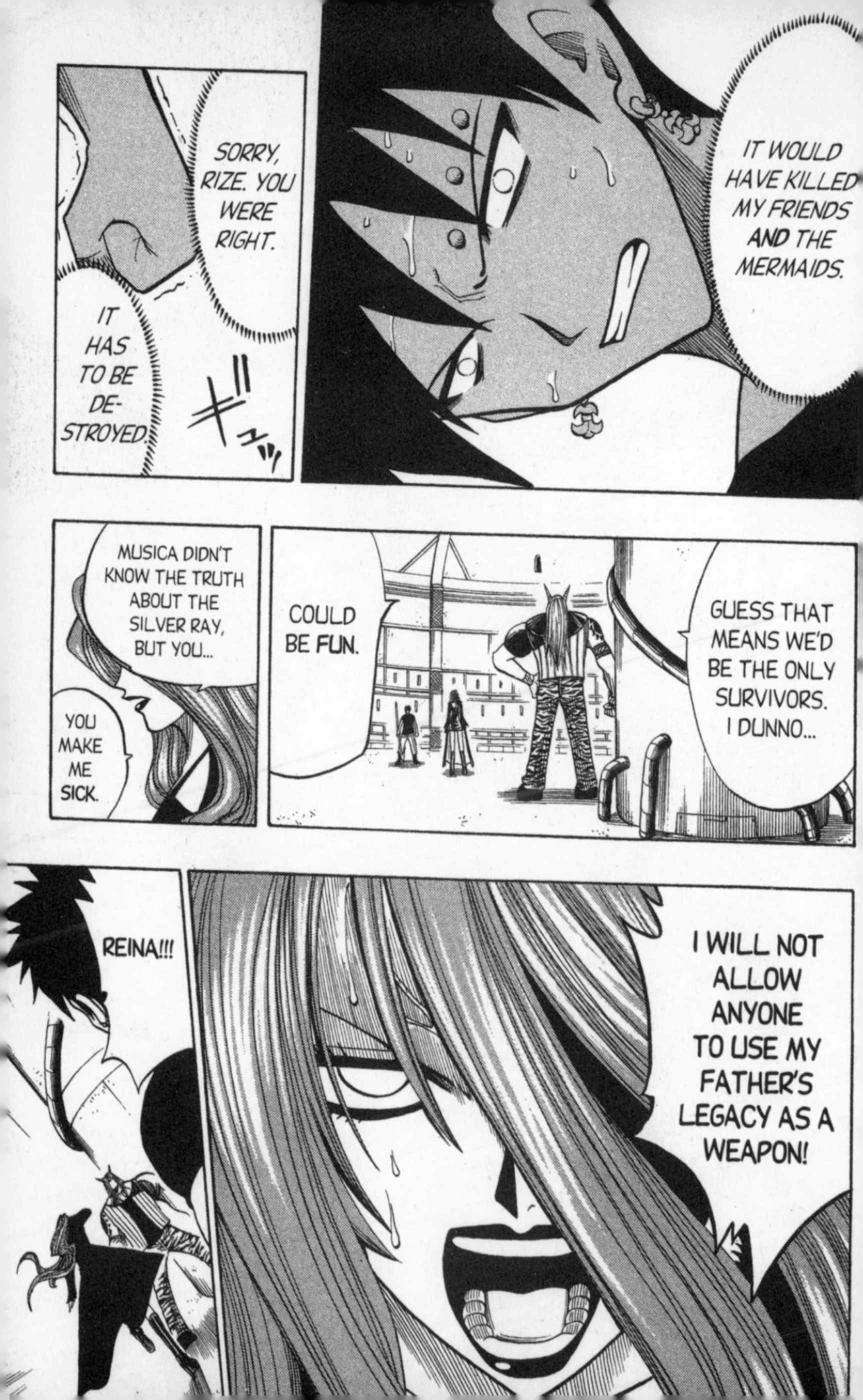
IT WOULD HAVE KILLED MY FRIENDS AND THE MERMAIDS.
SORRY, RIZE. YOU WERE RIGHT.
IT HAS TO BE DE-STROYED.
GUESS THAT MEANS WE'D BE THE ONLY SURVIVORS. I DUNNO...
COULD BE FUN.
MUSICA DIDN'T KNOW THE TRUTH ABOUT THE SILVER RAY, BUT YOU...
YOU MAKE ME SICK.
I WILL NOT ALLOW ANYONE TO USE MY FATHER'S LEGACY AS A WEAPON!
REINA!!!

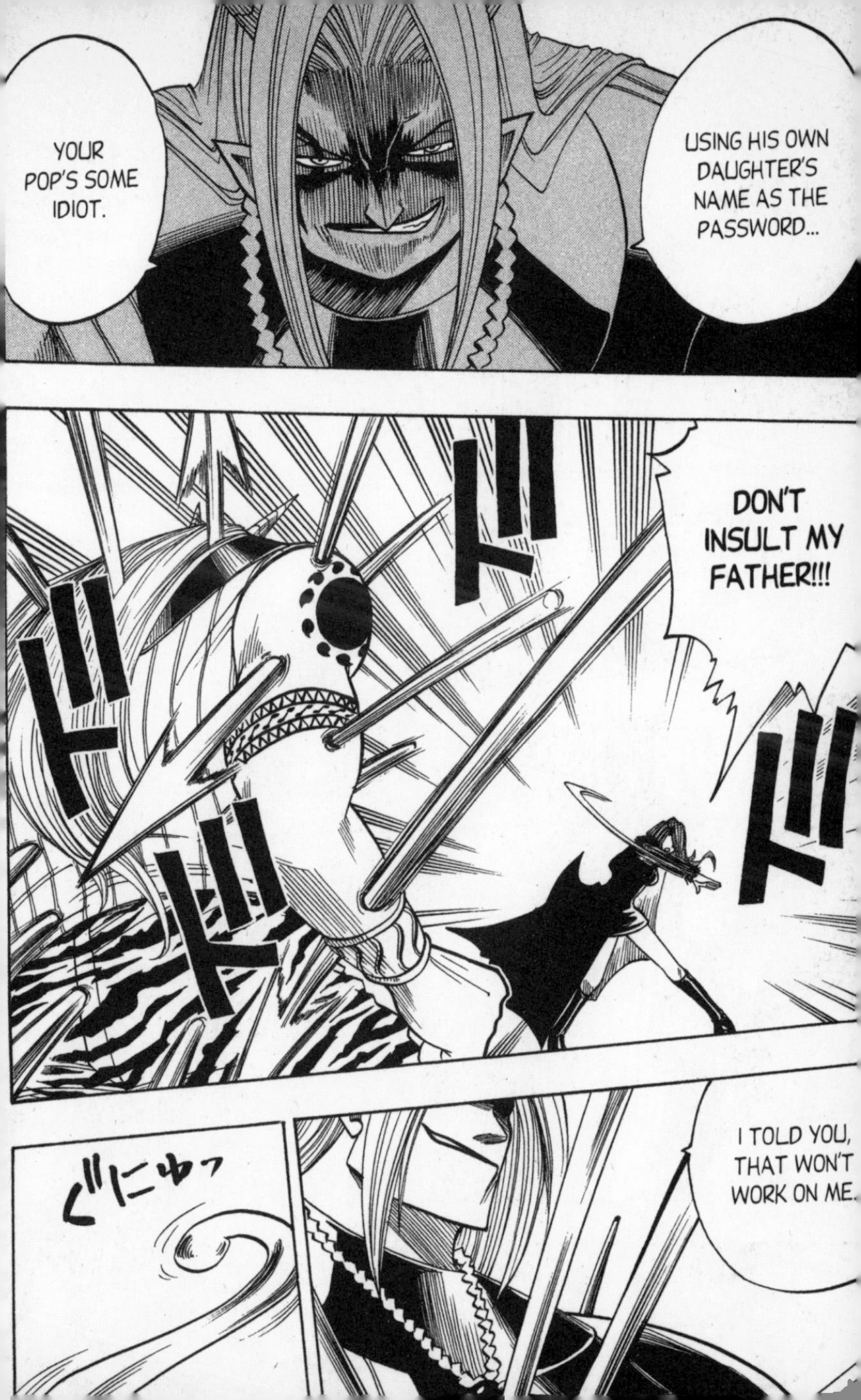
USING HIS OWN DAUGHTER'S NAME AS THE PASSWORD...
YOUR POP'S SOME IDIOT.
ド
DON'T INSULT MY FATHER!!!
ド
ド
ド
I TOLD YOU, THAT WON'T WORK ON ME.
ぐにゅっ

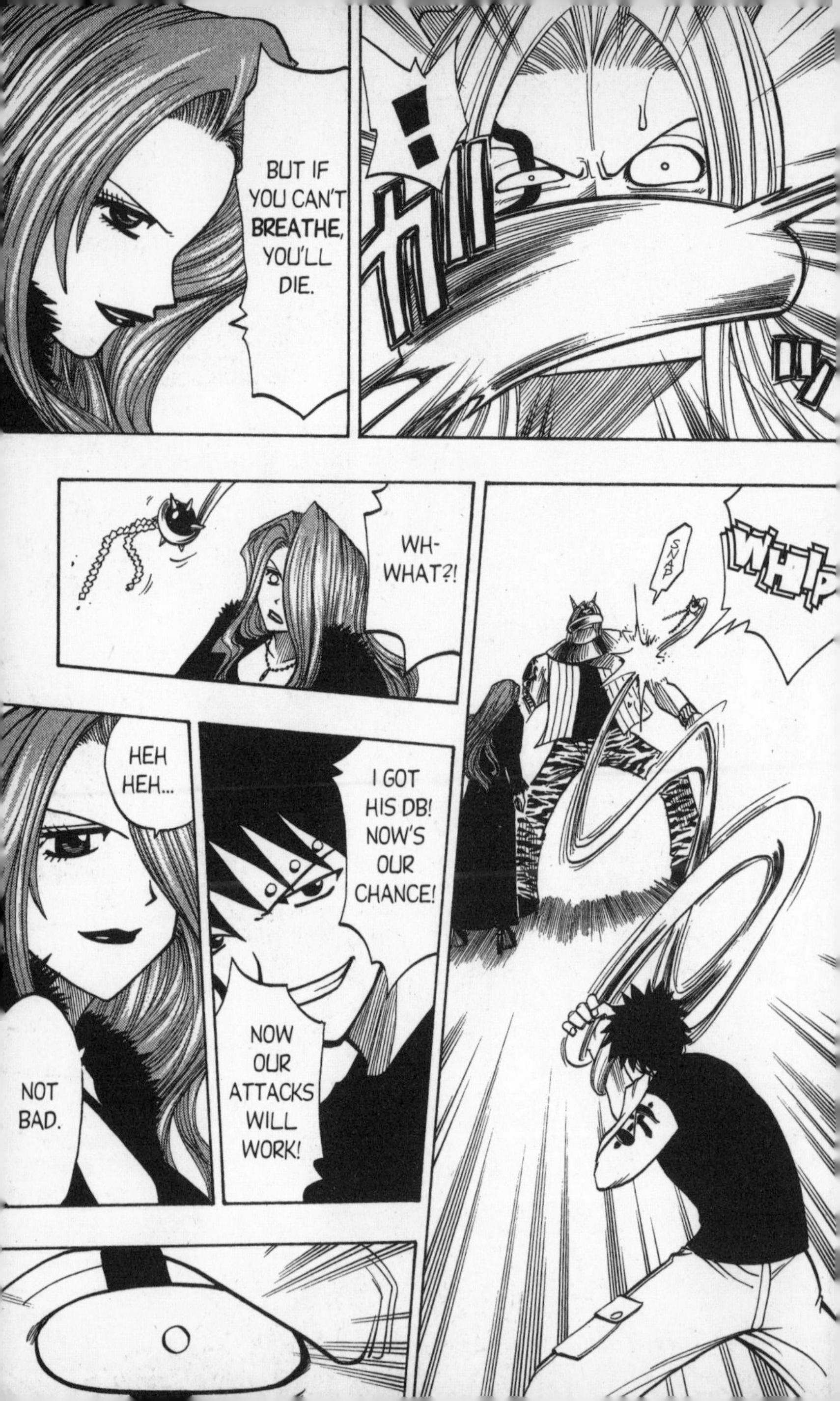
BUT IF YOU CAN'T BREATHE, YOU'LL DIE.
WHIP
SNAP
WH- WHAT?!
I GOT HIS DB! NOW'S OUR CHANCE!
NOW OUR ATTACKS WILL WORK!
HEH HEH...
NOT BAD.

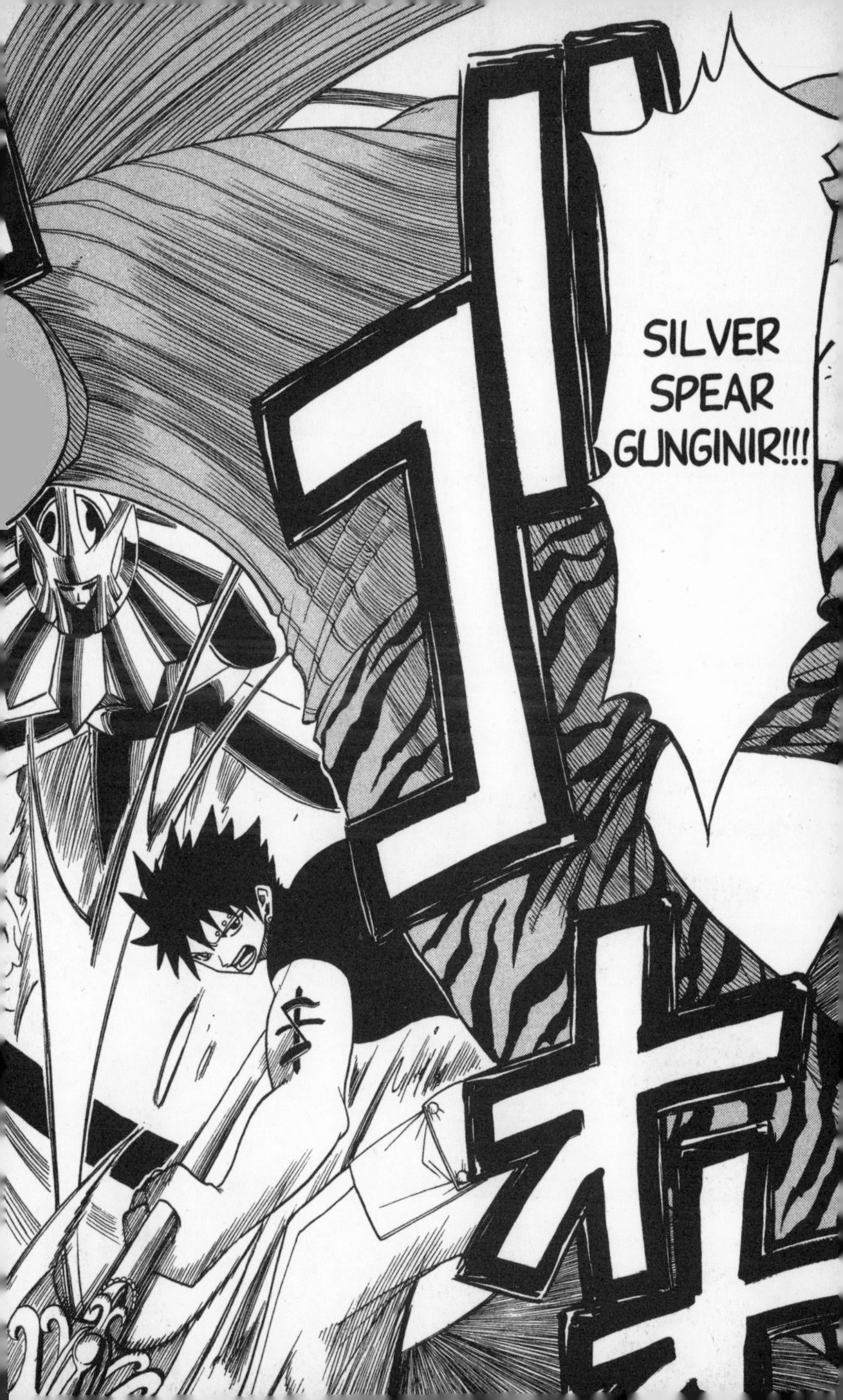
SILVER SPEAR GUNGINIR!!!

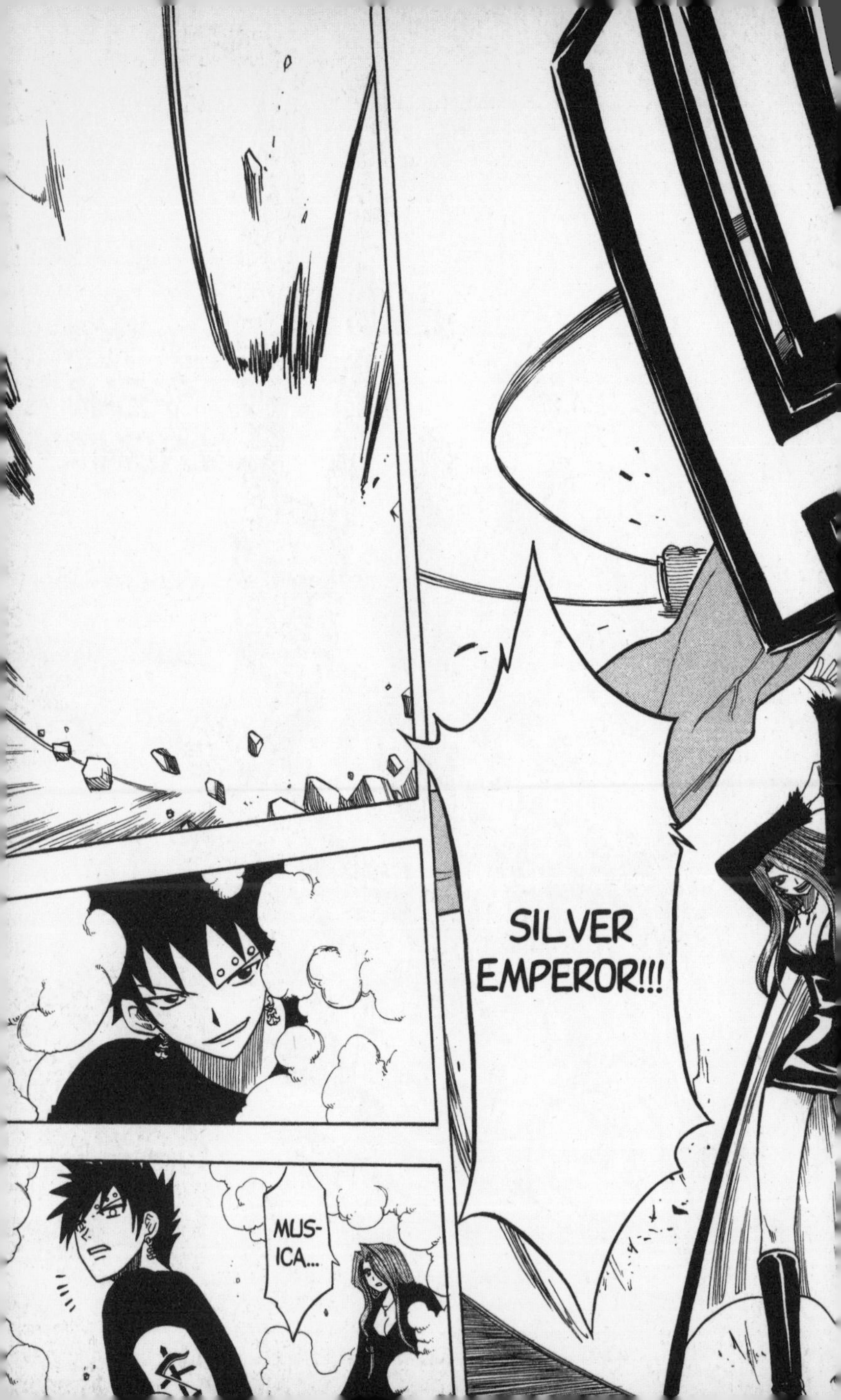
SILVER EMPEROR!!!
MUS-
ICA...

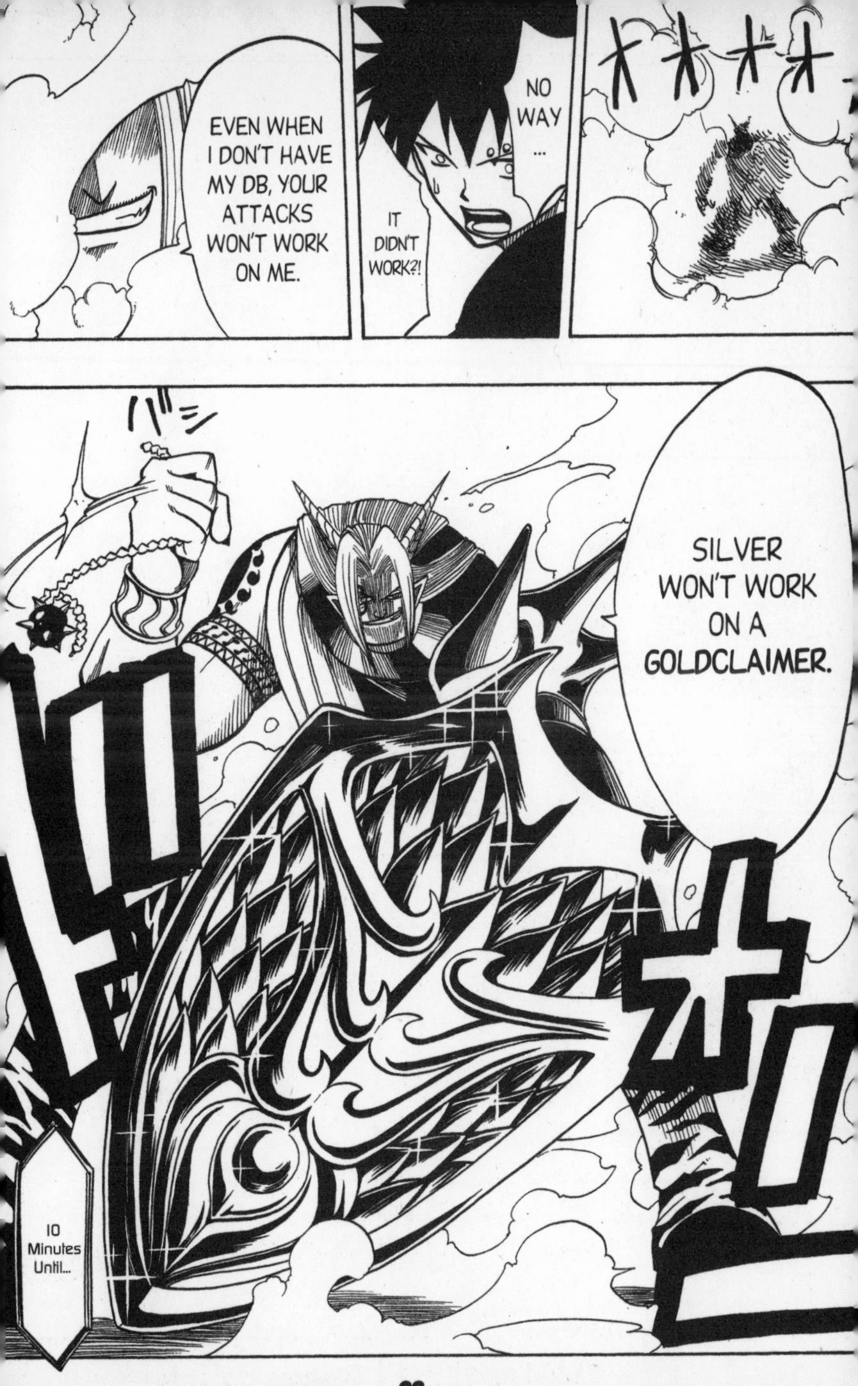
NO WAY ...
IT DIDN'T WORK?!
EVEN WHEN I DON'T HAVE MY DB, YOUR ATTACKS WON'T WORK ON ME.
SILVER WON'T WORK ON A GOLDCLAIMER.
10 Minutes Until...

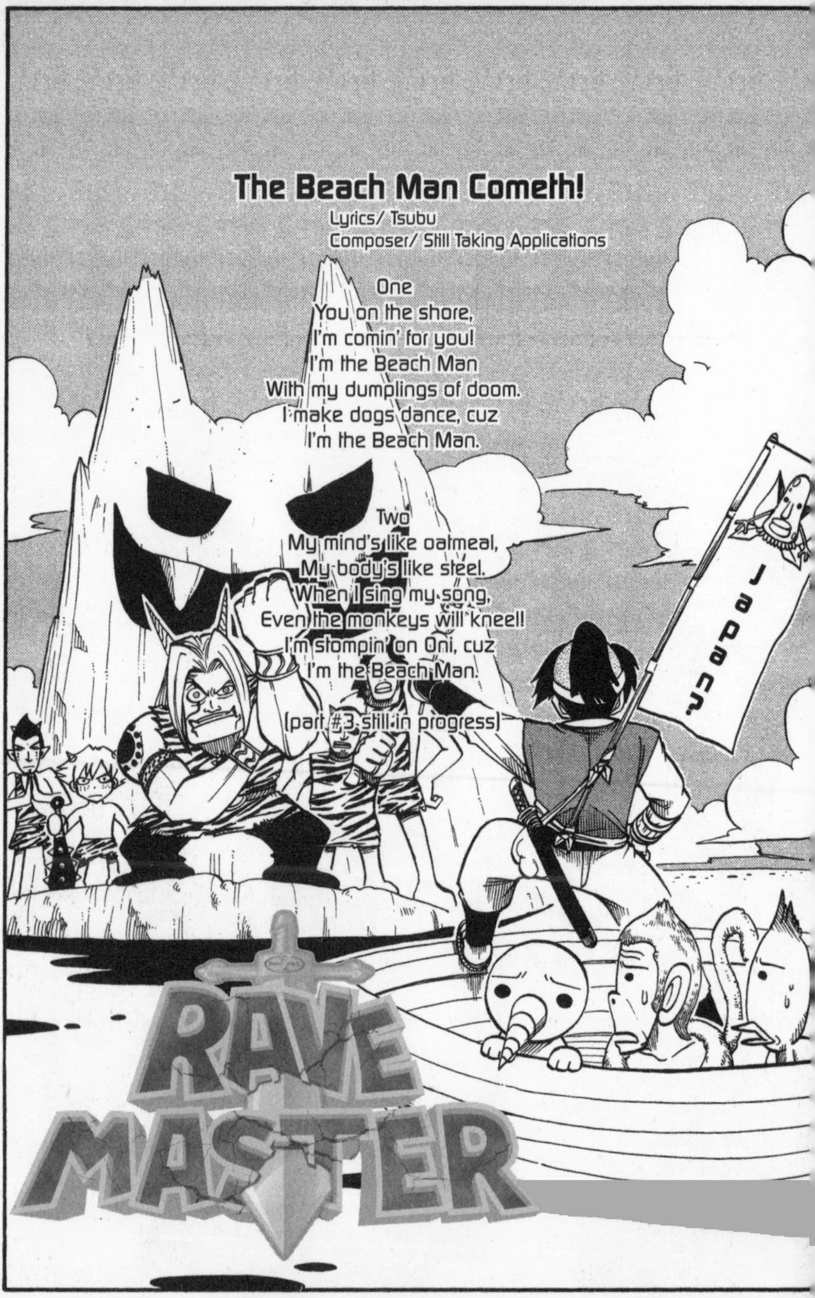
The Beach Man Cometh!
Lyrics/ Tsubu
Composer/ Still Taking Applications
One
You on the shore,
I'm comin' for you!
I'm the Beach Man
With my dumplings of doom.
I make dogs dance, cuz
I'm the Beach Man.
Two
My mind's like oatmeal,
My body's like steel.
When I sing my song,
Even the monkeys will kneel!
I'm stompin' on Oni, cuz
I'm the Beach Man.
(part #3 still in progress)
Japan.
RAVE MASTER

RAVE:127 ✚ Bonds of Silver

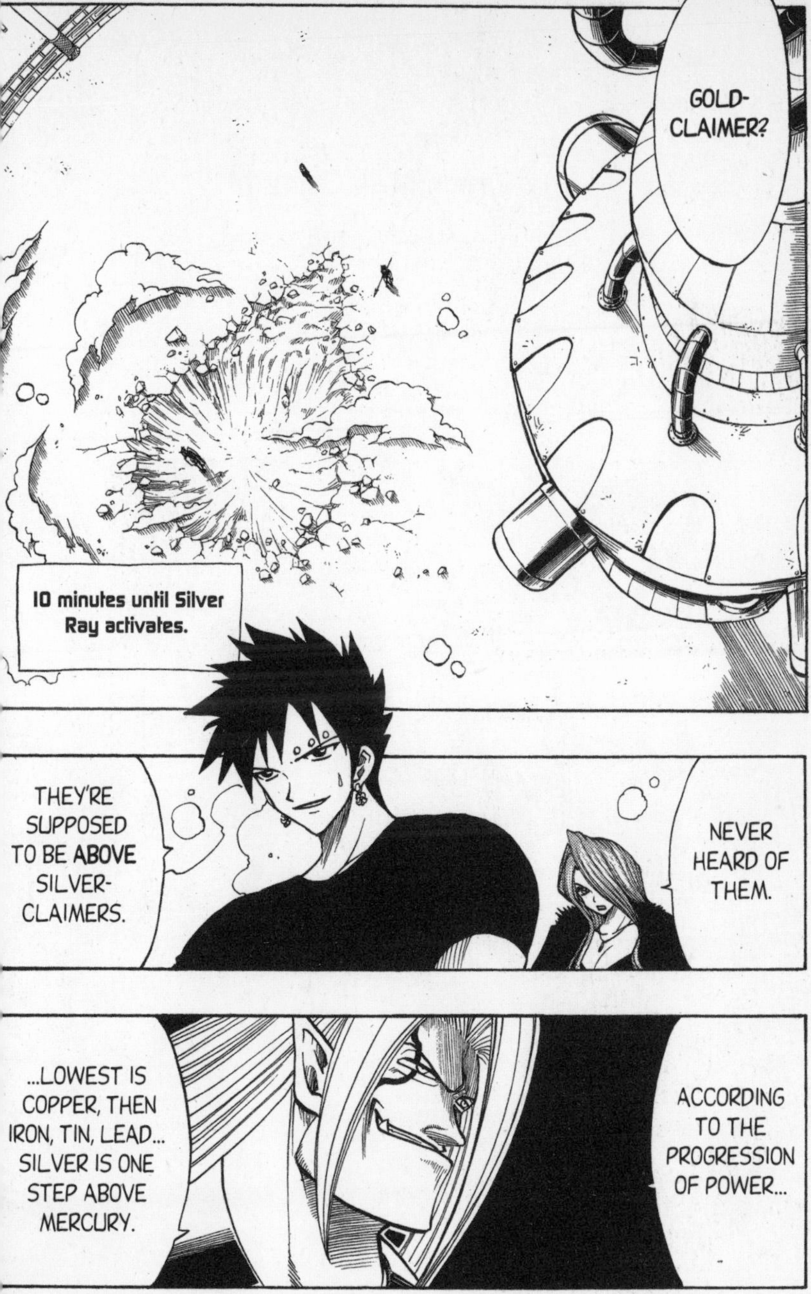
GOLD-CLAIMER?
10 minutes until Silver Ray activates.
NEVER HEARD OF THEM.
THEY'RE SUPPOSED TO BE ABOVE SILVER-CLAIMERS.
ACCORDING TO THE PROGRESSION OF POWER...
...LOWEST IS COPPER, THEN IRON, TIN, LEAD... SILVER IS ONE STEP ABOVE MERCURY.

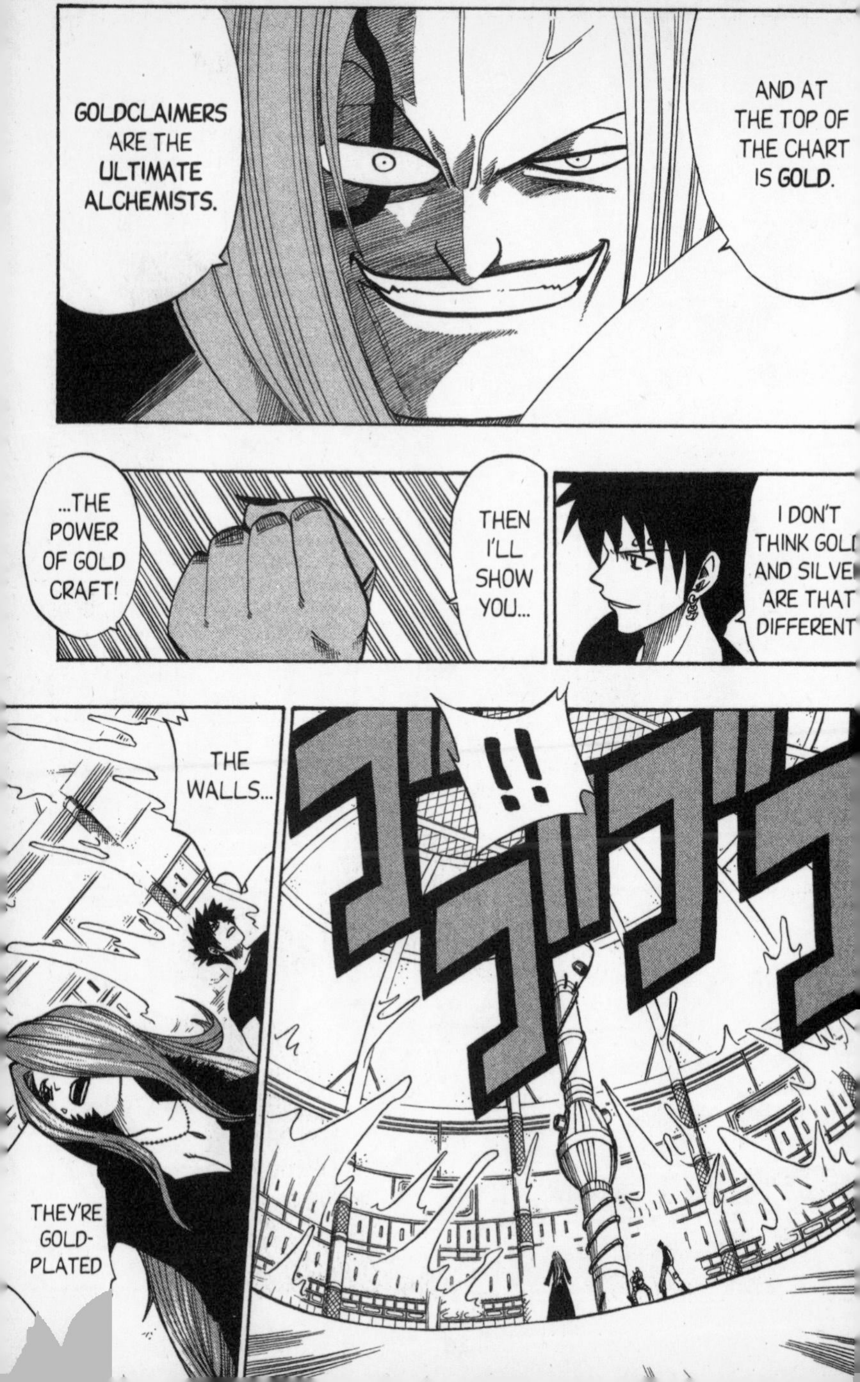
AND AT THE TOP OF THE CHART IS GOLD.
GOLDCLAIMERS ARE THE ULTIMATE ALCHEMISTS.
I DON'T THINK GOLI AND SILVE ARE THAT DIFFERENT
THEN I'LL SHOW YOU...
...THE POWER OF GOLD CRAFT!
!!
THE WALLS...
THEY'RE GOLD-PLATED

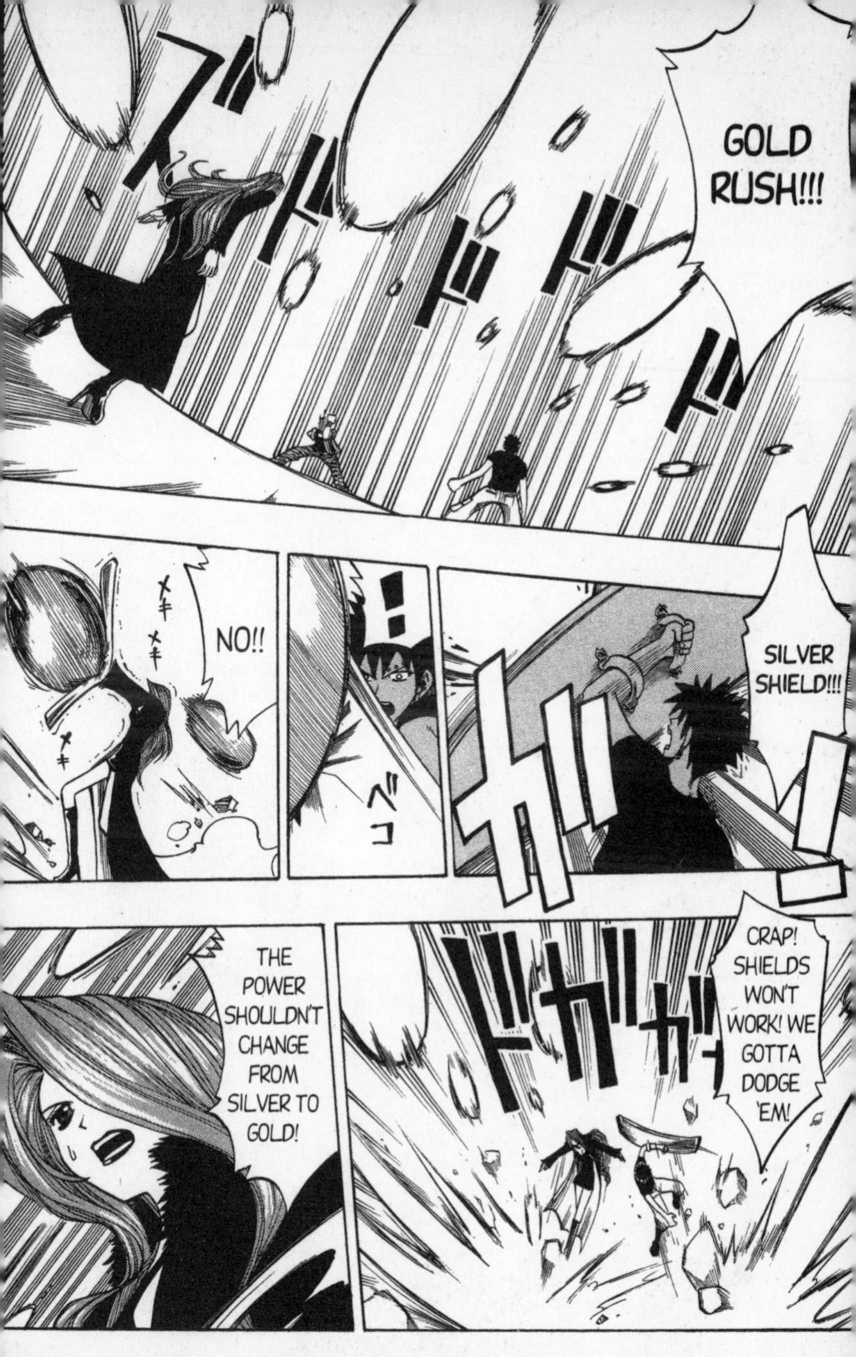
GOLD RUSH!!!
ドドドド
SILVER SHIELD!!!
ガッ
!
ベコ
NO!!
メキ メキ
メキ
CRAP! SHIELDS WON'T WORK! WE GOTTA DODGE 'EM!
ドガガガ
THE POWER SHOULDN'T CHANGE FROM SILVER TO GOLD!

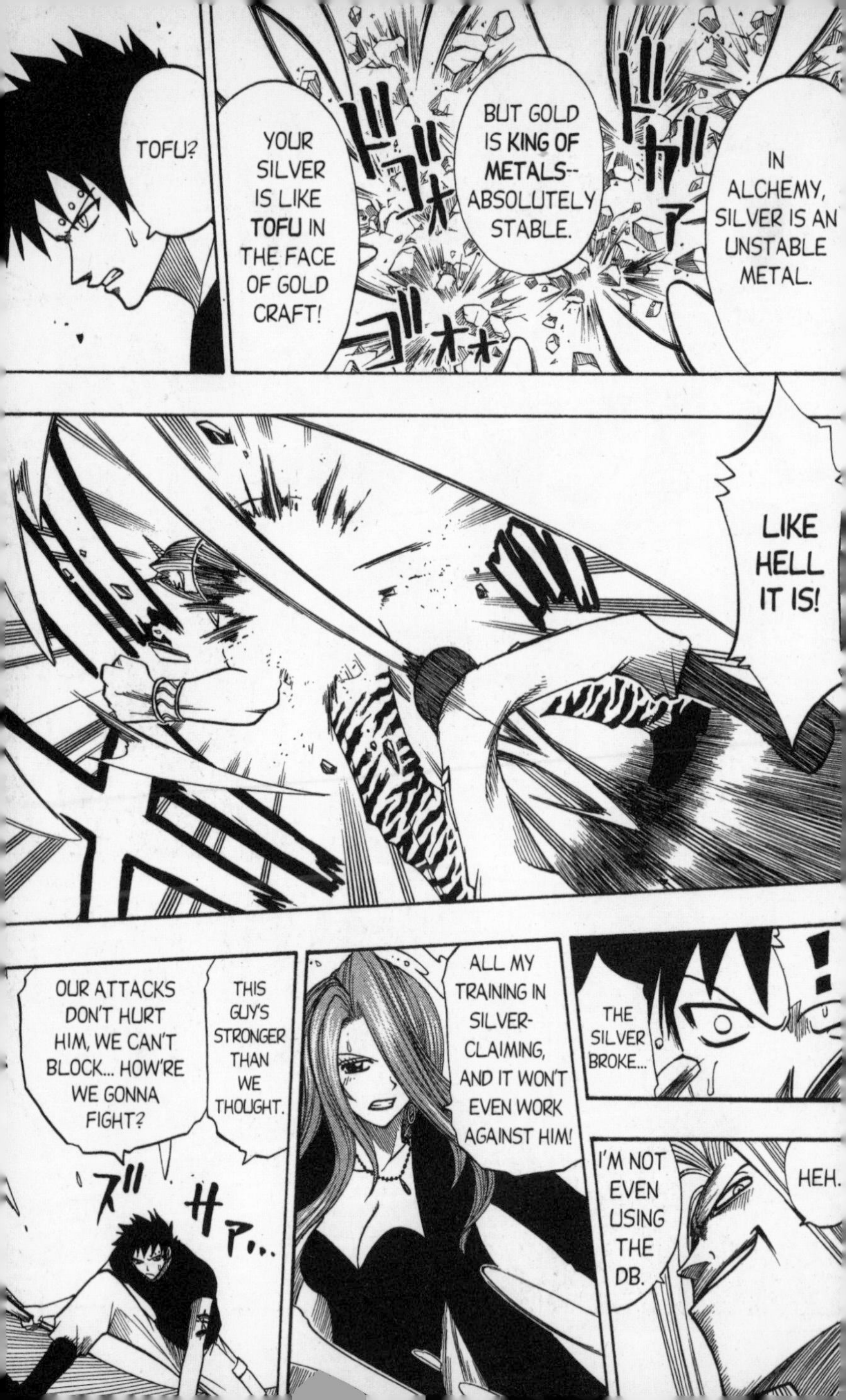
IN ALCHEMY, SILVER IS AN UNSTABLE METAL.
ドガァ
BUT GOLD IS KING OF METALS-- ABSOLUTELY STABLE.
ドゴォ
ゴォォ
YOUR SILVER IS LIKE TOFU IN THE FACE OF GOLD CRAFT!
TOFU?
LIKE HELL IT IS!
THE SILVER BROKE...
HEH.
I'M NOT EVEN USING THE DB.
ALL MY TRAINING IN SILVER-CLAIMING, AND IT WON'T EVEN WORK AGAINST HIM!
THIS GUY'S STRONGER THAN WE THOUGHT.
OUR ATTACKS DON'T HURT HIM, WE CAN'T BLOCK... HOW'RE WE GONNA FIGHT?
ズザァ...

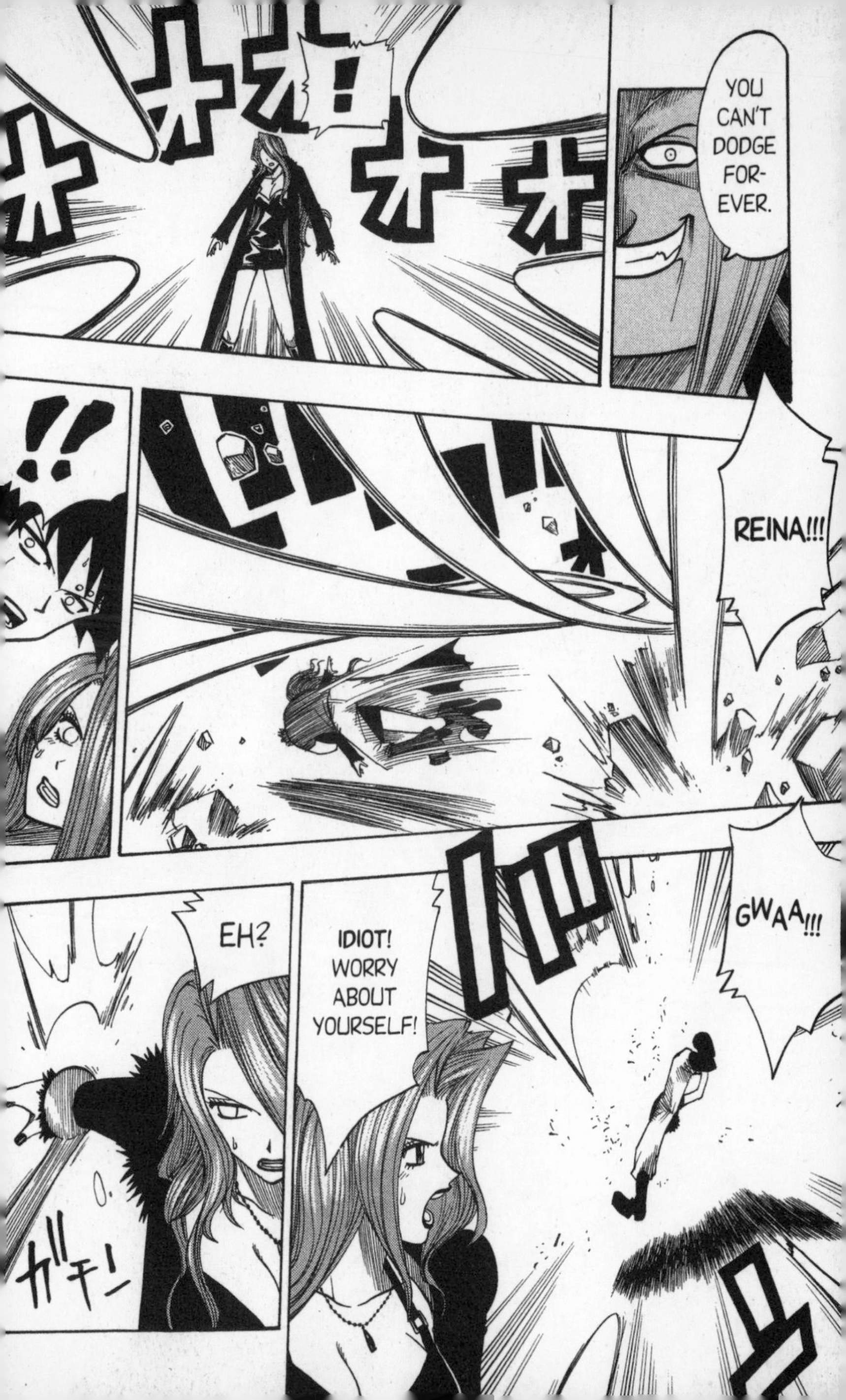
YOU CAN'T DODGE FOR-EVER.
REINA!!!
GWAA!!!
IDIOT! WORRY ABOUT YOURSELF!
EH?

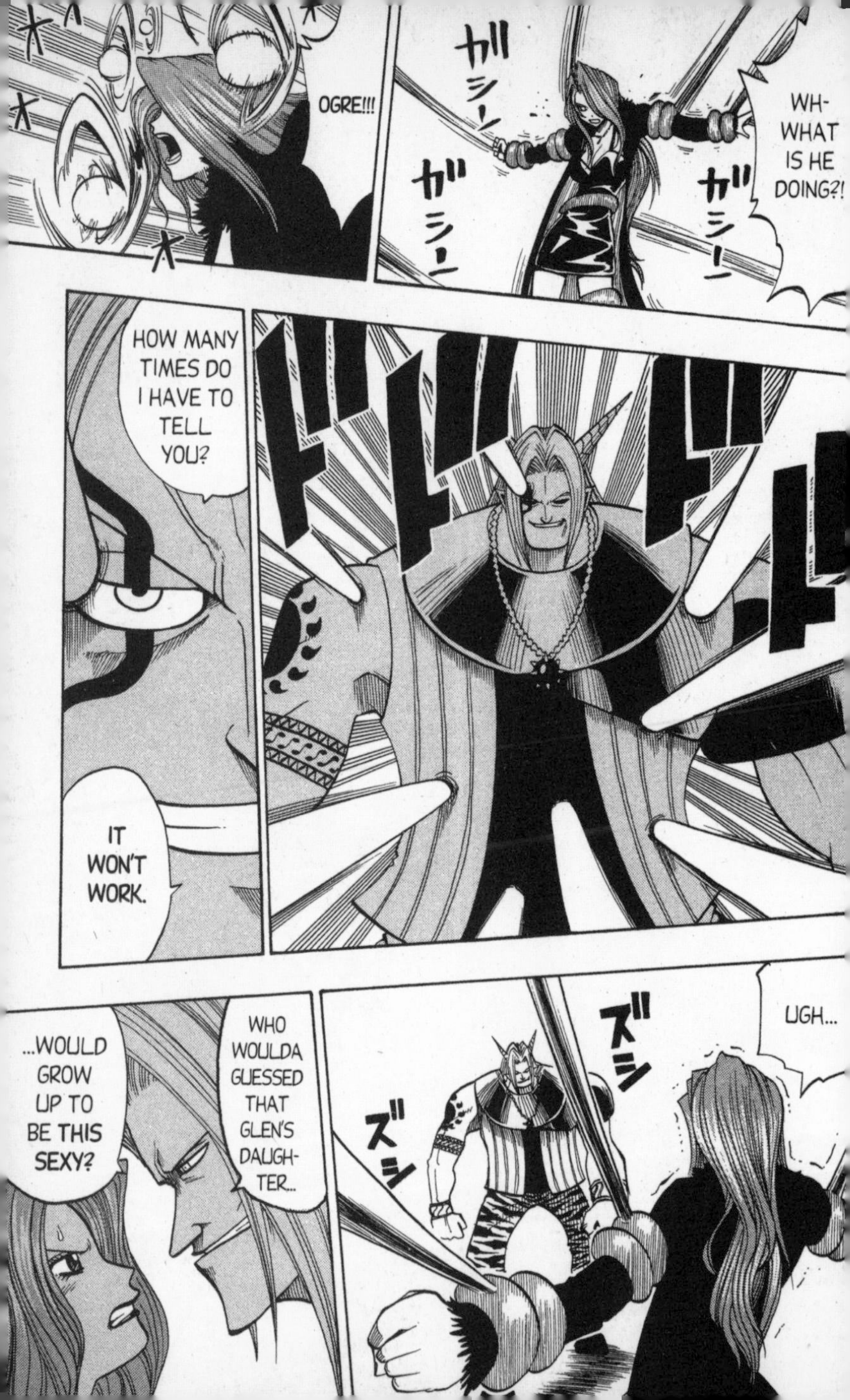

ガシーン
ガシーン
ガシーン
WH- WHAT IS HE DOING?!
OGRE!!!
HOW MANY TIMES DO I HAVE TO TELL YOU?
IT WON'T WORK.
ズシ
ズシ
UGH...
WHO WOULDA GUESSED THAT GLEN'S DAUGH-TER...
...WOULD GROW UP TO BE THIS SEXY?

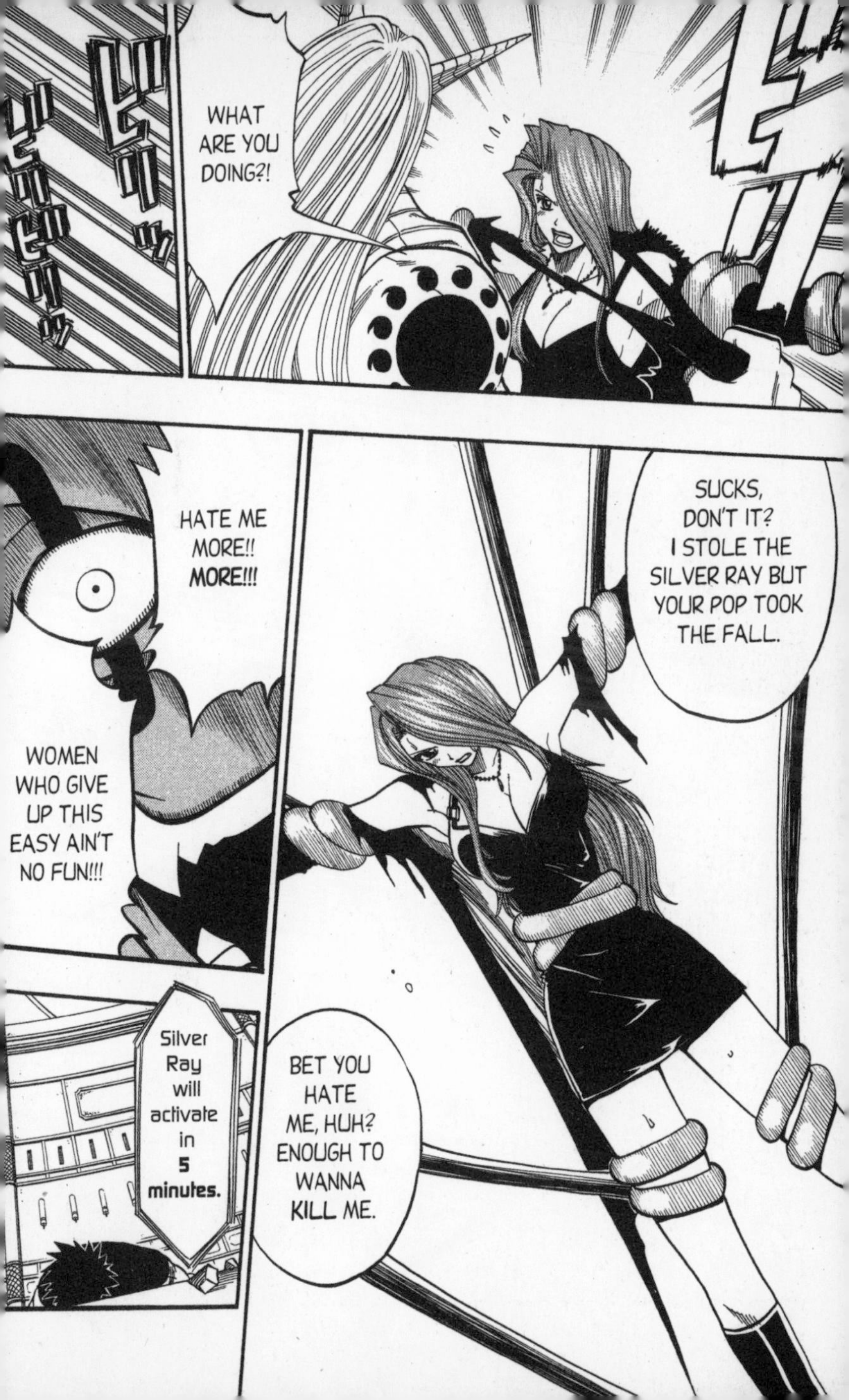
WHAT ARE YOU DOING?!
SUCKS, DON'T IT? I STOLE THE SILVER RAY BUT YOUR POP TOOK THE FALL.
BET YOU HATE ME, HUH? ENOUGH TO WANNA KILL ME.
HATE ME MORE!! MORE!!!
WOMEN WHO GIVE UP THIS EASY AIN'T NO FUN!!!
Silver Ray will activate in 5 minutes.

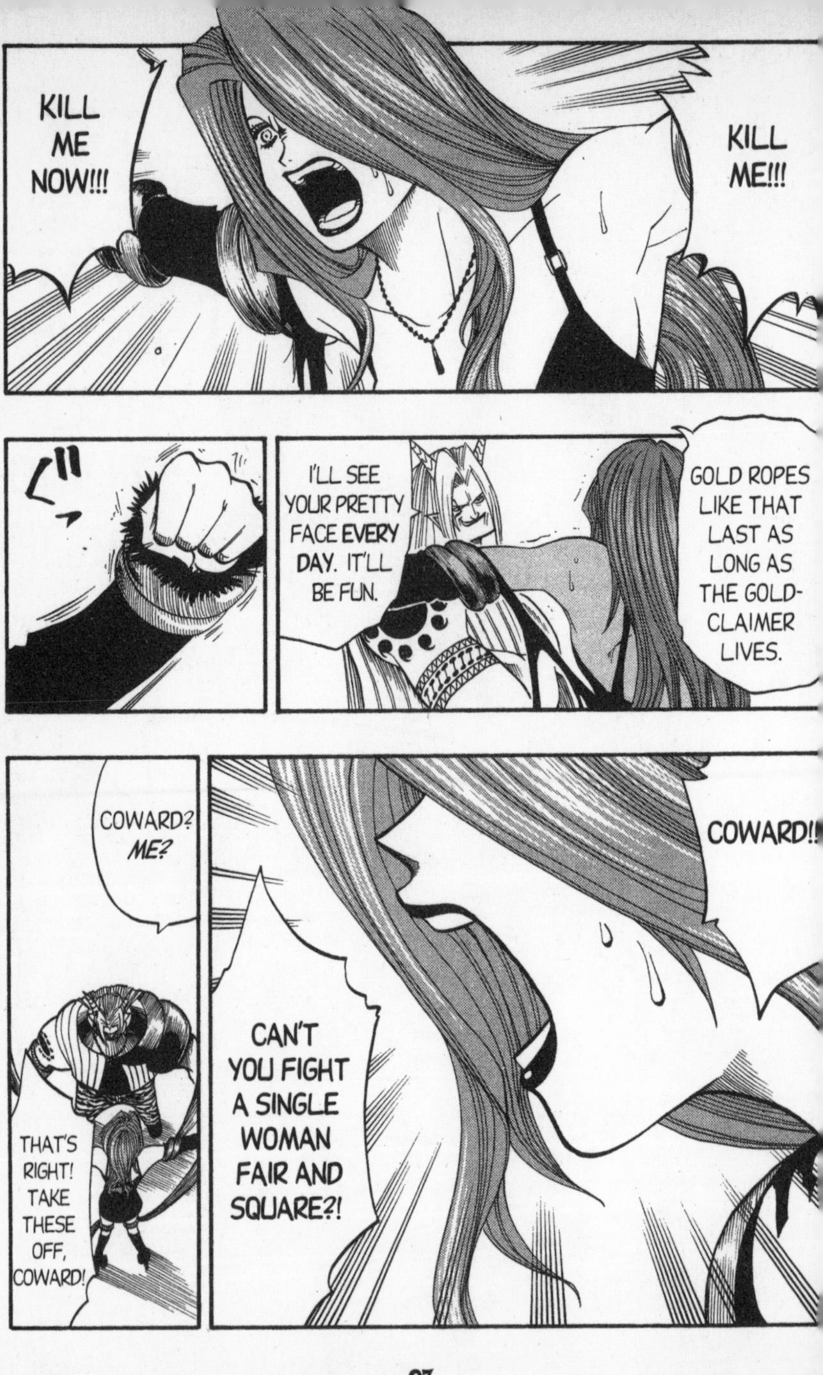
KILL ME!!!
KILL ME NOW!!!
GOLD ROPES LIKE THAT LAST AS LONG AS THE GOLD-CLAIMER LIVES.
I'LL SEE YOUR PRETTY FACE EVERY DAY. IT'LL BE FUN.
COWARD!!
CAN'T YOU FIGHT A SINGLE WOMAN FAIR AND SQUARE?!
COWARD? ME?
THAT'S RIGHT! TAKE THESE OFF, COWARD!

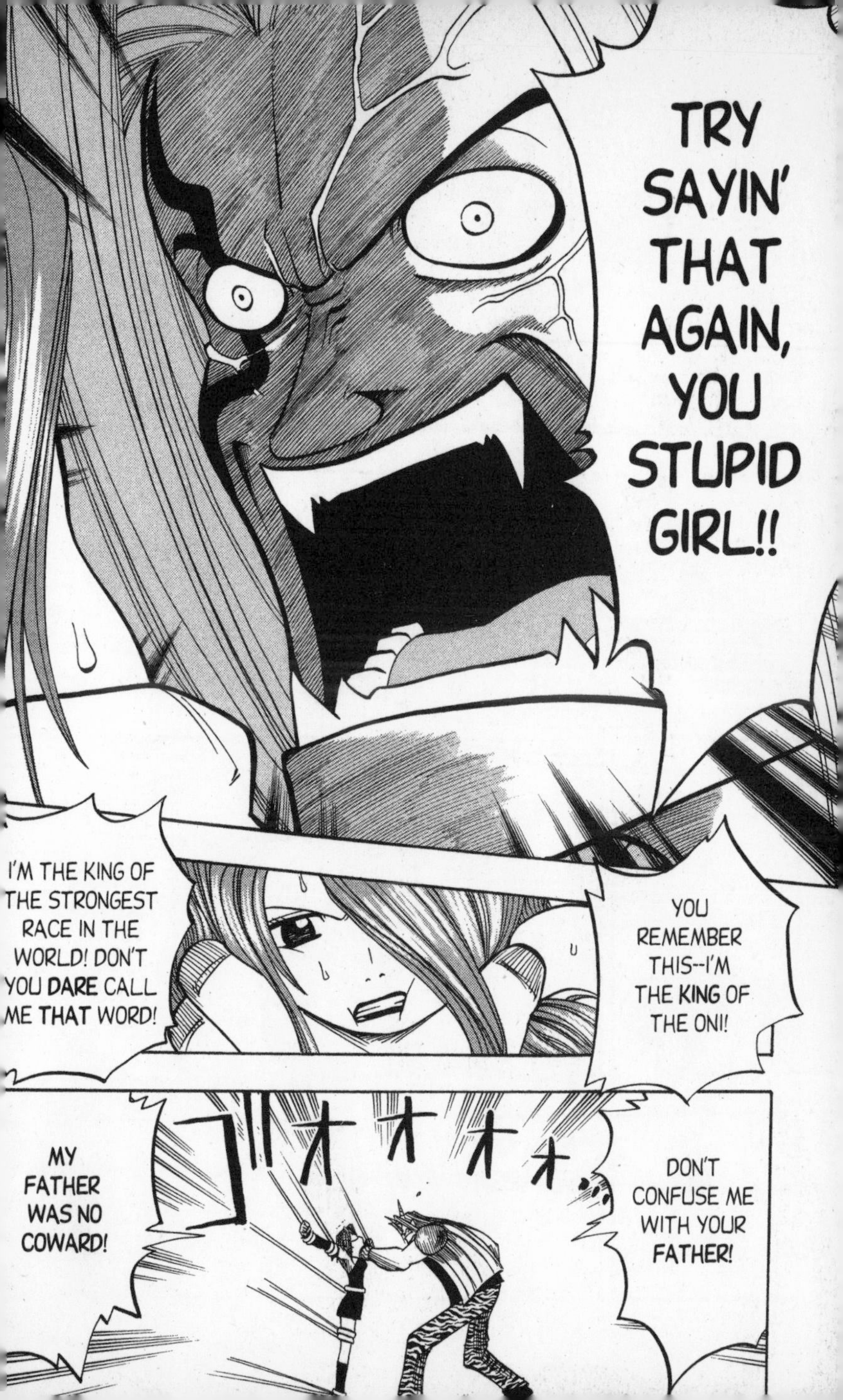
TRY SAYIN' THAT AGAIN, YOU STUPID GIRL!!
YOU REMEMBER THIS--I'M THE KING OF THE ONI!
I'M THE KING OF THE STRONGEST RACE IN THE WORLD! DON'T YOU DARE CALL ME THAT WORD!
ゴオオオオ
DON'T CONFUSE ME WITH YOUR FATHER!
MY FATHER WAS NO COWARD!

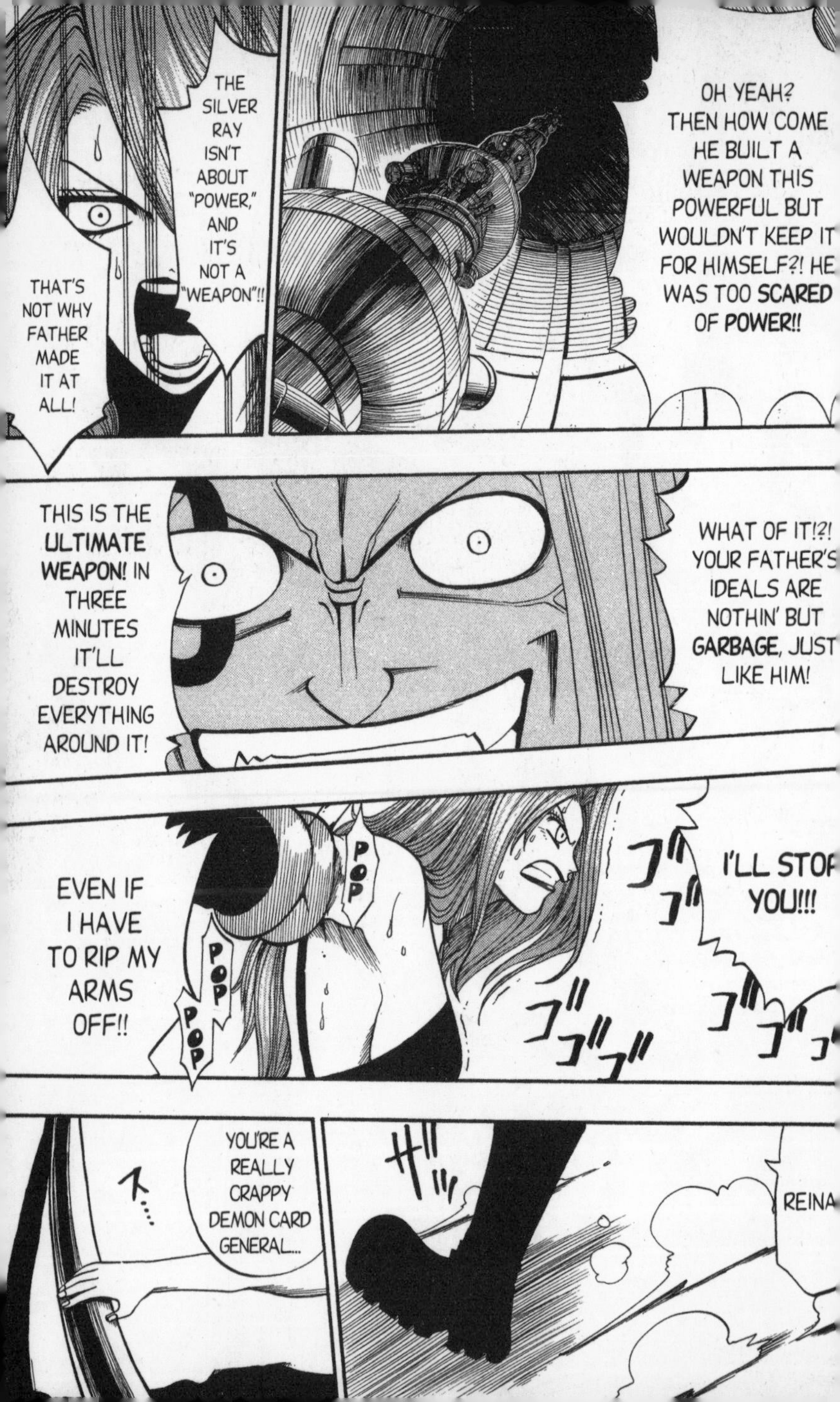
OH YEAH? THEN HOW COME HE BUILT A WEAPON THIS POWERFUL BUT WOULDN'T KEEP IT FOR HIMSELF?! HE WAS TOO SCARED OF POWER!!
THE SILVER RAY ISN'T ABOUT "POWER," AND IT'S NOT A "WEAPON"!!
THAT'S NOT WHY FATHER MADE IT AT ALL!
WHAT OF IT!?! YOUR FATHER'S IDEALS ARE NOTHIN' BUT GARBAGE, JUST LIKE HIM!
THIS IS THE ULTIMATE WEAPON! IN THREE MINUTES IT'LL DESTROY EVERYTHING AROUND IT!
I'LL STOP YOU!!!
POP
POP
POP
EVEN IF I HAVE TO RIP MY ARMS OFF!!
REINA
YOU'RE A REALLY CRAPPY DEMON CARD GENERAL...

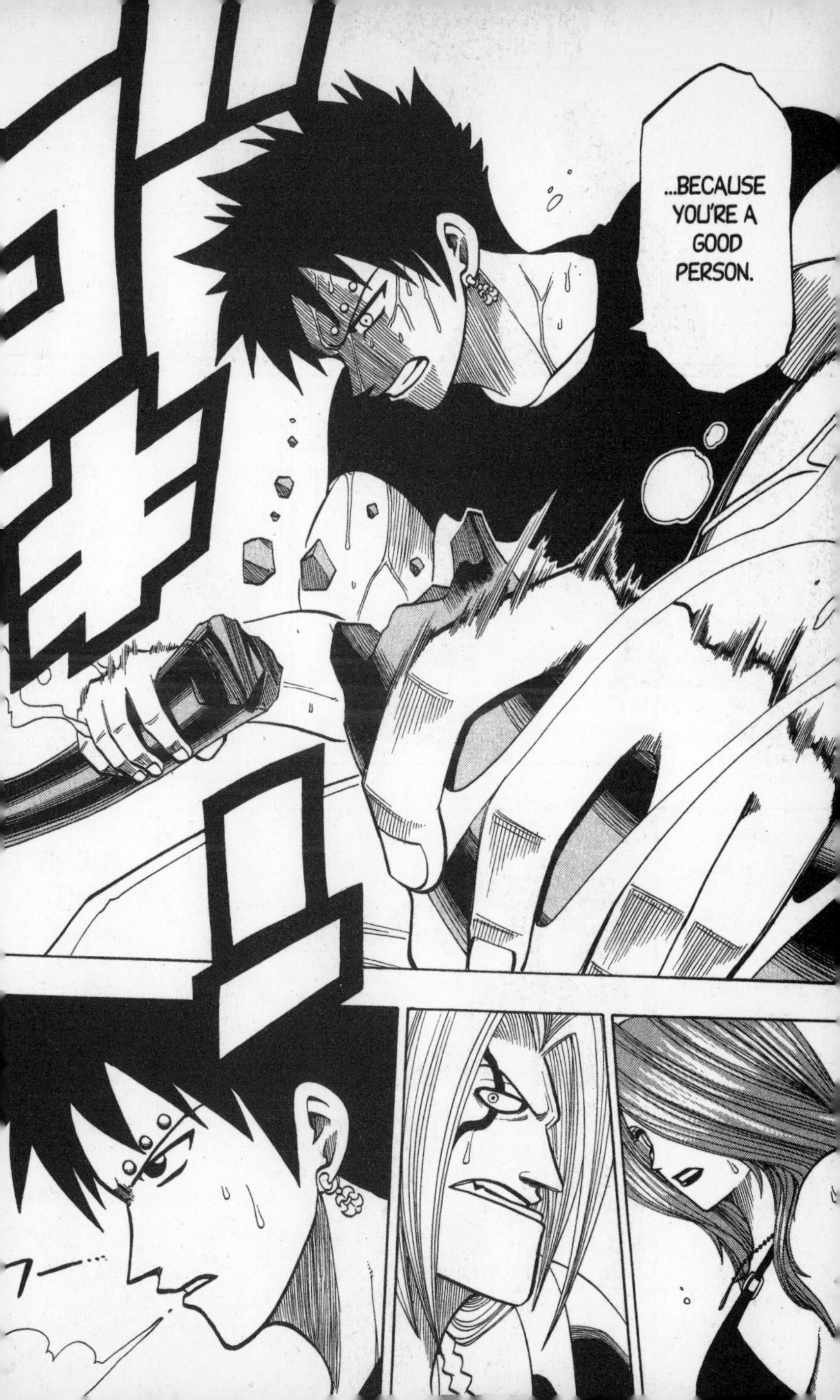
...BECAUSE YOU'RE A GOOD PERSON.
フー…

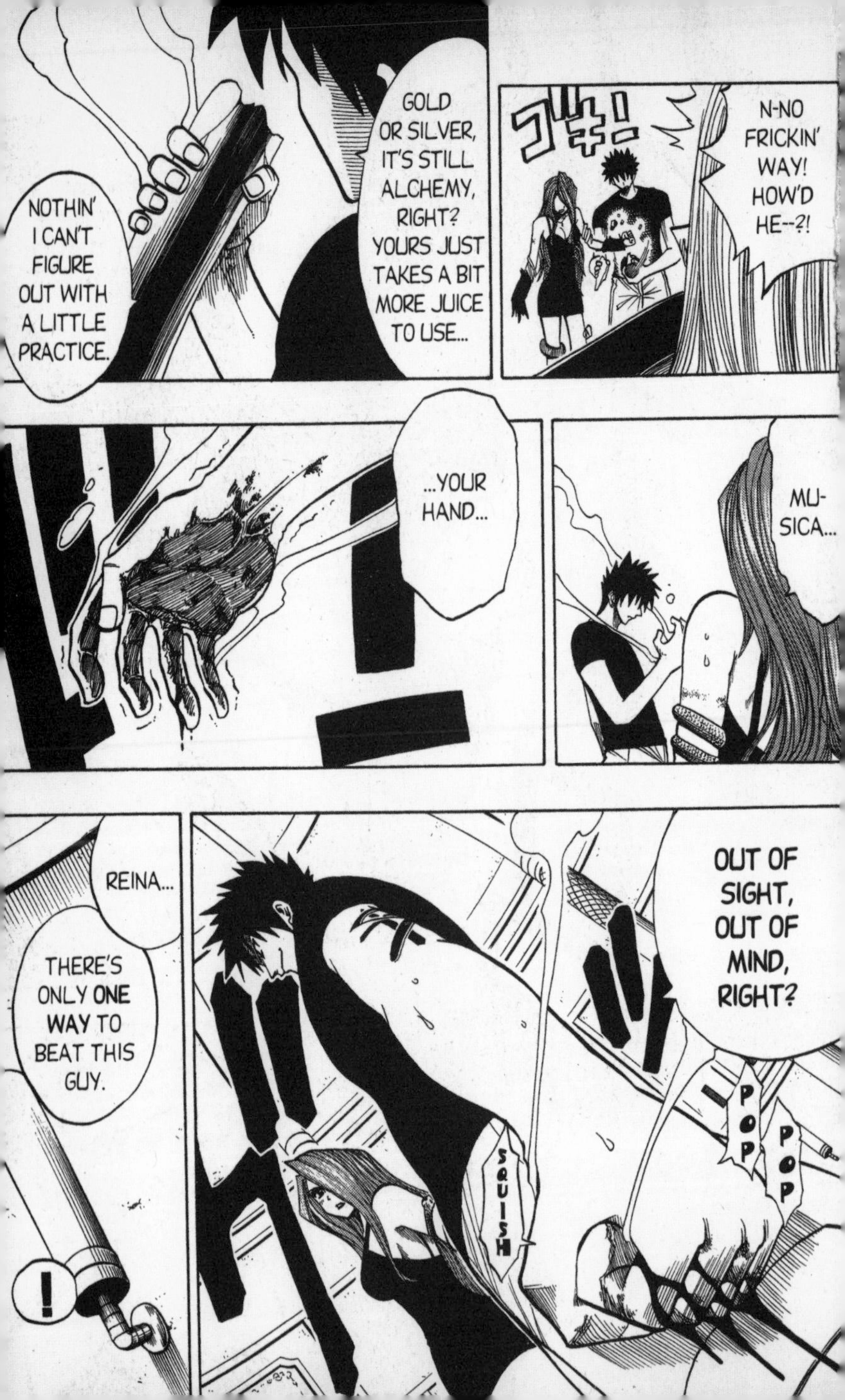

ゴキ!
N-NO FRICKIN' WAY! HOW'D HE--?!
GOLD OR SILVER, IT'S STILL ALCHEMY, RIGHT? YOURS JUST TAKES A BIT MORE JUICE TO USE...
NOTHIN' I CAN'T FIGURE OUT WITH A LITTLE PRACTICE.
MU-SICA...
...YOUR HAND...
OUT OF SIGHT, OUT OF MIND, RIGHT?
POP POP POP
SQUISH
REINA...
THERE'S ONLY ONE WAY TO BEAT THIS GUY.
!

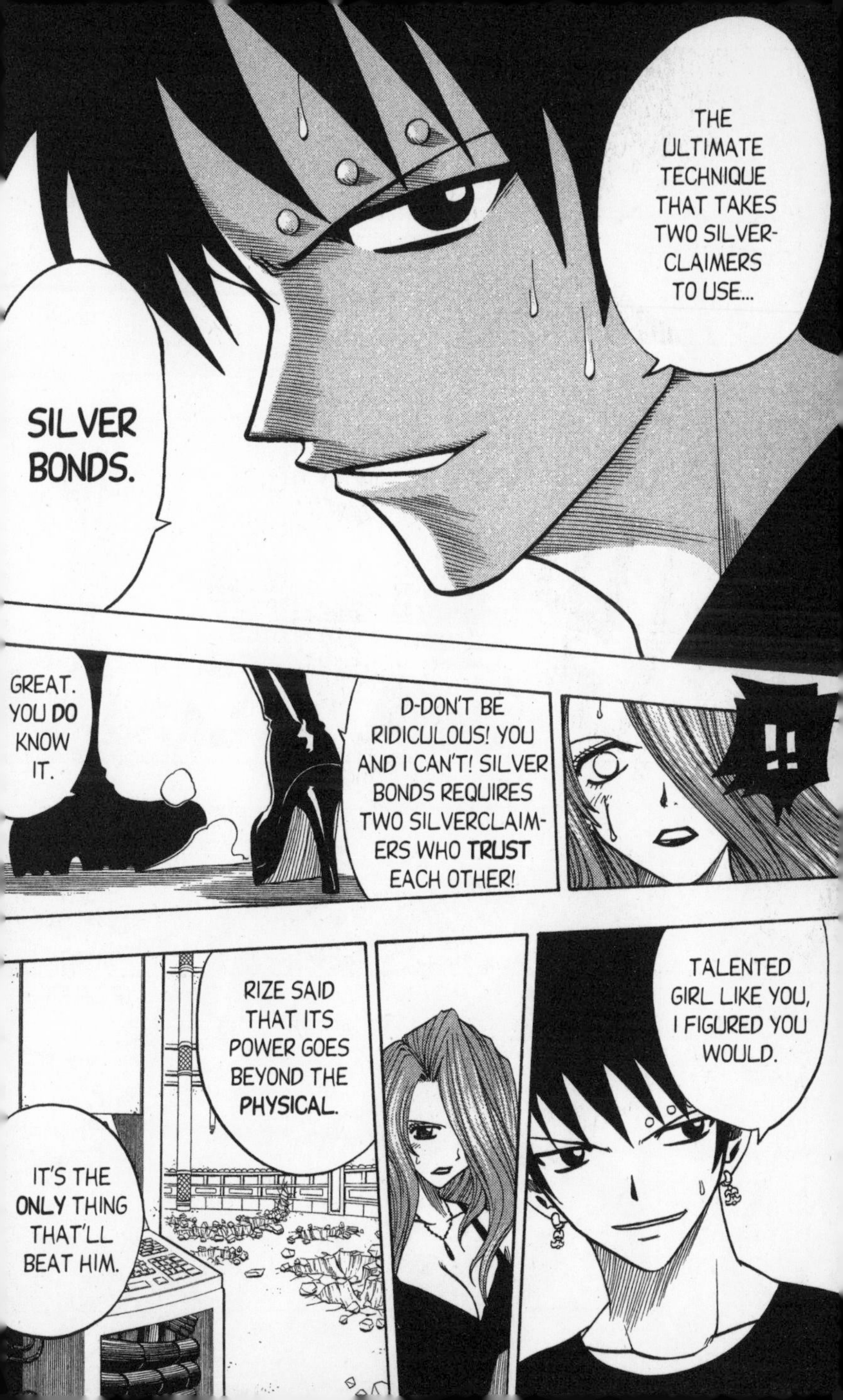
THE ULTIMATE TECHNIQUE THAT TAKES TWO SILVER-CLAIMERS TO USE...
SILVER BONDS.
!!
D-DON'T BE RIDICULOUS! YOU AND I CAN'T! SILVER BONDS REQUIRES TWO SILVERCLAIMERS WHO TRUST EACH OTHER!
GREAT. YOU DO KNOW IT.
TALENTED GIRL LIKE YOU, I FIGURED YOU WOULD.
RIZE SAID THAT ITS POWER GOES BEYOND THE PHYSICAL.
IT'S THE ONLY THING THAT'LL BEAT HIM.

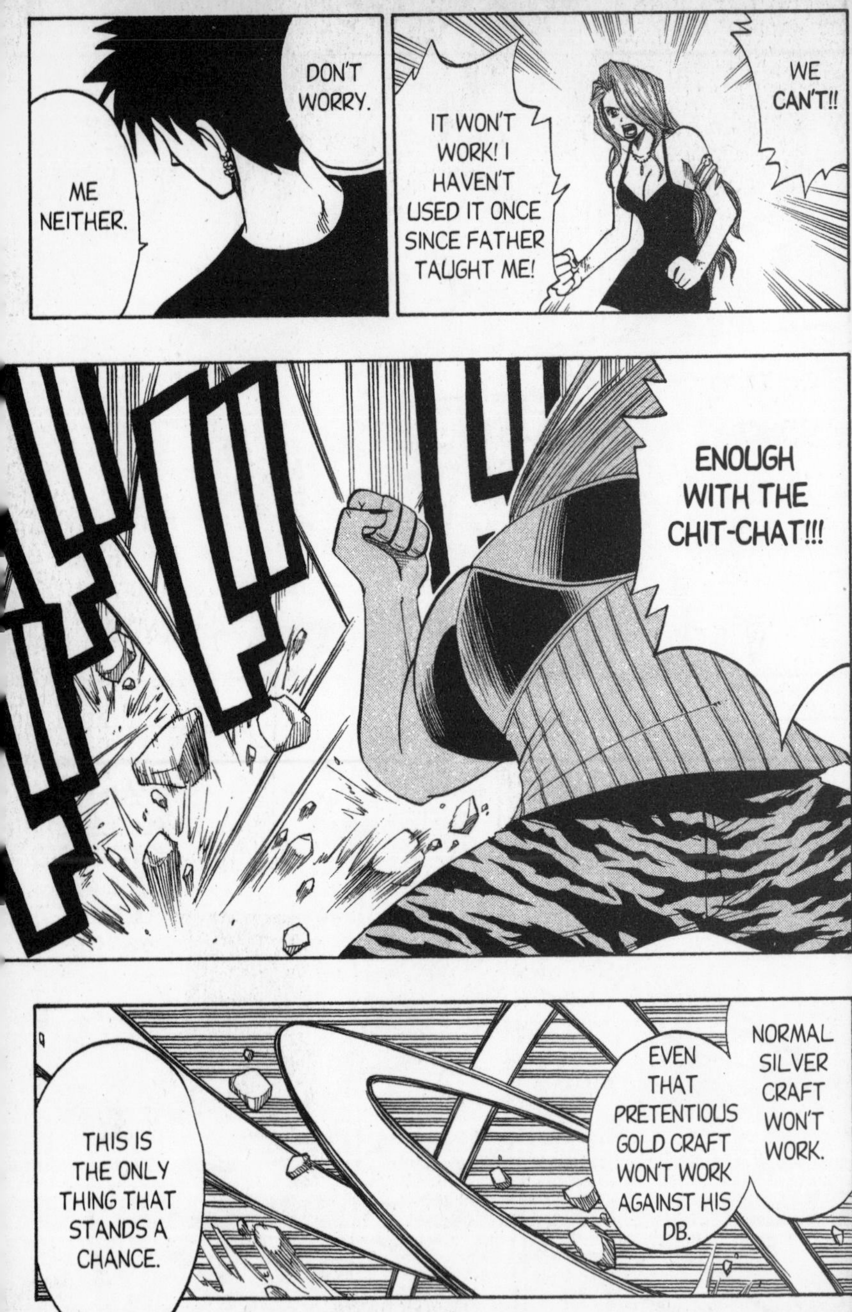
WE CAN'T!!
IT WON'T WORK! I HAVEN'T USED IT ONCE SINCE FATHER TAUGHT ME!
DON'T WORRY.
ME NEITHER.
ENOUGH WITH THE CHIT-CHAT!!!
NORMAL SILVER CRAFT WON'T WORK.
EVEN THAT PRETENTIOUS GOLD CRAFT WON'T WORK AGAINST HIS DB.
THIS IS THE ONLY THING THAT STANDS A CHANCE.

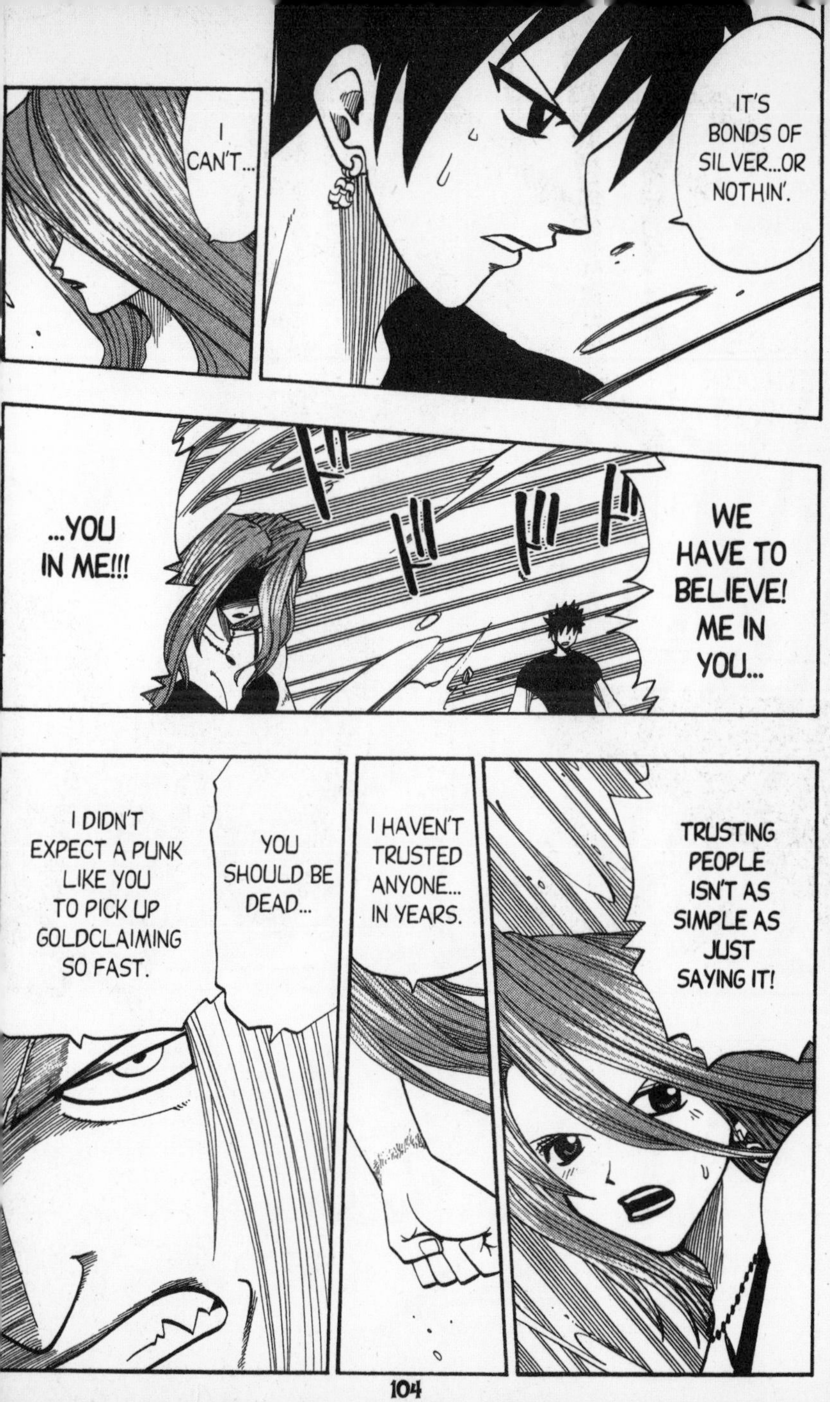
IT'S BONDS OF SILVER...OR NOTHIN'.
I CAN'T...
WE HAVE TO BELIEVE! ME IN YOU...
...YOU IN ME!!!
TRUSTING PEOPLE ISN'T AS SIMPLE AS JUST SAYING IT!
I HAVEN'T TRUSTED ANYONE... IN YEARS.
YOU SHOULD BE DEAD...
I DIDN'T EXPECT A PUNK LIKE YOU TO PICK UP GOLDCLAIMING SO FAST.

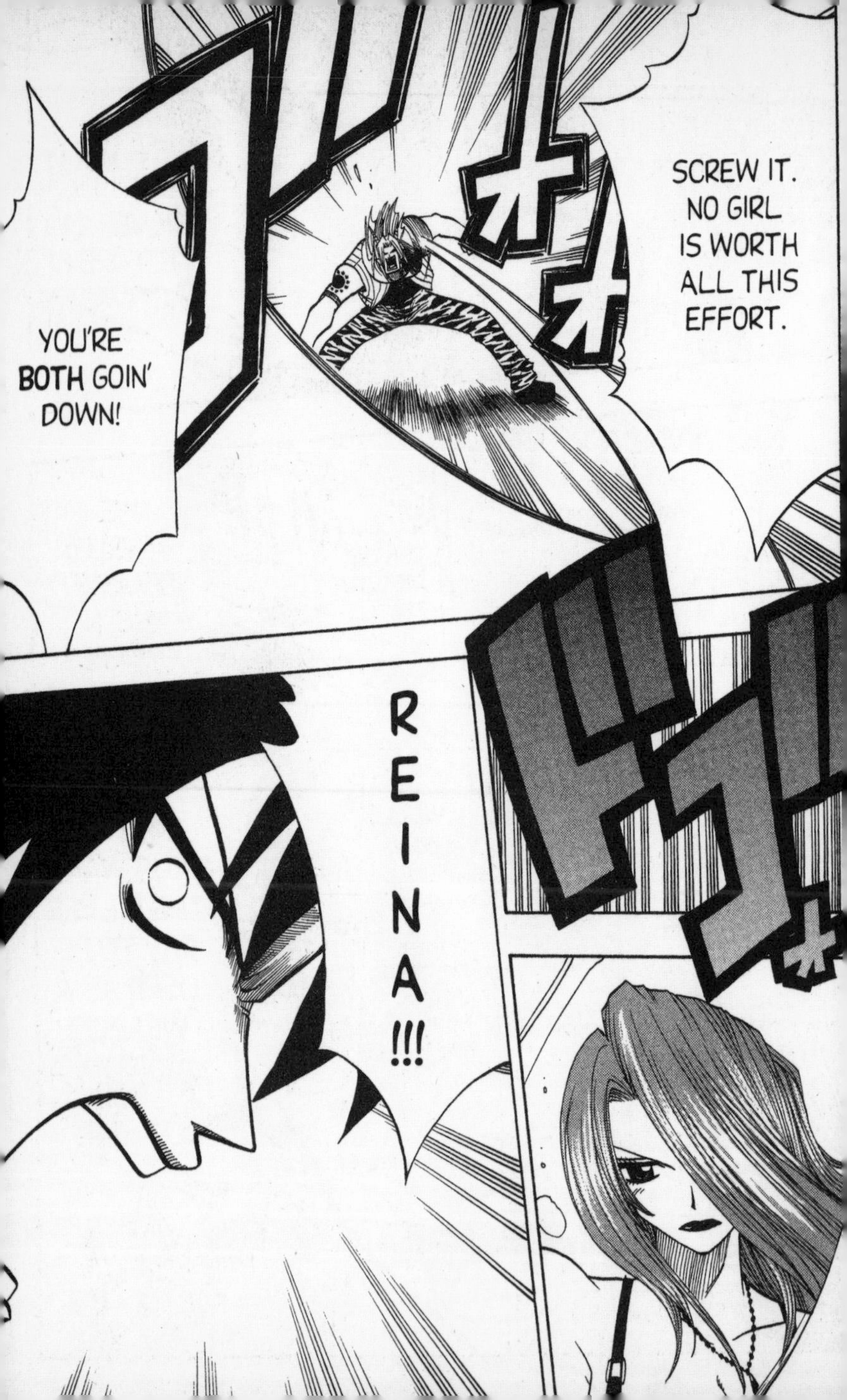
SCREW IT. NO GIRL IS WORTH ALL THIS EFFORT.
YOU'RE **BOTH** GOIN' DOWN!
REINA!!!

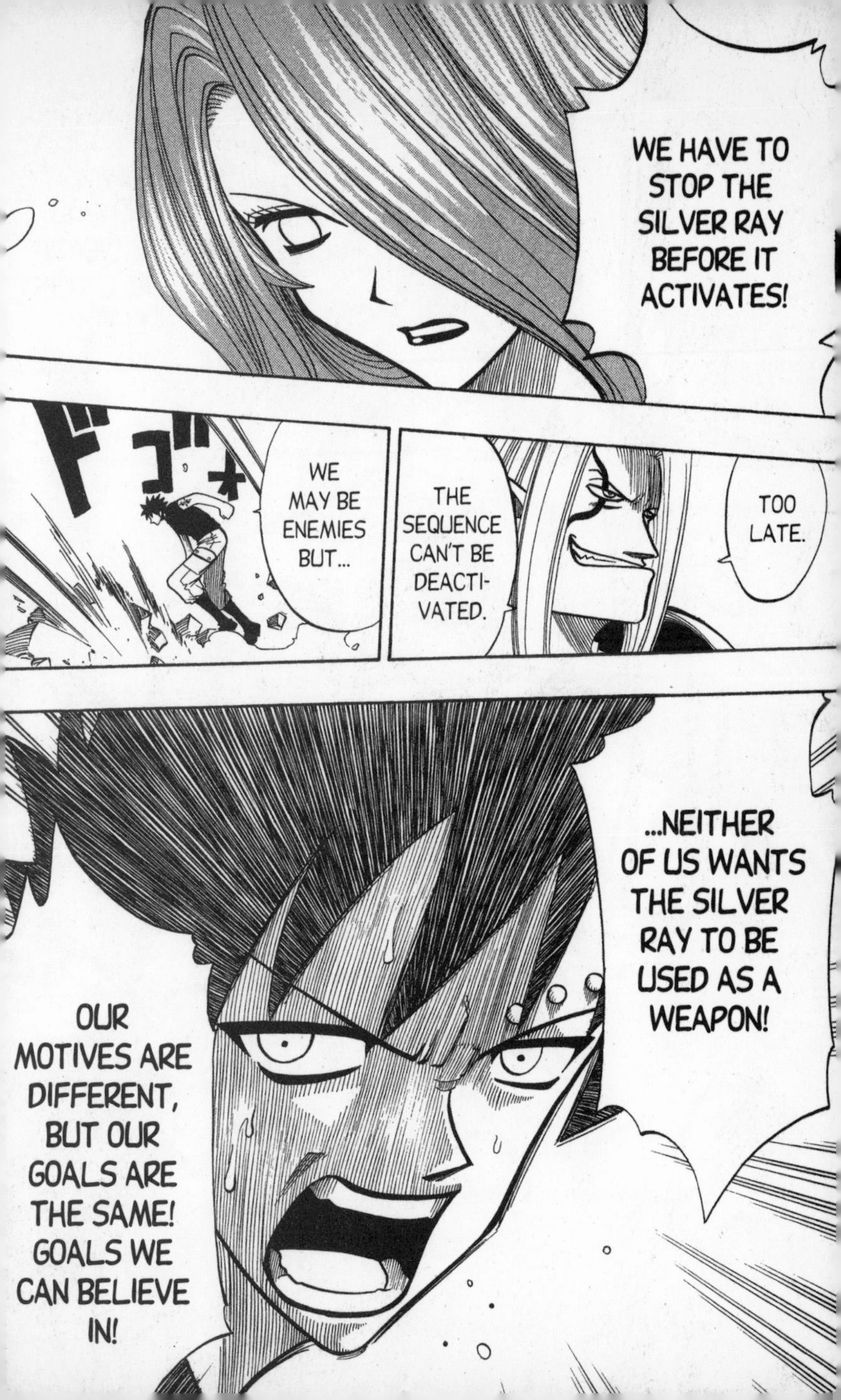
WE HAVE TO STOP THE SILVER RAY BEFORE IT ACTIVATES!
TOO LATE.
THE SEQUENCE CAN'T BE DEACTI-VATED.
WE MAY BE ENEMIES BUT...
...NEITHER OF US WANTS THE SILVER RAY TO BE USED AS A WEAPON!
OUR MOTIVES ARE DIFFERENT, BUT OUR GOALS ARE THE SAME! GOALS WE CAN BELIEVE IN!

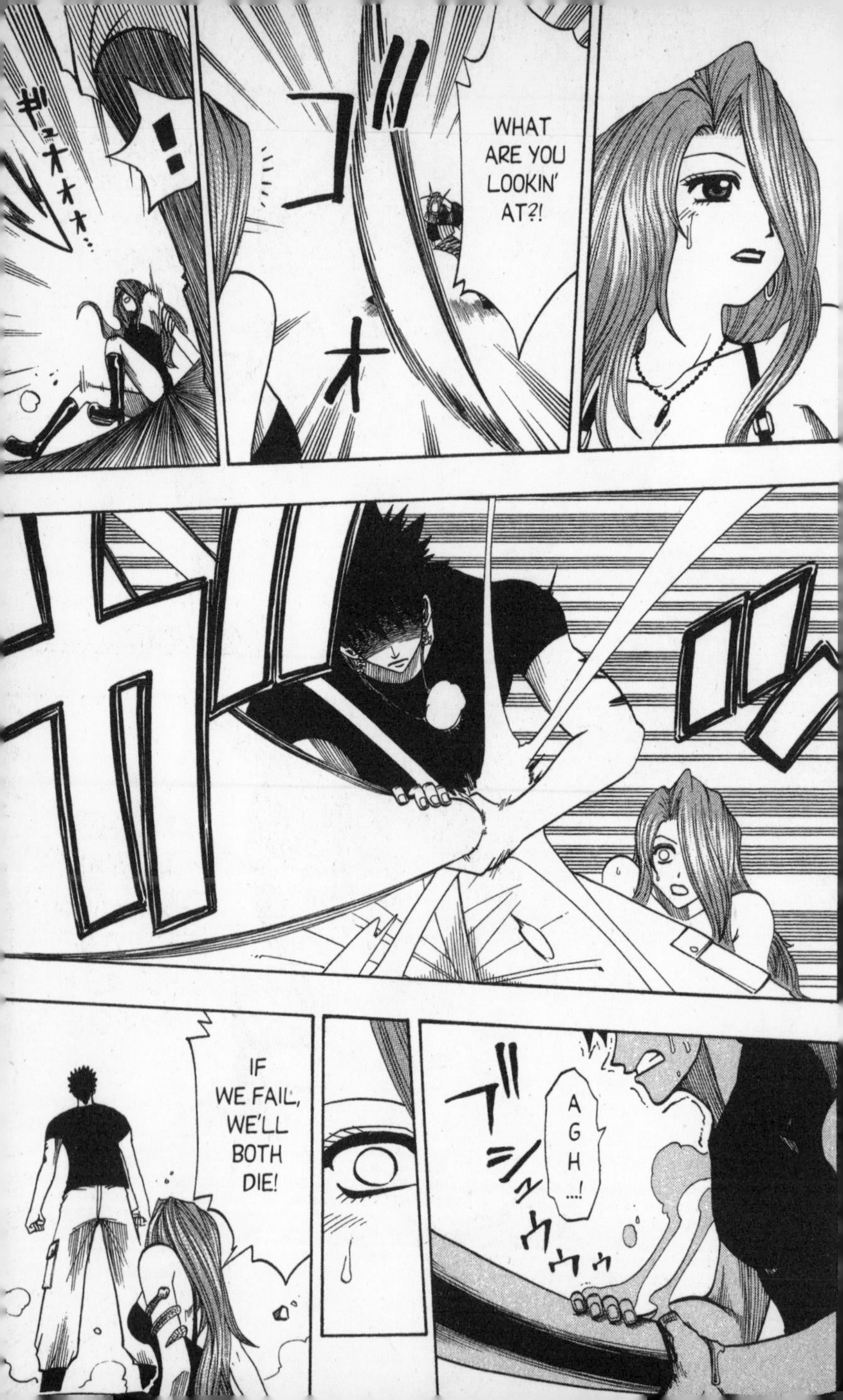
WHAT ARE YOU LOOKIN' AT?!
!
AGH...!
IF WE FAIL, WE'LL BOTH DIE!

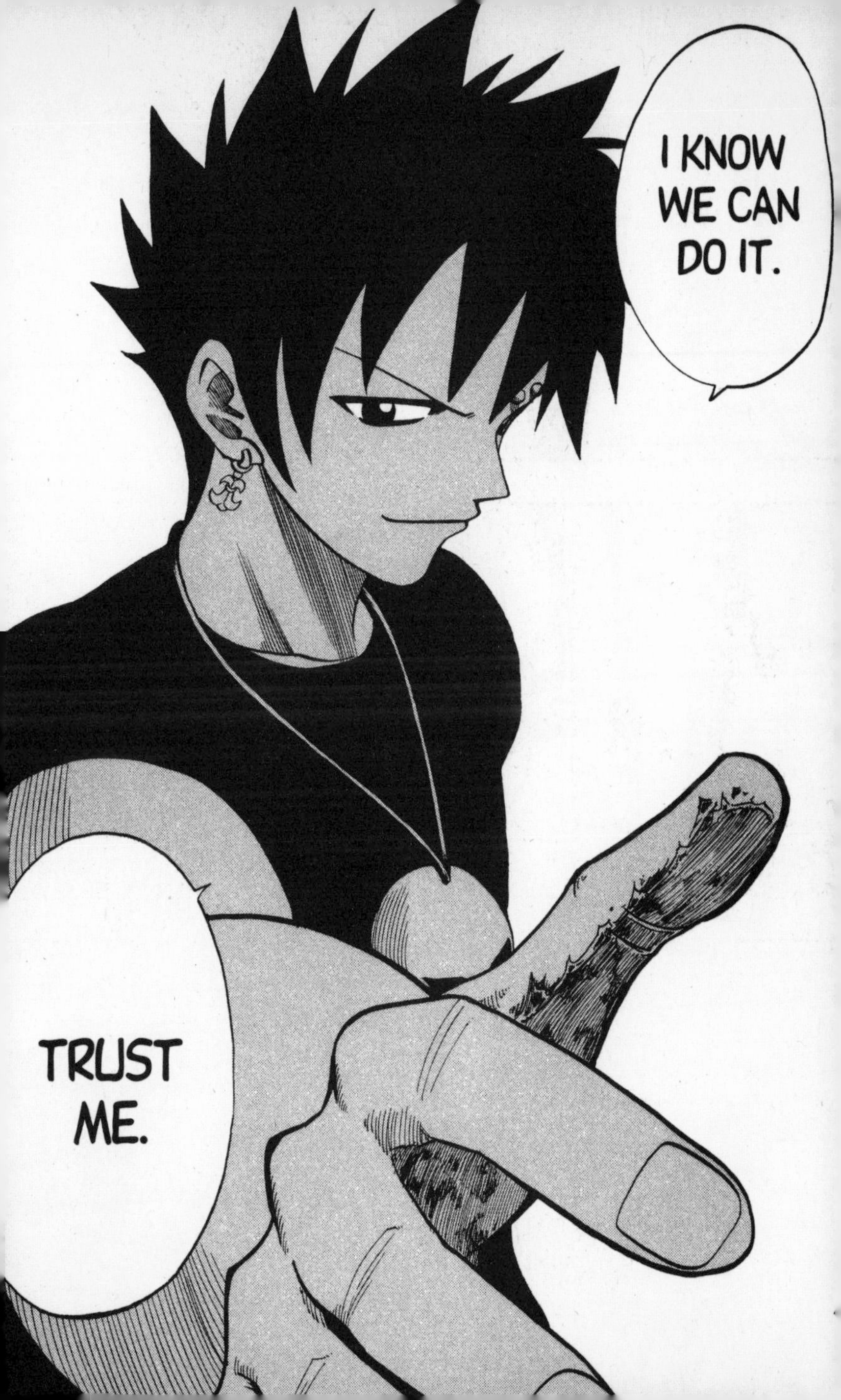
I KNOW WE CAN DO IT.
TRUST ME.

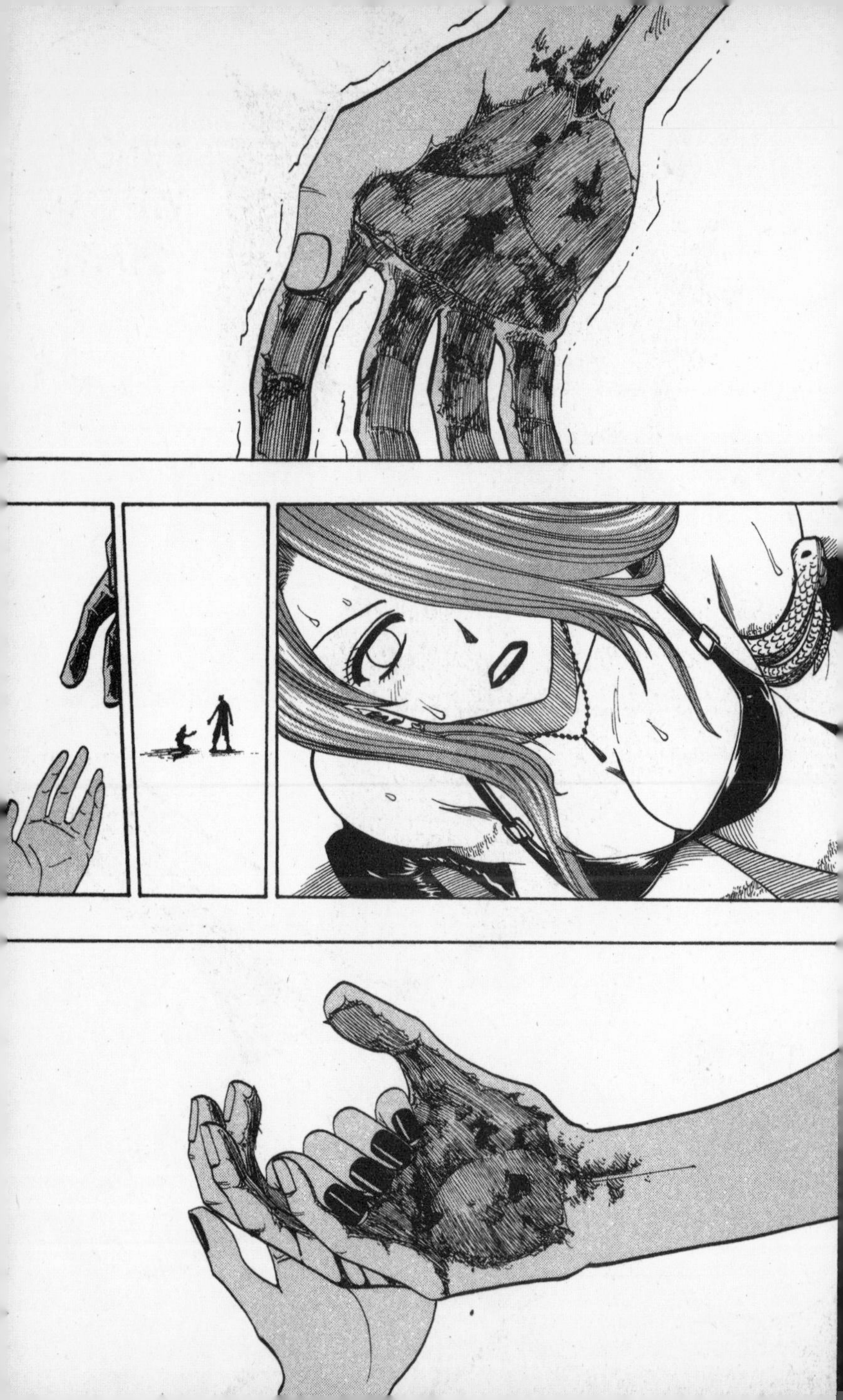

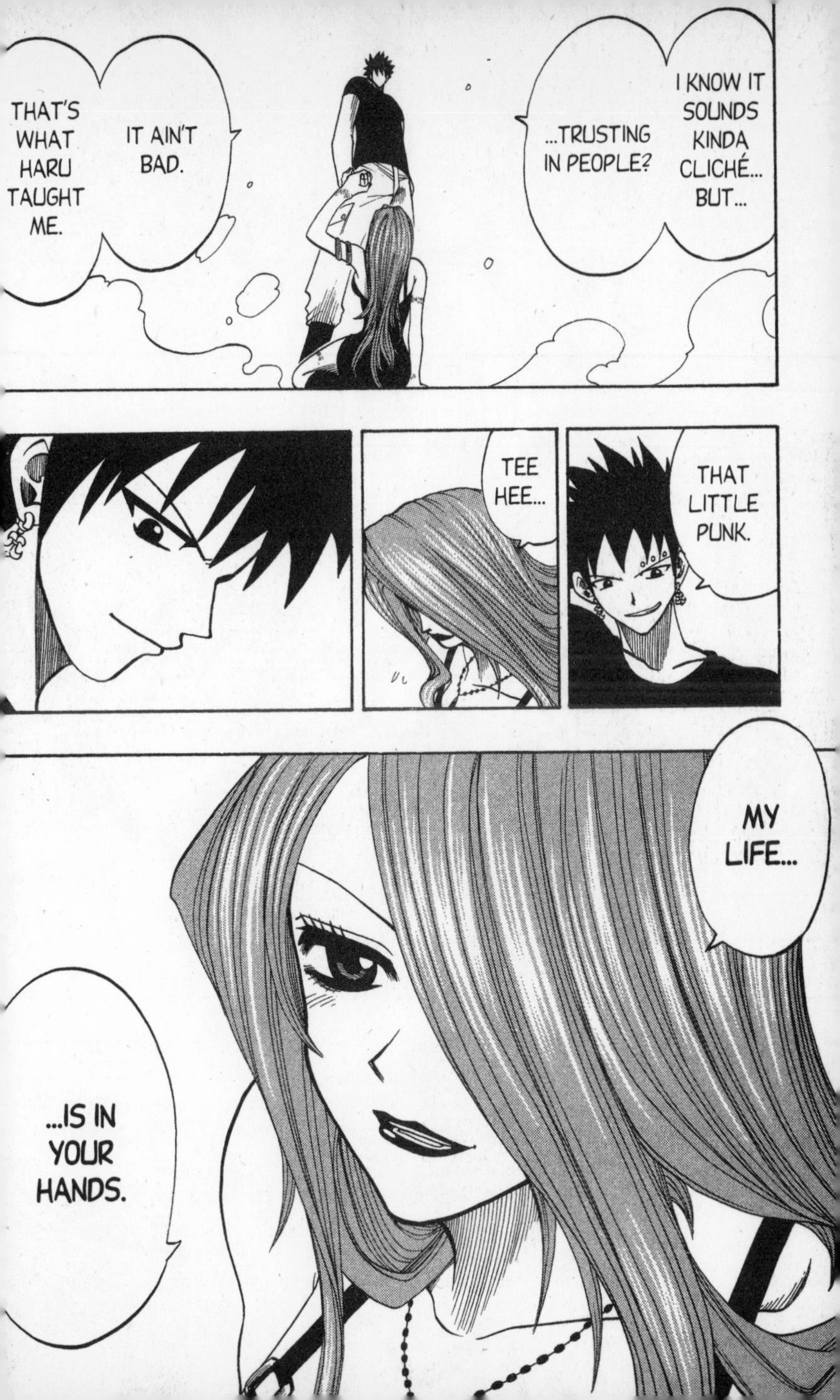
I KNOW IT SOUNDS KINDA CLICHÉ... BUT...
...TRUSTING IN PEOPLE?
IT AIN'T BAD.
THAT'S WHAT HARU TAUGHT ME.
THAT LITTLE PUNK.
TEE HEE...
MY LIFE...
...IS IN YOUR HANDS.

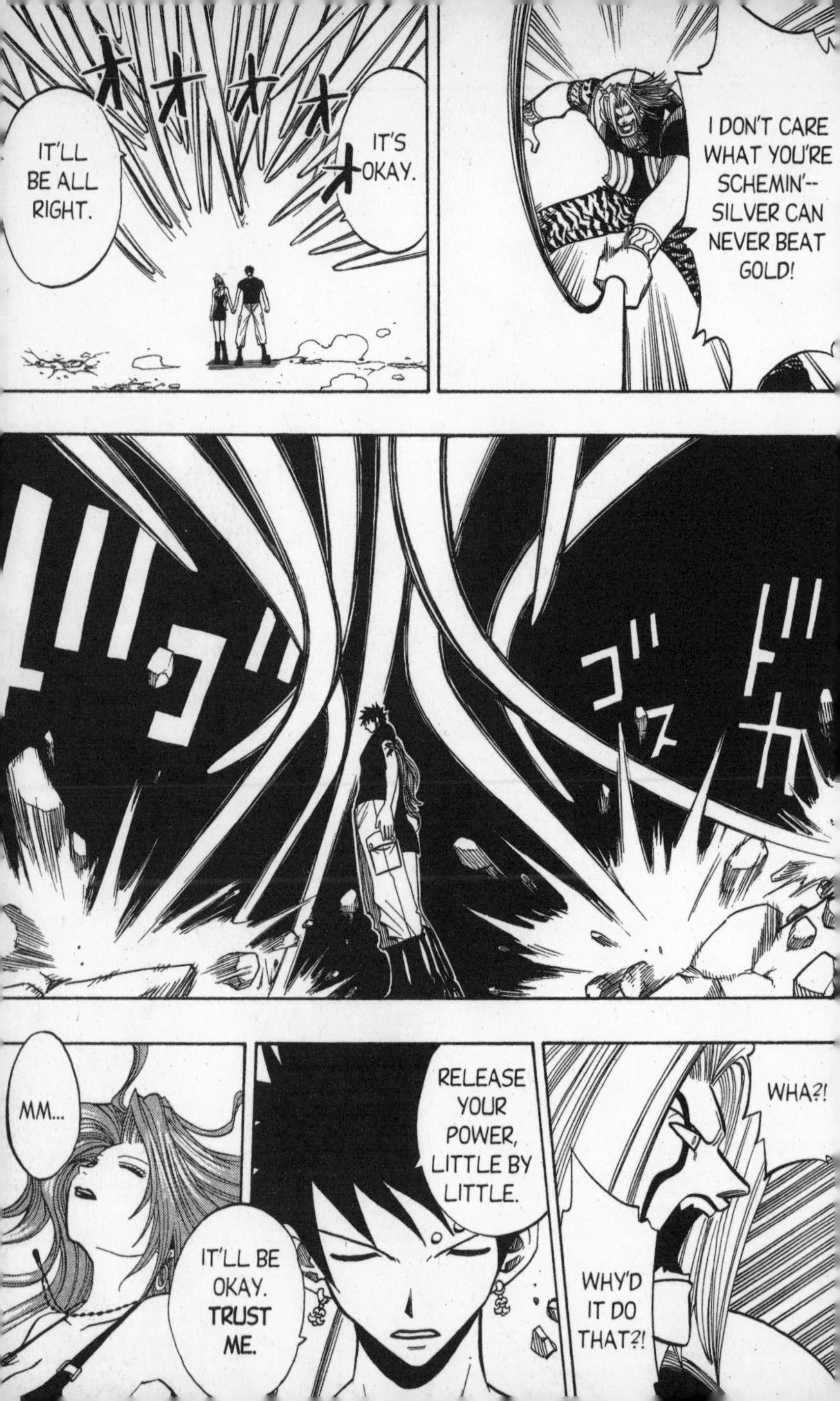
I DON'T CARE WHAT YOU'RE SCHEMIN'-- SILVER CAN NEVER BEAT GOLD!
IT'S OKAY.
IT'LL BE ALL RIGHT.
WHA?!
WHY'D IT DO THAT?!
RELEASE YOUR POWER, LITTLE BY LITTLE.
IT'LL BE OKAY. TRUST ME.
MM...

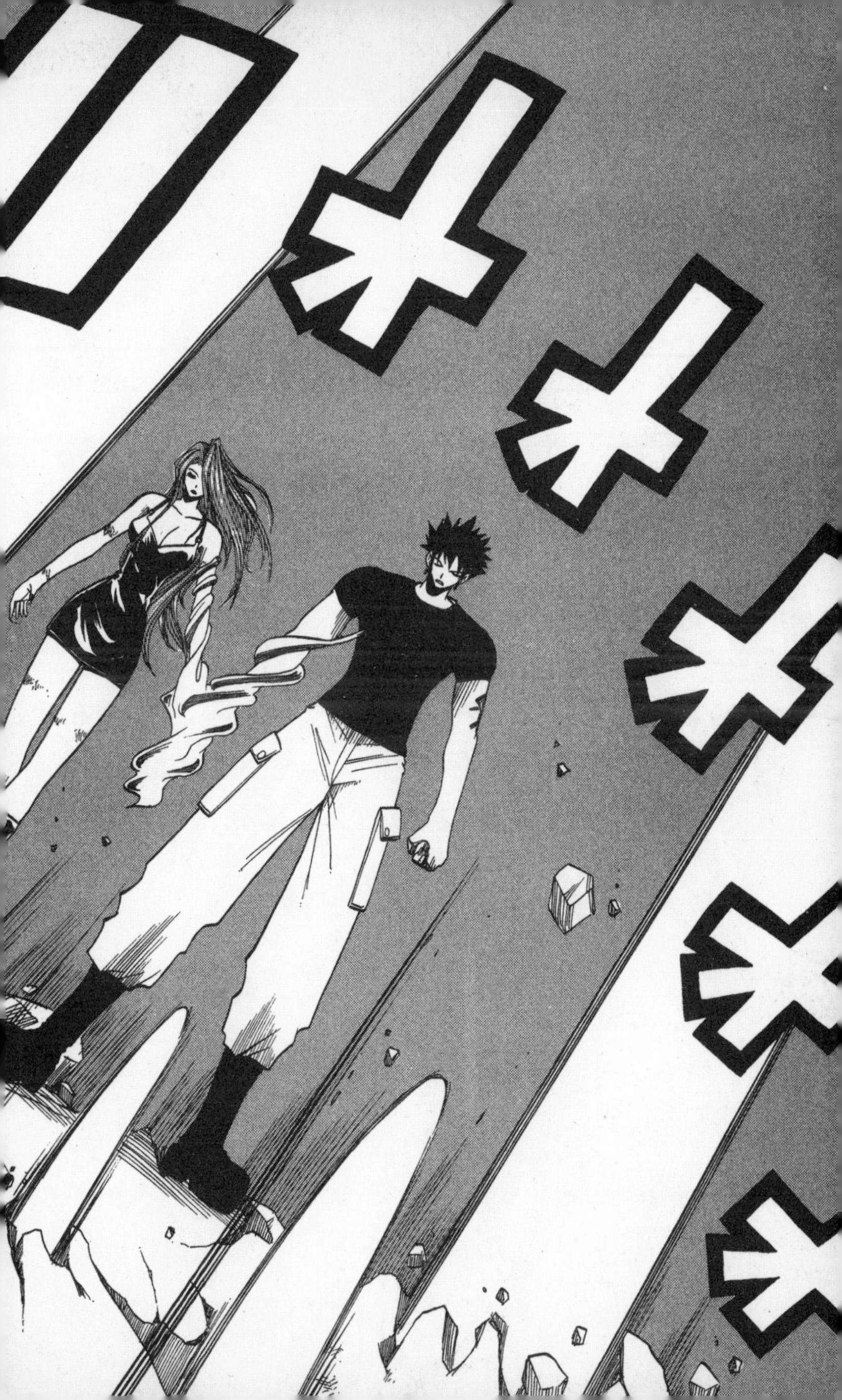
ロオオオオオ

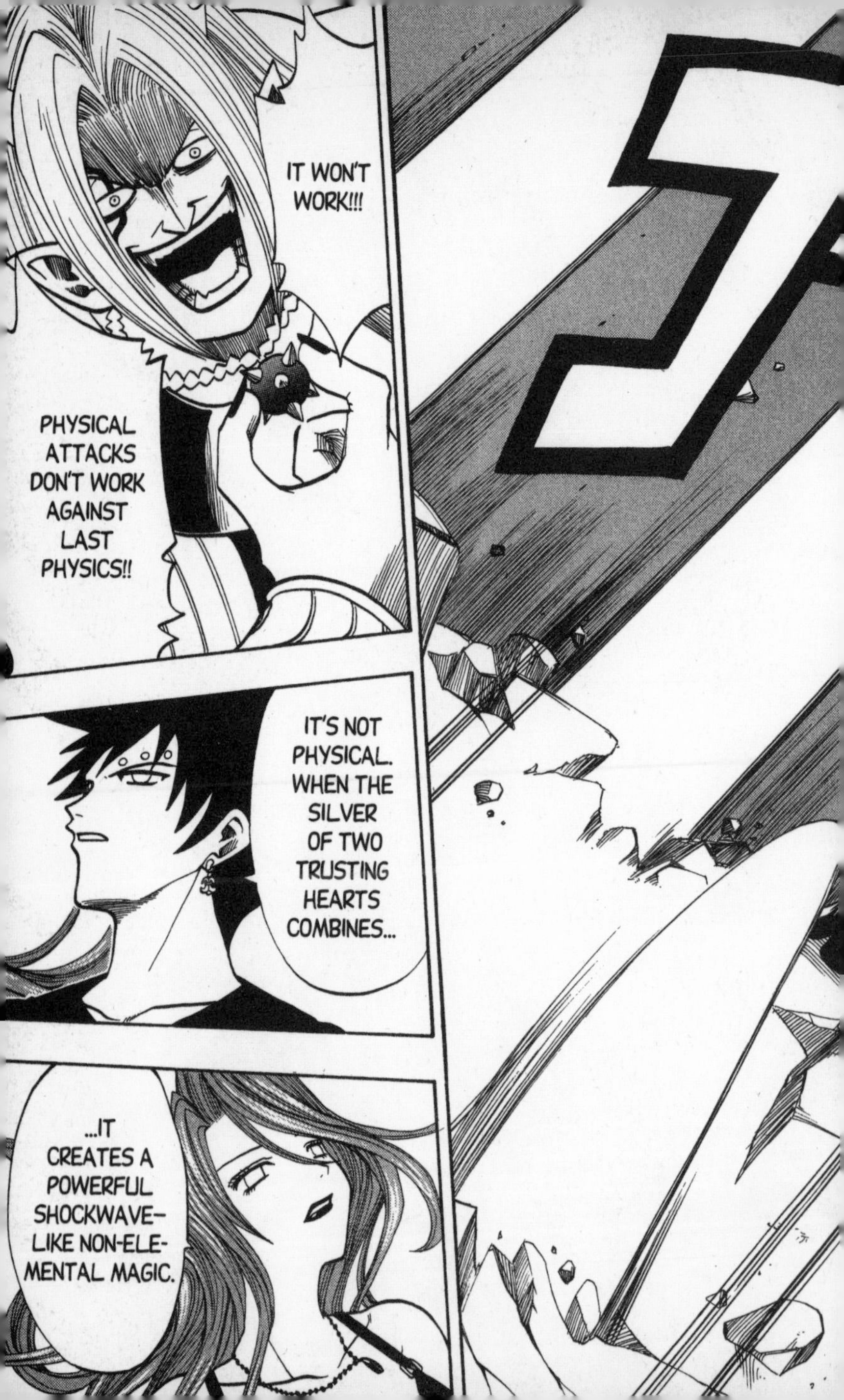
IT WON'T WORK!!!
PHYSICAL ATTACKS DON'T WORK AGAINST LAST PHYSICS!!
IT'S NOT PHYSICAL. WHEN THE SILVER OF TWO TRUSTING HEARTS COMBINES...
...IT CREATES A POWERFUL SHOCKWAVE-LIKE NON-ELE-MENTAL MAGIC.

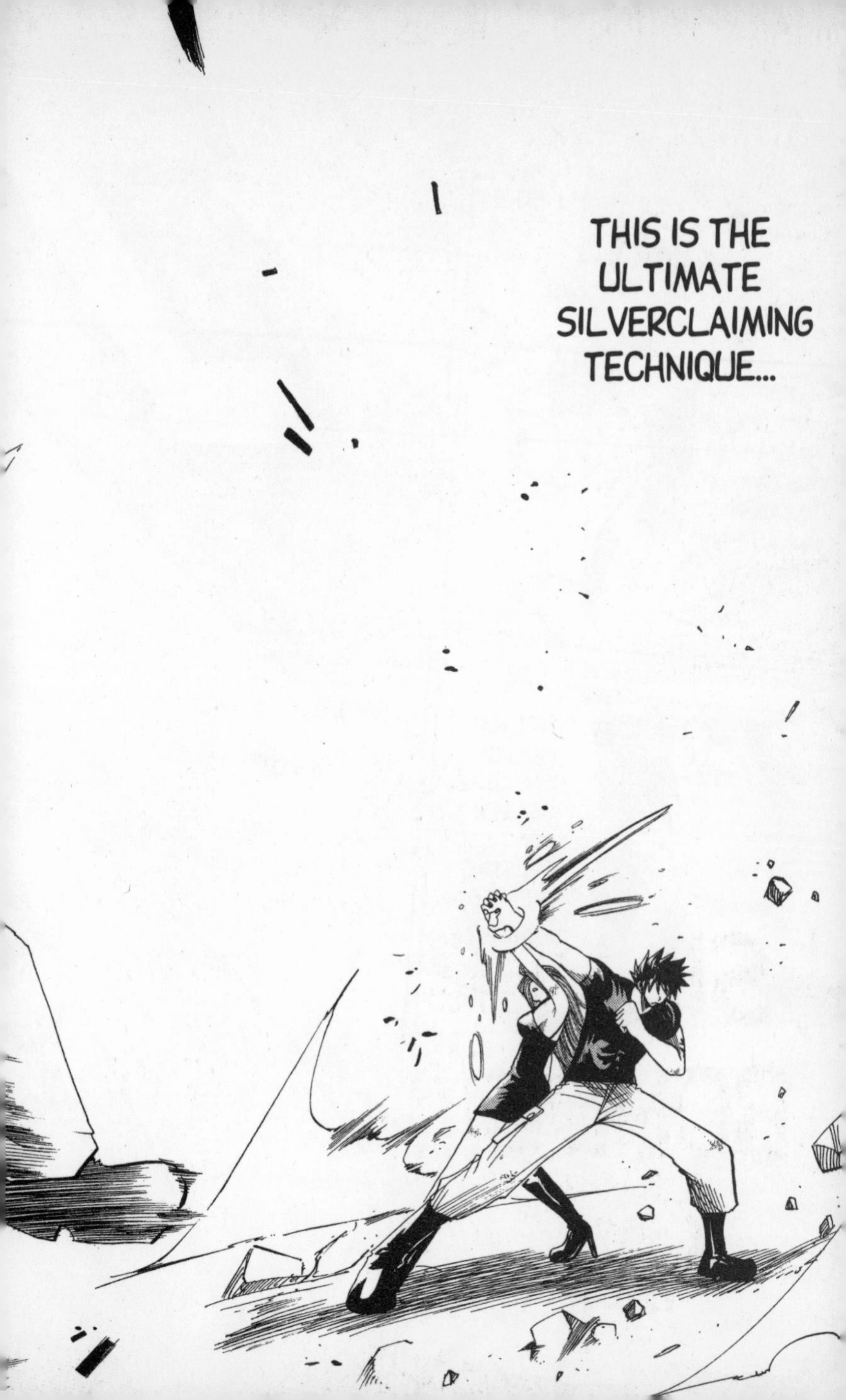
THIS IS THE ULTIMATE SILVERCLAIMING TECHNIQUE...

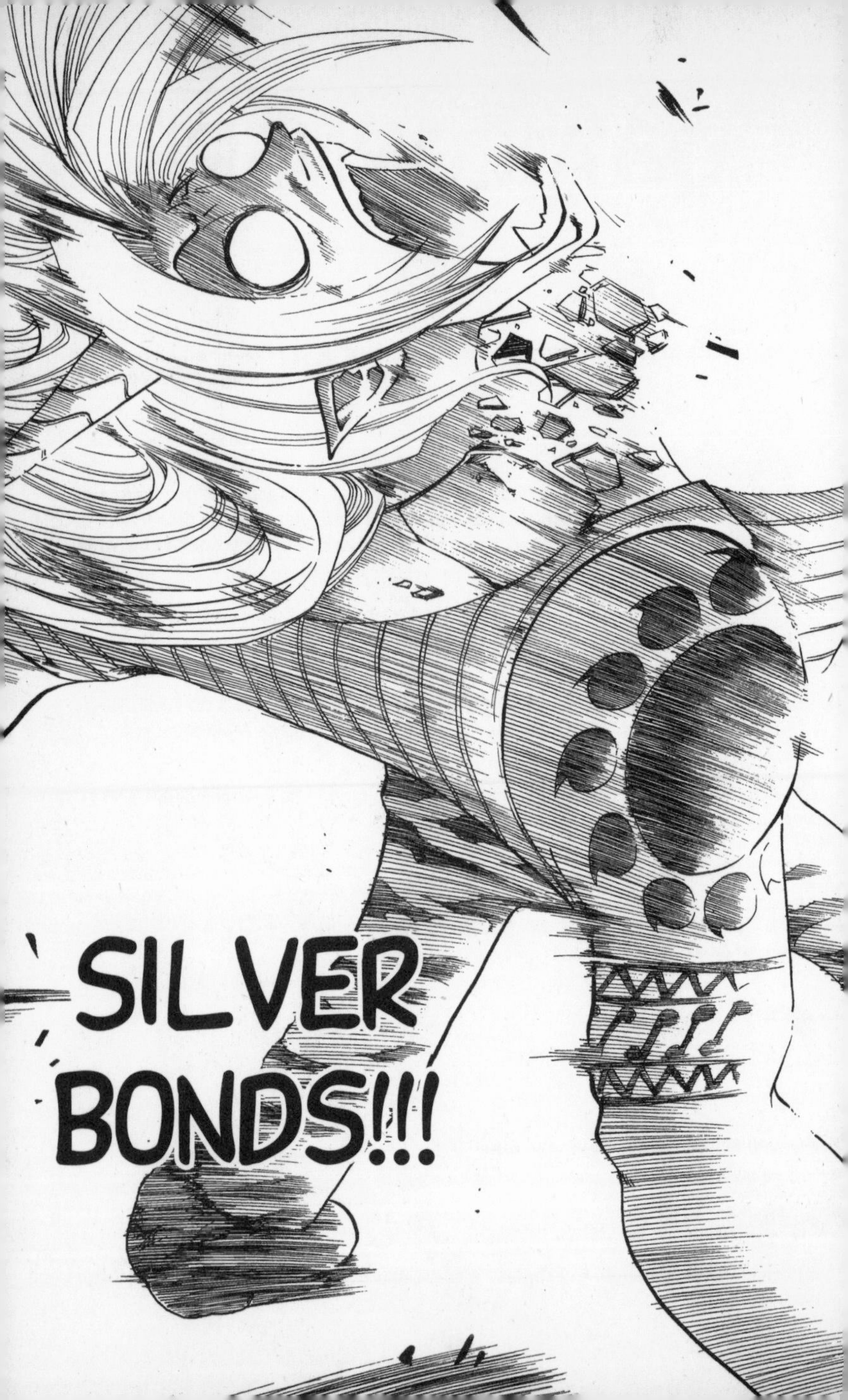
SILVER BONDS!!!

Q&A CORNER!!

q In Vol. I, Shiba seemed to recognize Haru's name. What was that all about?

(Tokyo City/ Remi & Others)

a A lot of people ask that. Er... you'll understand that later. That was really a strange place for those two... er, can't say that just yet. Foreshadowing, you know... I didn't think people would take note, but a lot of people seem to remember it. Oh, if you don't know what we're talking about, don't worry.

q In Vol. 15, Celia says, "I wanna turn into a human!" Couldn't she just do it with magic?

(Iwate-ken/ Makigo)

a Certainly, it could happen. (^_^) In this manga, you never know what'll happen week to week... I try.

q In Vol. 15, Cookie breaks the wall he smashes into. Why doesn't he just break the ground when he falls?

(Hokkaido/ Ushiushi)

a I TRY.

q Are you embarrassed to put your photo in the books?

(Nagazaki/Oota)

a It is embarrassing. (laugh) But I'm also a show-off... It's complicated. I'd never make a good celebrity.

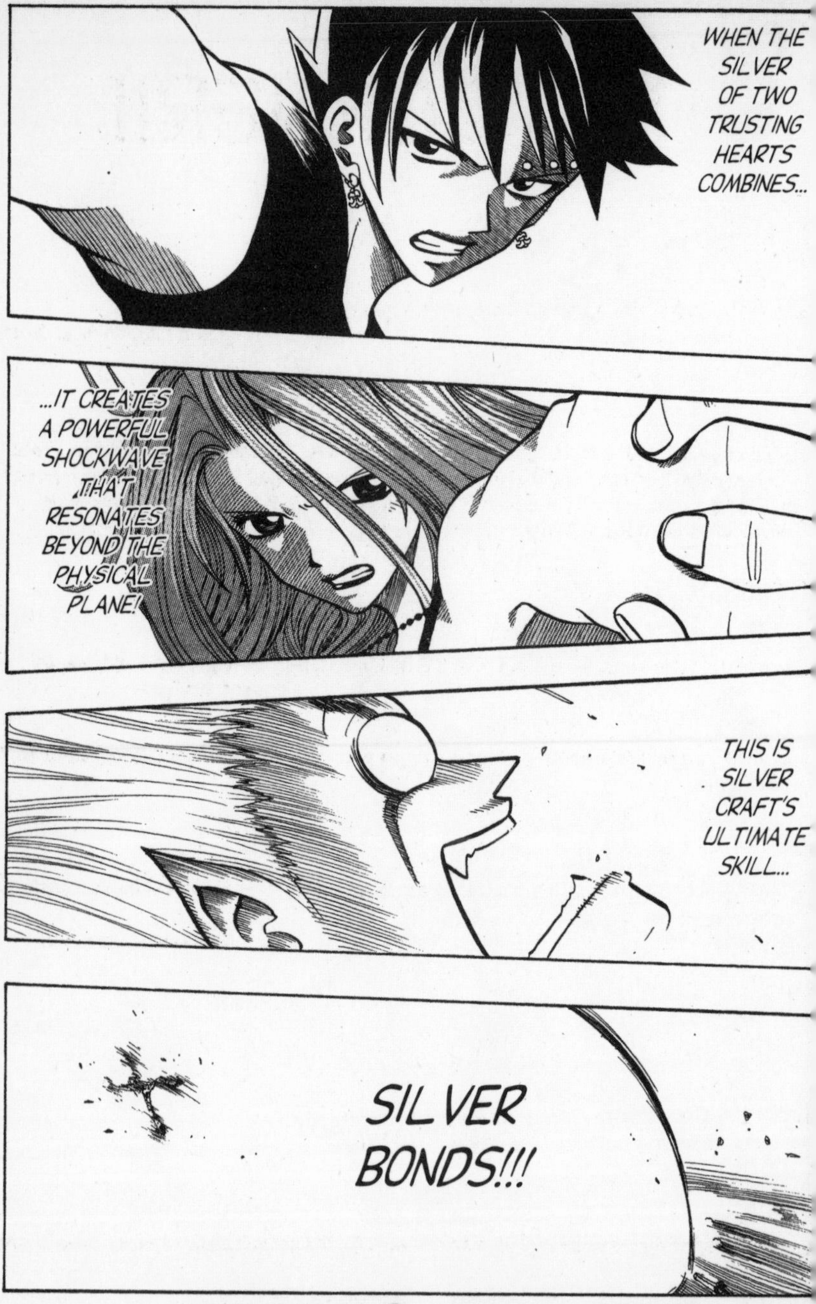
WHEN THE SILVER OF TWO TRUSTING HEARTS COMBINES...
...IT CREATES A POWERFUL SHOCKWAVE THAT RESONATES BEYOND THE PHYSICAL PLANE!
THIS IS SILVER CRAFT'S ULTIMATE SKILL...
SILVER BONDS!!!

RAVE:128 ✚ REINA'S HEART

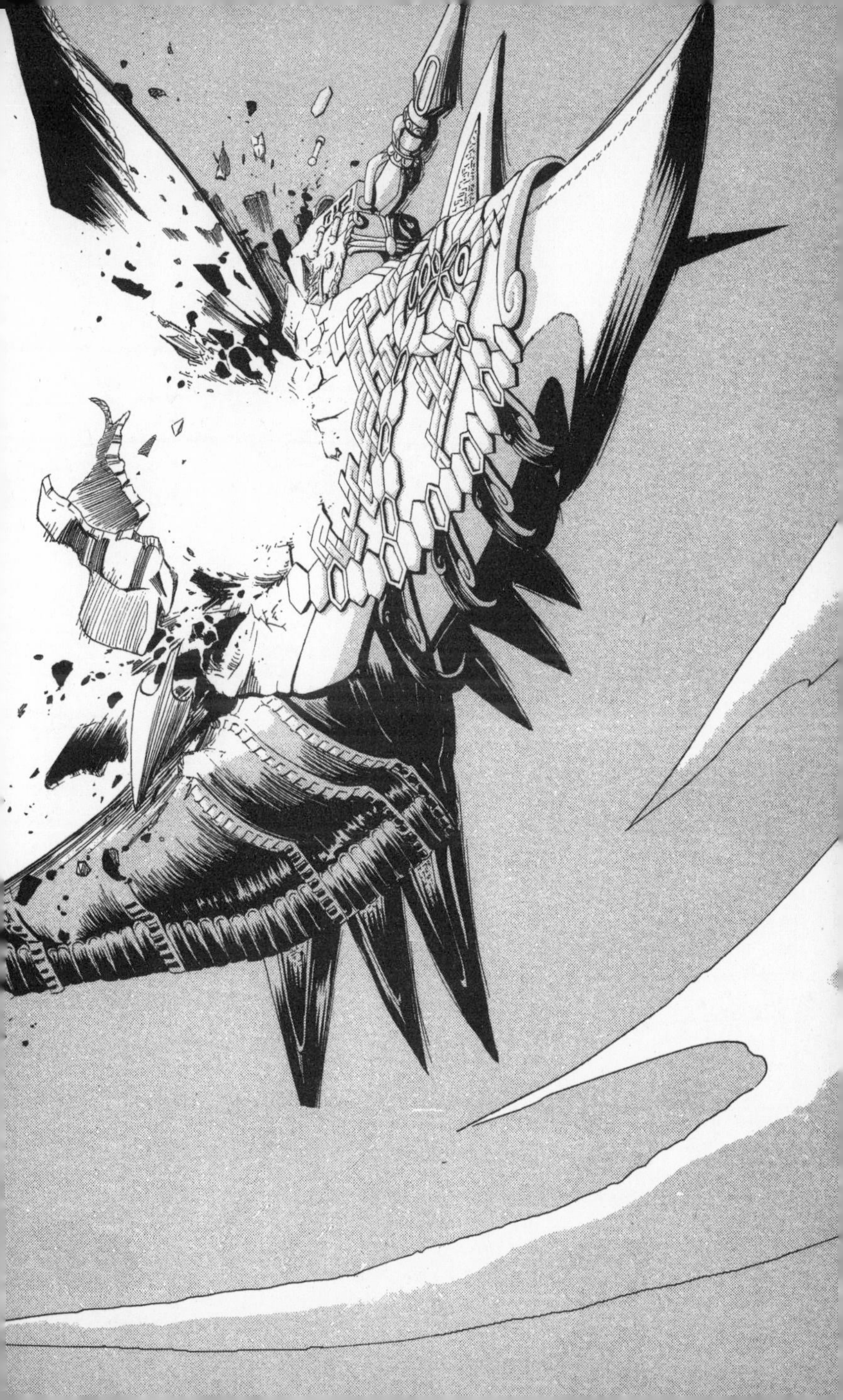

RAVE MASTER

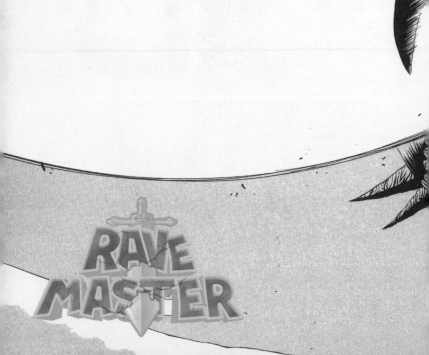

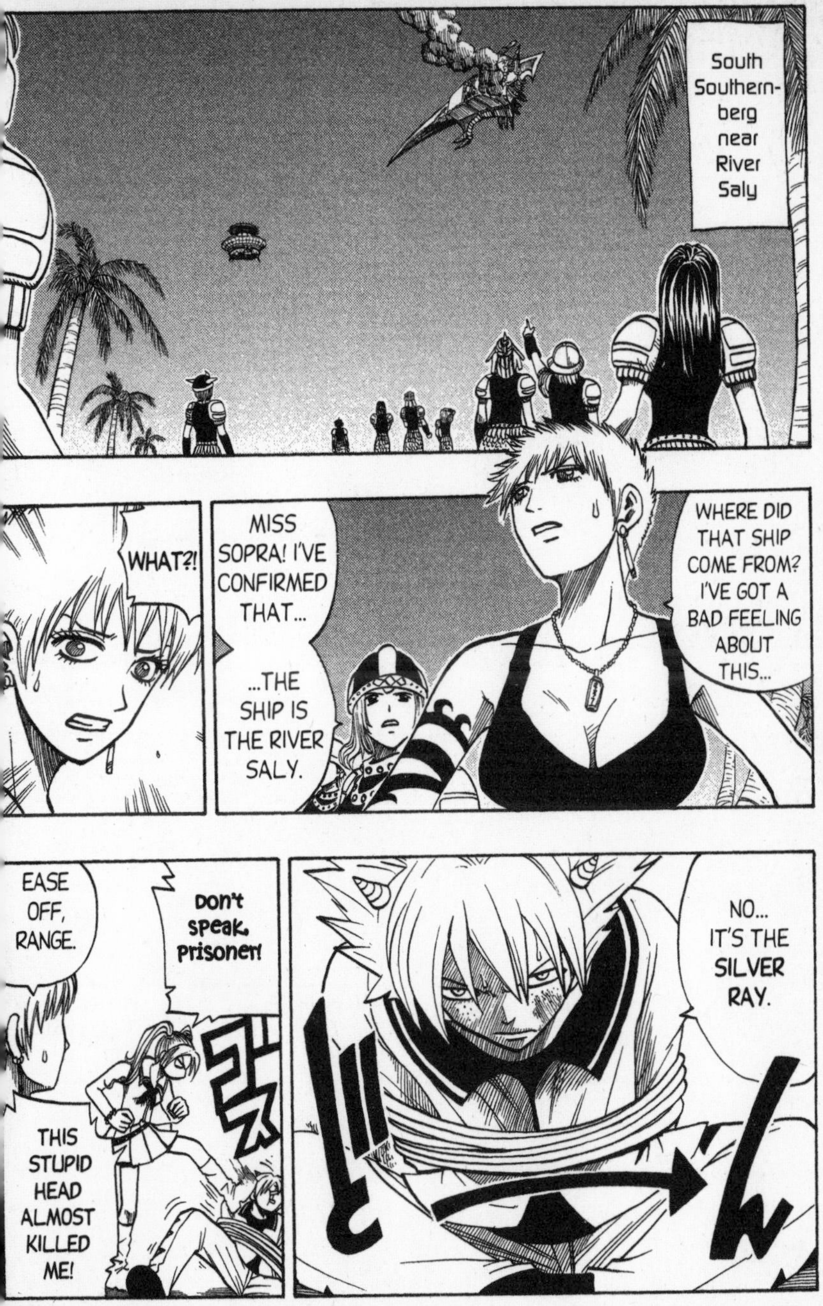
South Southernberg near River Saly
WHERE DID THAT SHIP COME FROM? I'VE GOT A BAD FEELING ABOUT THIS...
MISS SOPRA! I'VE CONFIRMED THAT...
...THE SHIP IS THE RIVER SALY.
WHAT?!
NO... IT'S THE SILVER RAY.
Don't speak, prisoner!
EASE OFF, RANGE.
THIS STUPID HEAD ALMOST KILLED ME!

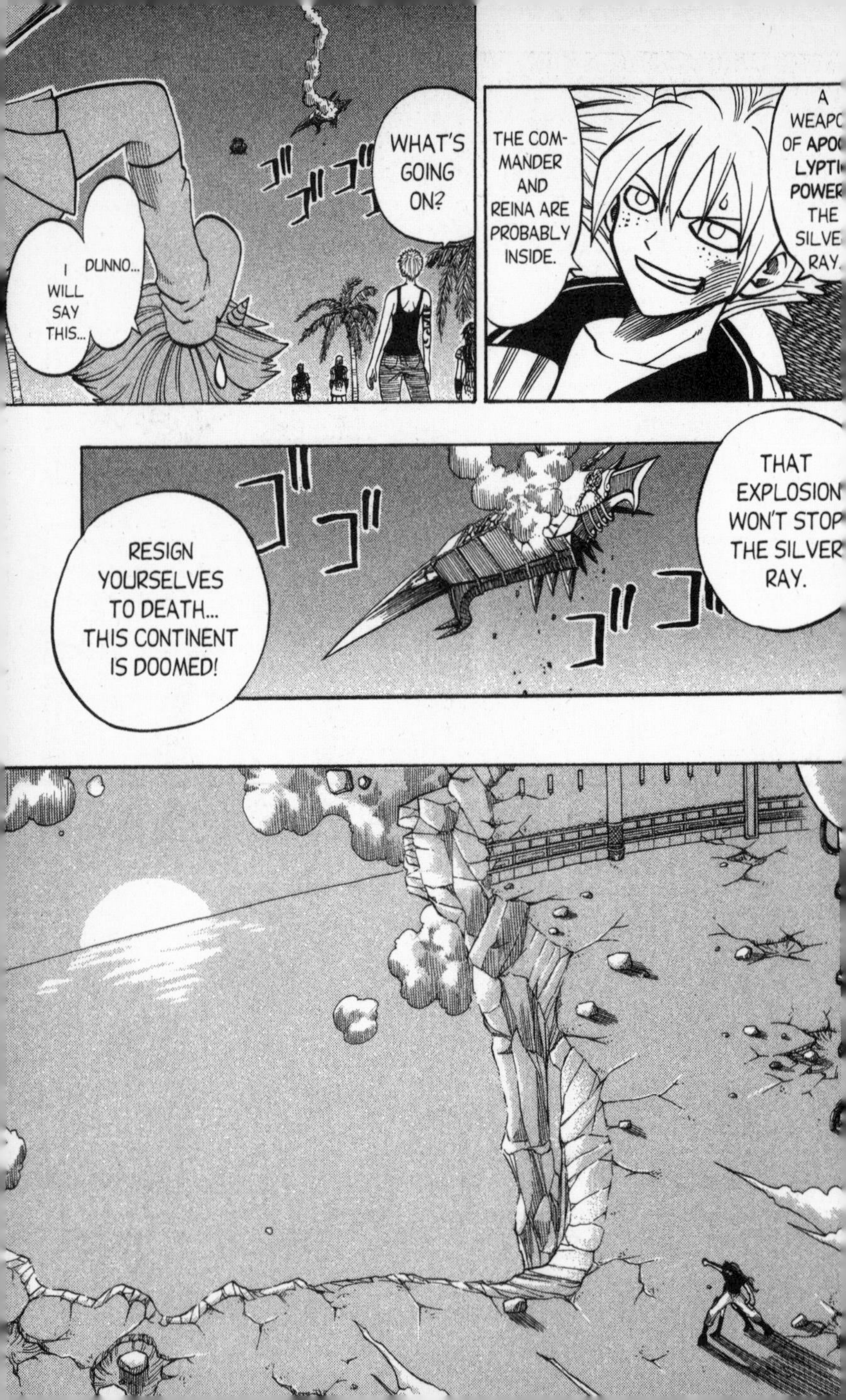

A WEAPO OF APOC LYPTI POWER THE SILVE RAY.
THE COMMANDER AND REINA ARE PROBABLY INSIDE.
ゴゴゴゴ
WHAT'S GOING ON?
DUNNO... I WILL SAY THIS...
THAT EXPLOSION WON'T STOP THE SILVER RAY.
ゴゴ
ゴゴ
RESIGN YOURSELVES TO DEATH... THIS CONTINENT IS DOOMED!

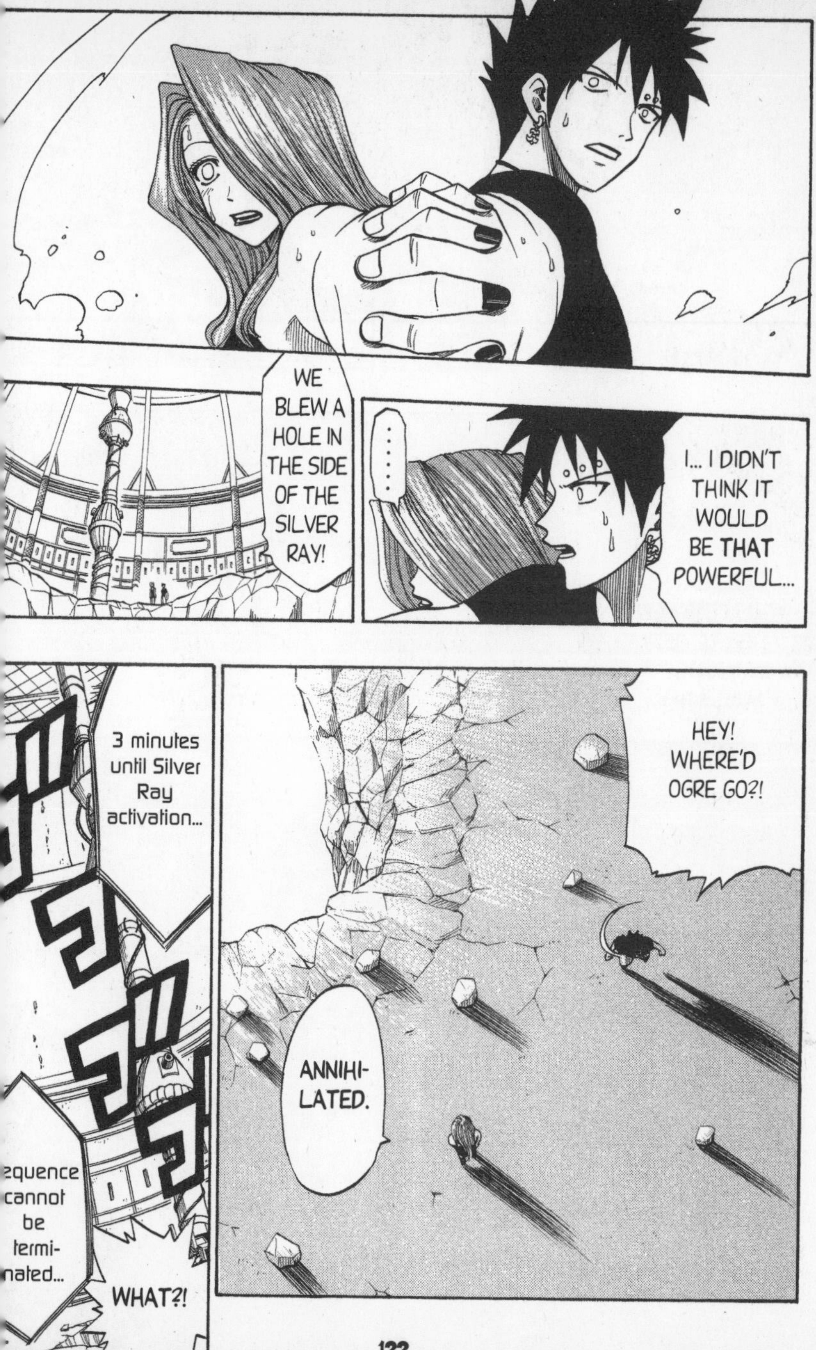
.....
I... I DIDN'T THINK IT WOULD BE THAT POWERFUL...
WE BLEW A HOLE IN THE SIDE OF THE SILVER RAY!
HEY! WHERE'D OGRE GO?!
ANNIHILATED.
3 minutes until Silver Ray activation...
equence cannot be terminated...
WHAT?!

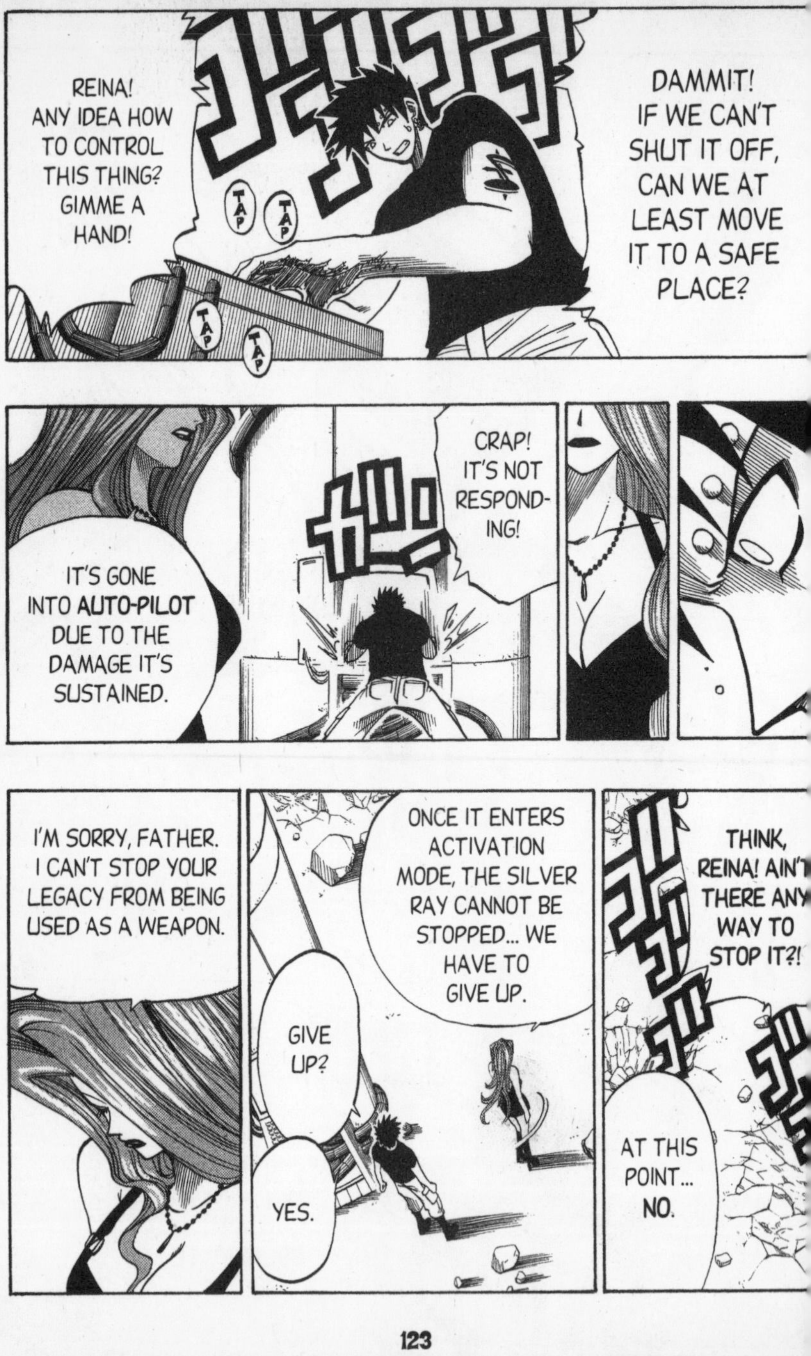
DAMMIT! IF WE CAN'T SHUT IT OFF, CAN WE AT LEAST MOVE IT TO A SAFE PLACE?
REINA! ANY IDEA HOW TO CONTROL THIS THING? GIMME A HAND!
TAP
TAP
TAP
TAP
CRAP! IT'S NOT RESPOND-ING!
IT'S GONE INTO **AUTO-PILOT** DUE TO THE DAMAGE IT'S SUSTAINED.
THINK, REINA! AIN'T THERE ANY WAY TO STOP IT?!
AT THIS POINT... **NO.**
ONCE IT ENTERS ACTIVATION MODE, THE SILVER RAY CANNOT BE STOPPED... WE HAVE TO GIVE UP.
GIVE UP?
YES.
I'M SORRY, FATHER. I CAN'T STOP YOUR LEGACY FROM BEING USED AS A WEAPON.

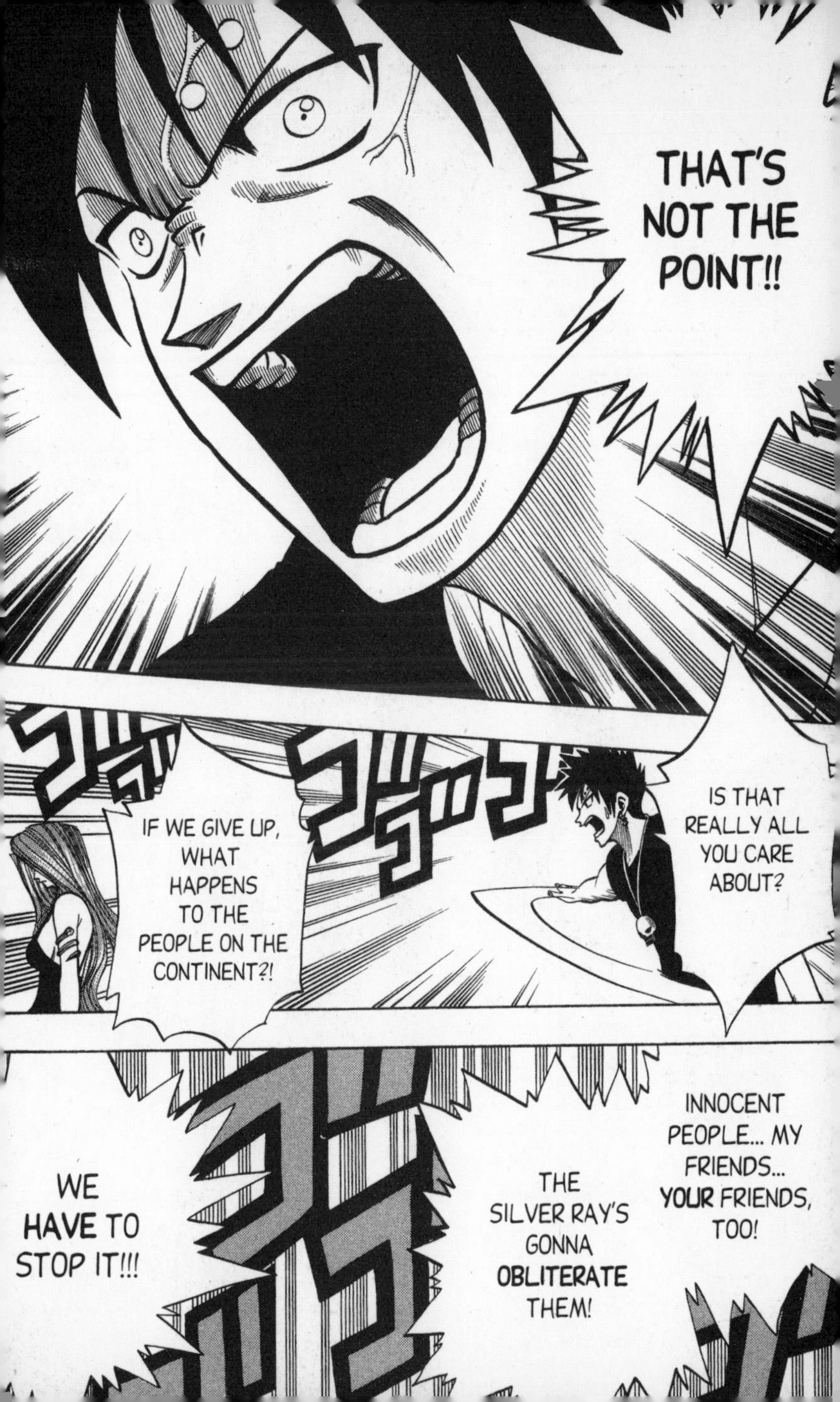
THAT'S NOT THE POINT!!
IS THAT REALLY ALL YOU CARE ABOUT?
IF WE GIVE UP, WHAT HAPPENS TO THE PEOPLE ON THE CONTINENT?!
INNOCENT PEOPLE... MY FRIENDS... **YOUR** FRIENDS, TOO!
THE SILVER RAY'S GONNA **OBLITERATE** THEM!
WE **HAVE** TO STOP IT!!!

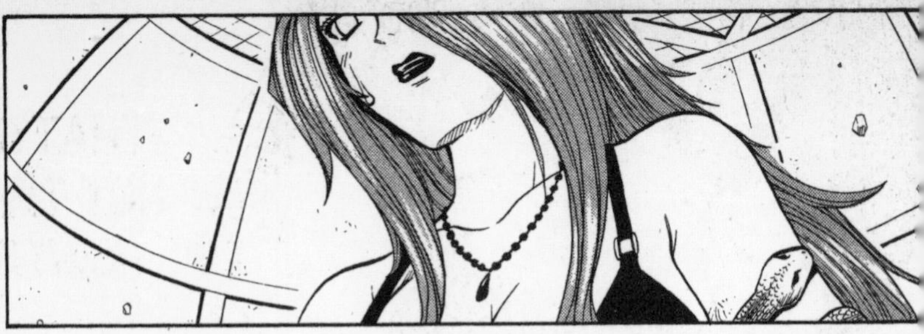
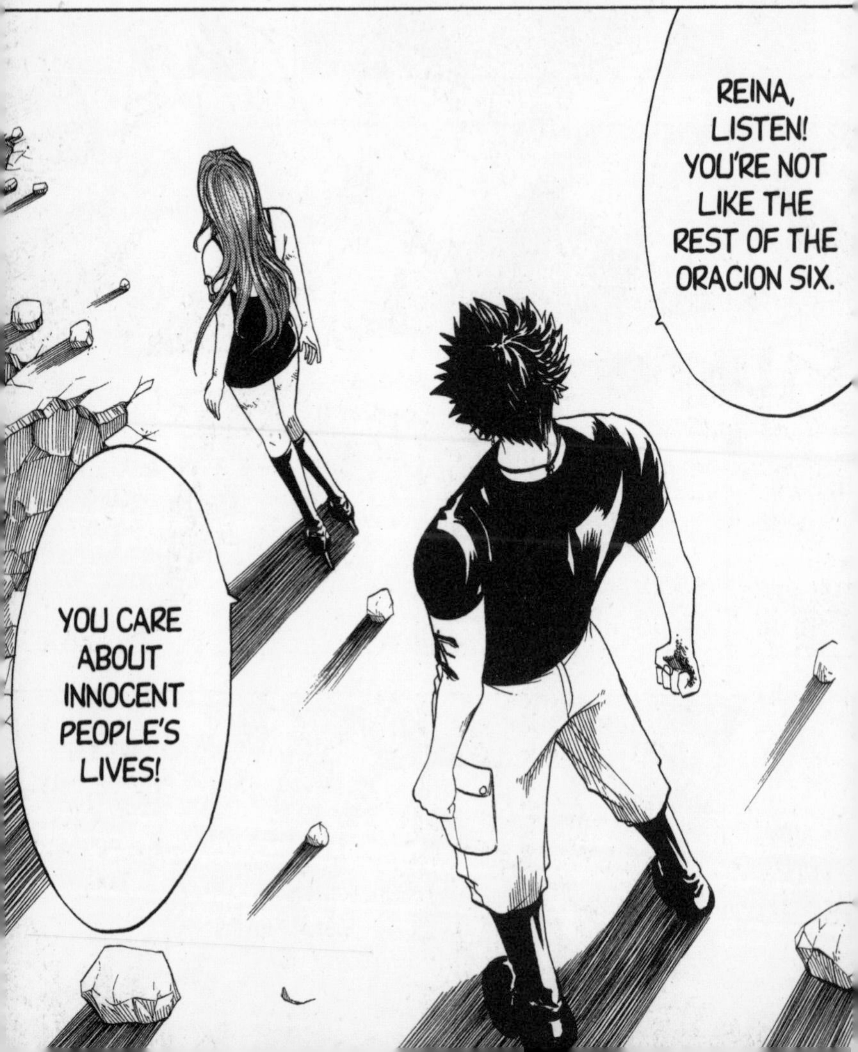
REINA, LISTEN! YOU'RE NOT LIKE THE REST OF THE ORACION SIX.
YOU CARE ABOUT INNOCENT PEOPLE'S LIVES!

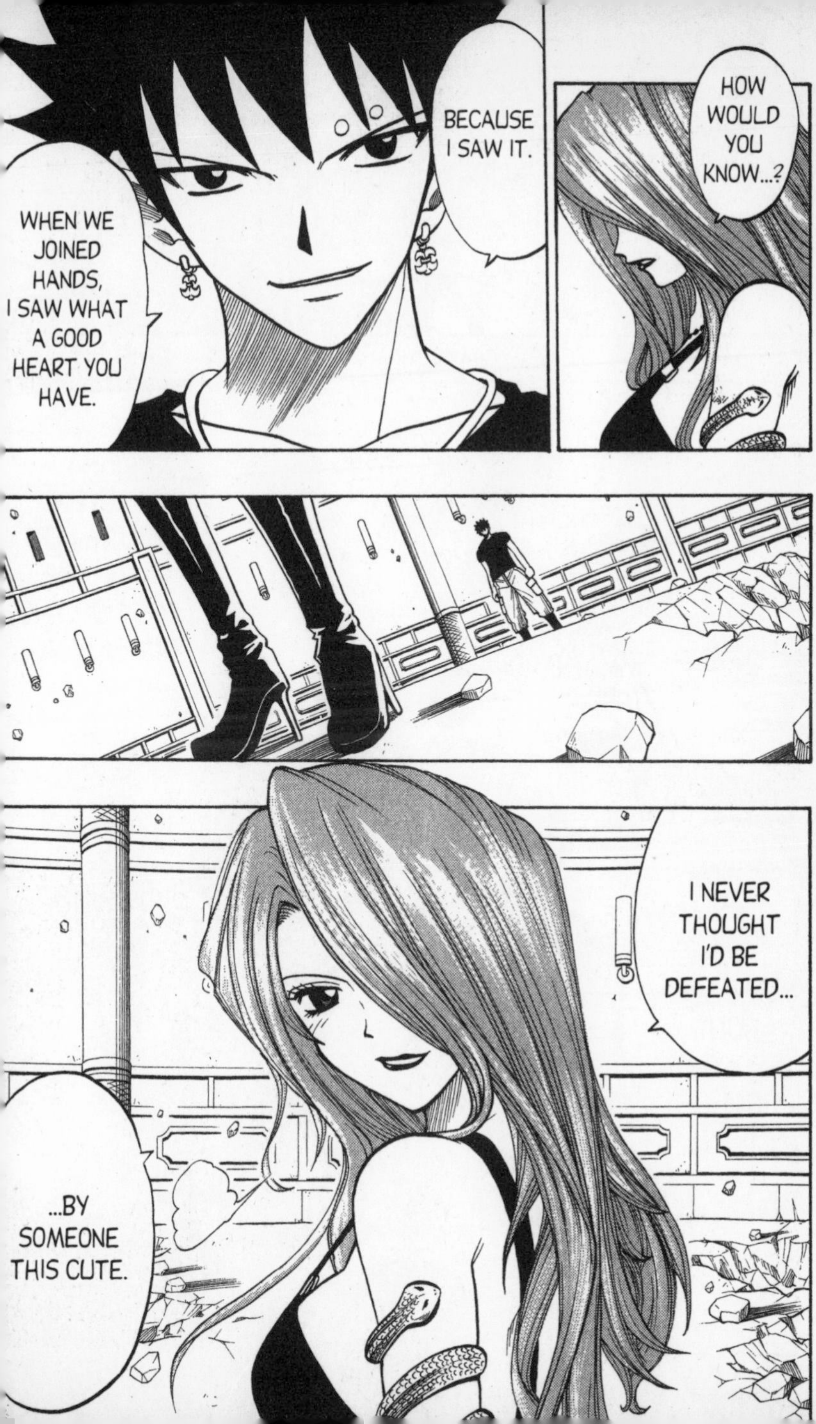
HOW WOULD YOU KNOW...?
BECAUSE I SAW IT.
WHEN WE JOINED HANDS, I SAW WHAT A GOOD HEART YOU HAVE.
I NEVER THOUGHT I'D BE DEFEATED...
...BY SOMEONE THIS CUTE.

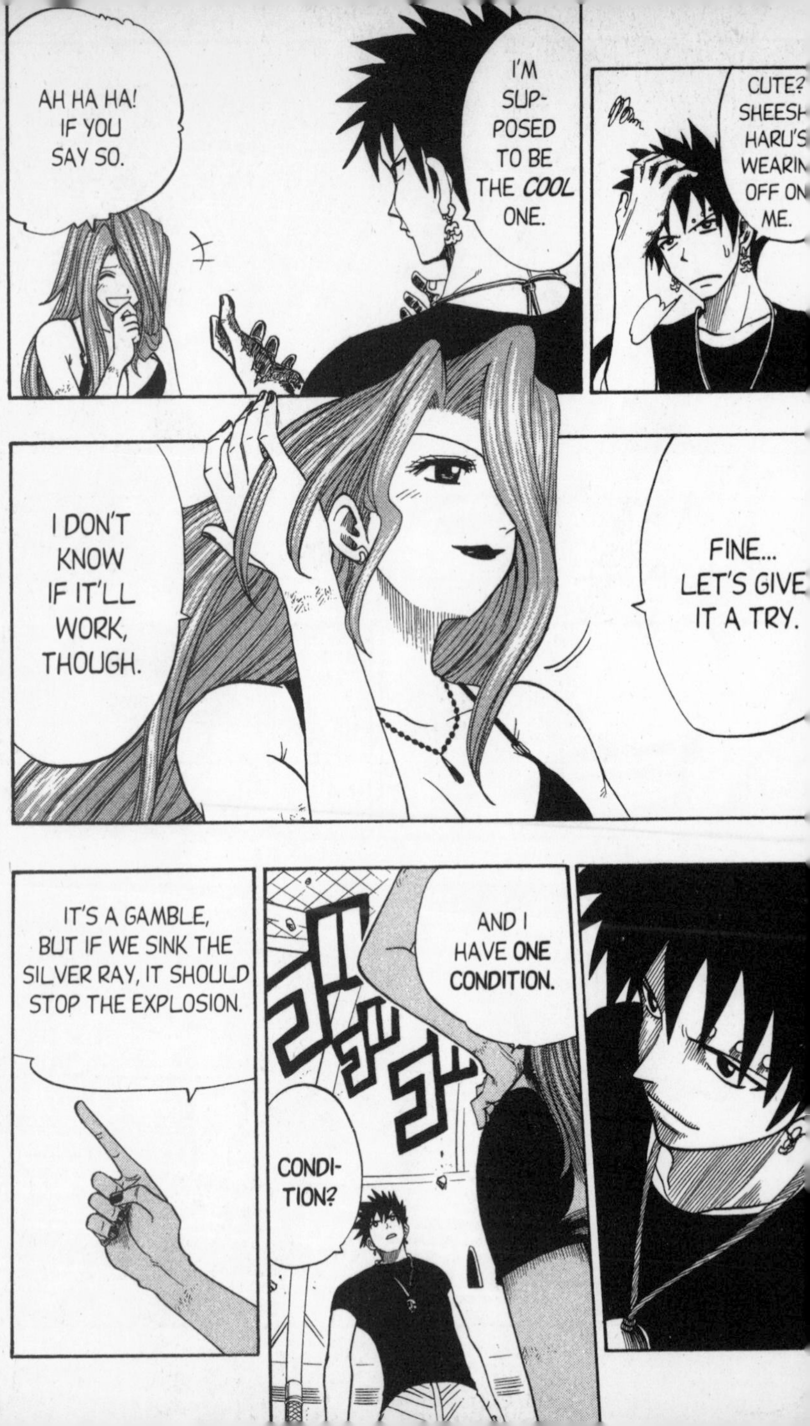
CUTE? SHEESH HARU'S WEARIN OFF ON ME.
I'M SUP-POSED TO BE THE *COOL* ONE.
AH HA HA! IF YOU SAY SO.
FINE... LET'S GIVE IT A TRY.
I DON'T KNOW IF IT'LL WORK, THOUGH.
AND I HAVE **ONE** CONDITION.
CONDI-TION?
IT'S A GAMBLE, BUT IF WE SINK THE SILVER RAY, IT SHOULD STOP THE EXPLOSION.

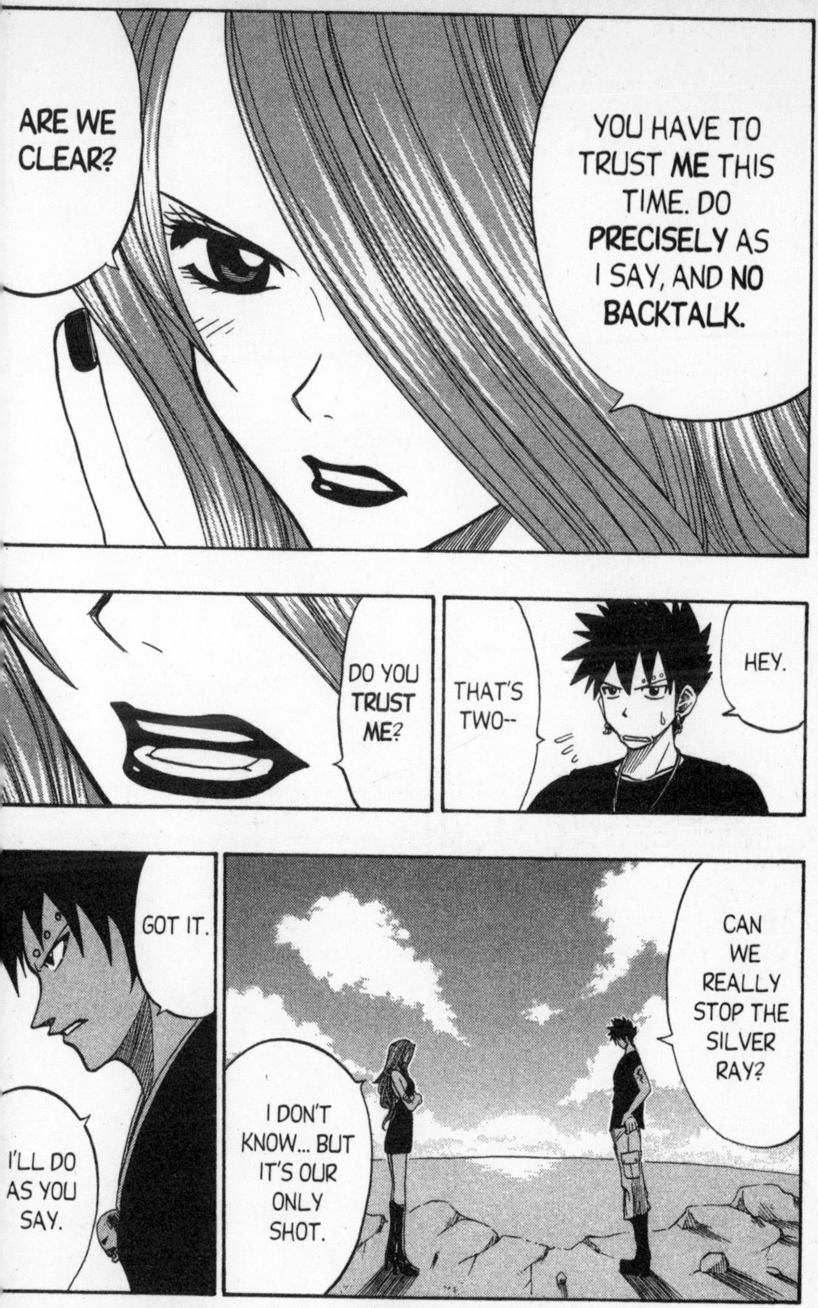
YOU HAVE TO TRUST ME THIS TIME. DO PRECISELY AS I SAY, AND NO BACKTALK.
ARE WE CLEAR?
HEY.
THAT'S TWO--
DO YOU TRUST ME?
CAN WE REALLY STOP THE SILVER RAY?
I DON'T KNOW... BUT IT'S OUR ONLY SHOT.
GOT IT.
I'LL DO AS YOU SAY.

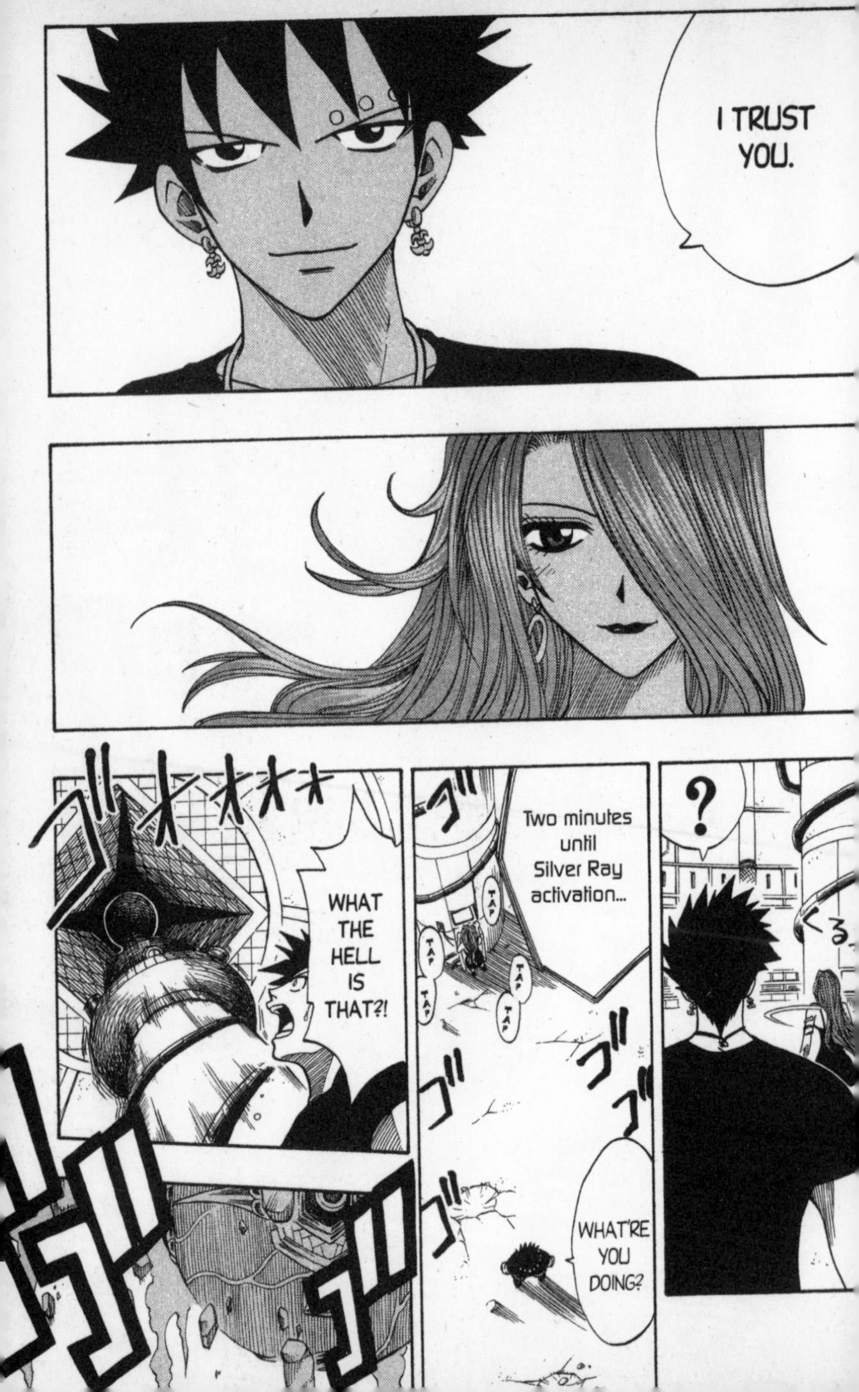
I TRUST YOU.
?
くる
Two minutes until Silver Ray activation...
TAP TAP TAP TAP TAP
WHAT'RE YOU DOING?
WHAT THE HELL IS THAT?!

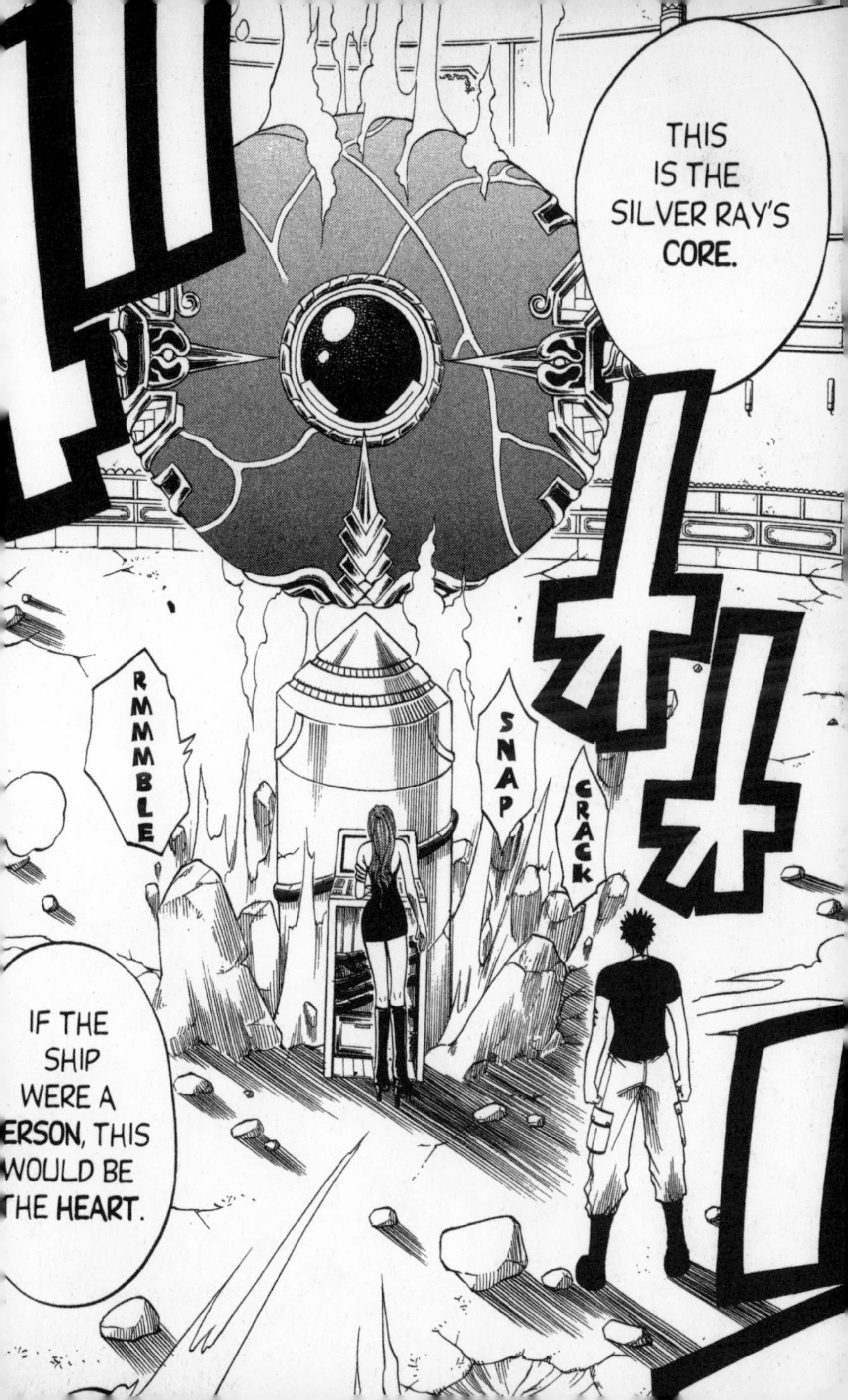
THIS IS THE SILVER RAY'S CORE.
CRACK
SNAP
RMMMBLE
IF THE SHIP WERE A ERSON, THIS WOULD BE THE HEART.

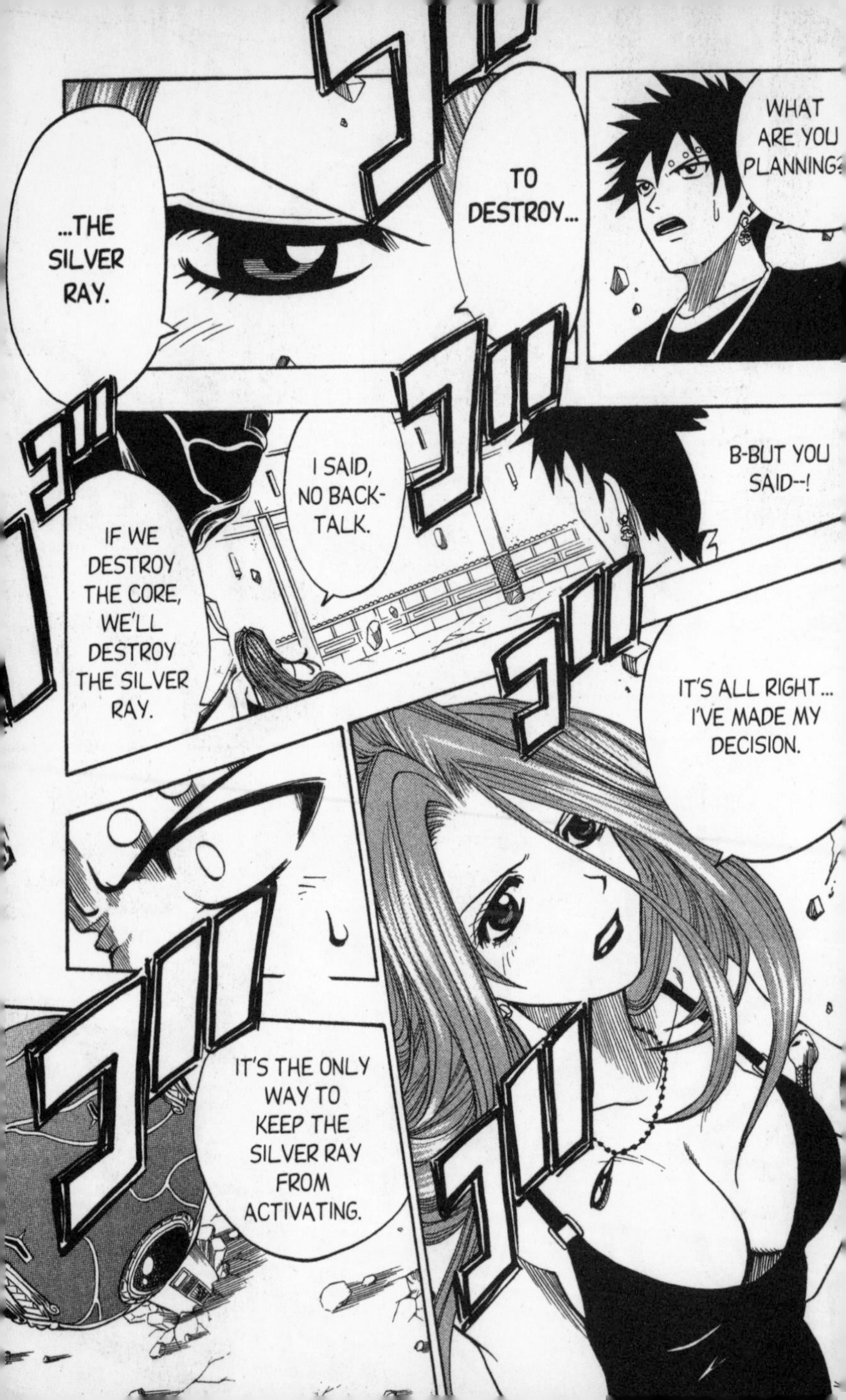
WHAT ARE YOU PLANNING?
TO DESTROY...
...THE SILVER RAY.
B-BUT YOU SAID--!
I SAID, NO BACK-TALK.
IF WE DESTROY THE CORE, WE'LL DESTROY THE SILVER RAY.
IT'S ALL RIGHT... I'VE MADE MY DECISION.
IT'S THE ONLY WAY TO KEEP THE SILVER RAY FROM ACTIVATING.

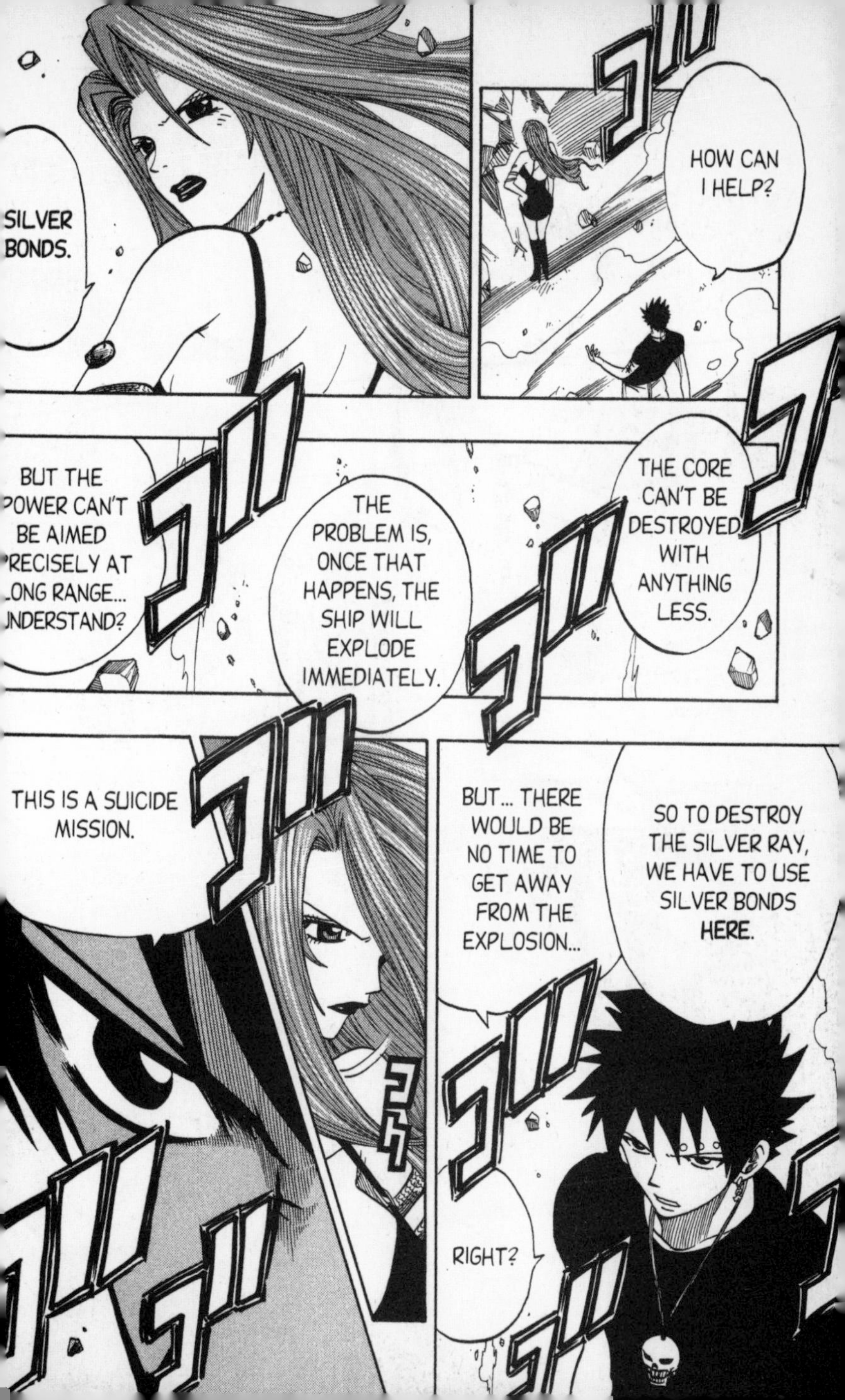
HOW CAN I HELP?
SILVER BONDS.
THE CORE CAN'T BE DESTROYED WITH ANYTHING LESS.
THE PROBLEM IS, ONCE THAT HAPPENS, THE SHIP WILL EXPLODE IMMEDIATELY.
BUT THE POWER CAN'T BE AIMED PRECISELY AT LONG RANGE... UNDERSTAND?
SO TO DESTROY THE SILVER RAY, WE HAVE TO USE SILVER BONDS HERE.
BUT... THERE WOULD BE NO TIME TO GET AWAY FROM THE EXPLOSION...
RIGHT?
THIS IS A SUICIDE MISSION.

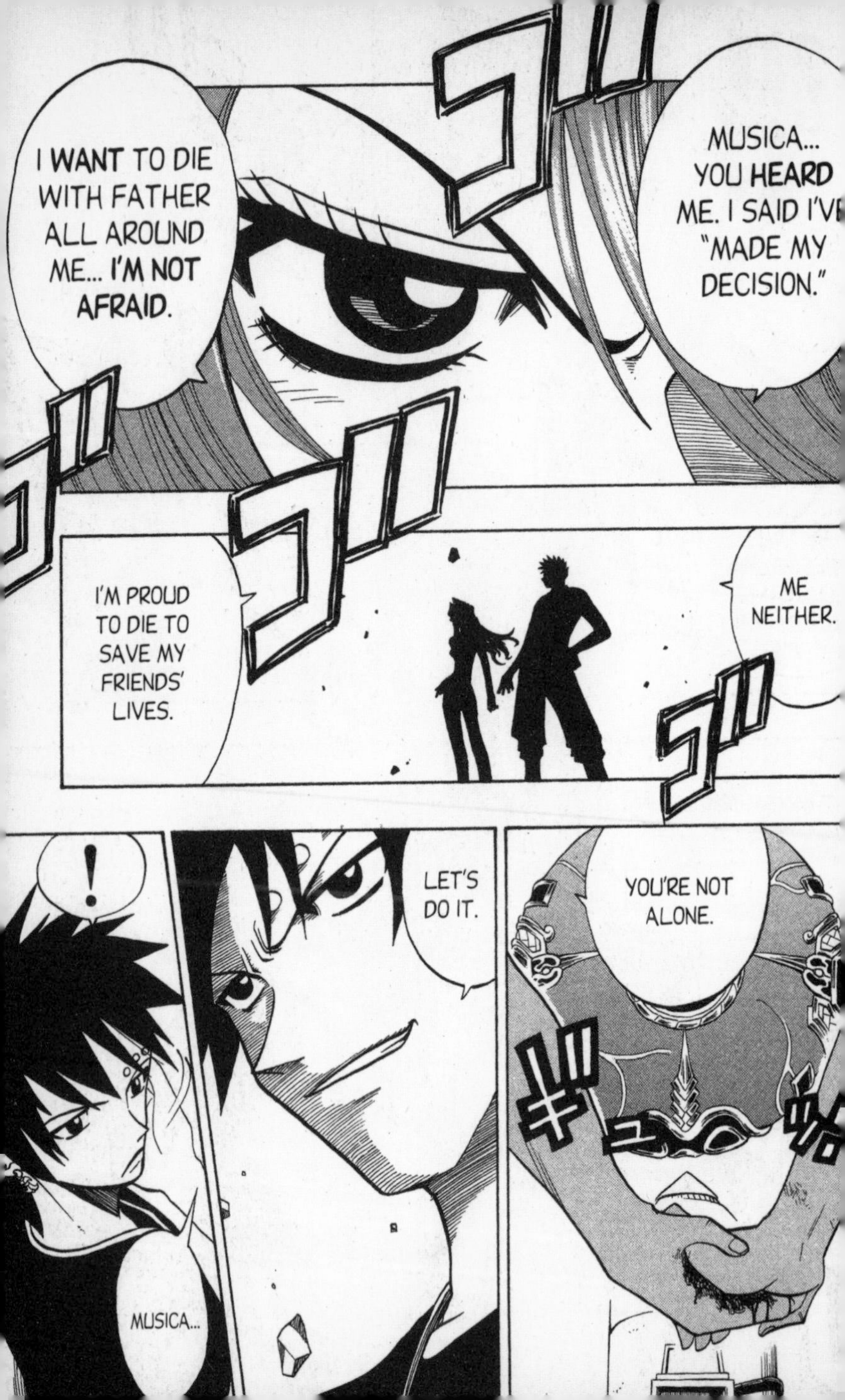
MUSICA... YOU **HEARD** ME. I SAID I'V "MADE MY DECISION."
I **WANT** TO DIE WITH FATHER ALL AROUND ME... **I'M NOT AFRAID.**
ME NEITHER.
I'M PROUD TO DIE TO SAVE MY FRIENDS' LIVES.
YOU'RE NOT ALONE.
LET'S DO IT.
!
MUSICA...

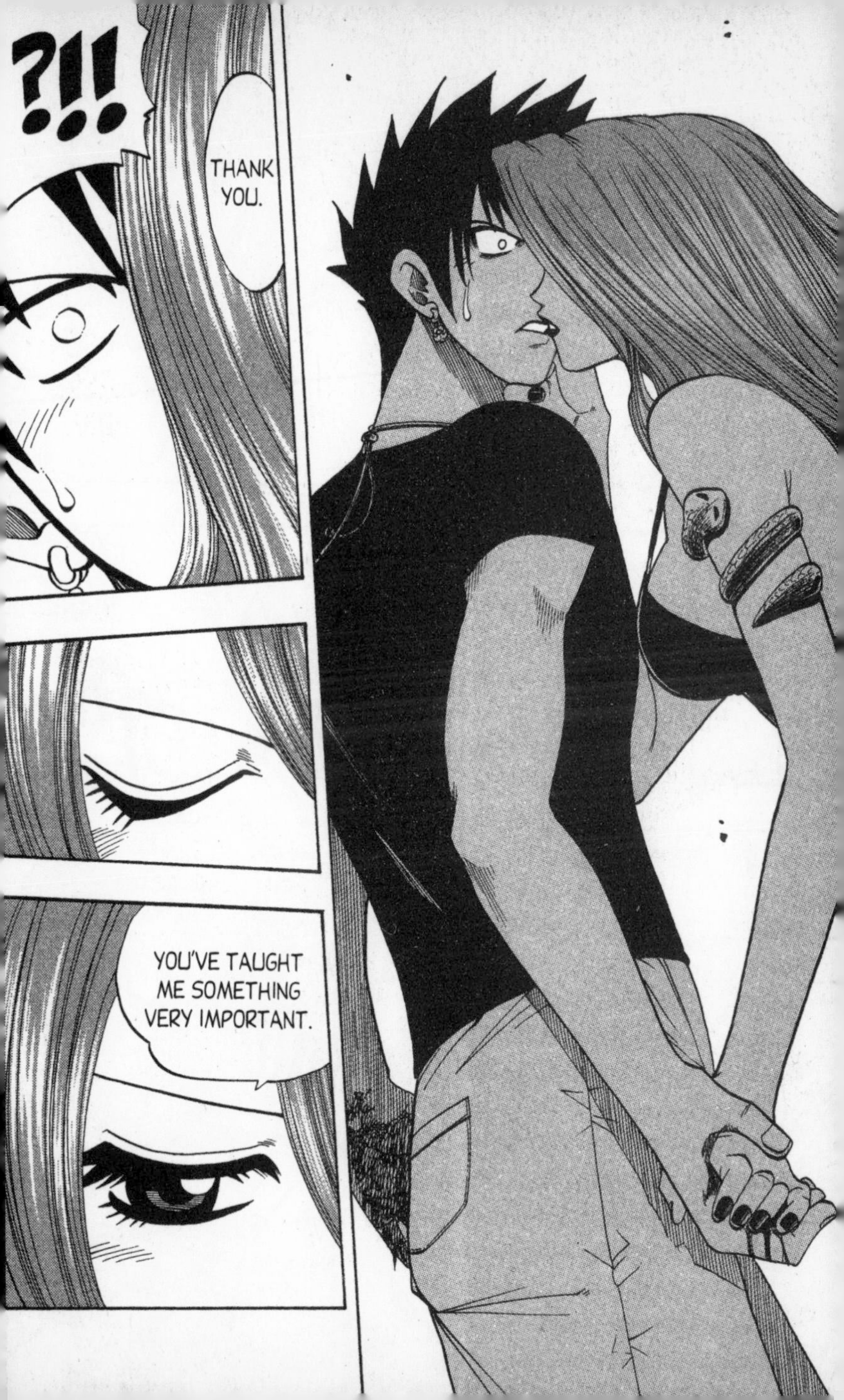
THANK YOU.
?!!
YOU'VE TAUGHT ME SOMETHING VERY IMPORTANT.

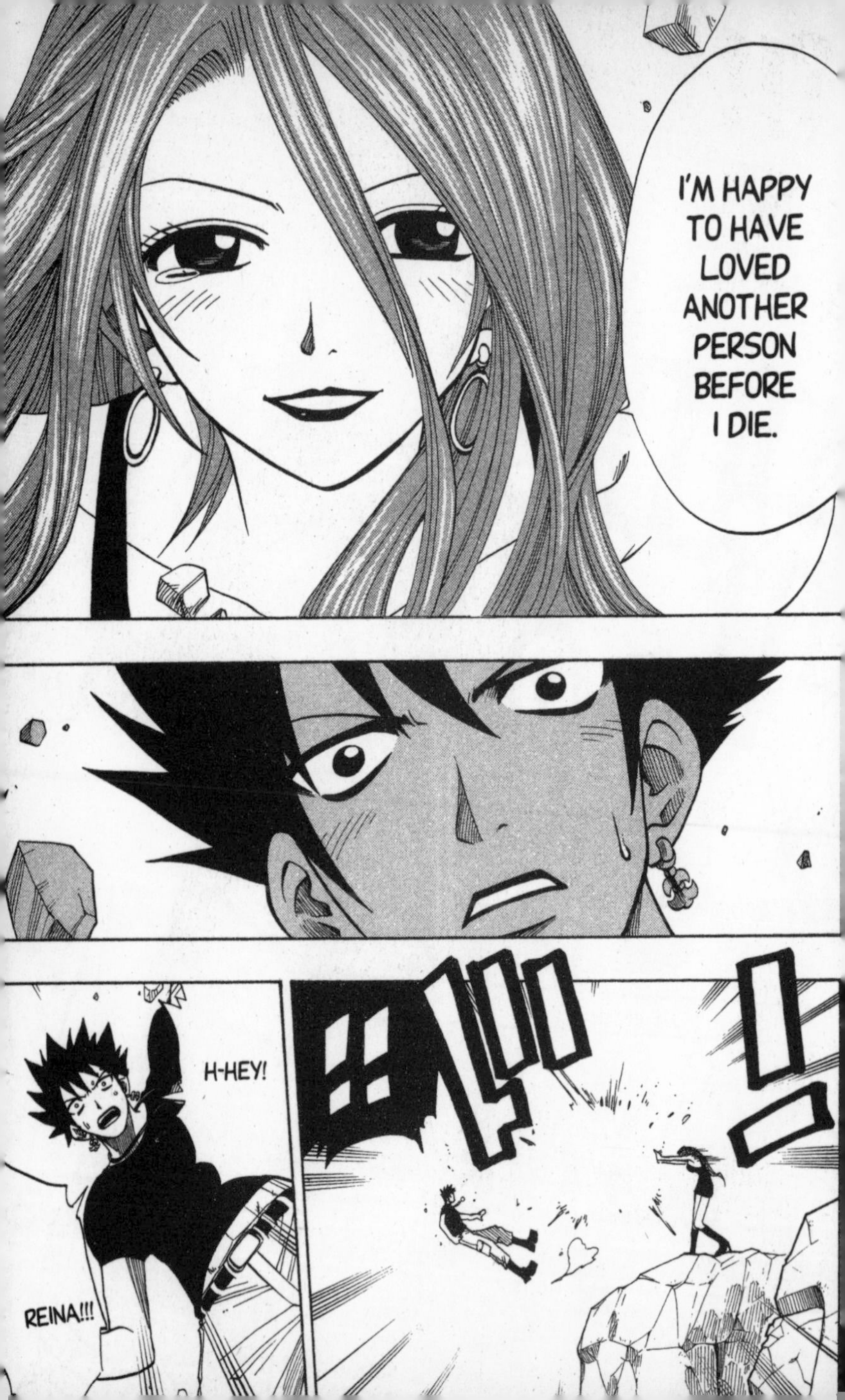
I'M HAPPY TO HAVE LOVED ANOTHER PERSON BEFORE I DIE.
H-HEY!
REINA!!!

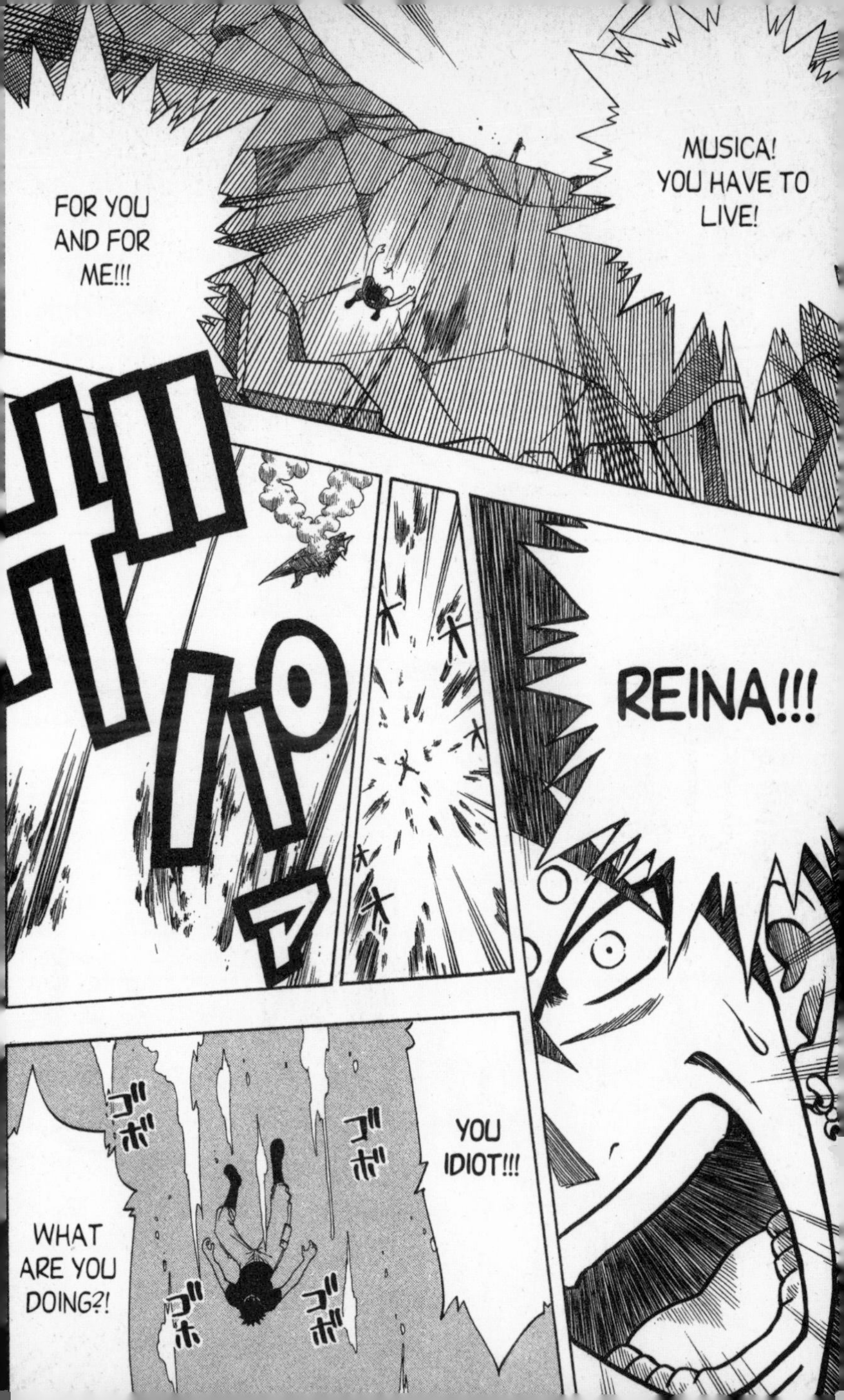

MUSICA! YOU HAVE TO LIVE!
FOR YOU AND FOR ME!!!
REINA!!!
YOU IDIOT!!!
WHAT ARE YOU DOING?!
ゴボ
ゴボ
ゴボ
ゴボ

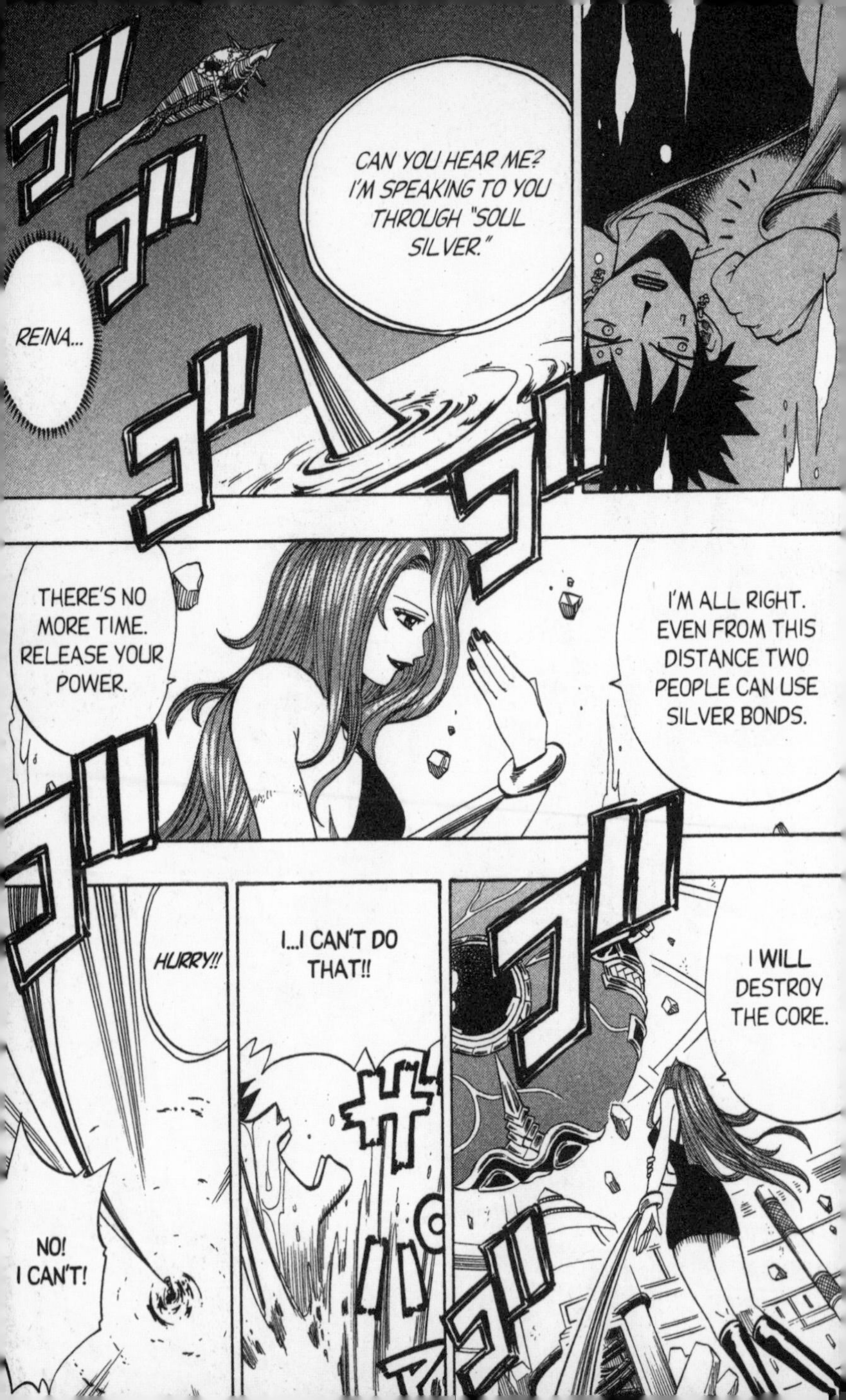
CAN YOU HEAR ME? I'M SPEAKING TO YOU THROUGH "SOUL SILVER."
REINA...
I'M ALL RIGHT. EVEN FROM THIS DISTANCE TWO PEOPLE CAN USE SILVER BONDS.
THERE'S NO MORE TIME. RELEASE YOUR POWER.
I WILL DESTROY THE CORE.
I...I CAN'T DO THAT!!
HURRY!!
NO! I CAN'T!

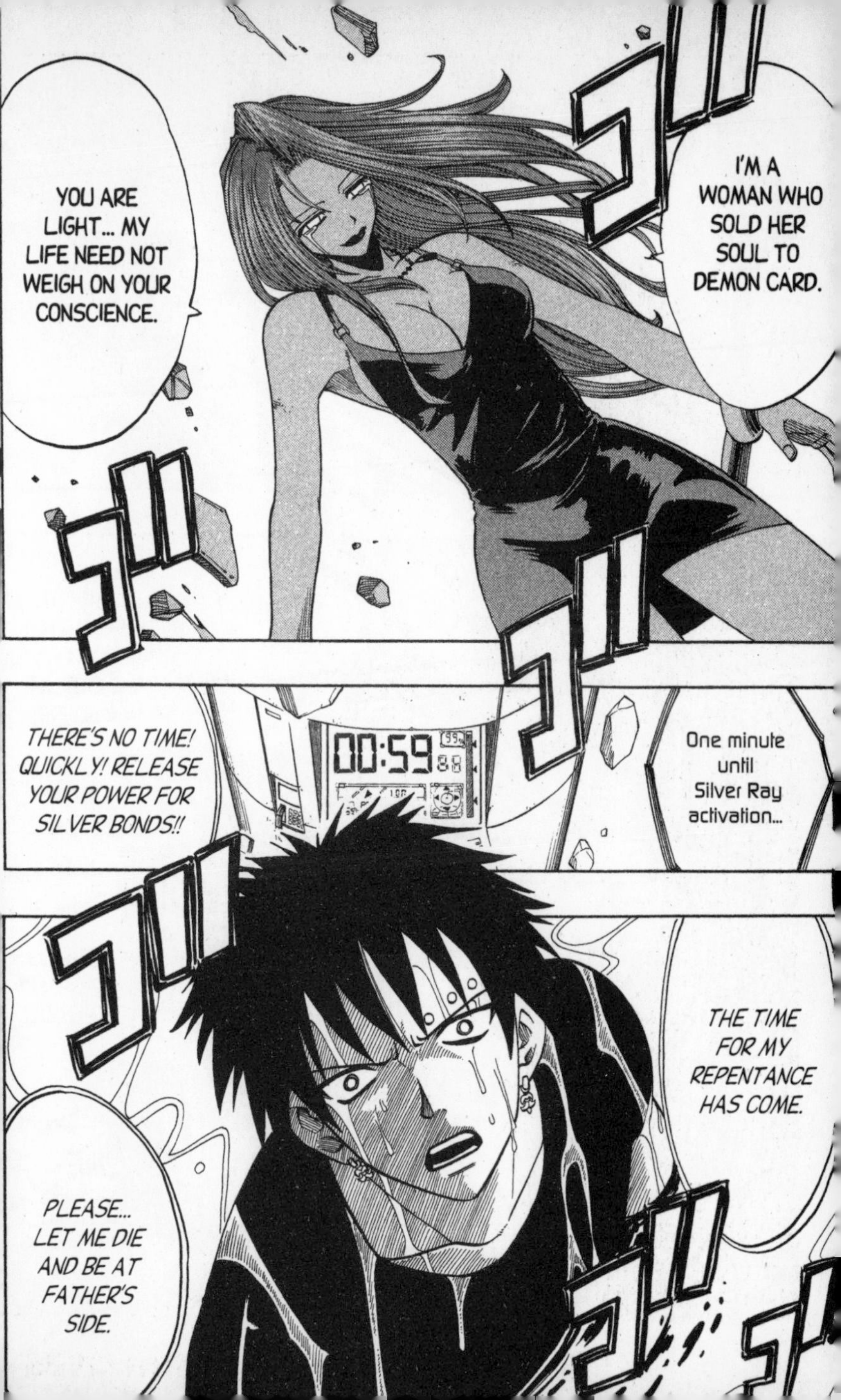
I'M A WOMAN WHO SOLD HER SOUL TO DEMON CARD.
YOU ARE LIGHT... MY LIFE NEED NOT WEIGH ON YOUR CONSCIENCE.
One minute until Silver Ray activation...
00:59
THERE'S NO TIME! QUICKLY! RELEASE YOUR POWER FOR SILVER BONDS!!
THE TIME FOR MY REPENTANCE HAS COME.
PLEASE... LET ME DIE AND BE AT FATHER'S SIDE.

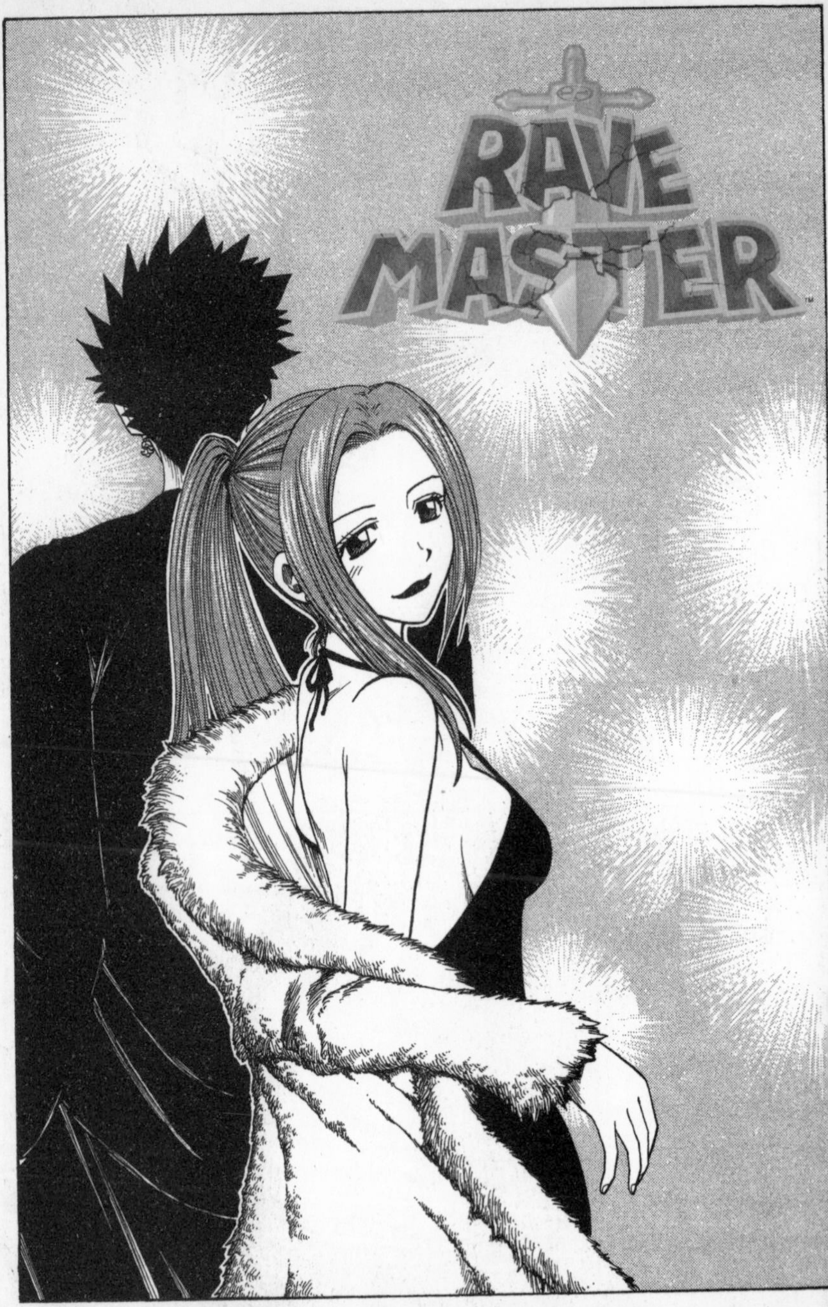
RAVE MASTER

RAVE:129 OVERLAPPING LIVES

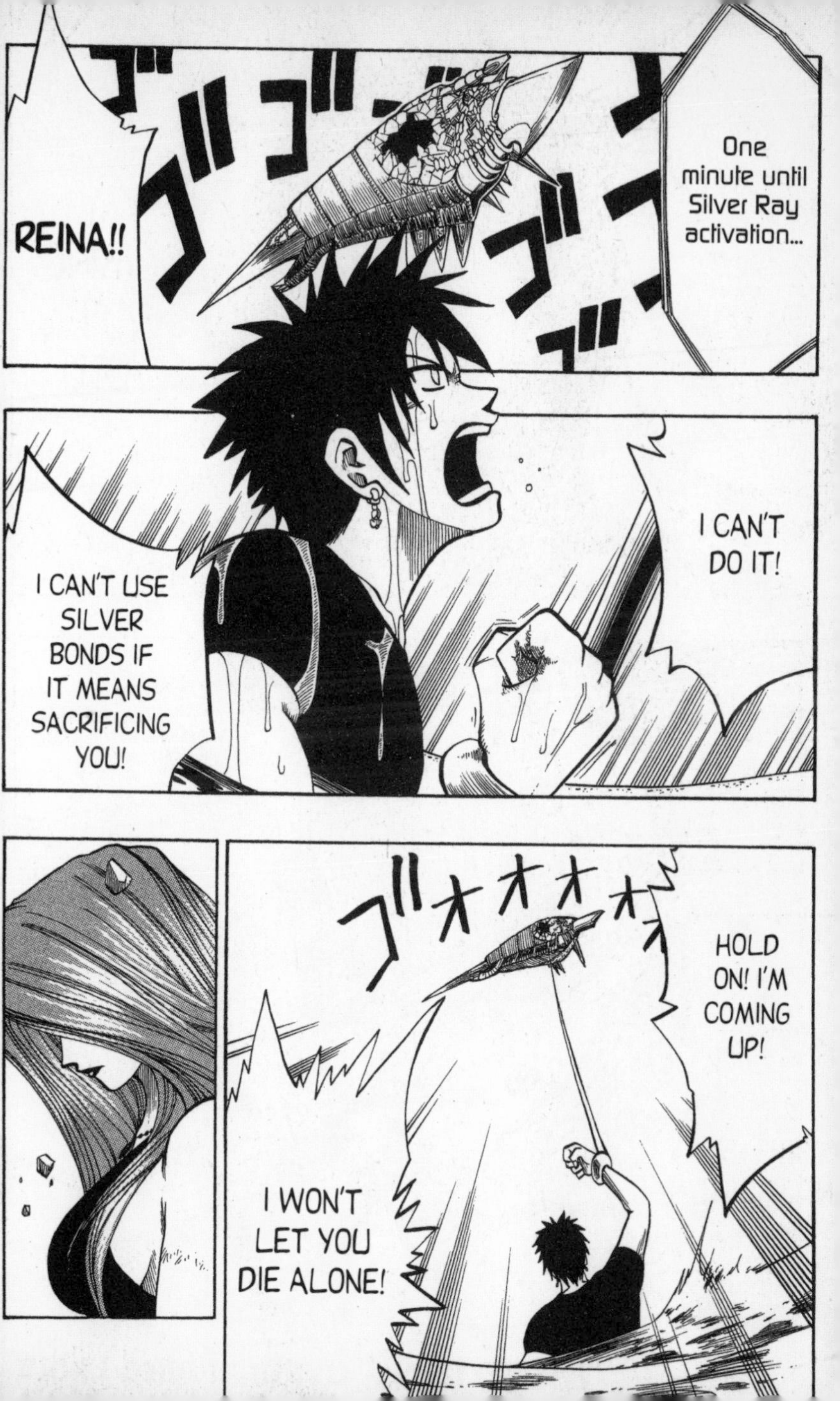
One minute until Silver Ray activation...
ゴゴゴゴ
REINA!!
I CAN'T DO IT!
I CAN'T USE SILVER BONDS IF IT MEANS SACRIFICING YOU!
ゴォォォォ
HOLD ON! I'M COMING UP!
I WON'T LET YOU DIE ALONE!

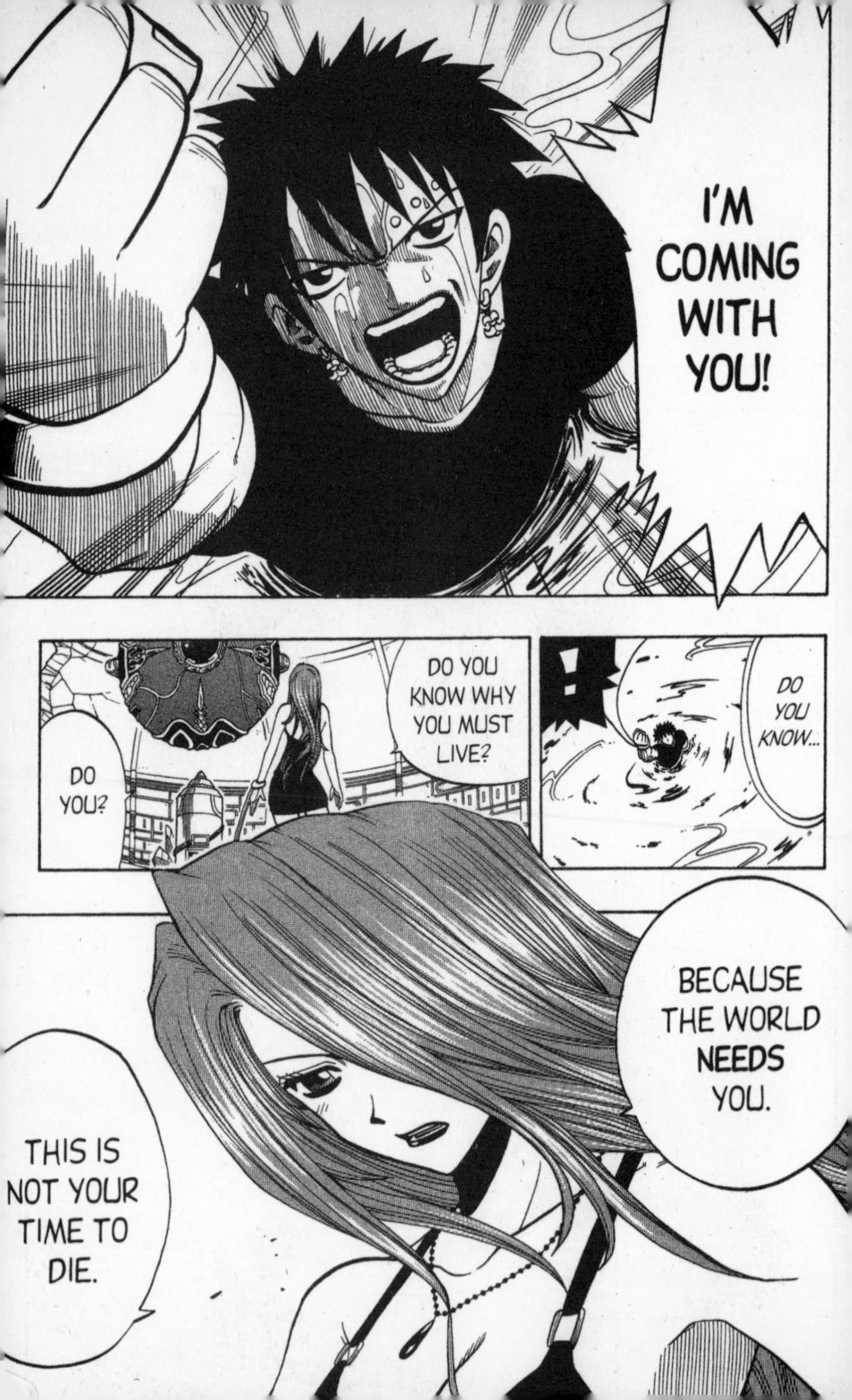
I'M COMING WITH YOU!
!
DO YOU KNOW...
DO YOU KNOW WHY YOU MUST LIVE?
DO YOU?
BECAUSE THE WORLD NEEDS YOU.
THIS IS NOT YOUR TIME TO DIE.

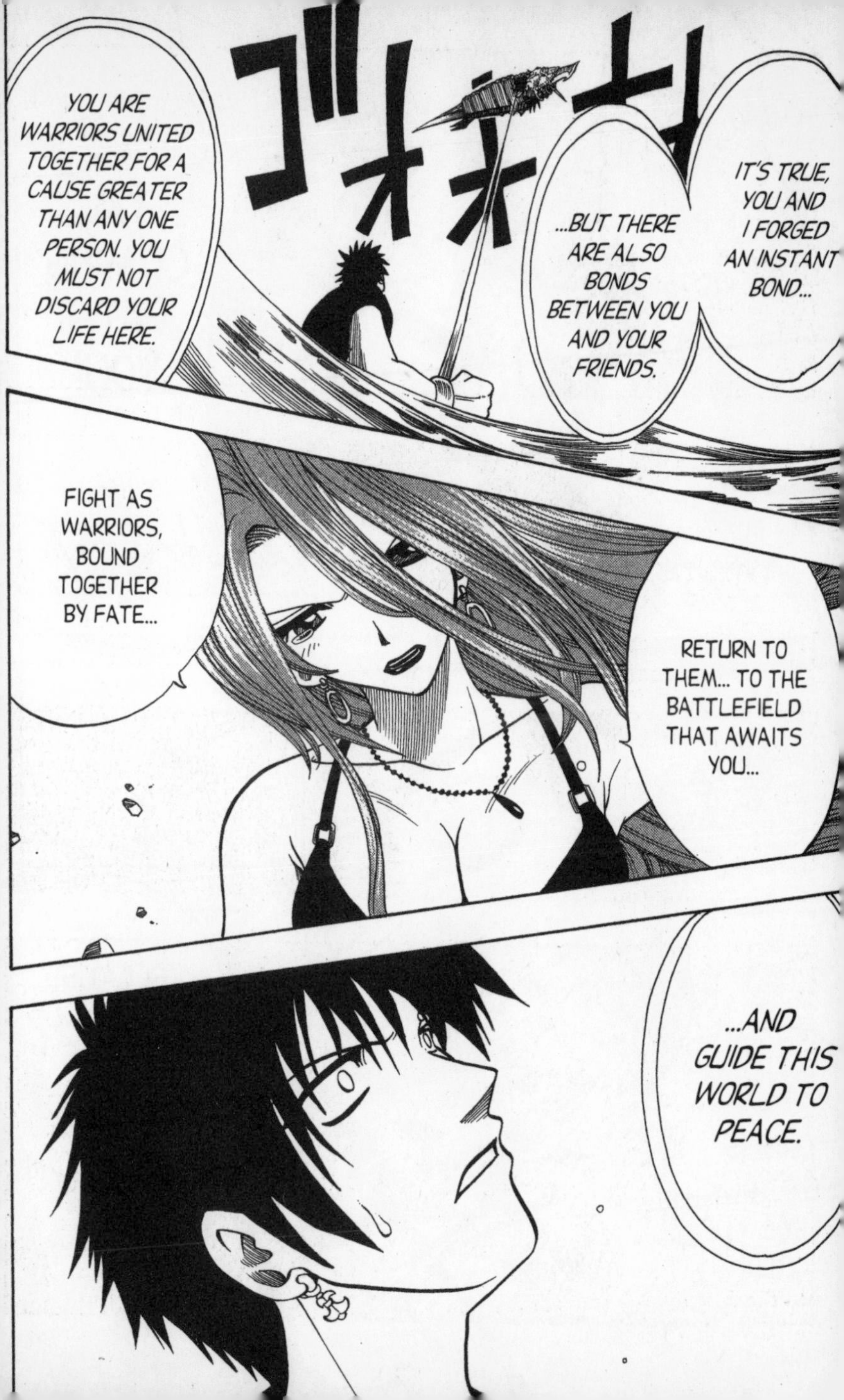
IT'S TRUE, YOU AND I FORGED AN INSTANT BOND...
...BUT THERE ARE ALSO BONDS BETWEEN YOU AND YOUR FRIENDS.
YOU ARE WARRIORS UNITED TOGETHER FOR A CAUSE GREATER THAN ANY ONE PERSON. YOU MUST NOT DISCARD YOUR LIFE HERE.
RETURN TO THEM... TO THE BATTLEFIELD THAT AWAITS YOU...
FIGHT AS WARRIORS, BOUND TOGETHER BY FATE...
...AND GUIDE THIS WORLD TO PEACE.

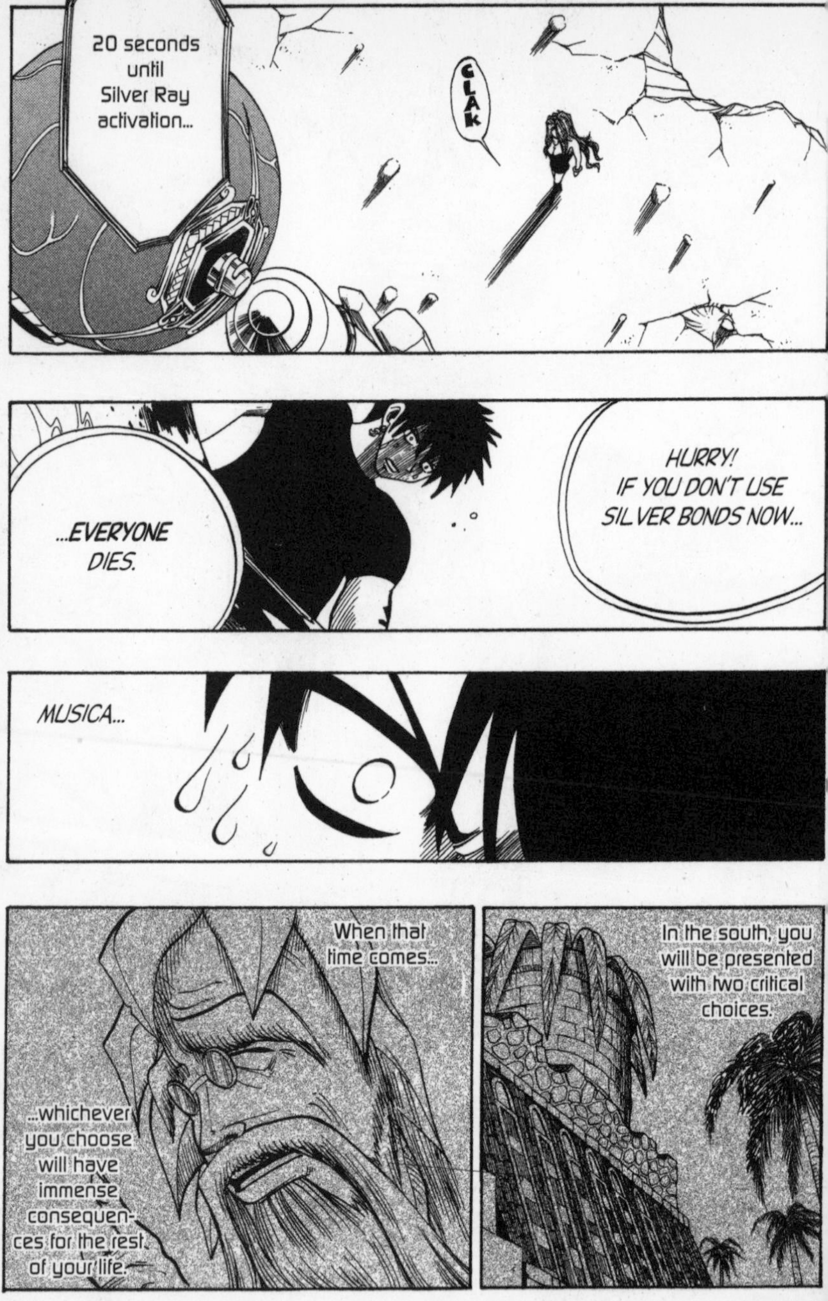
CLAK
20 seconds until Silver Ray activation...
HURRY! IF YOU DON'T USE SILVER BONDS NOW...
...EVERYONE DIES.
MUSICA...
In the south, you will be presented with two critical choices.
When that time comes...
...whichever you choose will have immense consequen-ces for the rest of your life.

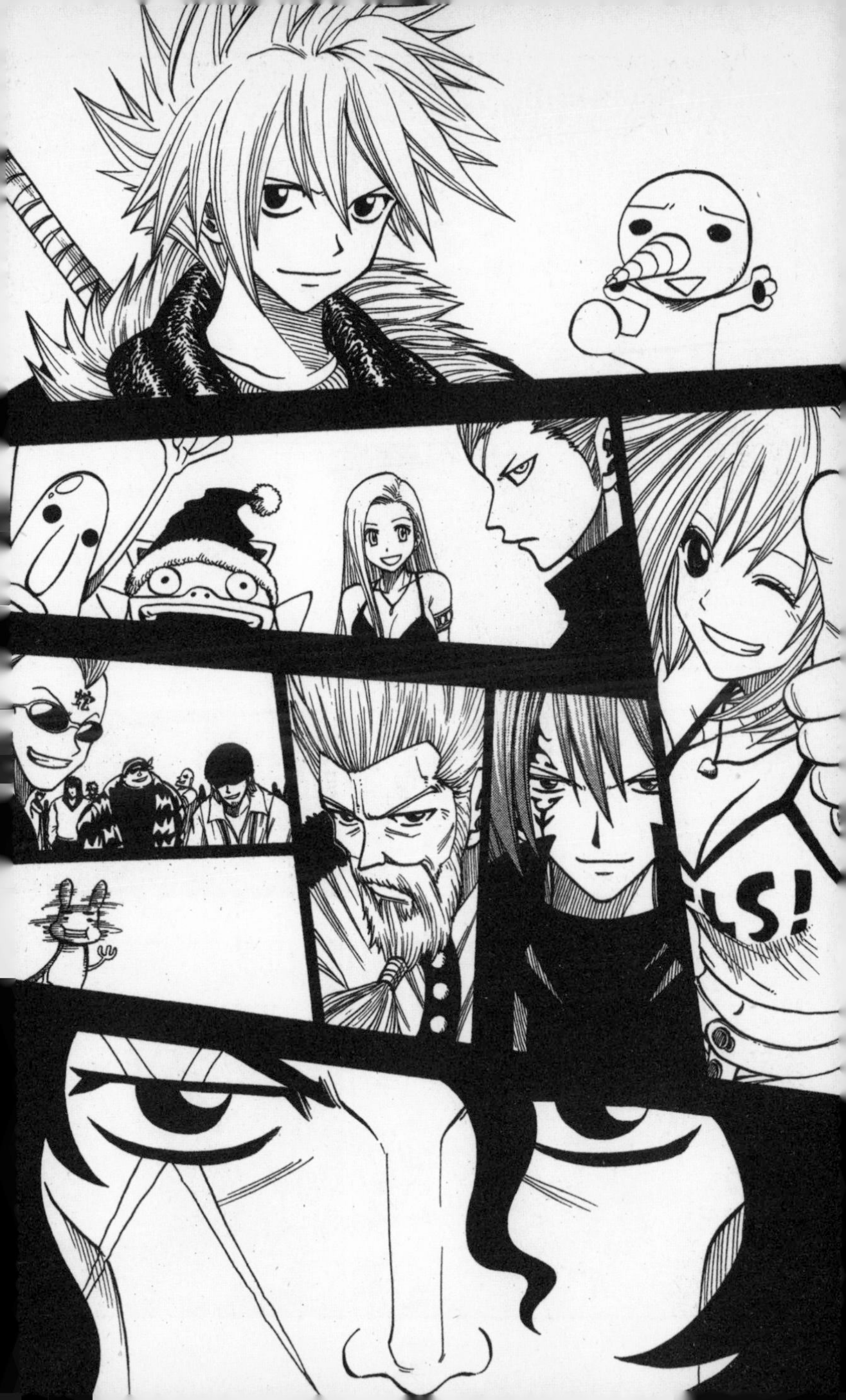

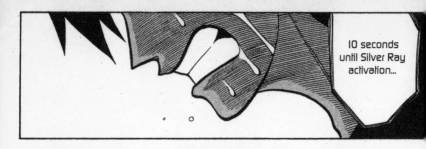

10 seconds until Silver Ray activation...

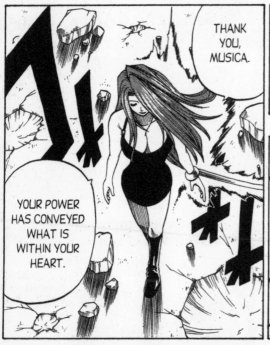

THANK YOU, MUSICA.

YOUR POWER HAS CONVEYED WHAT IS WITHIN YOUR HEART.

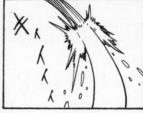

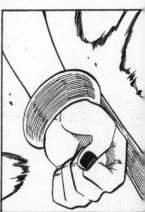

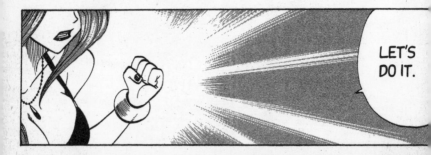

LET'S DO IT.

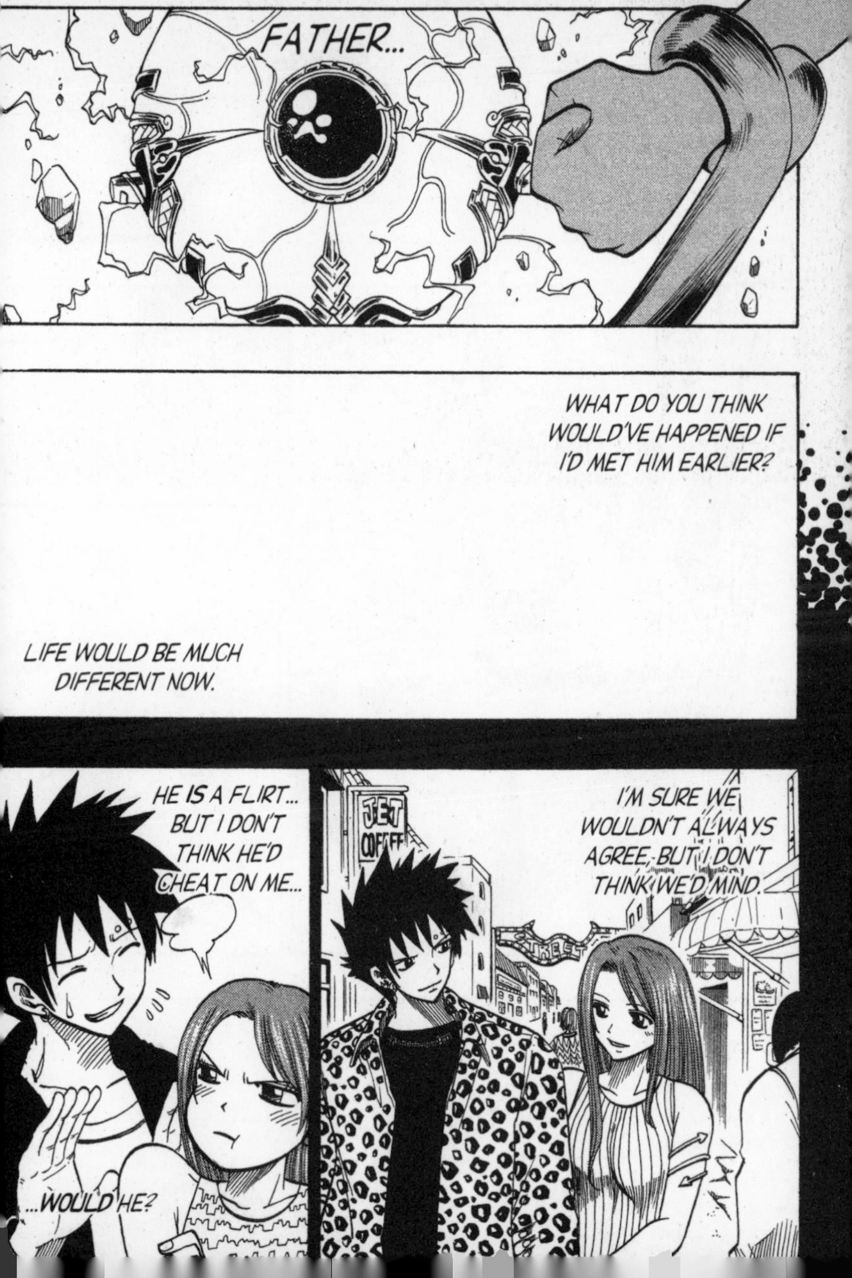
FATHER...
WHAT DO YOU THINK WOULD'VE HAPPENED IF I'D MET HIM EARLIER?
LIFE WOULD BE MUCH DIFFERENT NOW.
I'M SURE WE WOULDN'T ALWAYS AGREE, BUT I DON'T THINK WE'D MIND.
HE **IS** A FLIRT... BUT I DON'T THINK HE'D CHEAT ON ME...
...WOULD HE?

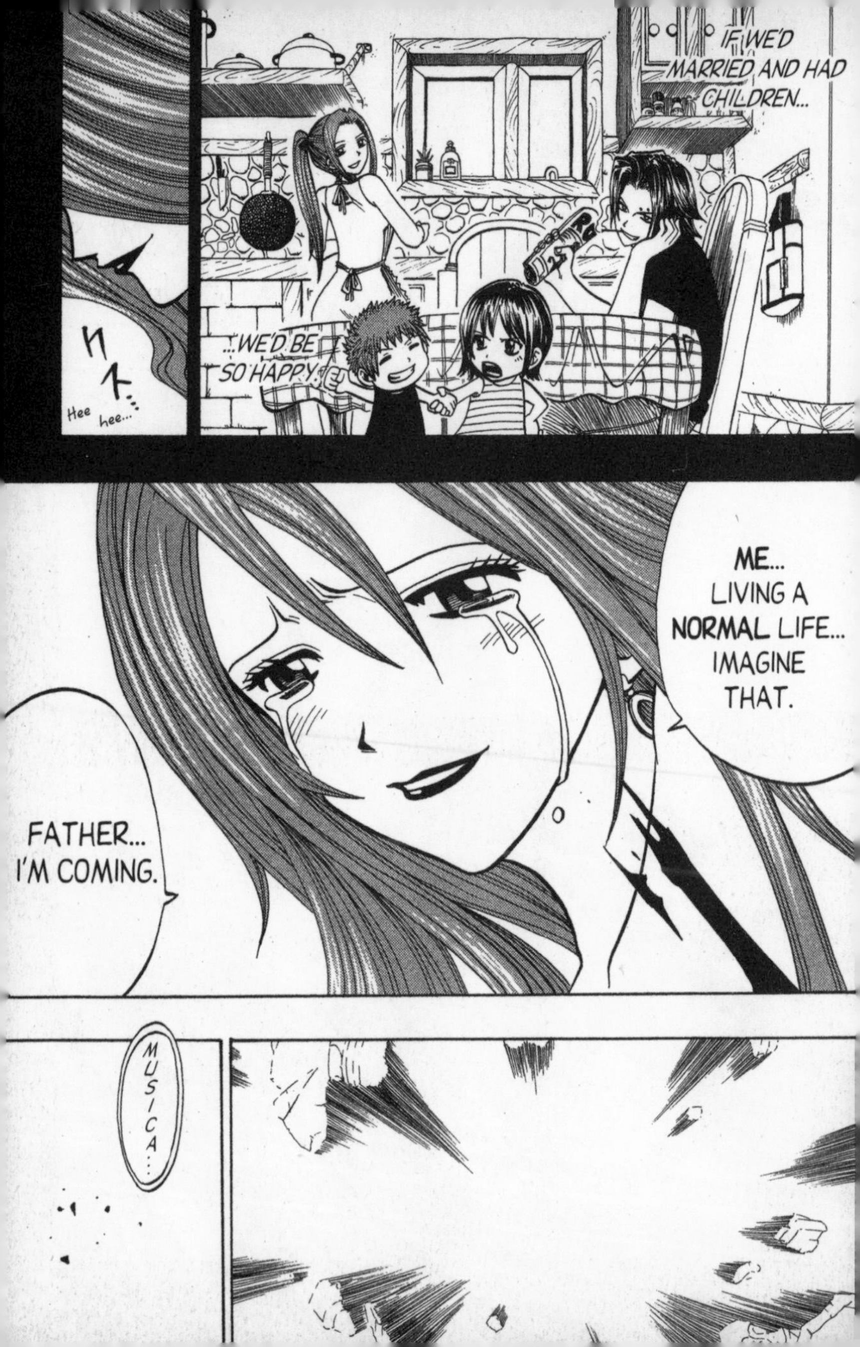
IF WE'D MARRIED AND HAD CHILDREN...
...WE'D BE SO HAPPY.
Hee hee...
ME... LIVING A NORMAL LIFE... IMAGINE THAT.
FATHER... I'M COMING.
MUSICA...

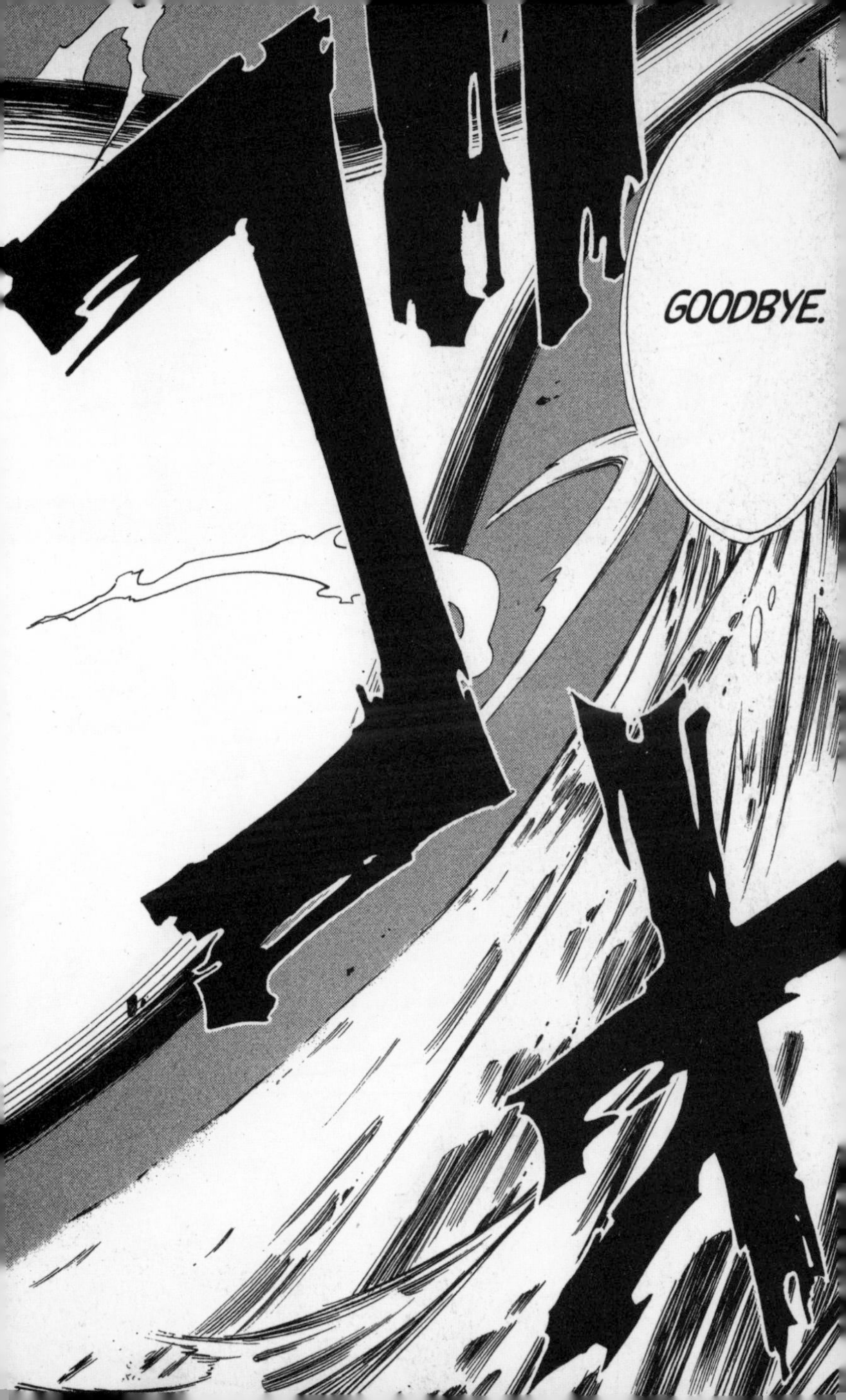
GOODBYE.

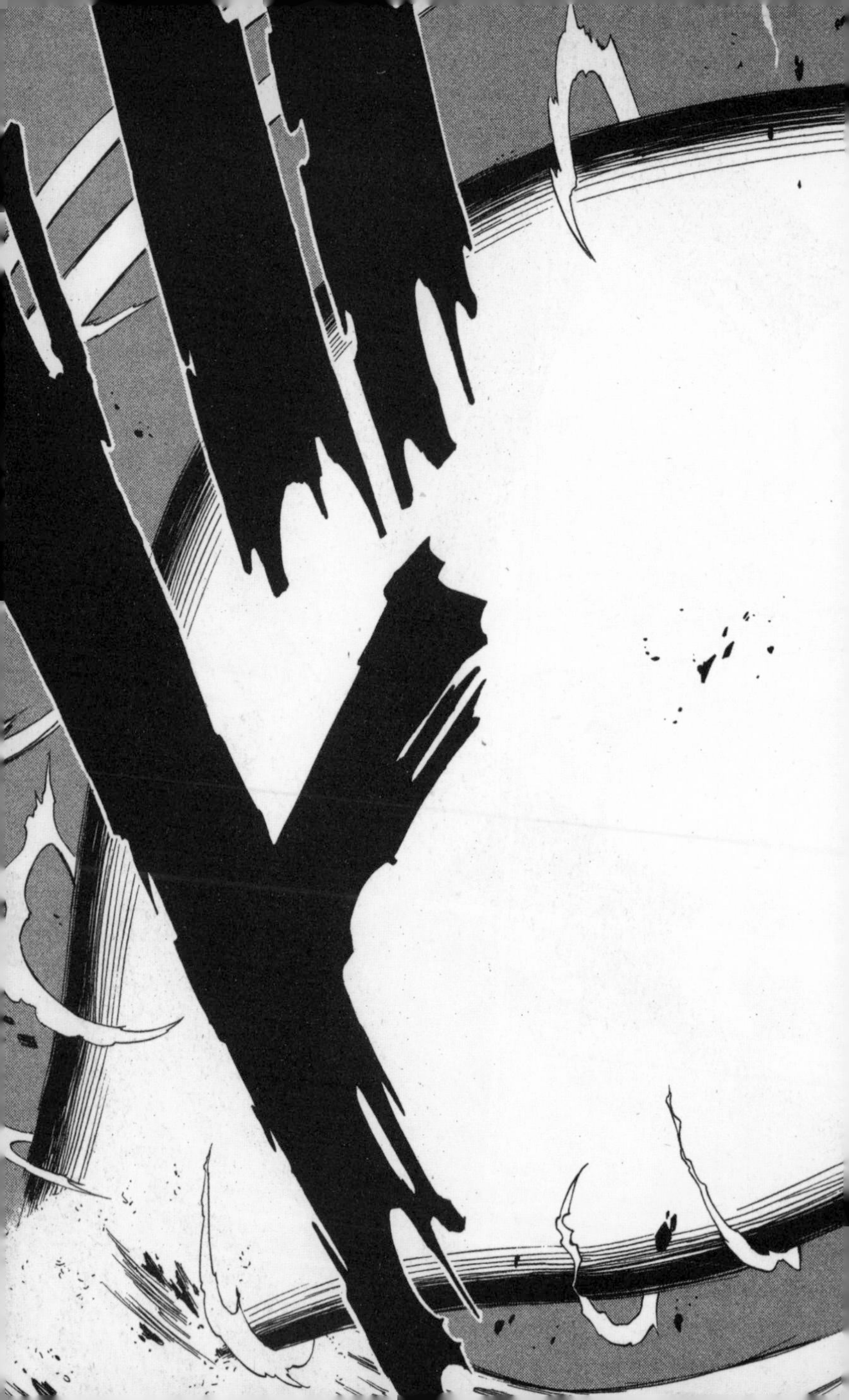

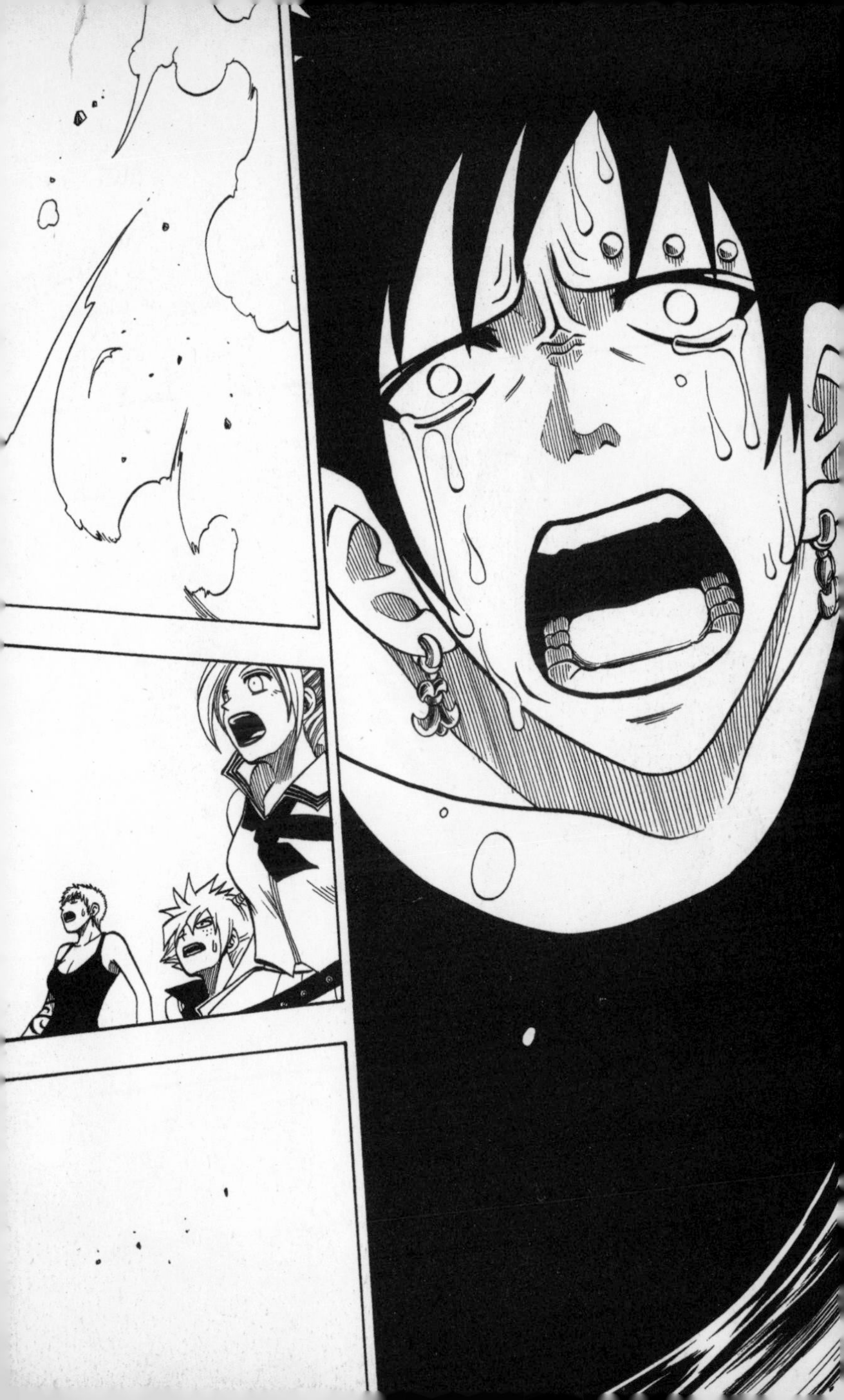

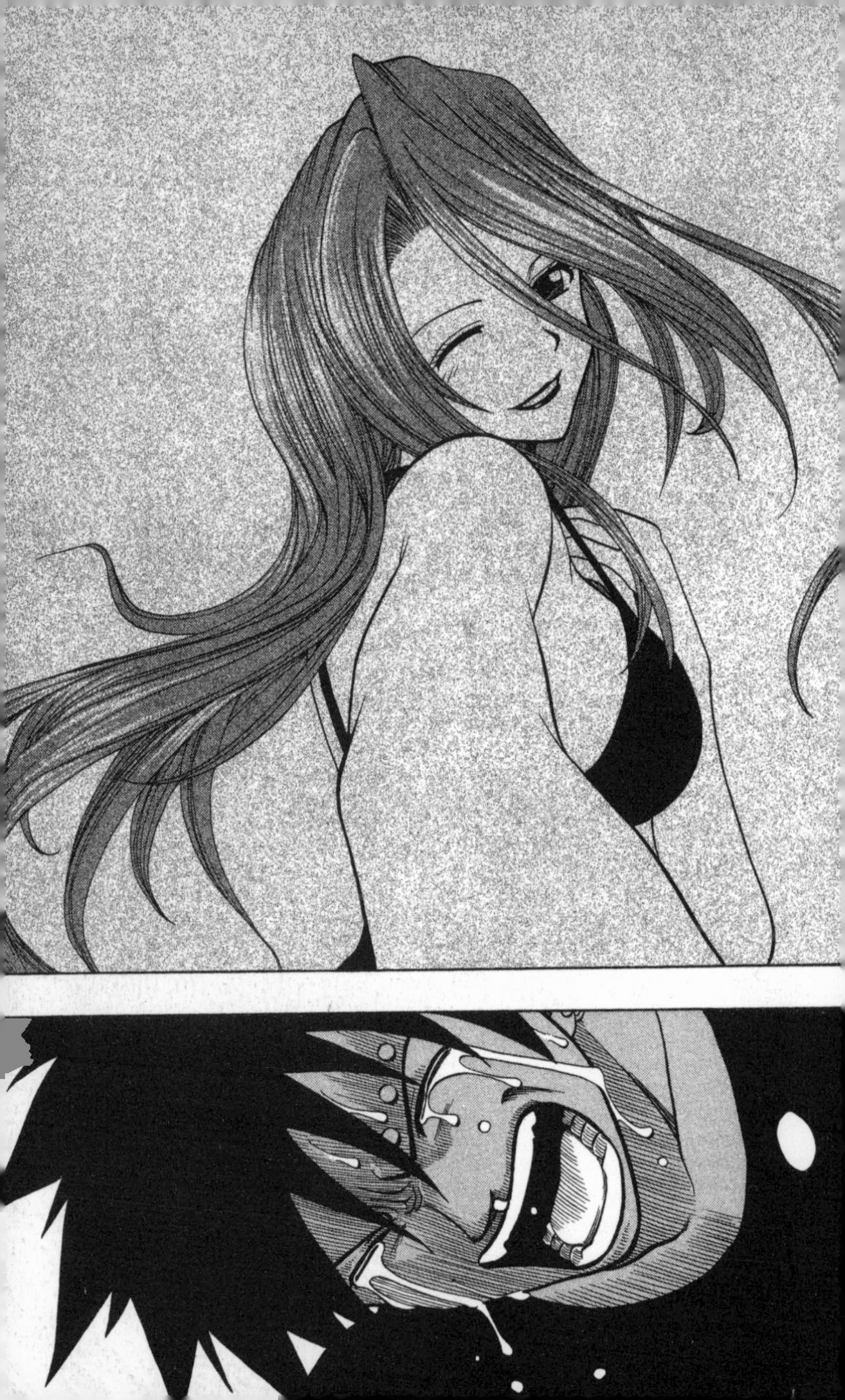

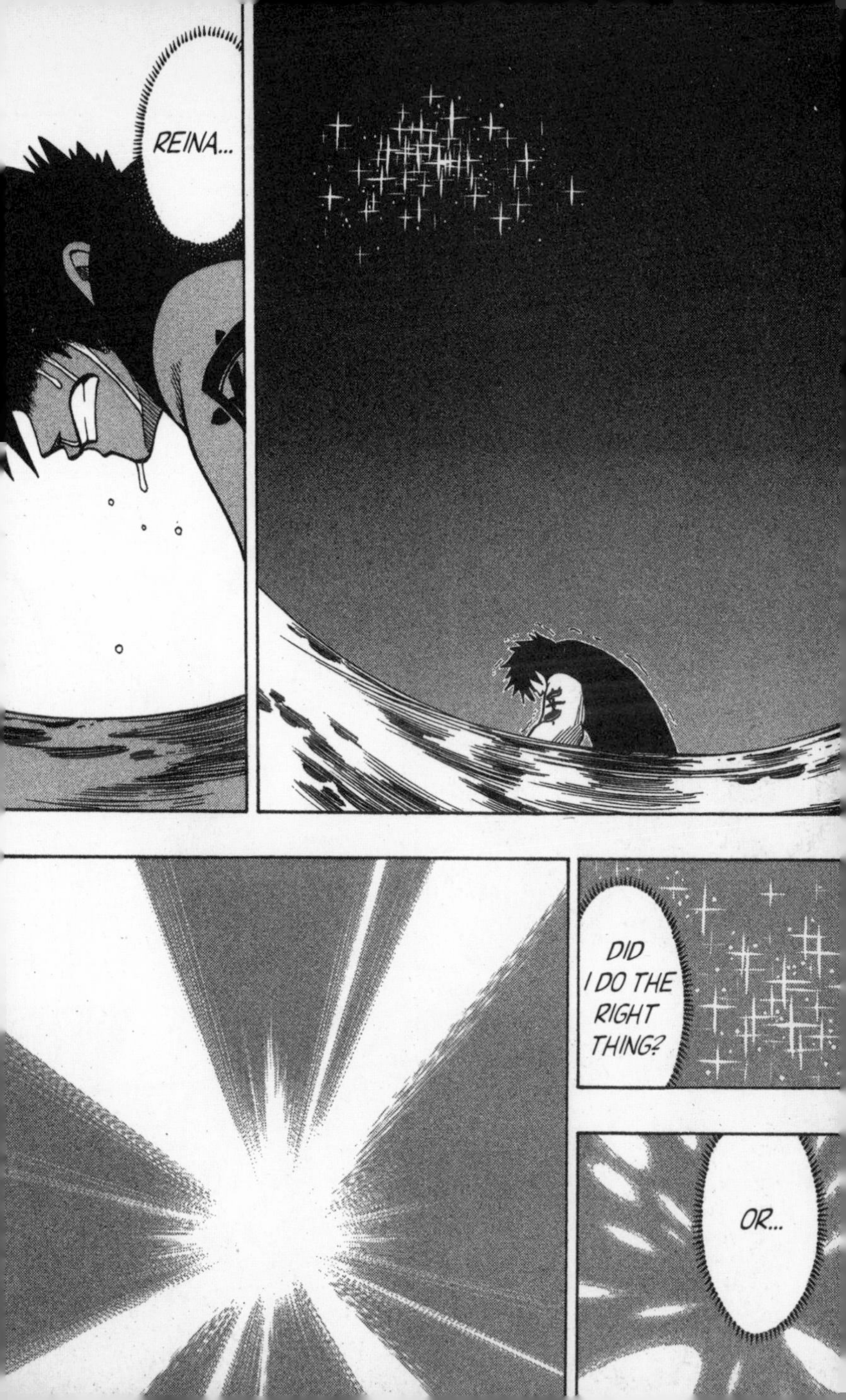
REINA...
DID I DO THE RIGHT THING?
OR...

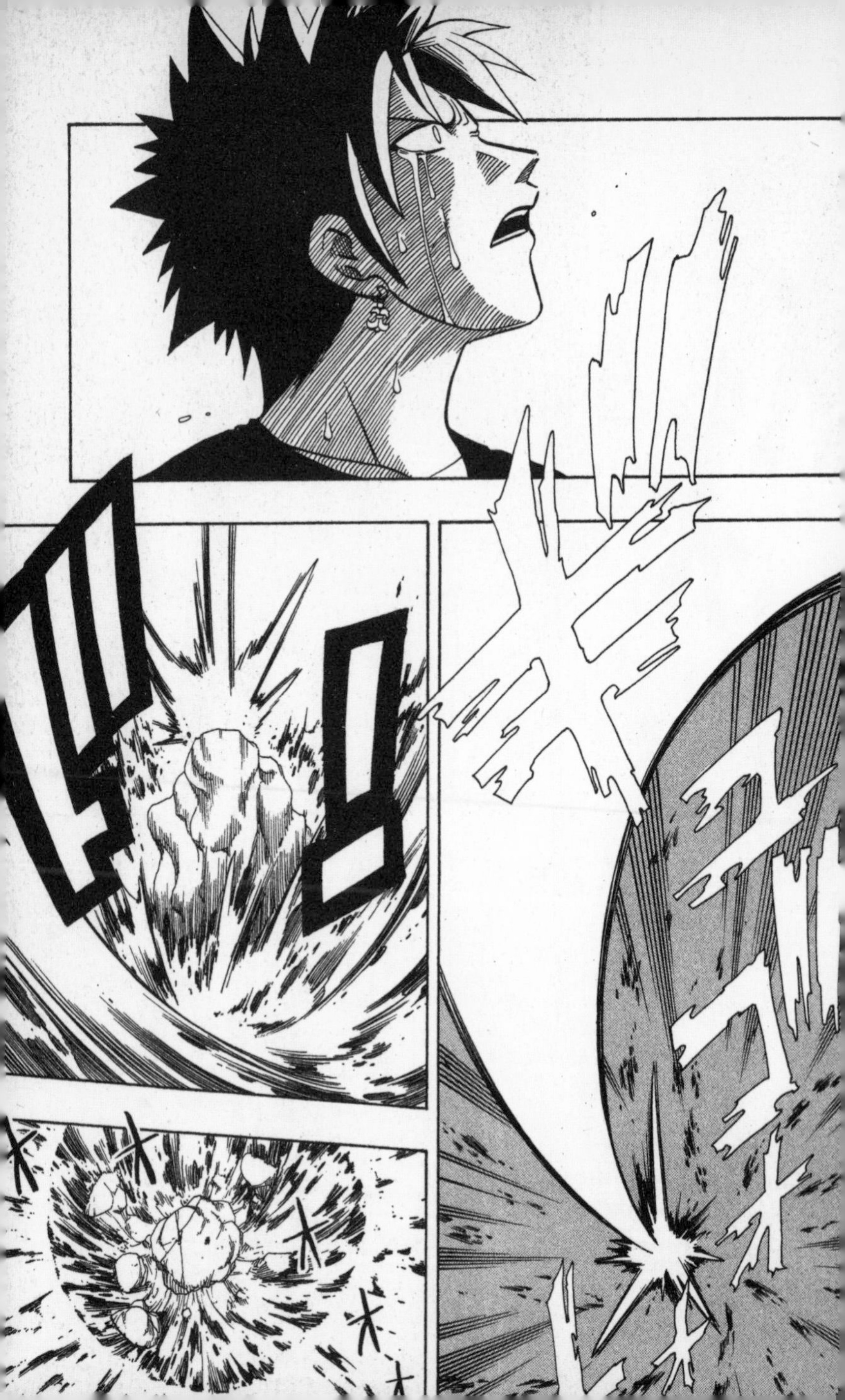

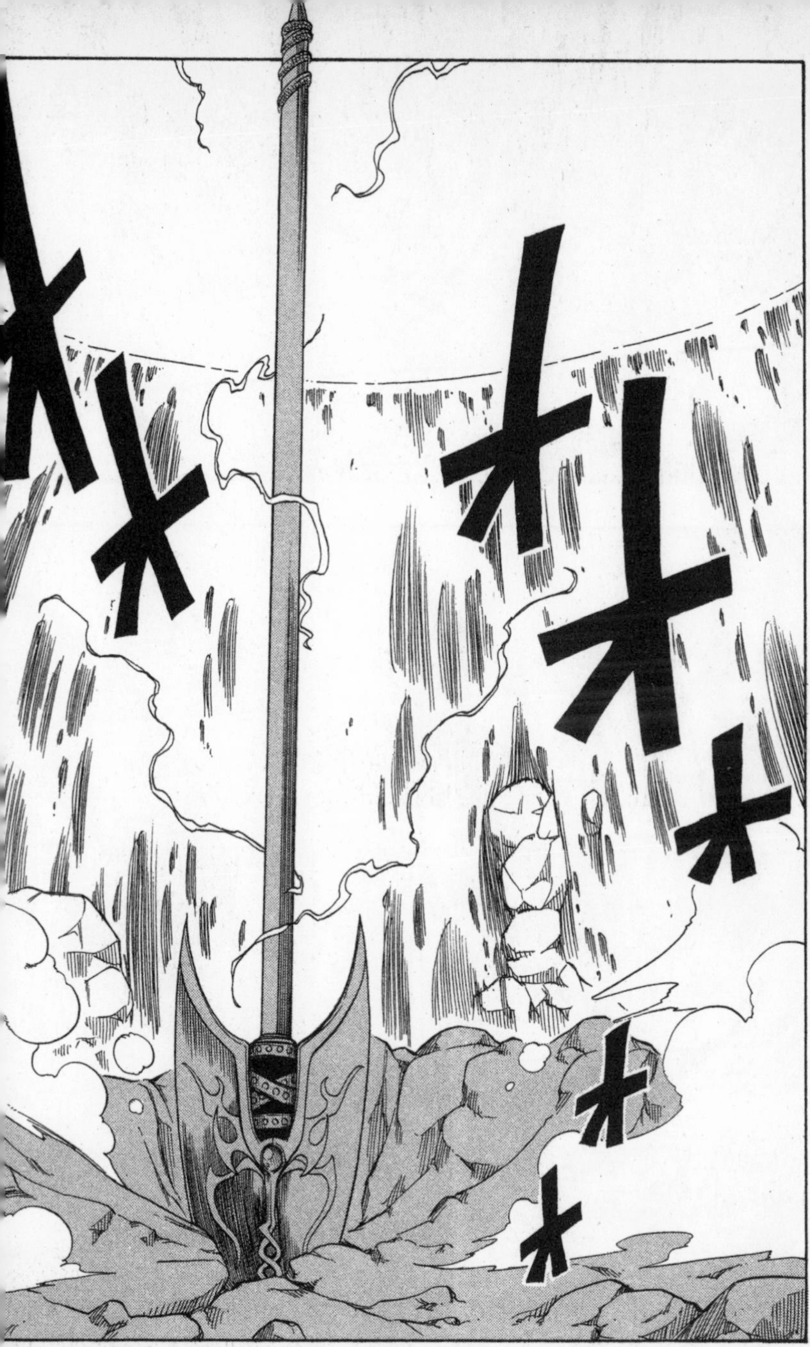

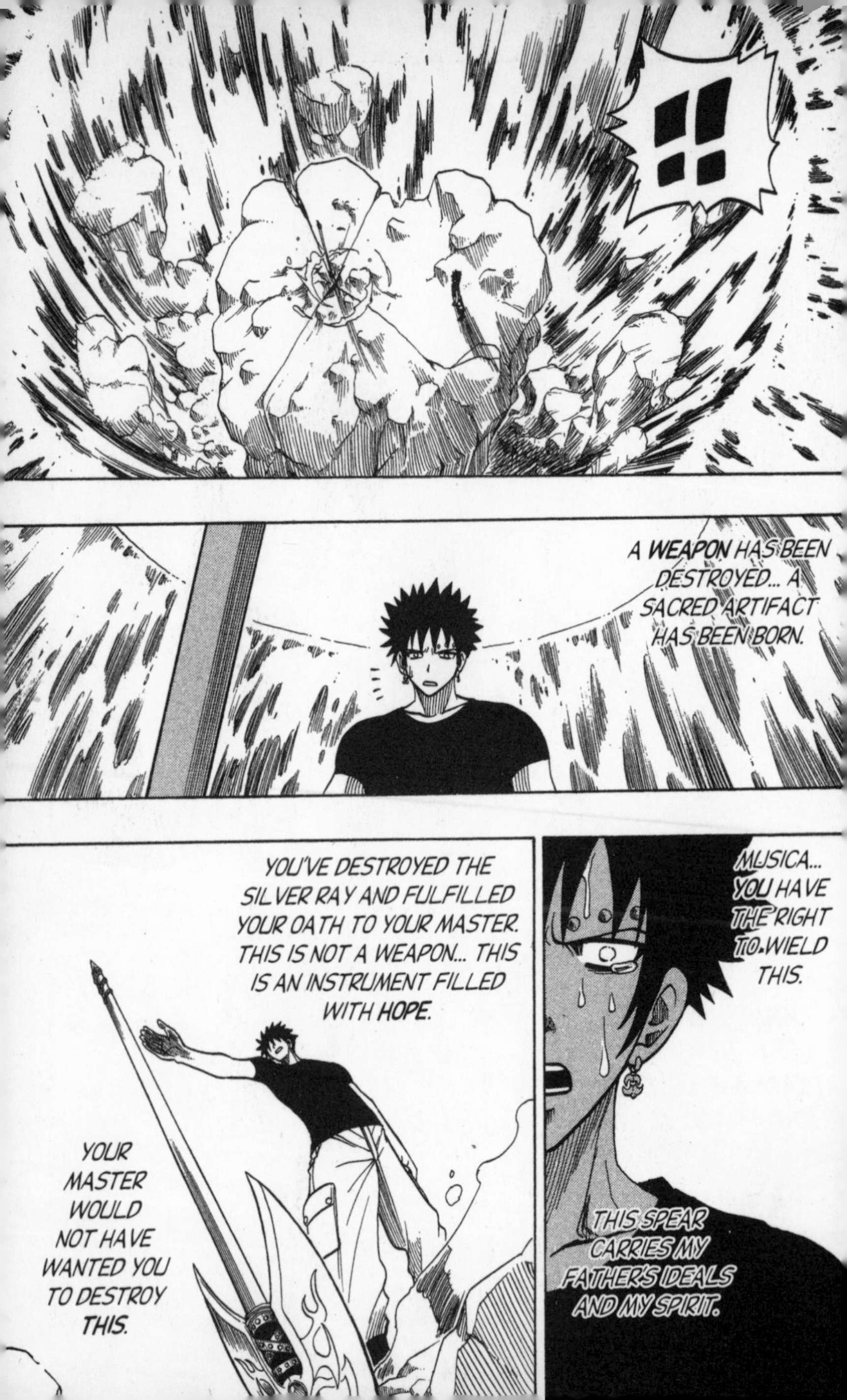
!!
A WEAPON HAS BEEN DESTROYED... A SACRED ARTIFACT HAS BEEN BORN.
MUSICA... YOU HAVE THE RIGHT TO WIELD THIS.
THIS SPEAR CARRIES MY FATHER'S IDEALS AND MY SPIRIT.
YOU'VE DESTROYED THE SILVER RAY AND FULFILLED YOUR OATH TO YOUR MASTER. THIS IS NOT A WEAPON... THIS IS AN INSTRUMENT FILLED WITH HOPE.
YOUR MASTER WOULD NOT HAVE WANTED YOU TO DESTROY THIS.

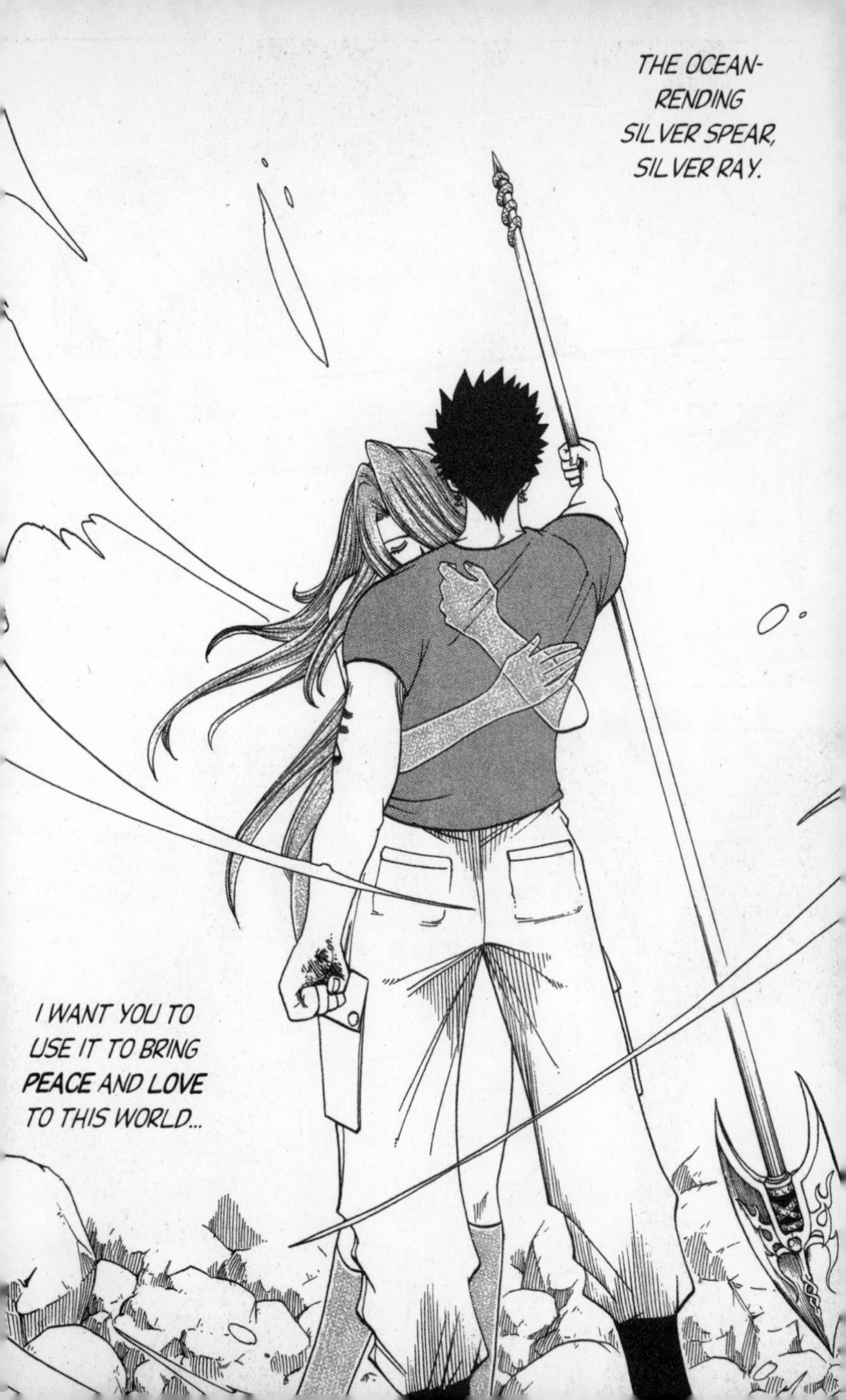
THE OCEAN-RENDING SILVER SPEAR, SILVER RAY.
I WANT YOU TO USE IT TO BRING PEACE AND LOVE TO THIS WORLD...

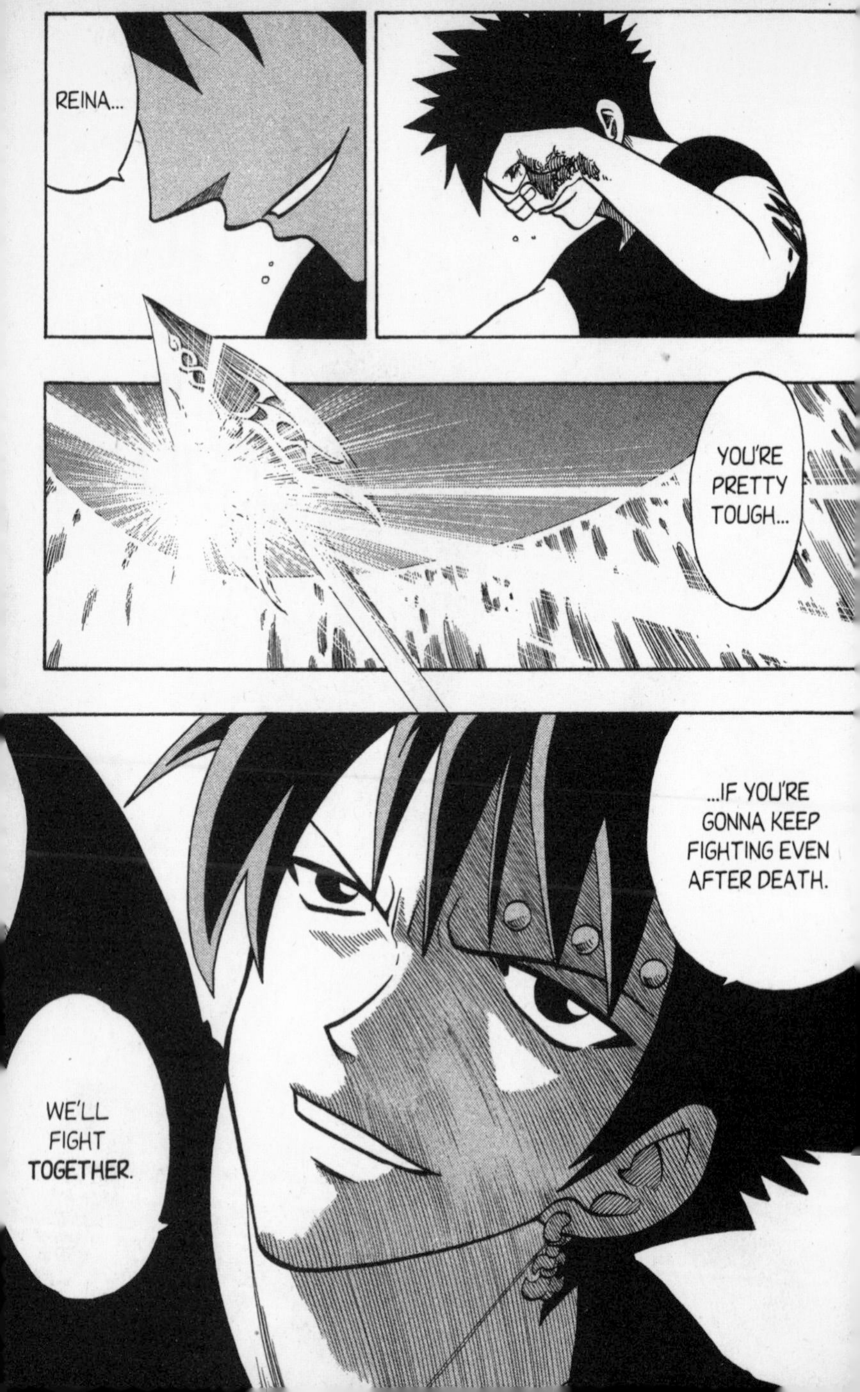
REINA...
YOU'RE PRETTY TOUGH...
...IF YOU'RE GONNA KEEP FIGHTING EVEN AFTER DEATH.
WE'LL FIGHT TOGETHER.

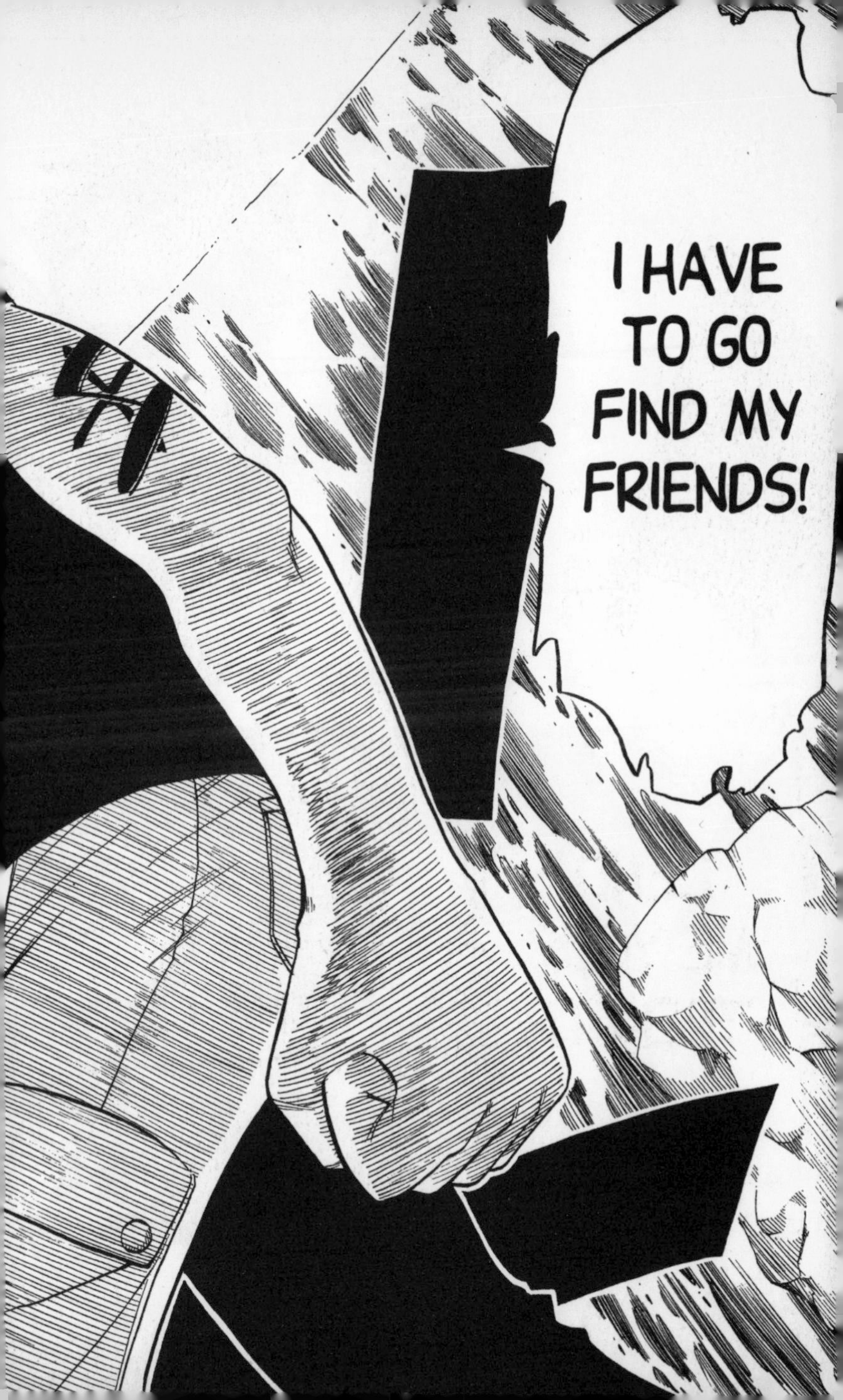
I HAVE TO GO FIND MY FRIENDS!

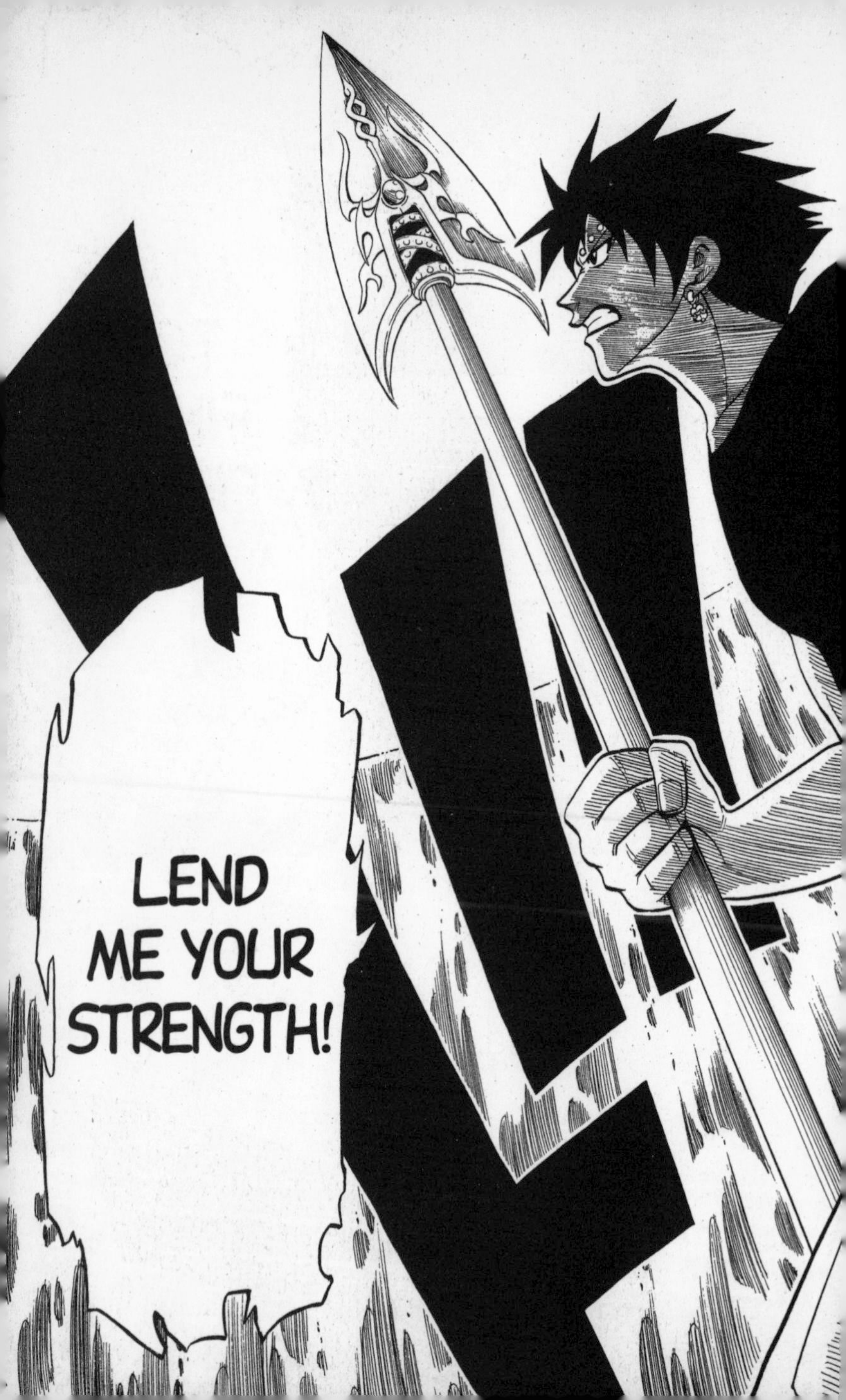
LEND ME YOUR STRENGTH!

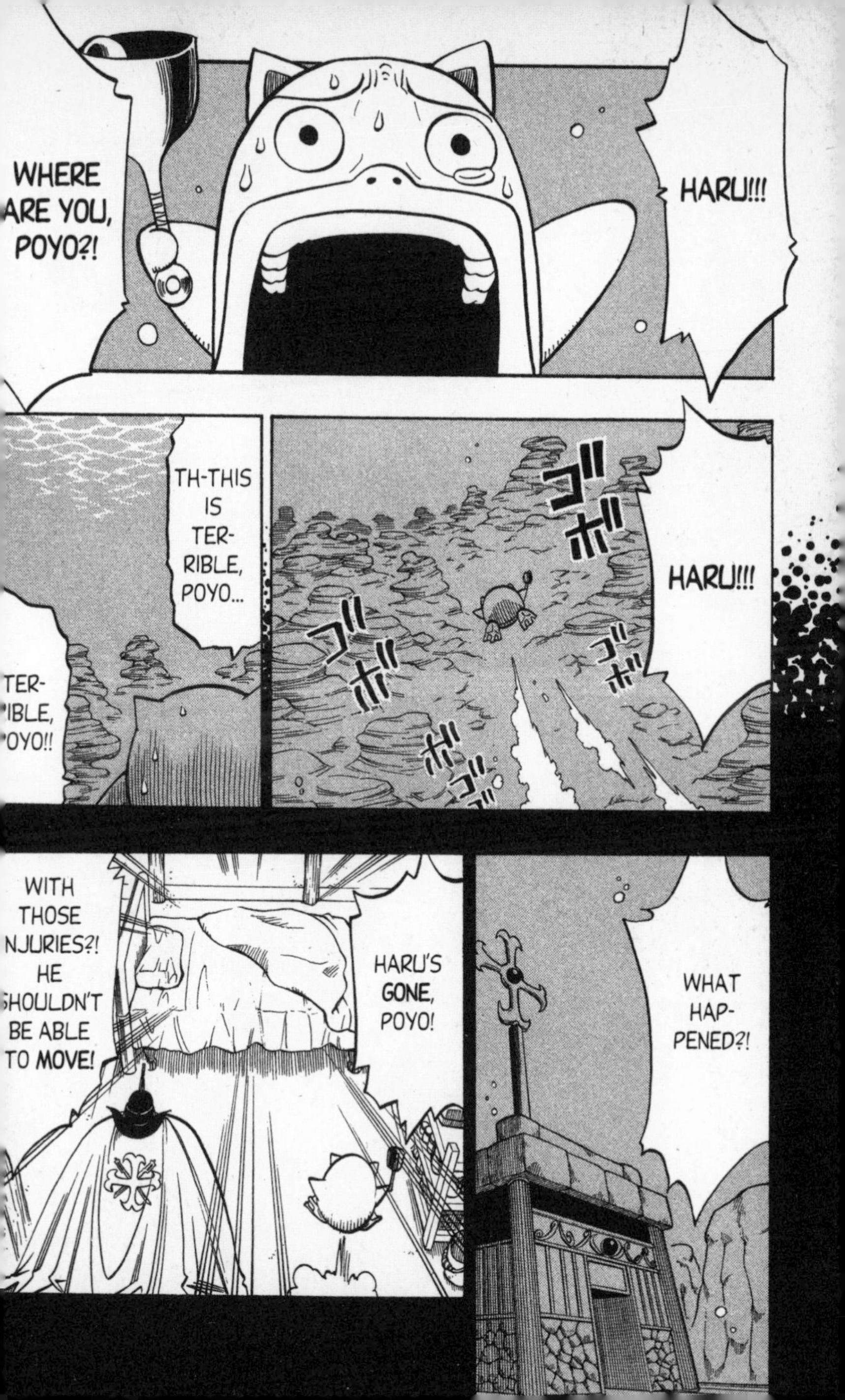
HARU!!!
WHERE ARE YOU, POYO?!
HARU!!!
ゴボ
ゴボ
ゴボ
ボゴ
TH-THIS IS TER-RIBLE, POYO...
TER-
IBLE,
OYO!!
WHAT HAP-PENED?!
HARU'S GONE, POYO!
WITH THOSE
NJURIES?! HE
SHOULDN'T BE ABLE TO MOVE!

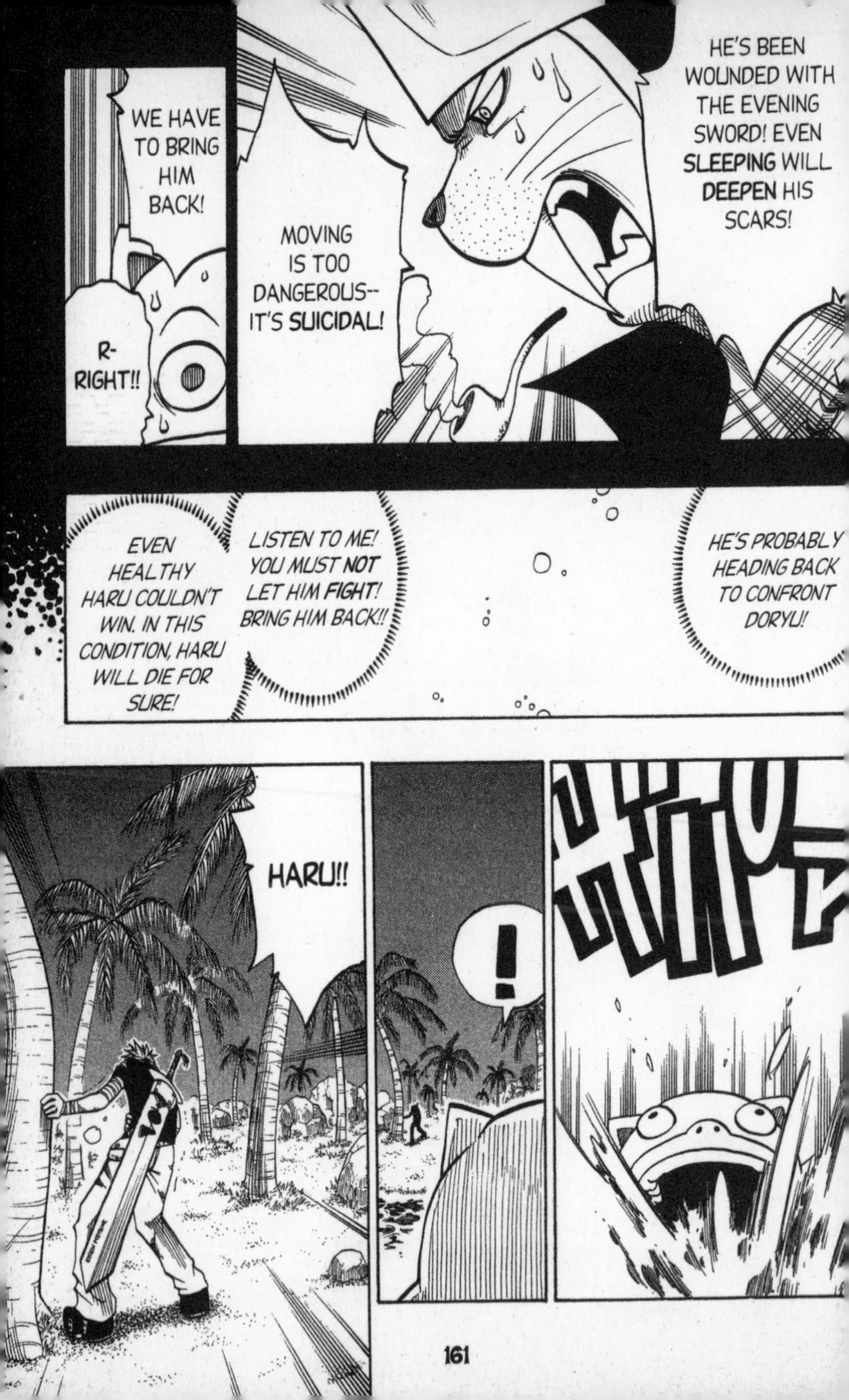
HE'S BEEN WOUNDED WITH THE EVENING SWORD! EVEN **SLEEPING** WILL **DEEPEN** HIS SCARS!
MOVING IS TOO DANGEROUS-- IT'S **SUICIDAL**!
WE HAVE TO BRING HIM BACK!
R- RIGHT!!
HE'S PROBABLY HEADING BACK TO CONFRONT DORYU!
*LISTEN TO ME! YOU MUST **NOT** LET HIM **FIGHT**! BRING HIM BACK!!*
EVEN HEALTHY HARU COULDN'T WIN. IN THIS CONDITION, HARU WILL DIE FOR SURE!
!
HARU!!

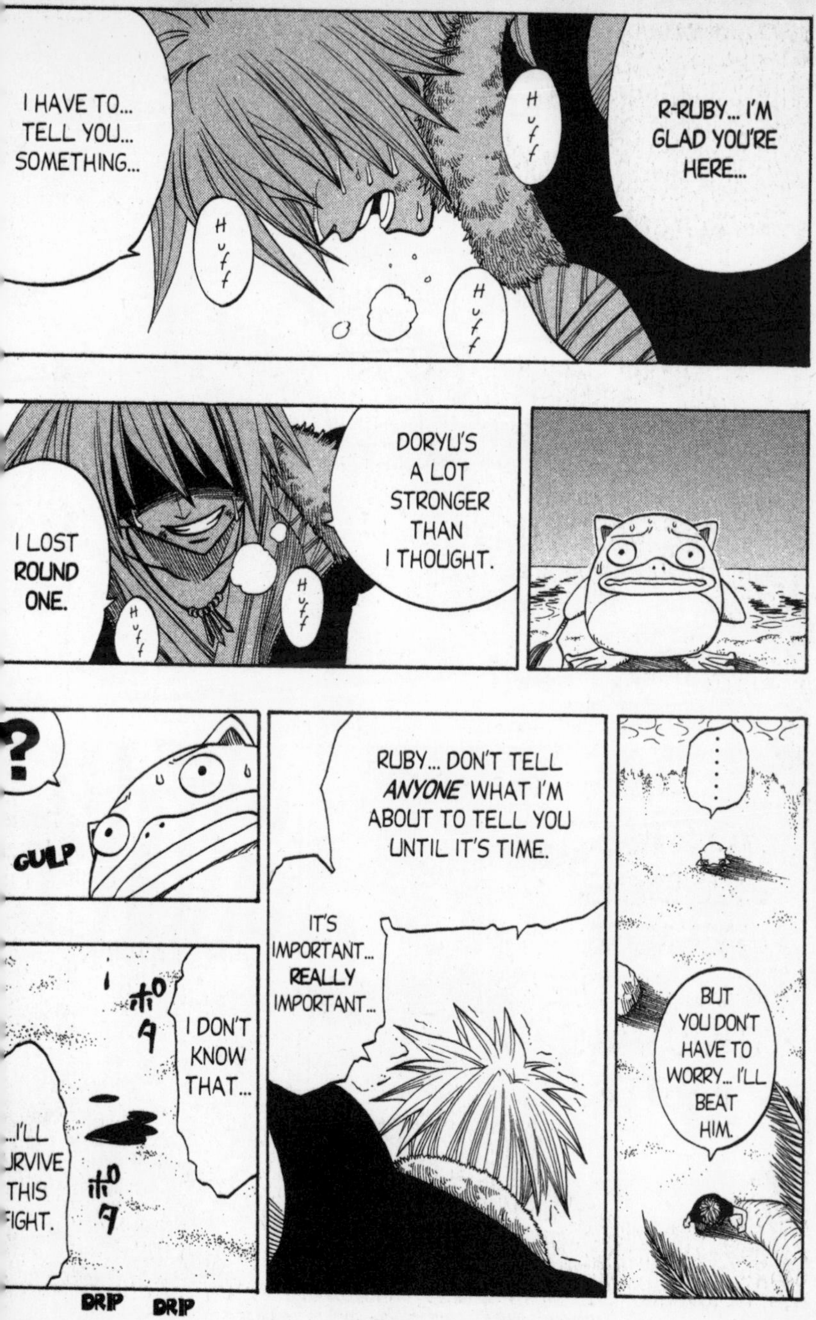
R-RUBY... I'M GLAD YOU'RE HERE...
Huff
Huff
Huff
I HAVE TO... TELL YOU... SOMETHING...
DORYU'S A LOT STRONGER THAN I THOUGHT.
Huff
I LOST ROUND ONE.
Huff
......
BUT YOU DON'T HAVE TO WORRY... I'LL BEAT HIM.
RUBY... DON'T TELL *ANYONE* WHAT I'M ABOUT TO TELL YOU UNTIL IT'S TIME.
IT'S IMPORTANT... **REALLY** IMPORTANT...
?
GULP
I DON'T KNOW THAT...
...I'LL URVIVE THIS FIGHT.
DRIP
DRIP

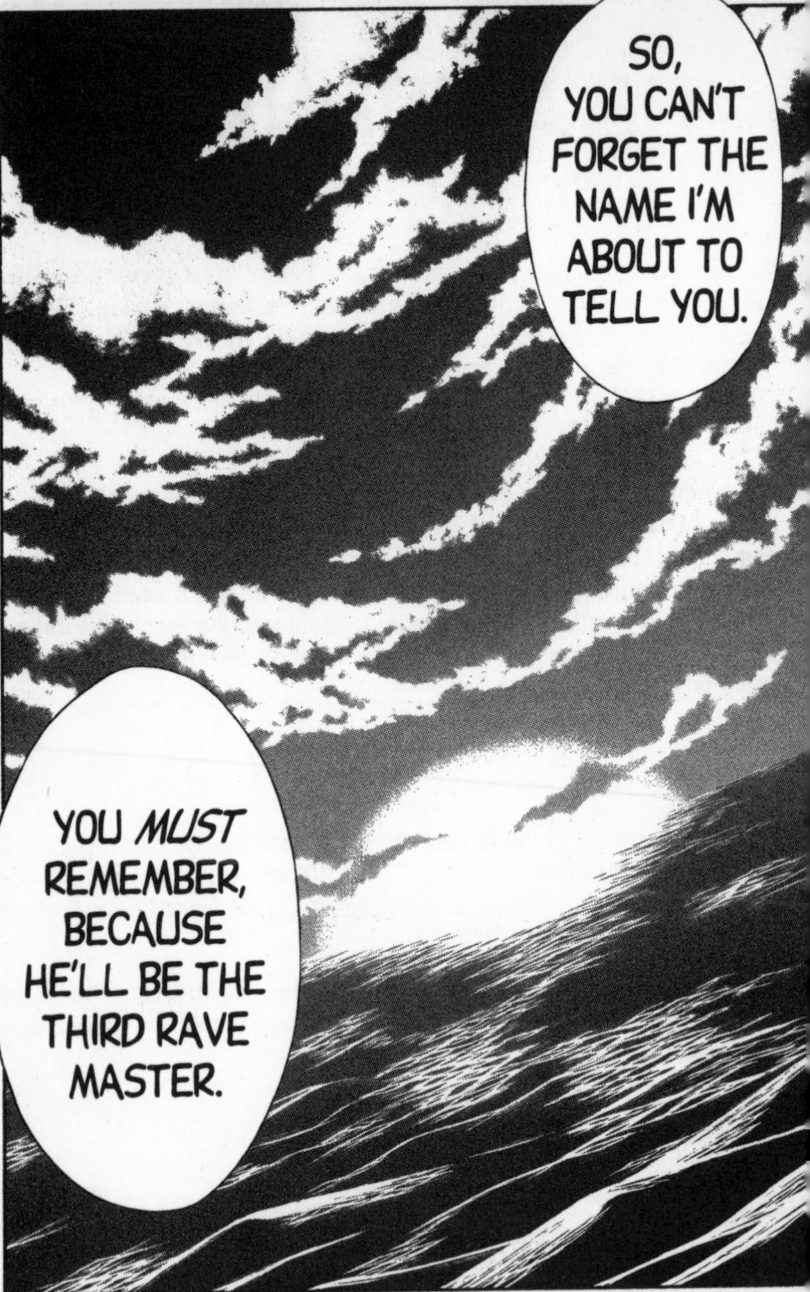
SO, YOU CAN'T FORGET THE NAME I'M ABOUT TO TELL YOU.
YOU *MUST* REMEMBER, BECAUSE HE'LL BE THE THIRD RAVE MASTER.

TO BE CONTINUED

Q&A CORNER!!

Q. Nice to meet you, Hiro Mashima-sensei!! I want to be a manga-ka like you, but, every time I start drawing something, I start thinking, "Can't I draw this just a little better?" Hiro Mashima-sensei, what do you think? (Shige-ken--He In Whom Insects Awaken The Urge To Kill)

A. Long pen name!! To be blunt, I think you've gotta draw even if you think you're no good at it. If you don't draw lots, you won't get better. Even now, I'm only somewhat satisfied with my own work. I still have lots of fun anyway. (^_^) Your work'll get better, you'll see!! But first you need to practice! If you're serious about being a manga-ka, take what you're drawing now and finish a portfolio and bring it over to an editorial dept! Good luck!

Q. Is it just me, or do all the female characters in Rave Master have big boobs? Do you have a thing for **GIANT BOOBS** or something?
(Chiba-ken/ Griff, Nakajima & Friends)

A. Nicely put. Not that I want to disappoint everyone, but...I'm actually not all that into breasts. Not that I have a particular *dislike*. (^_^) Just so you know.

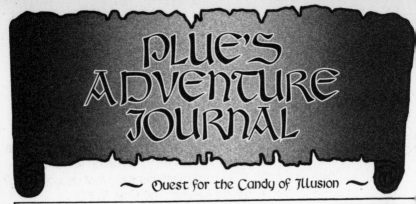

PLUE'S ADVENTURE JOURNAL

~ Quest for the Candy of Illusion ~

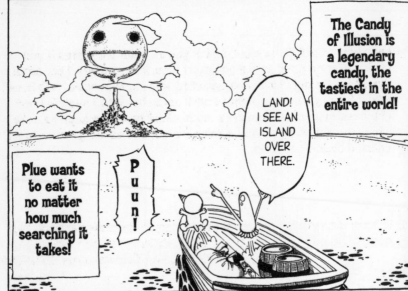

The Candy of Illusion is a legendary candy, the tastiest in the entire world!

LAND! I SEE AN ISLAND OVER THERE.

Puun!

Plue wants to eat it no matter how much searching it takes!

How To Read This Manga

* You can search for the **Candy of Illusion** with Plue!! Start at 1) on the next page. As you make your choices, follow the instructions and **jump to the next marker**!!! Ready, set... START!! --> Go to 1) on the next page.

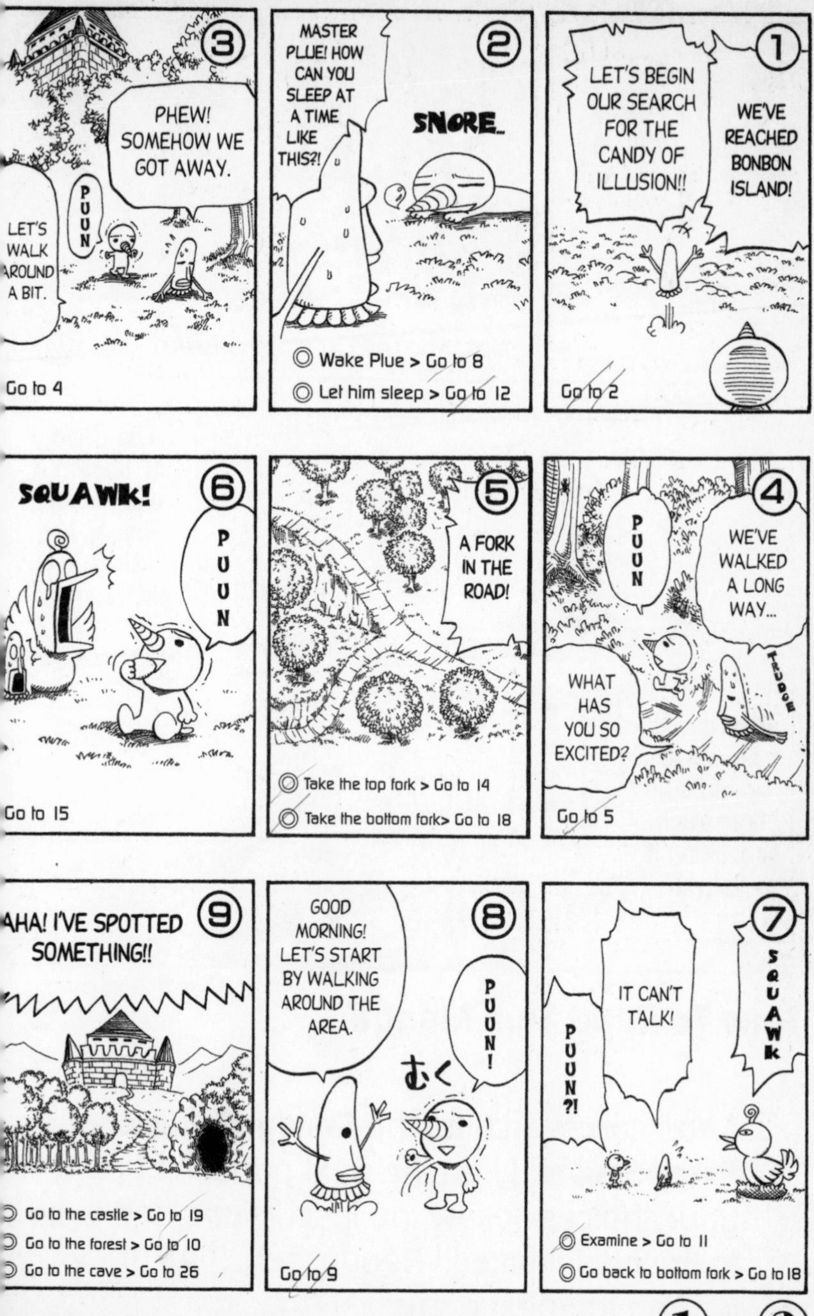
1
LET'S BEGIN OUR SEARCH FOR THE CANDY OF ILLUSION!!
WE'VE REACHED BONBON ISLAND!
Go to 2
2
SNORE...
MASTER PLUE! HOW CAN YOU SLEEP AT A TIME LIKE THIS?!
◎ Wake Plue > Go to 8
◎ Let him sleep > Go to 12
3
PHEW! SOMEHOW WE GOT AWAY.
PUUN
LET'S WALK AROUND A BIT.
Go to 4
4
WE'VE WALKED A LONG WAY...
PUUN
TRUDGE
WHAT HAS YOU SO EXCITED?
Go to 5
5
A FORK IN THE ROAD!
◎ Take the top fork > Go to 14
◎ Take the bottom fork> Go to 18
6
PUUN
SQUAWK!
Go to 15
7
SQUAWK
IT CAN'T TALK!
PUUN?!
◎ Examine > Go to 11
◎ Go back to bottom fork > Go to 18
8
PUUN!
むく
GOOD MORNING! LET'S START BY WALKING AROUND THE AREA.
Go to 9
9
AHA! I'VE SPOTTED SOMETHING!!
◎ Go to the castle > Go to 19
◎ Go to the forest > Go to 10
◎ Go to the cave > Go to 26

①~⑨

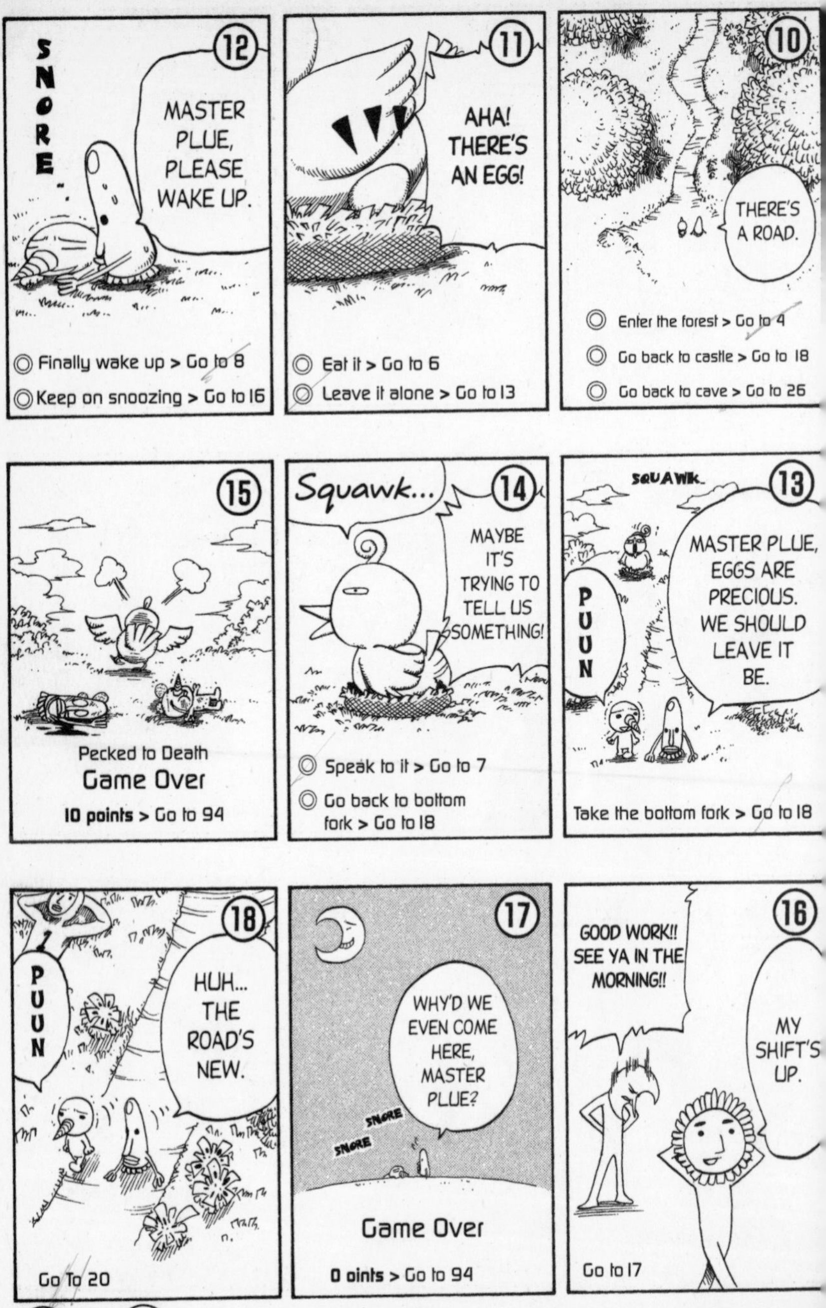
10
THERE'S A ROAD.
Enter the forest > Go to 4
Go back to castle > Go to 18
Go back to cave > Go to 26
11
AHA! THERE'S AN EGG!
Eat it > Go to 6
Leave it alone > Go to 13
12
SNORE
MASTER PLUE, PLEASE WAKE UP.
Finally wake up > Go to 8
Keep on snoozing > Go to 16
13
SQUAWK
MASTER PLUE, EGGS ARE PRECIOUS. WE SHOULD LEAVE IT BE.
PUUN
Take the bottom fork > Go to 18
14
MAYBE IT'S TRYING TO TELL US SOMETHING!
Squawk...
Speak to it > Go to 7
Go back to bottom fork > Go to 18
15
Pecked to Death
Game Over
10 points > Go to 94
16
MY SHIFT'S UP.
GOOD WORK!! SEE YA IN THE MORNING!!
Go to 17
17
WHY'D WE EVEN COME HERE, MASTER PLUE?
SNORE
SNORE
Game Over
0 oints > Go to 94
18
HUH... THE ROAD'S NEW.
PUUN
Go To 20

10~18

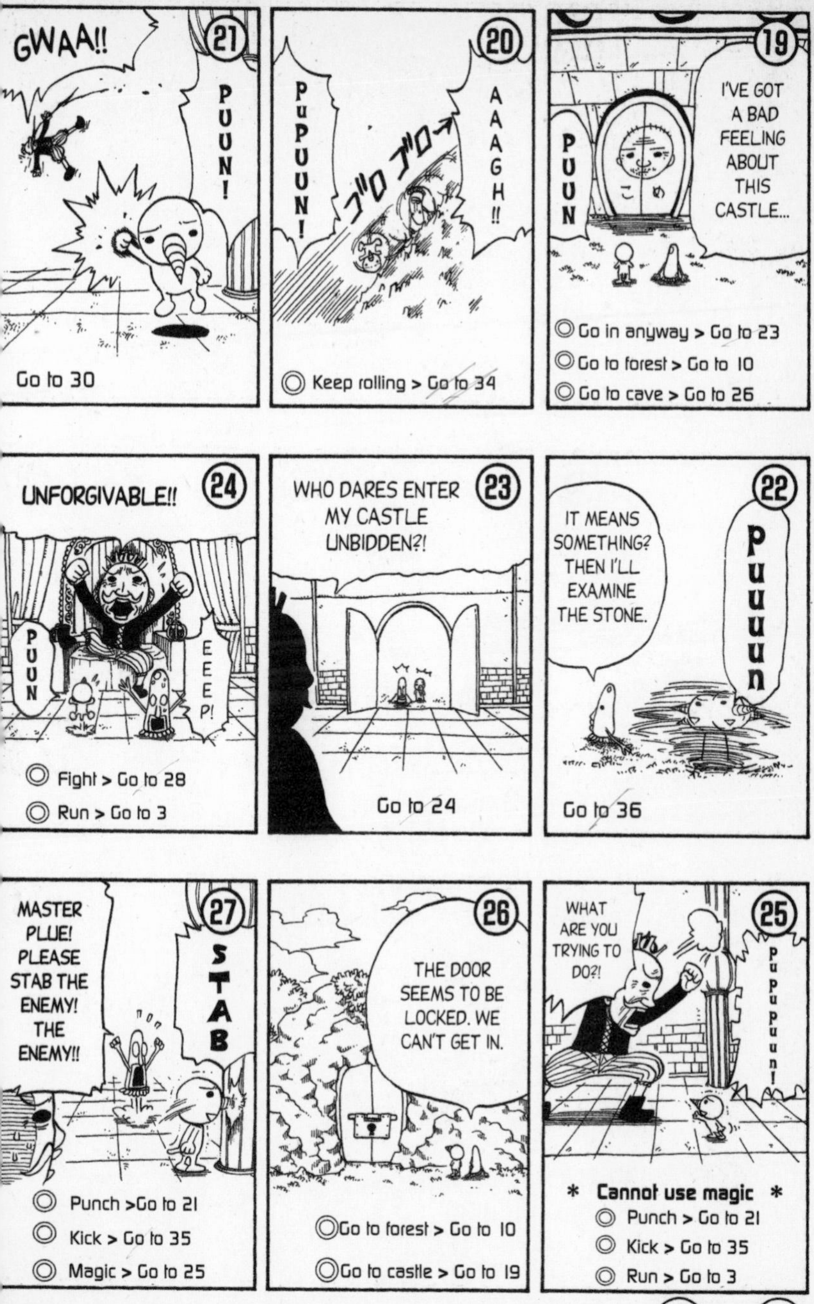
19
I'VE GOT A BAD FEELING ABOUT THIS CASTLE...
PUUN
Go in anyway > Go to 23
Go to forest > Go to 10
Go to cave > Go to 26
20
AAAGH!!
ゴロゴロ
PuPUUN!
Keep rolling > Go to 34
21
PUUN!
GWAA!!
Go to 30
22
Puuuun
IT MEANS SOMETHING? THEN I'LL EXAMINE THE STONE.
Go to 36
23
WHO DARES ENTER MY CASTLE UNBIDDEN?!
Go to 24
24
UNFORGIVABLE!!
EEEP!
PUUN
Fight > Go to 28
Run > Go to 3
25
PuPuPuun!
WHAT ARE YOU TRYING TO DO?!
* Cannot use magic *
Punch > Go to 21
Kick > Go to 35
Run > Go to 3
26
THE DOOR SEEMS TO BE LOCKED. WE CAN'T GET IN.
Go to forest > Go to 10
Go to castle > Go to 19
27
STAB
MASTER PLUE! PLEASE STAB THE ENEMY! THE ENEMY!!
Punch >Go to 21
Kick > Go to 35
Magic > Go to 25

19~27

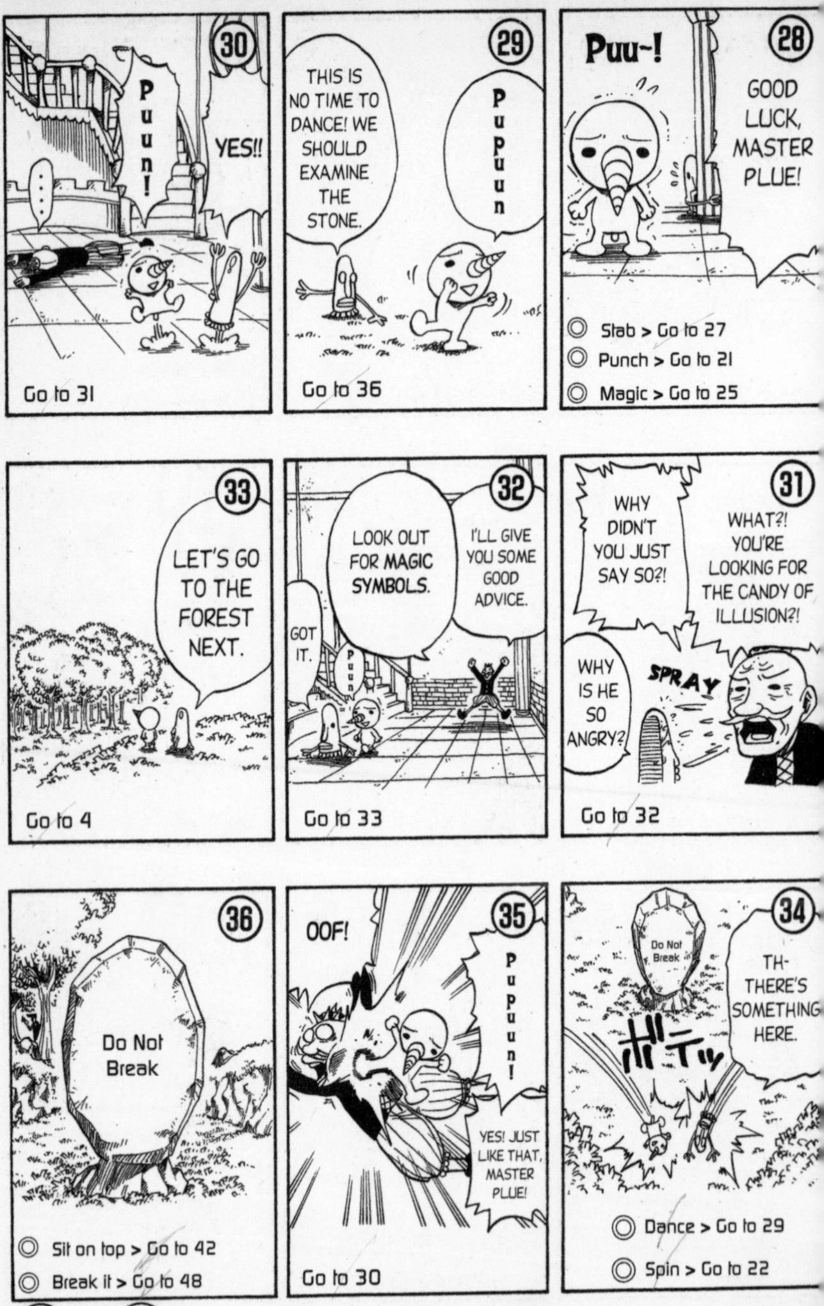
28
Puu~!
GOOD LUCK, MASTER PLUE!
Stab > Go to 27
Punch > Go to 21
Magic > Go to 25
29
Pupuun
THIS IS NO TIME TO DANCE! WE SHOULD EXAMINE THE STONE.
Go to 36
30
YES!!
Puun!
...
Go to 31
31
WHAT?! YOU'RE LOOKING FOR THE CANDY OF ILLUSION?!
WHY DIDN'T YOU JUST SAY SO?!
SPRAY
WHY IS HE SO ANGRY?
Go to 32
32
I'LL GIVE YOU SOME GOOD ADVICE.
LOOK OUT FOR MAGIC SYMBOLS.
Puun
GOT IT.
Go to 33
33
LET'S GO TO THE FOREST NEXT.
Go to 4
34
TH- THERE'S SOMETHING HERE.
Do Not Break
Dance > Go to 29
Spin > Go to 22
35
Pupuun!
OOF!
YES! JUST LIKE THAT, MASTER PLUE!
Go to 30
36
Do Not Break
Sit on top > Go to 42
Break it > Go to 48

28~36

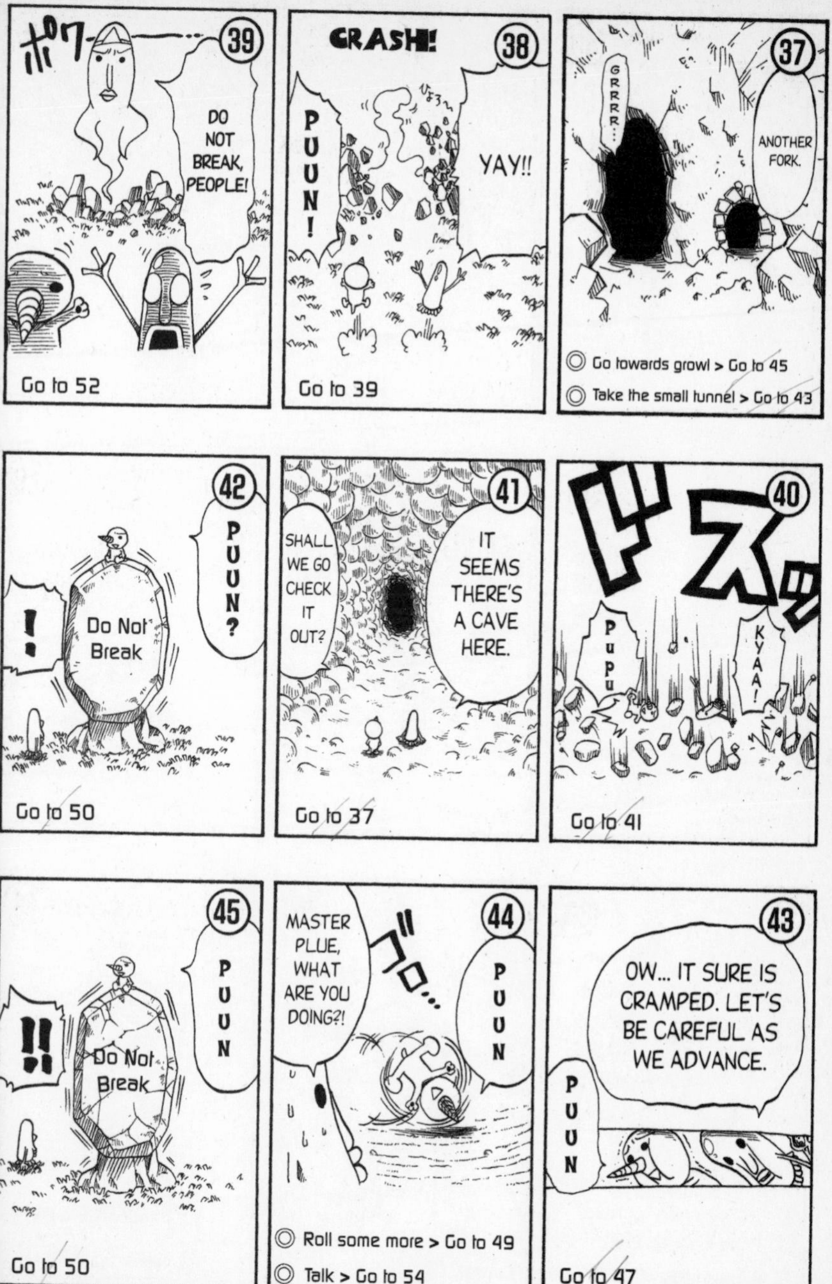
37
GRRRR...
ANOTHER FORK.
◎ Go towards growl > Go to 45
◎ Take the small tunnel > Go to 43
38
CRASH!
PUUN!
YAY!!
Go to 39
39
ポワ〜
DO NOT BREAK, PEOPLE!
Go to 52
40
ドスッ
Pupu
KYAAA!
Go to 41
41
IT SEEMS THERE'S A CAVE HERE.
SHALL WE GO CHECK IT OUT?
Go to 37
42
PUUN?
!
Do Not Break
Go to 50
43
OW... IT SURE IS CRAMPED. LET'S BE CAREFUL AS WE ADVANCE.
PUUN
Go to 47
44
PUUN
ゴロ...
MASTER PLUE, WHAT ARE YOU DOING?!
◎ Roll some more > Go to 49
◎ Talk > Go to 54
45
PUUN
!!
Do Not Break
Go to 50

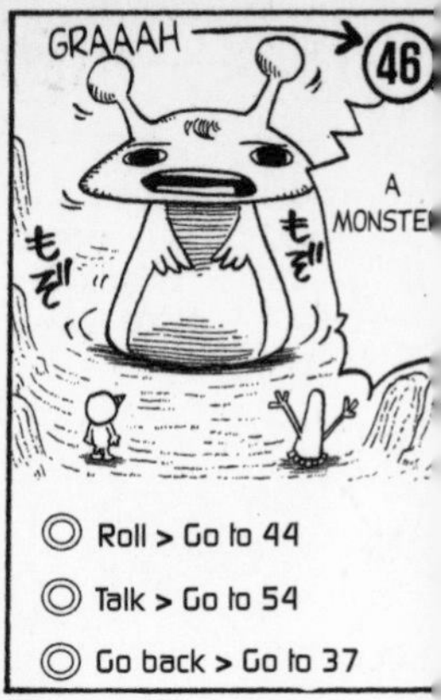

46
GRAAAH
A MONSTE
◎ Roll > Go to 44
◎ Talk > Go to 54
◎ Go back > Go to 37

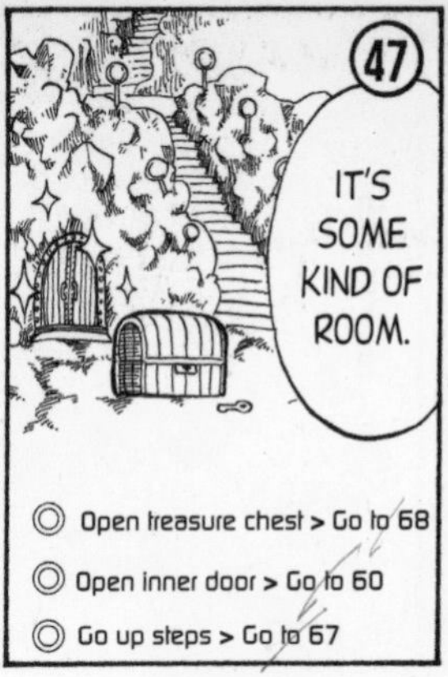

47
IT'S SOME KIND OF ROOM.
◎ Open treasure chest > Go to 68
◎ Open inner door > Go to 60
◎ Go up steps > Go to 67

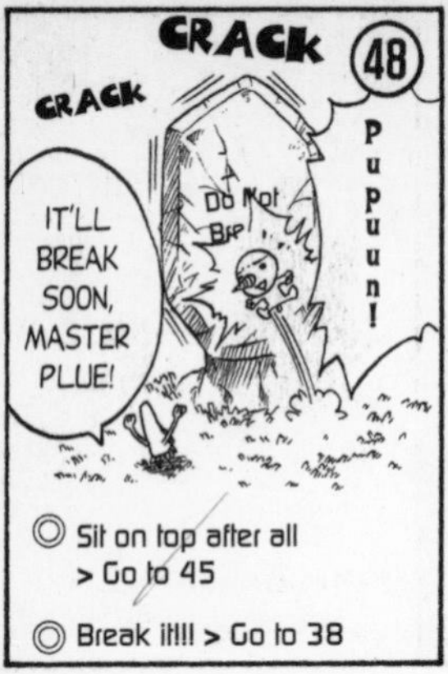

48
CRACK
CRACK
IT'LL BREAK SOON, MASTER PLUE!
Pupuun!
◎ Sit on top after all > Go to 45
◎ Break it!!! > Go to 38

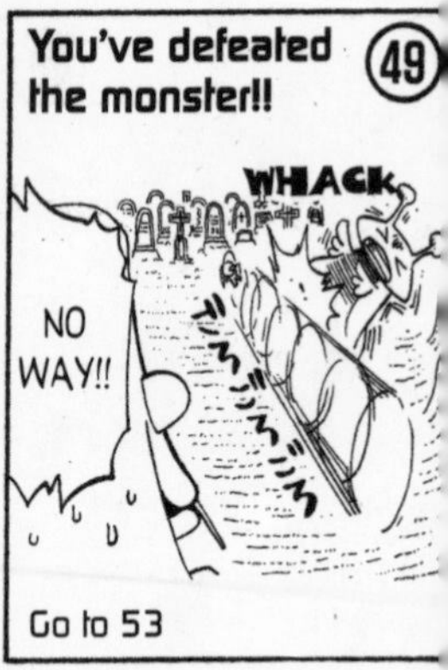

You've defeated the monster!!
49
WHACK
NO WAY!!
Go to 53

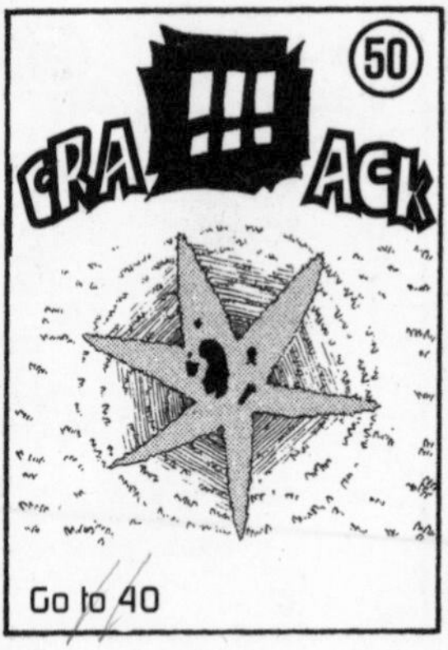

50
CRA!!!ACK
Go to 40

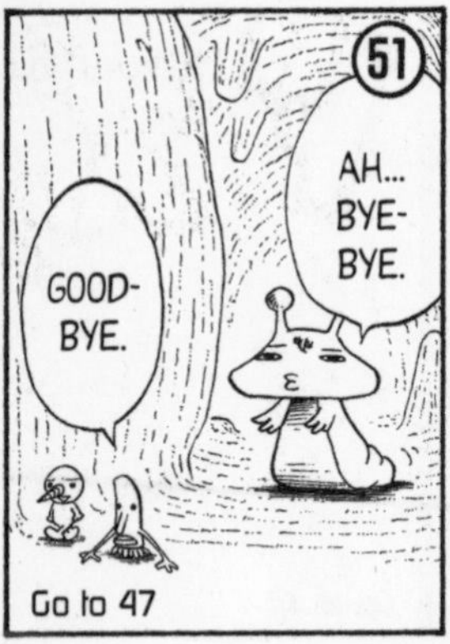

51
AH... BYE-BYE.
GOOD-BYE.
Go to 47

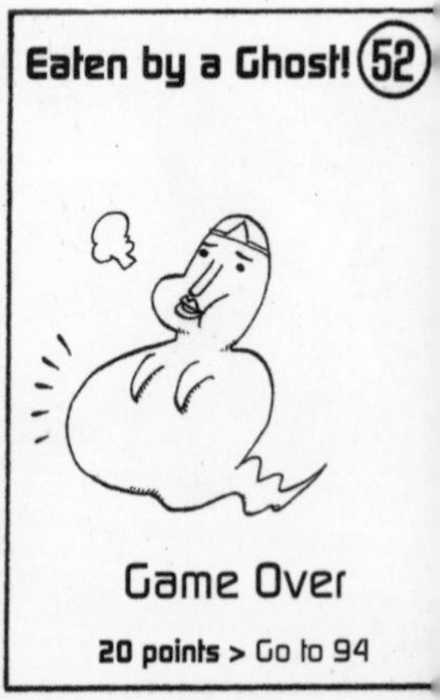

Eaten by a Ghost!
52
Game Over
20 points > Go to 94

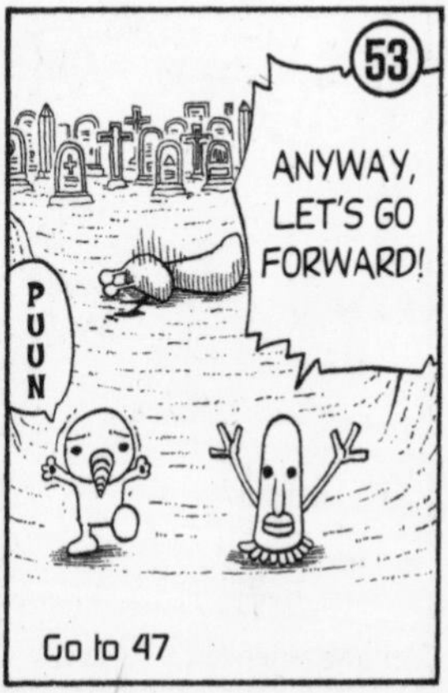

53
ANYWAY, LET'S GO FORWARD!
PUUN
Go to 47

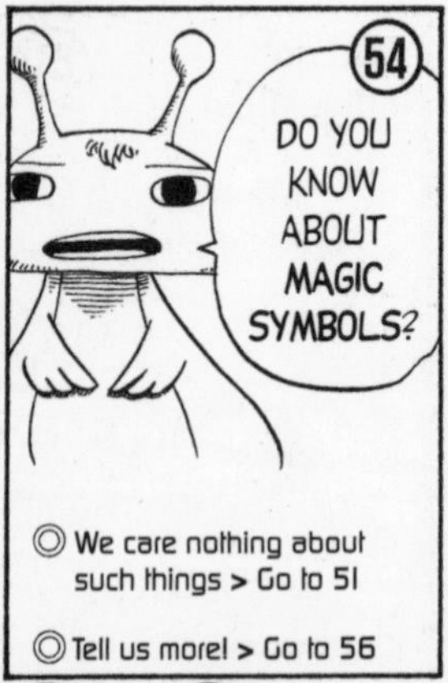

54
DO YOU KNOW ABOUT MAGIC SYMBOLS?
◎ We care nothing about such things > Go to 51
◎ Tell us more! > Go to 56

46~54

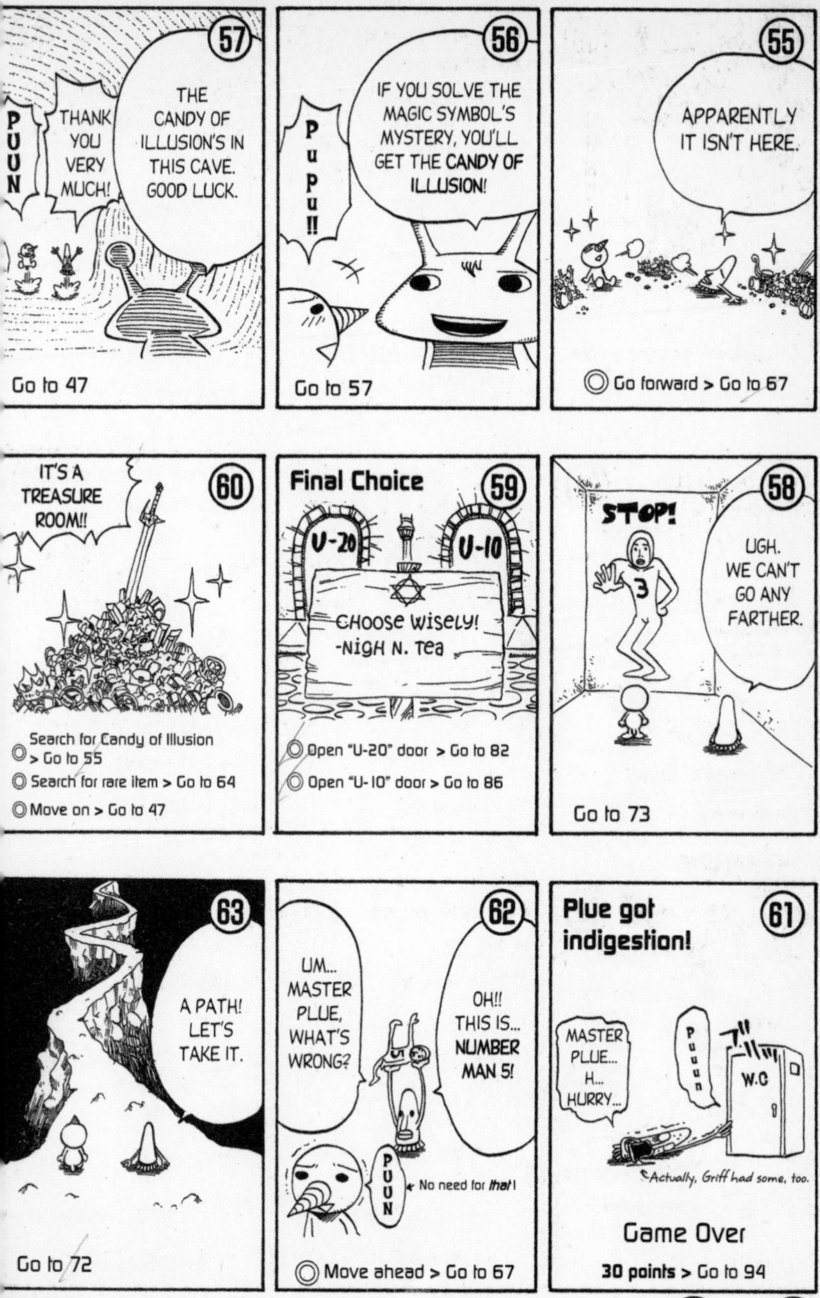
55
APPARENTLY IT ISN'T HERE.
Go forward > Go to 67
56
IF YOU SOLVE THE MAGIC SYMBOL'S MYSTERY, YOU'LL GET THE CANDY OF ILLUSION!
Pupu!!
Go to 57
57
THE CANDY OF ILLUSION'S IN THIS CAVE. GOOD LUCK.
THANK YOU VERY MUCH!
PUUN
Go to 47
58
UGH. WE CAN'T GO ANY FARTHER.
STOP!
3
Go to 73
Final Choice
59
U-10
U-20
CHOOSE WISELY! -NIGH N. TEA
Open "U-20" door > Go to 82
Open "U-10" door > Go to 86
60
IT'S A TREASURE ROOM!!
Search for Candy of Illusion > Go to 55
Search for rare item > Go to 64
Move on > Go to 47
Plue got indigestion!
61
Puuun
W.C
MASTER PLUE... H... HURRY...
Actually, Griff had some, too.
Game Over
30 points > Go to 94
62
OH!! THIS IS... NUMBER MAN 5!
UM... MASTER PLUE, WHAT'S WRONG?
PUUN
No need for that!
Move ahead > Go to 67
63
A PATH! LET'S TAKE IT.
Go to 72

55~63

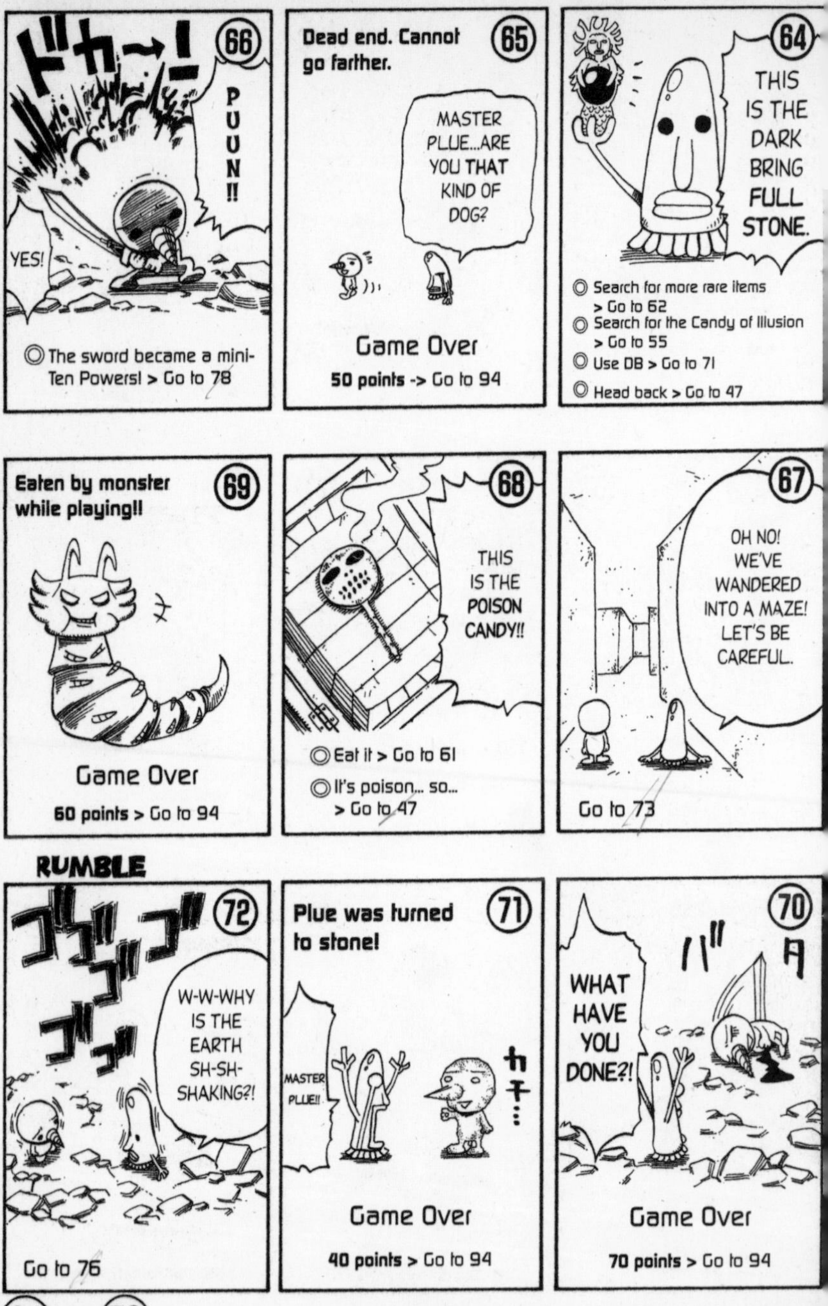
64
THIS IS THE DARK BRING FULL STONE.
◎ Search for more rare items > Go to 62
◎ Search for the Candy of Illusion > Go to 55
◎ Use DB > Go to 71
◎ Head back > Go to 47
65
Dead end. Cannot go farther.
MASTER PLUE...ARE YOU THAT KIND OF DOG?
Game Over
50 points -> Go to 94
66
PUUN!!
YES!
◎ The sword became a mini-Ten Powers! > Go to 78
67
OH NO! WE'VE WANDERED INTO A MAZE! LET'S BE CAREFUL.
Go to 73
68
THIS IS THE POISON CANDY!!
◎ Eat it > Go to 61
◎ It's poison... so... > Go to 47
69
Eaten by monster while playing!!
Game Over
60 points > Go to 94
70
WHAT HAVE YOU DONE?!
Game Over
70 points > Go to 94
71
Plue was turned to stone!
MASTER PLUE!!
Game Over
40 points > Go to 94
72
RUMBLE
W-W-WHY IS THE EARTH SH-SH-SHAKING?!
Go to 76

64~72

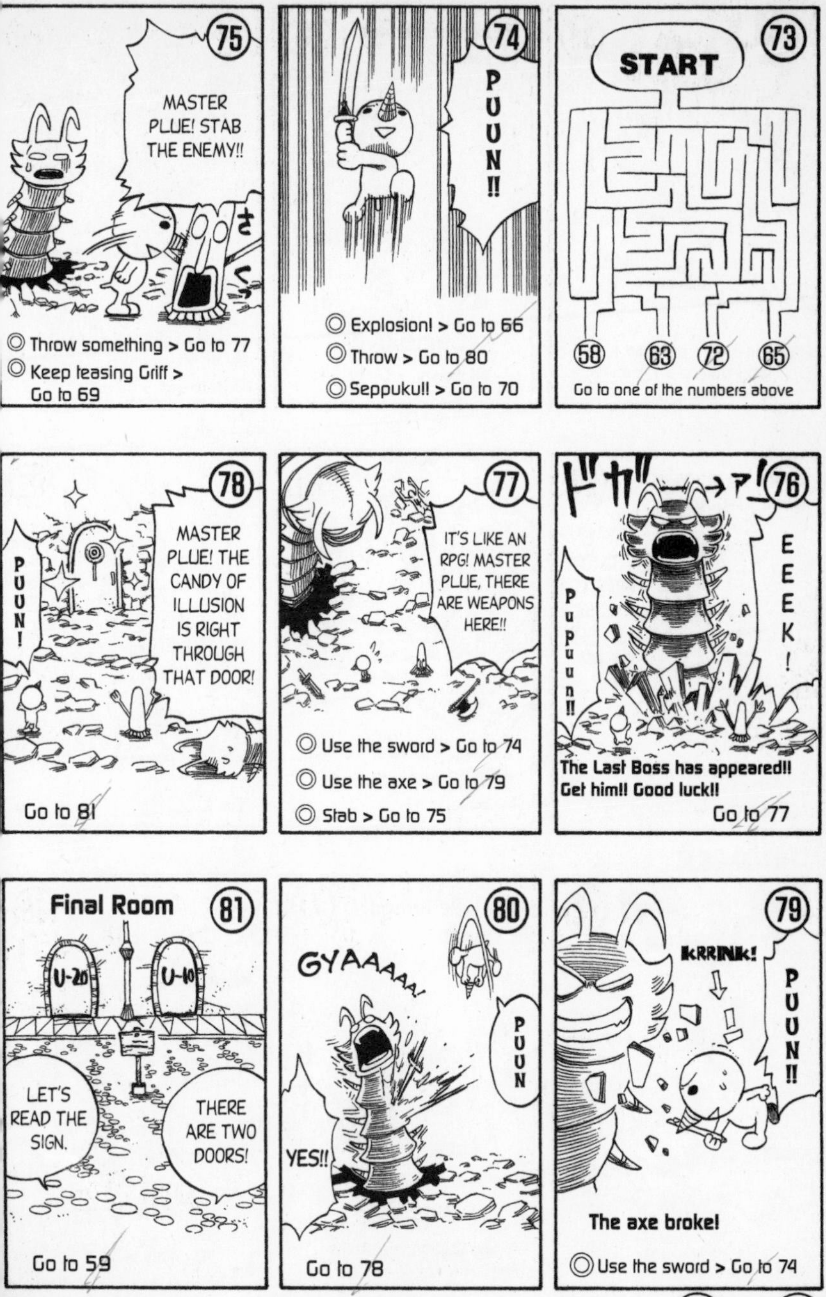
73
START
58
63
72
65
Go to one of the numbers above
74
PUUN!!
◎ Explosion! > Go to 66
◎ Throw > Go to 80
◎ Seppuku!! > Go to 70
75
MASTER PLUE! STAB THE ENEMY!!
◎ Throw something > Go to 77
◎ Keep teasing Griff > Go to 69
76
EEEK!
PuPuuun!!
The Last Boss has appeared!! Get him!! Good luck!!
Go to 77
77
IT'S LIKE AN RPG! MASTER PLUE, THERE ARE WEAPONS HERE!!
◎ Use the sword > Go to 74
◎ Use the axe > Go to 79
◎ Stab > Go to 75
78
MASTER PLUE! THE CANDY OF ILLUSION IS RIGHT THROUGH THAT DOOR!
PUUN!
Go to 81
79
KRRINK!
PUUN!!
The axe broke!
◎ Use the sword > Go to 74
80
GYAAAAAA!
PUUN
YES!!
Go to 78
Final Room
81
U-20
U-10
THERE ARE TWO DOORS!
LET'S READ THE SIGN.
Go to 59

73~81

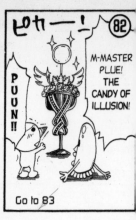

パッパッ

84

WHERE ARE WE?

?

Go to 87

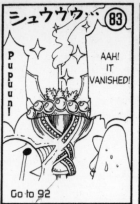

シュウウゥ…

83

Pupuun!

AAH! IT VANISHED!

Go to 92

ピカー！

82

PUUN!!

M-MASTER PLUE! THE CANDY OF ILLUSION!

Go to 83

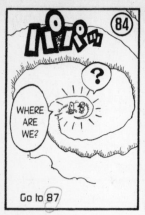

87

THIS IS THE CANDY KINGDOM. I AM THE CANDY GOD, KALMEIRA.

Go to 88

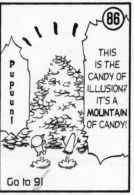

86

Pupuun!

THIS IS THE CANDY OF ILLUSION? IT'S A **MOUNTAIN** OF CANDY!

Go to 91

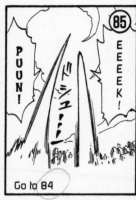

85

PUUN!

モシューッ！

EEEEK!

Go to 84

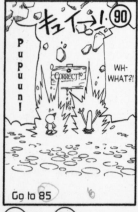

キュイーン！

90

Pupuun!

CORRECT!?

WH-WHAT?!

Go to 85

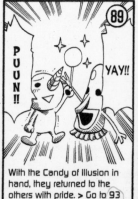

89

PUUN!!

YAY!!

With the Candy of Illusion in hand, they returned to the others with pride. > Go to 93

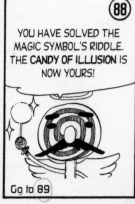

88

YOU HAVE SOLVED THE MAGIC SYMBOL'S RIDDLE. THE **CANDY OF ILLUSION** IS NOW YOURS!

Go to 89

82～90

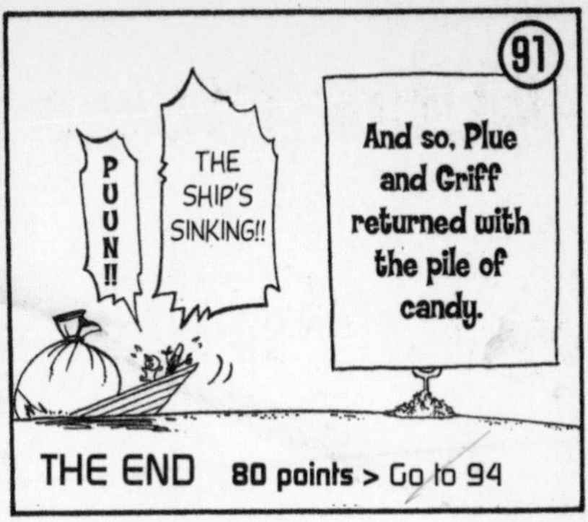
91
And so, Plue and Griff returned with the pile of candy.
THE SHIP'S SINKING!!
PUUN!!
THE END
80 points > Go to 94

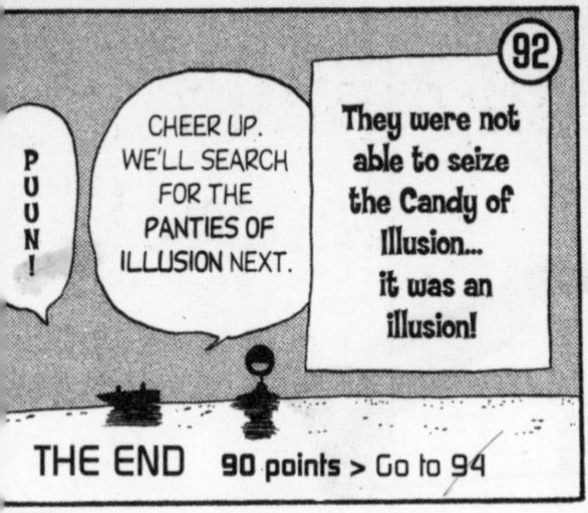
92
They were not able to seize the Candy of Illusion... it was an illusion!
CHEER UP. WE'LL SEARCH FOR THE PANTIES OF ILLUSION NEXT.
PUUN!
THE END
90 points > Go to 94

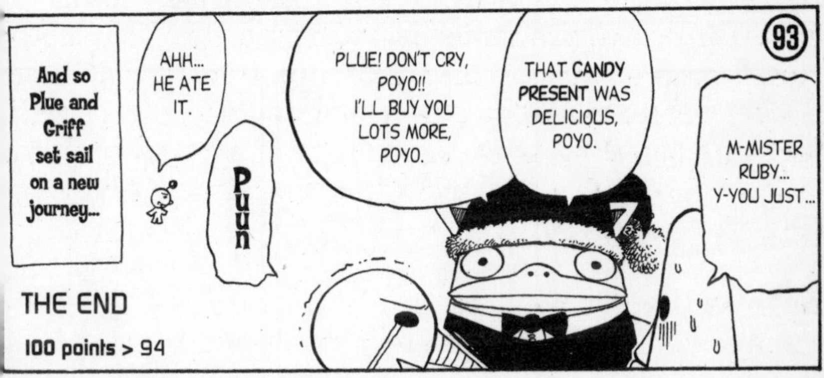
93
M-MISTER RUBY... Y-YOU JUST...
THAT CANDY PRESENT WAS DELICIOUS, POYO.
PLUE! DON'T CRY, POYO!! I'LL BUY YOU LOTS MORE, POYO.
Puun
AHH... HE ATE IT.
And so Plue and Griff set sail on a new journey...
THE END
100 points > 94

94

Points		Ranking
0	You sleep too much!	Sleeping Plue
10	Think of the parent!	Egg Lover
20	Don't break things.	Ghost Fodder
30	Yes, poison is bad.	Poison Man
40	DB's are bad stones.	Demon Card Trooper
50	Dead ends are bad.	Warp Man
60	You tease Griff too much.	Griff Killer
70	Why stab yourself?	Samurai
80	Better than 0 to 70.	Candy Merchant
90	Try for 100 points!	Candy Master
100	Congratulations! You solved the mystery!!	Dog of Legend

Hint ● You can't get to 100 normally, the hints are the King's words and your final choice!!

Extra ● If you got 100 points, try searching for Number Men 1 through 8!!

About Plue's Adventure Journal

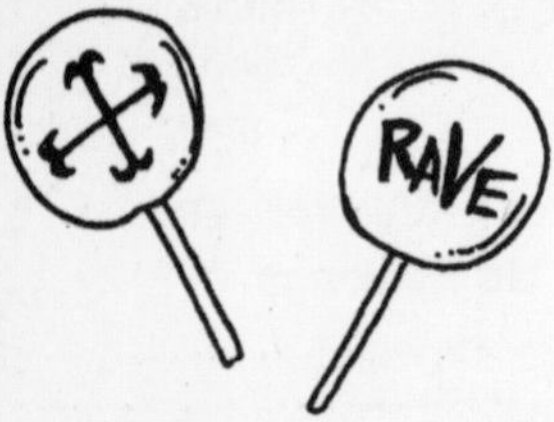
RAVE

This is just like one of those Choose Your Own Adventure books! When I was in elementary and middle school, I read those novels so much, I could recite them from memory in my sleep! I wanted to make my own someday, so I made one like this. It had to be short enough to be in a magazine serial, so instead of worrying about it, I just drew 12 pages of "What the heck?!" material.

If you had fun, then I'm glad. By the way, you can't get 100 points through normal straight-ahead progress.

So... this is ver. 1.0. I'll put out a ver. 2.0 when I have more material. I don't know yet which volume the next installment will appear in. If you catch it, lucky you.

Thanks so much for the fan art. People draw lots and lots of nice things and I'd love to publish them all, but there's only room to publish a few. Even if it's not for Rave Master, if some manga drawing or even a thought or suggestion strikes your fancy, send it along.

Hmm, I've said a lot as it is but... I suggest reading Plue's Adventure Journal more than one time.

RAVE *whatever* RANKINGS!!

☆ Rankings only of characters that have appeared to date.
Author's decisions are arbitrary.

◎ World of RAVE MASTER Mightiest Character Rankings

1. King (deceased)
2. Shiba (retired)
3. Gale Glory (deceased)
4. Pumpkin Doryu
5. Alpine Spaniel (deceased)
6. Lucia
7. Haja
8. Ogre
9. Sieg Hart
10. Deerhound (deceased)

◎ World of RAVE MASTER Secret DB Rankings

1. Last Physics
2. End of Earth
3. Monster Prison
4. Black Zenith
5. All Crush
6. The Earth
7. Ygdrassil
8. Smoke Bar
9. White Kiss
10. Decalogue

◎ Author's Best Battle Rankings

1. Haru & Friends vs. Doryu (Slated for vol. 17)
2. Musica & Reina vs. Ogre (vol. 16)
3. Haru & Gale vs. King (vols. 8~9)
4. Elie vs. Iulius (vol. 12)
5. Celia vs. Lilith (vol. 15)
6. Haru & Let vs. Cookie (vol. 15)
7. Elie vs. Rosa (vol. 4)
8. Haru vs. Shuda (vol. 5)
9. Haru vs. Let (vol. 8)
10. Haru vs. Demonoids (vol. 7)

◎ Author's Favorite Character Rankings

1. Plue
2. Haru Glory
3. Elie
4. Musica
5. Let
6. Griffon Kato
7. Ruby
8. Sieg Hart
9. King
10. Gob

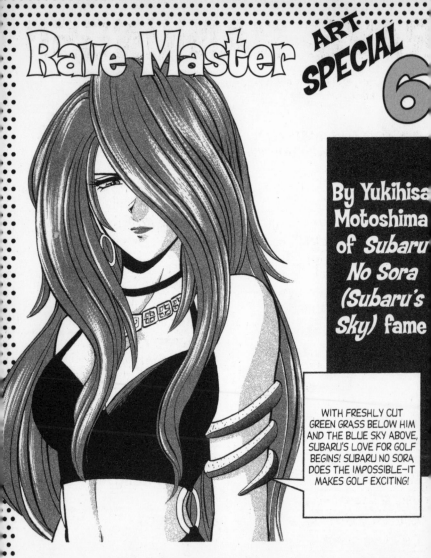

Rave Master ART SPECIAL 6

By Yukihisa Motoshima of *Subaru No Sora (Subaru's Sky)* fame

WITH FRESHLY CUT GREEN GRASS BELOW HIM AND THE BLUE SKY ABOVE, SUBARU'S LOVE FOR GOLF BEGINS! SUBARU NO SORA DOES THE IMPOSSIBLE—IT MAKES GOLF EXCITING!

MOTOSHIMA-SENSEI!!! I KNOW HOW BUSY YOU ARE, SO THANK YOU SO MUCH FOR THE ILLUSTRATION. I DIDN'T THINK YOU'D GO WITH REINA! (LAUGHS) MY MOTHER IS ACTUALLY A HUGE FAN OF YOURS (ME TOO, OF COURSE), SO THAT'S WHY I WANTED YOU TO CONTRIBUTE TO THIS PAGE. THANK YOU SO MUCH! DID YOU SEE THIS, MOM?

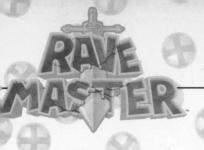

RAVE MASTER Fan Art

HEY, ASPIRING MANGA ARTISTS! WANT TO SEE YOUR PICTURES IN PRINT? WELL, IF YOU THINK YOU CAN DRAW A COOL-LOOKING HARU, A SEXY ELIE OR A FUNNY PLUE, SEND 'EM THIS WAY! WE'LL PICK ONE LUCKY WINNER FROM EACH ROUND AND SEND THEM A SPECIAL PRIZE! WHAT DO HAVE TO LOSE? NOTHING!

HOW TO SUBMIT:

1) SEND YOUR WORK VIA REGULAR MAIL (NOT E-MAIL) TO:

RAVE MASTER FAN ART
C/O TOKYOPOP
5900 WILSHIRE BLVD.
SUITE 2000
LOS ANGELES, CA 90036

2) ALL WORK SUBMITTED SHOULD BE IN BLACK-AND-WHITE AND NO LARGER THAN 8.5" X 11". (AND TRY NOT TO FOLD IT TOO MANY TIMES!)

3) ANYTHING YOU SEND WILL NOT BE RETURNED. IF YOU WANT TO KEEP YOUR ORIGINAL, IT'S FINE TO SEND US A COPY.

4) PLEASE INCLUDE YOUR FULL NAME, AGE, CITY AND STATE FOR US TO PRINT WITH YOUR WORK. IF YOU'D RATHER WE USE A PEN NAME, PLEASE INCLUDE THAT TOO.

5) IMPORTANT: IF YOU'RE UNDER THE AGE OF 18, YOU MUST HAVE YOUR PARENT'S PERMISSION IN ORDER FOR US TO PRINT YOUR WORK. ANY SUBMISSIONS WITHOUT A SIGNED NOTE OF PARENTAL CONSENT CANNOT BE USED.

6) FOR FULL DETAILS, PLEASE CHECK OUT HTTP://WWW.TOKYOPOP.COM/ABOUTUS/FANART.PHP

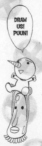

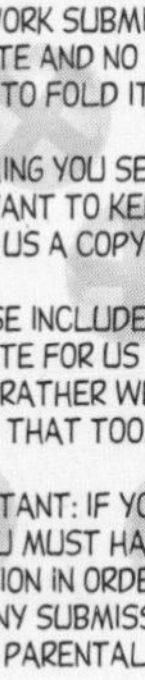

DRAW US! PUUN!

DISCLAIMER: ANYTHING YOU SEND TO US BECOMES THE PROPERTY OF TOKYOPOP INC. AND, AS WE SAID BEFORE, WILL NOT BE RETURNED TO YOU. WE WILL HAVE THE RIGHT TO PRINT, REPRODUCE, DISTRIBUTE OR MODIFY THE ARTWORK FOR USE IN FUTURE VOLUMES OF RAVE MASTER OR ON THE WEB WITHOUT PAYMENT TO YOU.

17

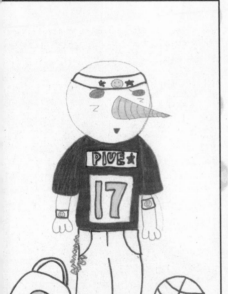

PLUE IS GEARED UP AND IS READY TO LEAD HIS TEAM TO VICTORY! NICE DRAWING, GEORGE. HE SHOOTS, HE SCORES!

GEORGE V.
AGE 12
MONROE, NC

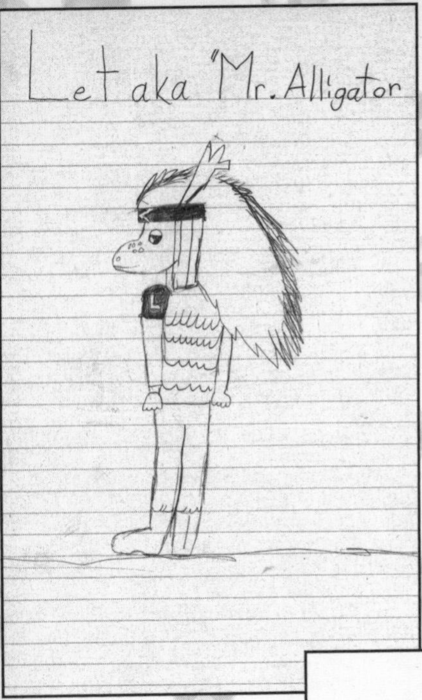
Let aka "Mr. Alligator

LET GETS GATORIZED! CONSIDERING HE'S VERY PROUD OF BEING DRAGON CLAN, I'M NOT SURE IF LET WOULD LIKE YOUR LITTLE NICKNAME FOR HIM, EMILY. BUT PERSONALLY, I THINK IT'S AS CUTE AS YOUR DRAWING!

EMILY J.
AGE 11
CHULA VISTA, CA

WHOA, BRANDON! THAT'S INTENSE! HARU IS ANGRY AND LOOKS OUT FOR BLOOD IN THIS VOLUME 12-INSPIRED DRAWING. (AND LOOK FOR ANOTHER OF BRANDON'S RAVE MASTER DRAWINGS IN ISSUE 2 OF TOKYOPOP'S TAKUHAI!)

BRANDON N.
AGE 13

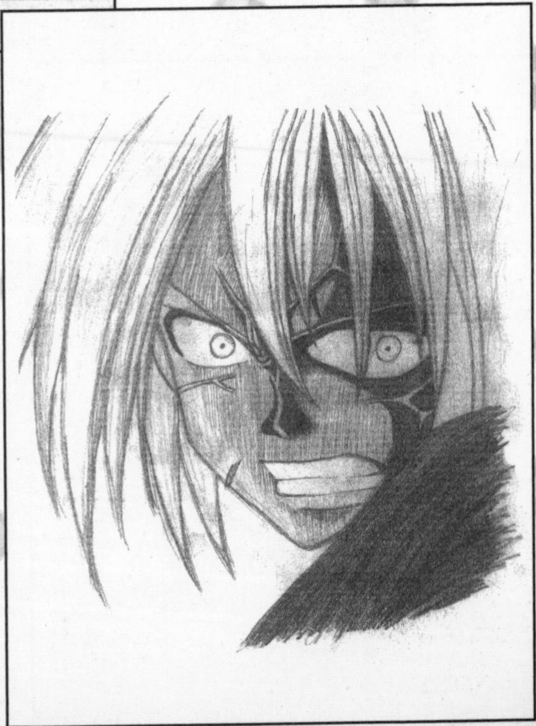

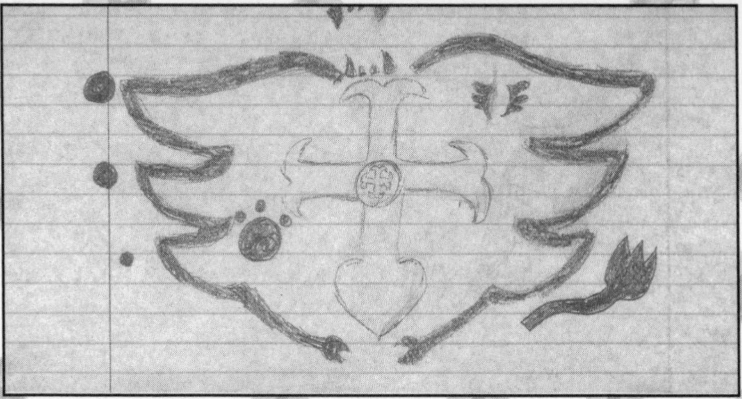

THIS ONE IS FOR ALL THE HARDCORE RAVE MASTER FANS. TYLER'S CLEVER DOODLE IS COMPRISED ENTIRELY OF IMPORTANT SYMBOLS FOUND THROUGHOUT PAST VOLUMES. CAN YOU SPOT THEM ALL? THERE ARE EIGHT DIFFERENT ONES.

TYLER P.
AGE 13
EVANSVILLE, IN

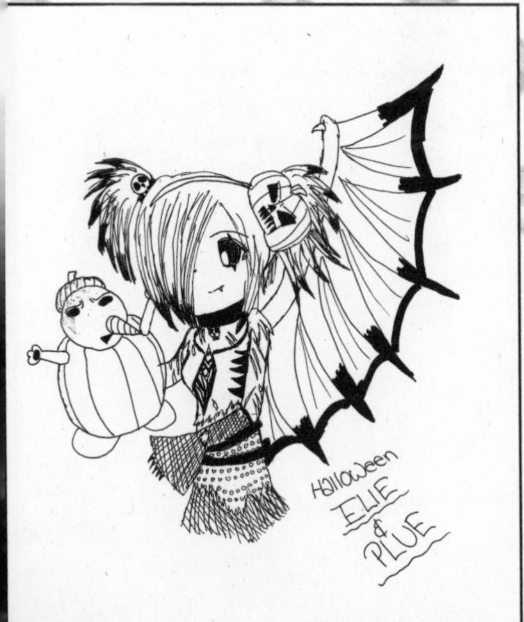
Halloween
ELIE
&
PLUE

HALLOWEEN IS JUST AROUND THE CORNER, AND CAMILLE'S GETTING US IN THE SPIRIT EARLY WITH THIS SLIGHTLY GOTHIC DRAWING OF ELIE AND PLUE DECKED OUT FOR PLUE'S FAVORITE HOLIDAY. TRICK OR TREAT!

CAMILLE W.
AGE 11
SAN ANTONIO, TX

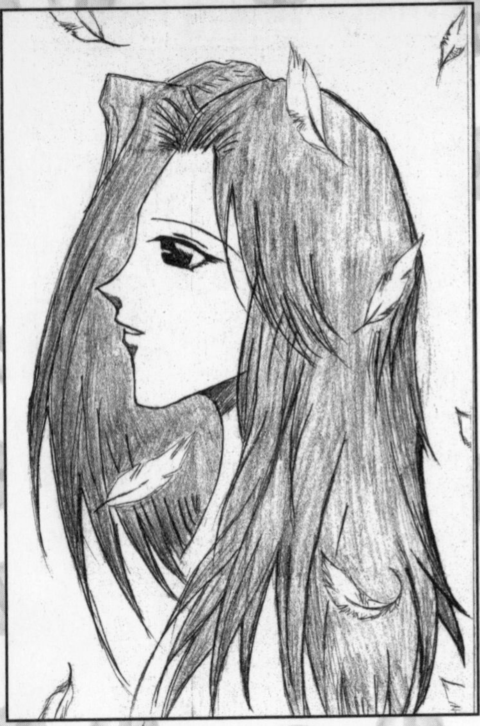

JOYCE'S LOVELY DRAWING OF SAKURA GLORY IS BOTH BEAUTIFUL AND SAD. HER DEATH AT THE HANDS OF THE YOUNG GALE RAREGROOVE REMAINS ONE OF RAVE MASTER'S MOST DRAMATIC MOMENTS.

JOYCE T.
AGE 15
CANTON, MI

PLUE AND HIS LOVE FOR LOLLIPOPS TAKE CENTER STAGE IN THIS FUN DRAWING OF FIVE OF OUR HEROES. GREAT JOB, ELIZABETH!

ELIZABETH N.
AGE 14
HOUSTON, TX

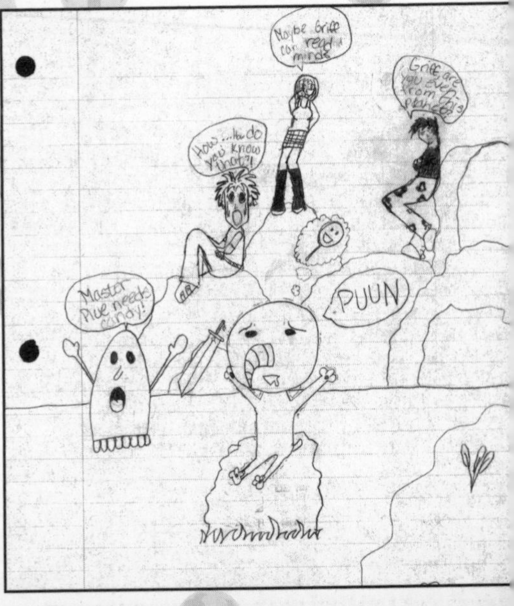
Griff, are you even from this planet?
Maybe Griff can read minds
How ... how do you know that?!
PUUN
Master Plue needs candy!

#16 - Things Taking Form

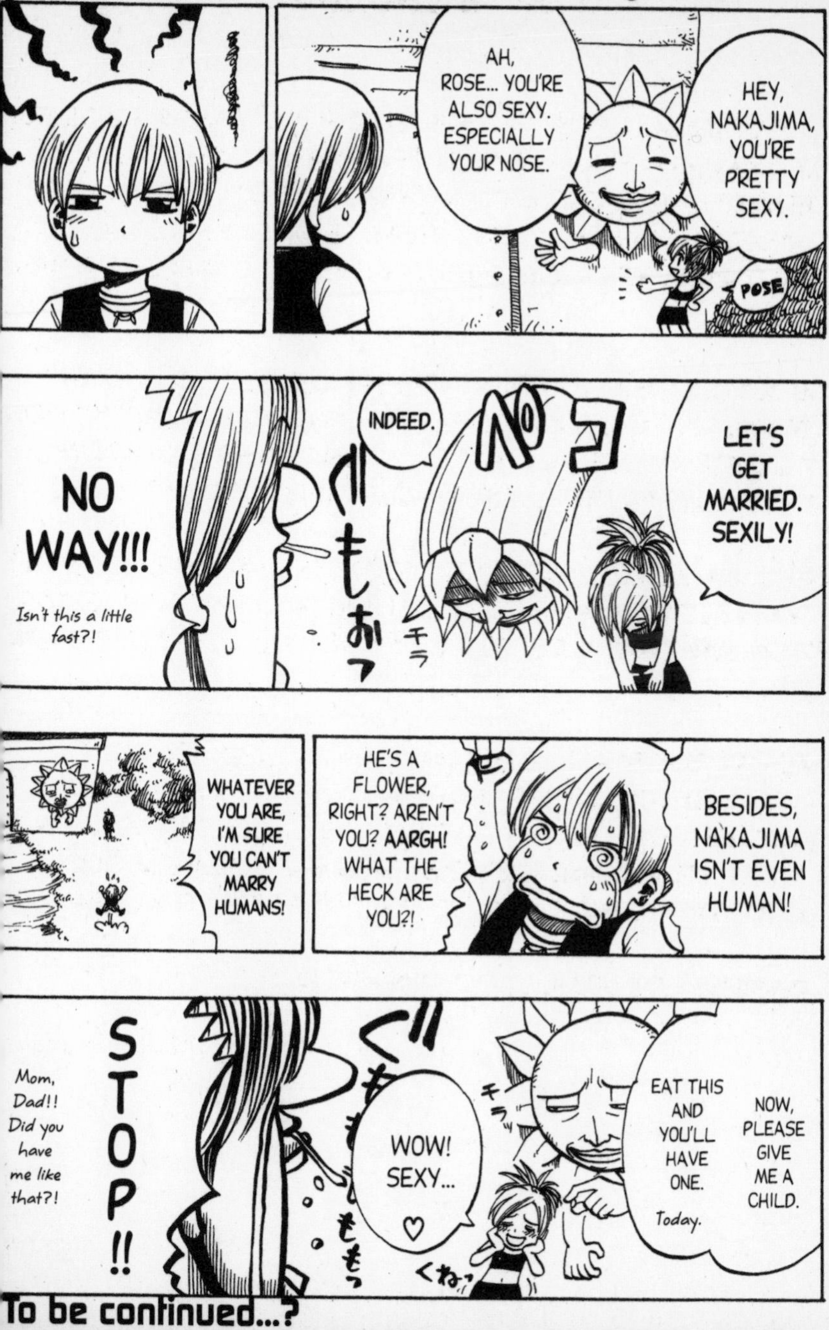
HEY, NAKAJIMA, YOU'RE PRETTY SEXY.
POSE
AH, ROSE... YOU'RE ALSO SEXY. ESPECIALLY YOUR NOSE.
LET'S GET MARRIED. SEXILY!
ペコ
INDEED.
チラ
NO WAY!!!
Isn't this a little fast?!
BESIDES, NAKAJIMA ISN'T EVEN HUMAN!
HE'S A FLOWER, RIGHT? AREN'T YOU? AARGH! WHAT THE HECK ARE YOU?!
WHATEVER YOU ARE, I'M SURE YOU CAN'T MARRY HUMANS!
NOW, PLEASE GIVE ME A CHILD.
EAT THIS AND YOU'LL HAVE ONE.
Today.
WOW! SEXY... ♡
STOP!!
Mom, Dad!! Did you have me like that?!

To be continued...?

"AFTERWORDS"

DID YOU LIKE VOLUME 16? A RATHER TRAGIC STORY, I'M AFRAID. I GOT LOTS OF "I WANTED MUSICA AND REINA TO BE HAPPY!" LETTERS. I REALLY LIKE REINA, SO I HAD SOME REGRET ENDING THINGS THIS WAY. NEIM (WHO GOES THROUGH THE FAN MAIL) IS STILL SEEING "REINA- SHE'S STILL ALIVE, RIGHT?" IN LETTERS, BUT NO, SHE'S NOT ALIVE. HER JOURNEY ENDS IN THIS VOLUME.

RAVE MASTER IS A STORY WITH THEMES OF LIFE AND DEATH. THOUGH SOMEWHAT HEAVY, IF NO ONE EVER DIES, HOW CAN THE CHARACTERS KNOW THE IMPORTANCE OF LIFE? THAT'S WHAT I HAD IN MIND WHEN I WROTE THIS VOLUME. (I'M KIDDING. I ONLY THOUGHT IT UP JUST NOW.)

WELL, ERR...REALLY, IT WOULD BE NICE IF NO ONE HAD TO DIE. YOU'D THINK THAT AT LEAST IN MANGA, WE COULD COUNT ON A HAPPY ENDING. BUT YOU KNOW- **SORRY! I DID IT JUST TO MAKE YOU CRY!** OKAY, BUSTED. THAT'S HOW IT IS.

ANYWAY, REINA'S LAST MOMENT WAS A MOMENT WHEN HER SOUL WAS FILLED WITH LOVE FOR ANOTHER PERSON. THAT'S THE GREATEST HAPPINESS OF ALL, ISN'T IT? LOVE IS BEAUTIFUL! ALTHOUGH YOU KNOW, WHAT I WROTE JUST NOW...IT'S **EMBARRASSING!** IT'S MAKING ME **SICK.** MMM... I NEED TO END THIS ON THE PROPER NOTE WITH A REALLY BAD LINE

READERS!! I LOVE YOU ALL!!! (INCLUDING THE MEN.)

- HIRO MASHIM

The evil Pumpkin Doryu is painting the world black one Rave Master at a time!

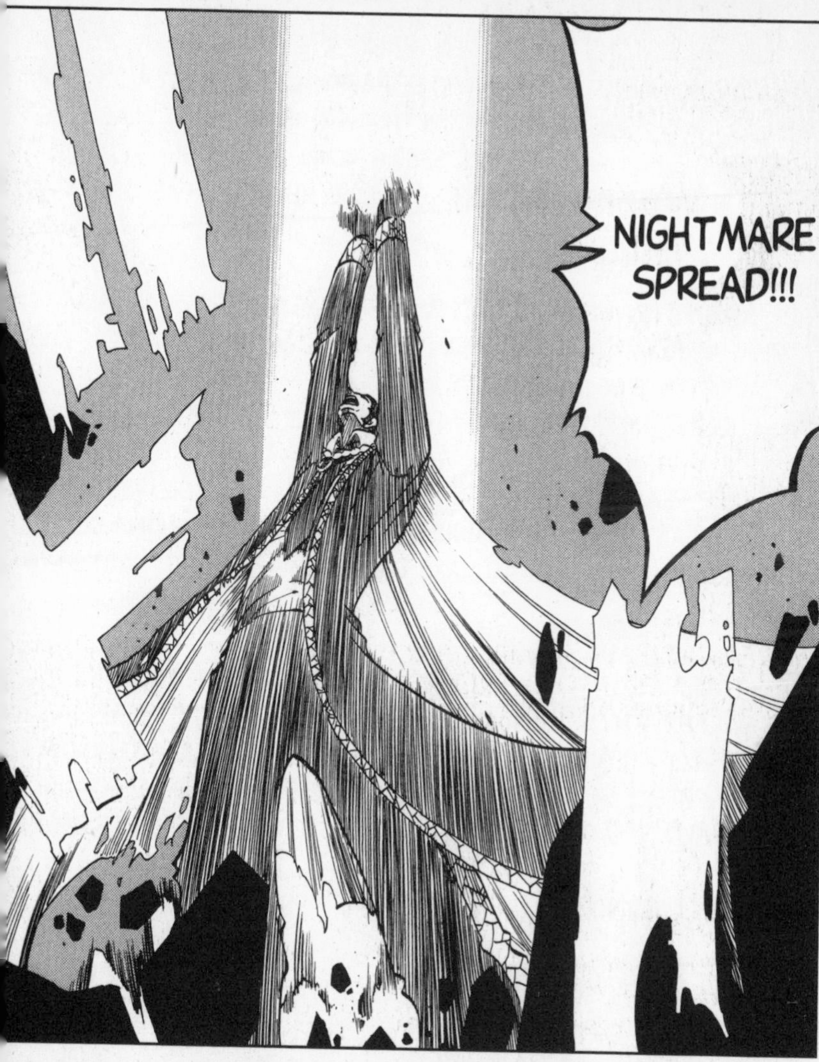
NIGHTMARE SPREAD!!!

This is like a bad dream! The commander of the Ghost Attack Squad won't stop until the world's been enveloped by darkness. But he'll have to go through Haru to do it. Does this mean lights out for our Rave Master?!

Rave Master Volume 17
Available October 2005

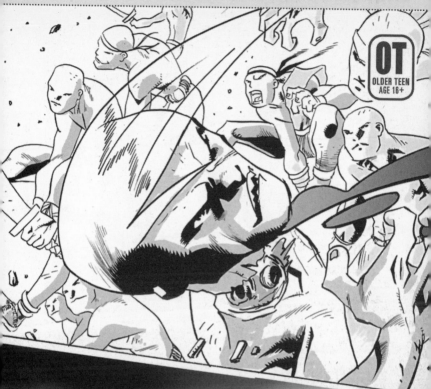

In the deep South, an ancient voodoo curse unleashes the War on Flesh—a hellish plague of voracious Ew Chott hornets that raises an army of the walking dead. This undead army spreads the plague by ripping the hearts out of living creatures to make room for a Black Heart hive, all in preparation for the most awesome incarnation of evil ever imagined... An unlikely group of five mismatched individuals have to put their differences aside to try to destroy the onslaught of evil before it's too late.

VOODOO MAKES A MAN NASTY!

WAR ON FLESH

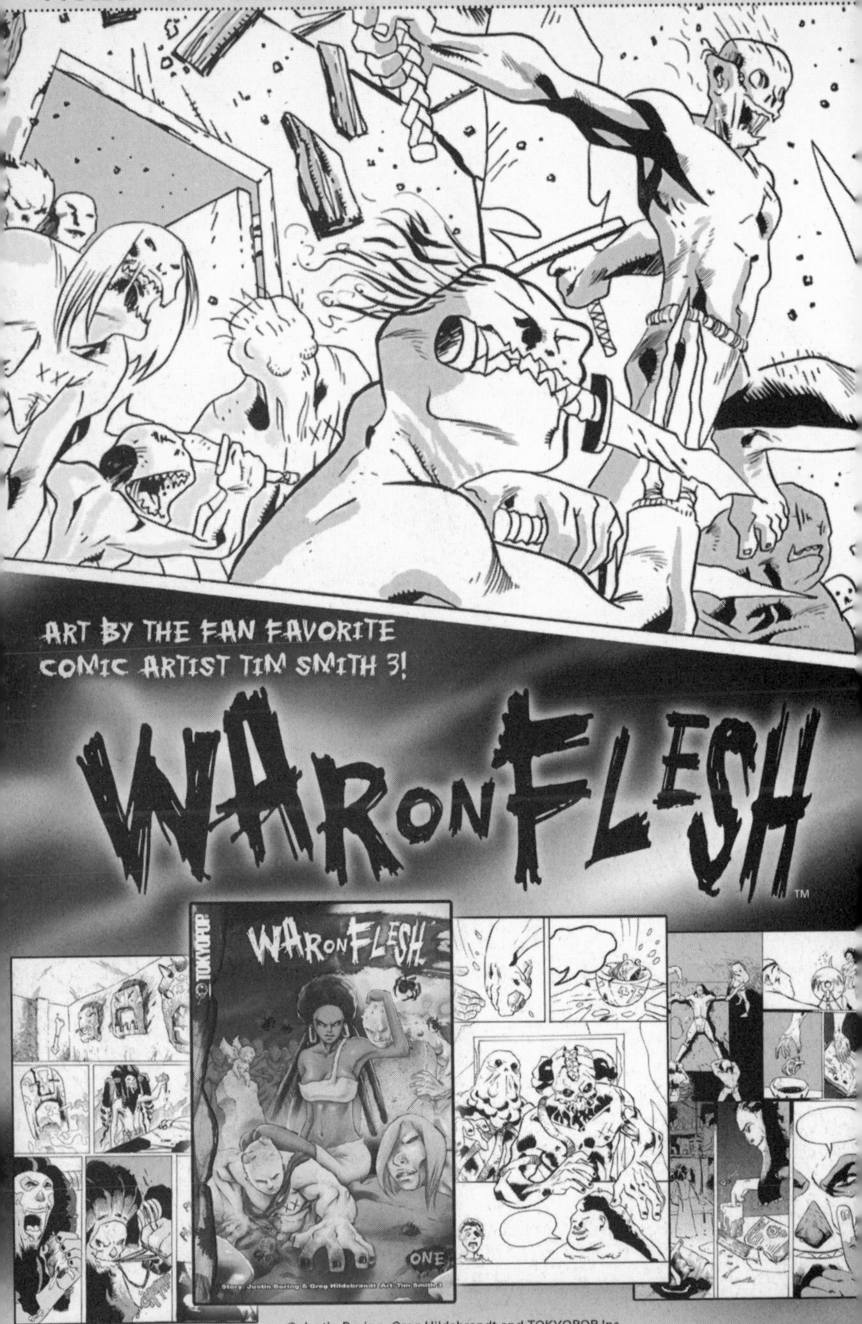
ART BY THE FAN FAVORITE
COMIC ARTIST TIM SMITH 3!
WAR ON FLESH™
TOKYOPOP
WAR ON FLESH
ONE
Story: Justin Boring & Greg Hildebrandt Art: Tim Smith 3

TOKYOPOP SHOP

WWW.TOKYOPOP.COM/SHOP

HOT NEWS!
Check out the
TOKYOPOP SHOP!
The world's best
collection of manga in
English is now available
online in one place!

SAIYUKI RELOAD

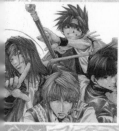

HACK NOVEL

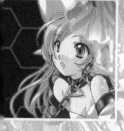

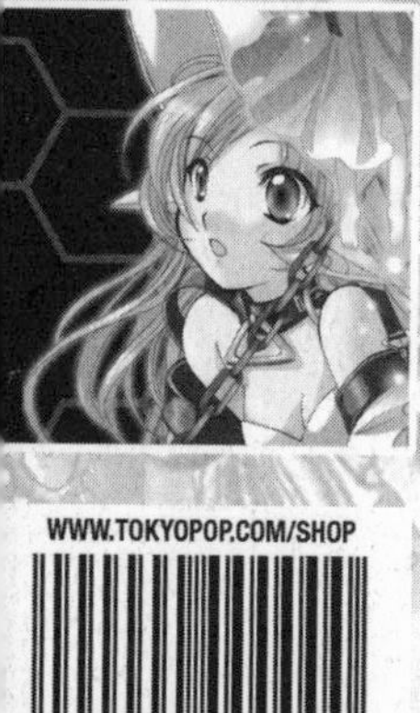

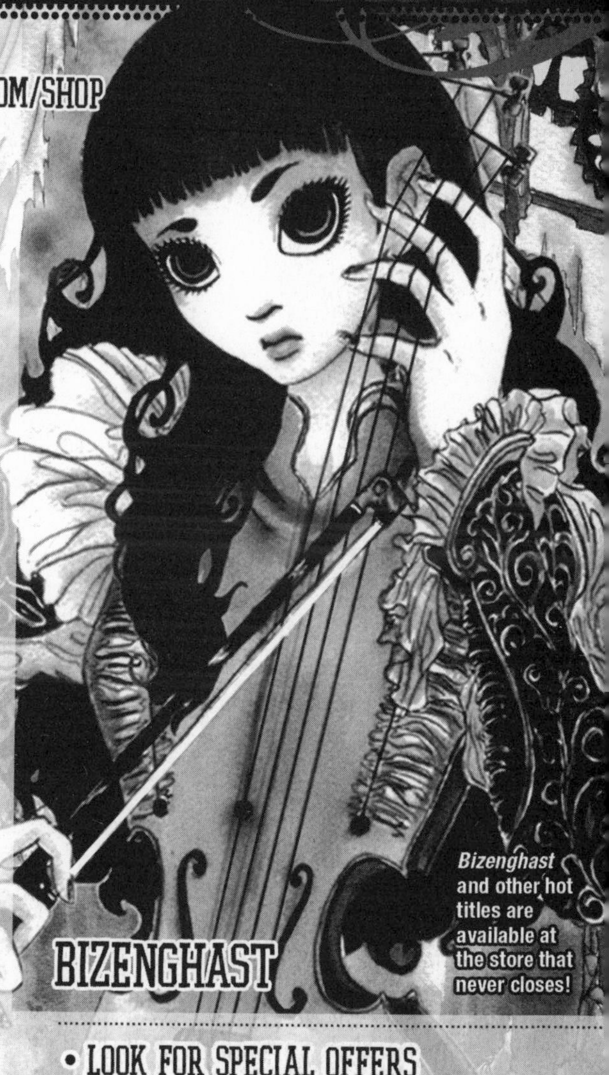

WWW.TOKYOPOP.COM/SHOP

BIZENGHAST

Bizenghast
and other hot
titles are
available at
the store that
never closes!

- LOOK FOR SPECIAL OFFERS
- PRE-ORDER UPCOMING RELEASES
- COMPLETE YOUR COLLECTIONS

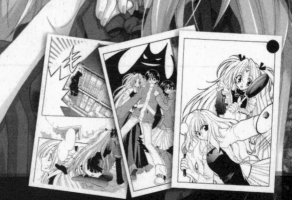

STOP!

This is the back of the book.
You wouldn't want to spoil a great ending!

This book is printed "manga-style," in the authentic Japanese right-to-left format. Since none of the artwork has been flipped or altered, readers get to experience the story just as the creator intended. You've been asking for it, so TOKYOPOP® delivered: authentic, hot-off-the-press, and far more fun!

DIRECTIONS

1
2
3
4
5
6
7
8
9
10

If this is your first time reading manga-style, here's a quick guide to help you understand how it works.

It's easy... just start in the top right panel and follow the numbers. Have fun, and look for more 100% authentic manga from TOKYOPOP®!

100% AUTHENTIC MANGA
品質第一公式商品

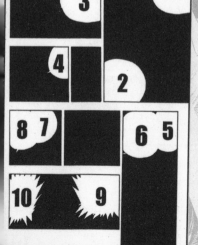

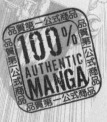